THE
DAME
IN THE
KIMONO

THE DAME IN THE KIMONO

Hollywood, Censorship, and the Production Code from the 1920s to the 1960s

LEONARD J. LEFF
and
JEROLD L. SIMMONS

ANCHOR BOOKS
DOUBLEDAY
NEW YORK   LONDON   TORONTO   SYDNEY   AUCKLAND

AN ANCHOR BOOK

PUBLISHED BY DOUBLEDAY

a division of Bantam Doubleday Dell Publishing Group, Inc.
666 Fifth Avenue, New York, New York 10103

ANCHOR BOOKS, DOUBLEDAY, and the portrayal of an anchor
are trademarks of Doubleday, a division of Bantam Doubleday
Dell Publishing Group, Inc.

The Dame in the Kimono was originally published in hardcover
by Grove Weidenfeld in 1990.
The Anchor Books edition is published by arrangement
with Grove Weidenfeld.

Published in Canada by General Publishing Company, Ltd.

Portions of this book have appeared in American Film.

Library of Congress Cataloging-in-Publication Data

Leff, Leonard J.
   The dame in the kimono: Hollywood, censorship,
and the production code from the 1920s to the
1960s / Leonard J. Leff and Jerold L. Simmons.
   —1st Anchor Books ed.
      p.   cm.
   Includes bibliographical references and index.
   1. Motion pictures—Censorship—United States.
2. Motion pictures—California—Los Angeles—
History.   3. Hollywood (Calif.) History.
I. Simmons, Jerold, 1941–   . II. Title.
[PN1995.62.L4   1990b]   91-12052
791.43'0973—dc20   CIP
ISBN 0-385-41722-5

for
LINDA RINGER LEFF
and
SCARLETT SIMMONS

ACKNOWLEDGMENTS

The research and writing of *The Dame in the Kimono* involved numerous persons who generously offered their assistance. At the Margaret Herrick Library of the Academy of Motion Picture Arts and Sciences, which houses the Motion Picture Association Production Code Administration Collection, archivist Samuel Gill and his assistants Barbara Hall and Val Almendarez lent their experience, intelligence, and good humor to the project.

We are equally grateful to Daniel Selznick of Selznick Properties, Ltd., which granted permission to cite from materials in the Selznick Archive; John Hall at RKO Pictures; Judith Singer at Warner Bros.; Robert Knudson, Leith Adams, and Ned Comstock of Special Collections at the University of Southern California; Nicholas B. Scheetz of Special Collections at Georgetown University; W. H. Crain, Raymond Daum, and Paul Bailey of the Humanities Research Center, the University of Texas at Austin; Josephine Savaro of the St. Joseph's University Archives, Philadelphia; the staff of Special Collections at the University of California at Los Angeles; Michael Gallagher of the Department of Communication, United States Catholic Conference; and James Ferman and Ken Penry of the British Board of Film Censors.

Marc Wanamaker of the Bison Archives; Jan-Christopher Horak of the George Eastman House; Mary Corliss, Stills Archivist of the Museum of Modern Art; Ron Mandelbaum of Photofest; and Linda Beyer of the

Acknowledgments

Wisconsin Center for Film and Theater Research offered us their expertise. So did the staffs of the Margaret Herrick Library and the American Film Institute, Los Angeles; the Film Study Center (Museum of Modern Art) and the Billy Rose Theatre Collection (Lincoln Center Library for the Performing Arts), New York; and the British Film Institute, London. We are especially grateful to the librarians and staff of the Oklahoma State University and University of Nebraska at Omaha libraries.

Men who served the studios as Production Code Administration liaisons—Luigi Luraschi (Paramount), Frank McCarthy (Twentieth Century–Fox), and Robert M. W. Vogel (Metro-Goldwyn-Mayer)—shared with us their memories of Joseph Breen and Geoff Shurlock. Screenwriters Niven Busch, Philip Dunne, John Michael Hayes, Arthur Laurents, Ernest Lehman, and Daniel Taradash; producers Pandro Berman, James B. Harris, and Stanley Kramer; and Loew's vice-president J. J. Cohn and RKO vice-president William Dozier also granted interviews. Martin S. Quigley answered some important questions about his father, the co-author of the Production Code. Former staff members of the Production Code Administration were helpful: Jack Vizzard, Robert Watkins, and especially Al Van Schmus. We are indebted to these three men and all of the others for their assistance.

Mark Polizzotti, our editor, improved the manuscript in countless important ways; like Nat Sobel, our agent, he also supported the project from the onset. Richard Jewell of the University of Southern California and Garth Jowett of the University of Houston read the manuscript and offered constructive criticism; almost ten years ago, Skip Landen at Ithaca College led us to Al Van Schmus and the *Gone With the Wind* files. Jacqueline McGlade provided invaluable research assistance at a critical moment. Our thanks to them all.

Through Summer Stipends and Travel to Collections grants, the National Endowment for the Humanities helped fund the project; so did the South Central Modern Language Association. At Oklahoma State University, Dean Smith Holt and Associate Dean Neil Hackett as well as Gordon Weaver, John Crane, and E. P. Walkiewicz provided considerable support. At the University of Nebraska at Omaha, deans John Newton and Margaret Gessaman and the University Committee on Research were also supportive.

CONTENTS

PREFACE

WHEN IVA ARCHER rapped at the door of the swank flat, she sensed that she had not awakened Samuel Spade but had somehow interrupted him. The middle of a phone call? A cheese danish and coffee? What was it? He seemed less the occupant of the flat than a precinct cop assigned to guard it. He talked as he always talked: reserved, under control. But the reserve and control now seemed forced. Then Iva saw the woman in the bedroom, the woman in dishabille. The woman who had thrown on a robe that Spade had perhaps tossed her. It looked bad for Spade. Iva turned to the private eye and asked one hard question: "Who is that dame wearin' my kimono?"

Mark it! Joe Breen hollered to the projectionist. In the arid screening room of the Hollywood "Hays Office," where in summer 1934 he monitored even rereleases, Breen had had enough of the 1931 *Maltese Falcon*. The foul language (a stage-whispered "S.O.B.") and homosexual riffs (Joel Cairo with an arm around his buddy) were bad. The low morals of Spade and the women were worse. In one scene, Spade dangled a DO NOT DISTURB sign in one hand and fluffed pillows with the other; later Spade's dame dropped her kimono and slipped into the bath with "breasts partially exposed and one leg raised the height of the side of the tub."

Though the screening ended well after seven o'clock, Breen marched into his office to dictate a stern memorandum for the

Warner brothers. The picture could not be rereleased, he ordered; the studio must return *The Maltese Falcon*—kimonos and all—to the vault. A battle over the *Falcon* would leave Breen and Jack Warner scarred, but for now, confident and exhausted, Breen could head home.

Breen doused the lights and looked around. Even in shadow the Production Code office on Hollywood Boulevard resembled that of a third-rate Sam Spade: the rugs were matted, the paint yellowed, the chairs hand-me-down; the antique switchboard belonged on the set of a 1920s melodrama, not at the hub of an important Hollywood agency. But Breen could smile. Across the threshold of the Production Code Administration passed the scripts and release prints of virtually every motion picture made. Within those dingy walls, Breen and the Production Code staff shaped the content of America's most vital cultural medium.

Breen could well recall the days before 1934 and the formation of the Production Code Administration, the days of easy morals and *Maltese Falcon*s. "I am so enthusiastic about this whole business and so willing to work that I'd be tempted *to bite the legs* off anybody who might dare to cross us at this stage of the game," Breen had told his boss, Will Hays. But in 1930 the Irishman had then been a public relations flack for the Production Code, not an enforcer, and the studios had scorned both the Code and its guardians.

Charged with Production Code enforcement in 1931, the West Coast Hays Office staff had been ministers without portfolio. When they asked Motion Picture Association president Will Hays for "some help in cleaning up" the *Falcon,* he did not respond; he was too busy "cleaning up" the Depression-whipped balance sheets of the studios. So strapped for funds were the major companies in 1932 that they could not even pay Association dues. The remedy was sex, and the pictures were wanton. The wisecracks and double entendres exposed the Production Code as one more Hollywood facade, a public relations gimmick that allowed the studios to preach morality and purvey sin.

"The pest hole that infects the entire country with its obscene and lascivious moving pictures must be cleansed and disinfected," a Catholic church group commanded in 1933. Along with rumblings of federal censorship and a strengthening of local and state censor boards, the threat of a nationwide Catholic boycott paralyzed the movie capital. In response, the company presidents formed the agency that for three decades was as integral to moviemaking as soundstages and back lots.

The success of the Production Code Administration was assured. The company presidents made the Production Code Seal the passport that a film needed to enter the largest and most profitable theaters in America. They fined those who distributed or exhibited a picture without the Seal. They also named Joe Breen the Production Code Administration director. In 1934, the kimono era ended.

Hollywood annals portray Breen as town bully, a cross between desperado and marshal whose six-shooter was the Production Code. Striving to balance freedom and control, Breen veered more toward the latter than the former. Yet he served the ends of commercial entertainment: he smoothed the assembly line operation of the studio system, he helped secure a reasonably uniform product for conservative American exhibitors, and he hindered the quick-buck producers and bandwagon jumpers whose pictures could whet the censors' knives for *all* releases. Rather like "Props" or "Casting," the Production Code Administration was generally accepted as a department within the studio structure. Many respected Breen as a Hollywood veteran, someone who loved motion pictures and who could help make—not break—them. Good writing demands "adroit indirection," noted one famous screenwriter, and the Code "forced writers not only to be cleaner but also to be cleverer." Perhaps because they understood that the movies were a collaborative art, Breen and Geoff Shurlock, his successor, were less doctrinaire than reporters and scholars or producers and directors have painted them. The East Coast moguls cast the Production Code director as the heavy; they employed him to defend the Production Code, to protect the studios—as the studios could not or would not protect themselves—from the excesses of established and independent filmmakers. For better and worse, Breen and Shurlock gave Oscar-caliber performances.

The Production Code Administration was run much like an American court. "We like to think that the decisions of the Production Code Administration are, in reality, the decisions of a private judicial tribunal," Breen explained, "duly instituted and empowered to interpret a set of fundamental laws. These decisions, even as the decisions of public courts, have the force of law for the industry and are carefully considered in adjudicating subsequent cases." Judges Breen and Shurlock saw thousands of pictures, and like tough court cases that shape the law and illuminate the judicial process, those films that resisted the Production Code form a kaleidoscope of shifting values, an extraordinary body of case law that traces the relationship between Hollywood, the Code, and American culture.

While dozens of pictures shaped the Production Code and the Production Code Administration, eleven "tough cases" tell the agency's story with notable clarity. These eleven pictures show how morals and personalities clashed, and how rules were made, applied, and stretched. They show how producers were chastened and how they rebelled; how appeals were processed and how the damage from reversals was contained; how the Production Code was born and how, three decades later, the Production Code expired and the Motion Picture Association Ratings were born.

From *Dead End* to *Who's Afraid of Virginia Woolf?*, these eleven movies produced a raucous debate, at once familial and divisive, creative and destructive. More than dames in kimonos were at stake: the Production Code wars concerned nothing less than the nature of the Hollywood studio system, the content of American movies, and a half-century dialogue over the morals and ideals of a nation.

THE PRODUCTION CODE

1922–1934

1

Welcome Will Hays!

IN THE LATE teens of the twentieth century, America lost her innocence. The Great War not only tarnished her ideals but cast doubt on her national goals. Painters and poets, reporters and Rotarians, laborers and politicians—all experienced the bitter aftershock of the war. Some turned to God, some to pessimism, and some, especially in Hollywood, to the hot-cha-cha.

The California sun warmed the innocent and the corrupt, both of whom could overheat. By the 1920s, scandal seemed rife. ACTRESS DIES AT DRUNKEN PARTY, one 1921 headline shouted. FAMOUS COMEDIAN CHARGED WITH MURDER. For the Labor Day weekend, Fatty Arbuckle had taken a suite at the St. Francis Hotel. As the hooch flowed, he disappeared into the bedroom with model Virginia Rappe. Hours later, the young woman became ill and, after a short hospitalization, died. The autopsy report led the San Francisco district attorney to hold Arbuckle responsible. With kinky sex as the main attraction, the rape and murder trial of Fatty Arbuckle drove Hollywood from the entertainment section of American newspapers to the front page.

The Arbuckle affair was not the only "drunken party" of the decade. The murder of director William Desmond Taylor and the deaths of young actors Olive Thomas and Wallace Reid from narcotics abuse fed the suspicion that film artists were bohemians and

3

debauchees, perhaps even criminals. The torrid films that brought
Sodom and Gomorrah to the provinces confirmed the suspicion.
Bluenoses led the assault against the movies; yellow journalists
followed; then came antagonistic legislators waving censorship
proposals. In 1921 alone, solons in thirty-seven states introduced
nearly one hundred bills designed to censor motion pictures. The
rules of the extant censor boards were mine fields. Women could
not smoke on-screen in Kansas but could in Ohio; a pregnant
woman could not appear on-screen in Pennsylvania but could in
New York. All six censorship states—which controlled over thirty
percent of the theater seats in America—condemned illegitimacy
and sexual deviance. After producers cut their films, censors recut
them. The outcome was mutilated prints and adverse publicity.

Local exhibitors bore the cost of censor cuts and the abuse of
press and patrons. Why should producers care? Washington and
Wall Street offered one answer: by 1922, the motion picture business had become an industry. Famous Players studios (later Paramount) had merged with a theater chain, while First National
Exhibitors planned a Burbank studio. Other companies that
wanted to integrate production, distribution, and exhibition understood a formula as true as Bronco Billy's aim: expansion meant
capital, capital meant Wall Street, and Wall Street meant conservative business practices. The movie companies could not afford
scandal or the federal probes of Hollywood high finance that might
follow. Neither could they afford clean movies. They *could* afford—
and very much needed—an astute public relations campaign that
would content Washington and strengthen motion picture securities. With Wall Street assured that the industry was stable, Hollywood would never have to choose between Fatty Arbuckle and
venture capital.

In 1922, the movie company presidents formed a trade association with Postmaster General Will Hays as head. An ex-Republican
national chairman with White House connections, Hays was a
booster straight out of *Babbitt*. He was an elder of the Presbyterian
Church and had a shrill voice that could assume an evangelical roar.
He also had enormous ears and asked photographers to use "an ear-
reduction lens" when snapping him. Ring Lardner whimsically
noted that the youthful Hays had been a traffic cop in his native

Sullivan, Indiana. Whenever he wished to stop northbound vehicles, he faced north and nothing could pass. At Sunset and Vine, the oncoming traffic included professional do-gooders, crusading reporters, and vindictive congressmen. Could the General halt them?

Within months of the formation of the Motion Picture Producers and Distributors of America (henceforth, "the Association"), Hays not only helped the moguls defeat a Massachusetts censorship law but also persuaded many industry critics to join the Association's Committee on Public Relations, an advisory group on "public demands and moral standards." He later created the "Formula," which made Association members "exercise every possible care that only books or plays which are of the right type are used for screen presentation." As the public continued to agitate for control over the movies, the General assured the National Council of Catholic Women, the Boy Scouts of America, and others that with their support he could purify the movies. Studio executives cheered him when he traveled west; after all, his gospel of Main Street morals promised to blunt the censors and warm the investment climate. Hollywood was "decorated with bunting and flags," Hays later recalled, "and big signs reading WELCOME WILL HAYS!"

Signs were elsewhere as well. Under Hays, Hollywood had instituted a morals clause that, as part of the standard employment contract, regulated performers' offscreen lives:

> The artist agrees to conduct himself with due regard to public conventions and morals and agrees that he will not do or commit any act or thing that will tend to degrade him in society or bring him into public hatred, contempt, scorn or ridicule, or that will tend to shock, insult or offend the community or ridicule public morals or decency or prejudice the producer or the motion picture industry in general.

Among many directors and actors, the prospect of sanitized movies, of artistic freedom tempered with restraint and self-regulation, evoked even more contempt than the morals clause. "We are against any kind of censorship, and particularly against Presbyterian censorship," Charlie Chaplin told friends at a private party. According to an FBI informant at the affair, the comedian also "showed his guests a pennant with the words: 'Welcome WILL

HAYS,' which he had fastened over the door of the men's toilet in his studio."

Pace Chaplin, Hays did not want to turn the Little Tramp into the Little Puritan. Rather, he wanted Hollywood to become mature enough to bear censure, conservative enough to value goodwill, and shrewd enough to advocate middle-class morals. He also wanted Hollywood to see how the press and censors rewarded an absence of self-control.

Ironically, with Hays' Committee on Public Relations and the Formula as shield, producers roared through the twenties. De Mille's "studies in diminishing draperies" and "It Girl" Clara Bow's teasing sexuality wowed the flappers. Erich von Stroheim's *The Merry Widow* brought moviegoers, among other pleasures, a sexual fetishist who died atop his bride on their honeymoon. For one scene in *The Dancer of Paris,* Dorothy MacKaill wore merely stones and beadwork; for the finale she donned cloak, loincloth, and breast-plates—then stripped. In *Black Paradise,* Madge Bellamy showed "all of her legs and 82 percent of everything else," de rigueur for desert-island pictures awash with bare brown breasts. A callow David Selznick quit Metro because of a dispute with boss Hunt Stromberg over *White Shadows in the South Seas:* "David thought it an idyllic story; Hunt said he wanted lots of tits."

The handful of producers who cooperated with Hays found themselves handcuffed. In April 1927, Universal president Carl Laemmle confided in one executive that the company was losing business because of its reputation for "namby-pamby" movies: "Invariably they are too damned clean, and they [the public] stay away on account of it." Pressured by his marketing staff for more-competitive product, Laemmle concluded that "much as I hate to admit it, I am beginning to think our clean-picture policy was a mistake." The studios that produced such fare as *The Merry Widow* or *Exclusive Rights* (a crime story with bare women and an electric-chair finish) exposed the Hays nostrums for what they were: the remedies of a quack. While social protesters called for federal regu-lation, the censor boards accelerated their demands for emendations and cuts.

The cost of the boards' dictums soon added over $3 million each year to overhead. Faced with demands for cuts, technicians could patch sound-on-film prints with relative ease, but they could not alter sound-on-disc without expensive retakes. "Cutting has often resulted in the ruin of a picture to an extent where grosses on these pictures, in the six censorship states, have been negligible," *Variety* reported. "A recent case was Harry Langdon's *The Chaser,* from which five or six sequences were cut, spoiling the entire continuity." The East and West coasts wanted Hays to rout the censors, but the General could not: according to one Association staff member in spring 1927, the boards were so proliferous that without drastic action "the motion picture industry will be hogtied and strangled in 25 states before May 1." With the need for self-regulation ever more apparent, Hays established the Studio Relations office. The distance between California (where the producers worked) and New York (where Hays worked) helped scuttle previous forms of control; perhaps an administrator at the source would make Hollywood see how urgent matters had become. Conversant with censorship laws around the country, Hays appointee Jason Joy would read scenarios and scripts, then advise producers on potential problems with local authorities. The former Wesleyan University student had earned a reputation for courage, especially (one of his classmates recalled) "in situations where unpopular causes were concerned." Now this former War Department public relations man would test that reputation in Hollywood.

Colonel Joy helped evolve three dozen proscriptions based on the rules of censor boards around the country. These "Don'ts and Be Carefuls" included pointed profanity, nudity, drug trafficking, sex perversion, white slavery, miscegenation, sex hygiene and venereal diseases, scenes of actual childbirth, children's sex organs, ridicule of the clergy, and offenses against a nation, race, or creed. Endorsed by the Motion Picture Association in October 1927, the Don'ts and Be Carefuls allowed Hays once more to claim that Hollywood had cleaned house. His office sent copies of the industry's code of ethics to every newspaper editor in the nation, along with a personally signed letter that promised a new era in screen history. Though Hays also forwarded the code to producers, many scribbled RE-TURN TO SENDER across the envelope. Producers were always suspicious of outside interference, even from the East Coast company presidents. They also found the threat of censorship laws and board–imposed cuts remote from the world of film production. In 1929, they sent Joy only twenty percent of their scenarios.

The studios were in heat. Metro had a sweaty Joan Crawford drop her skirt for a hot Charleston in *Our Dancing Daughters,* while First National set afire a theater in *Paris* so that chorines could flee the dressing rooms undressed. In *Mating Call,* Renée Adorée swam nude, then wore a sheer wet chemise homeward. *Mad Hour* was the story of a drunken couple who awoke in a hotel double bed. "And if you don't hear those on the side lines at Burbank hollering, 'Make it hotter!' " *Variety* noted in its review, "then you have no imag." Though some producers slapped EDUCATIONAL or DOCUMENTARY across the posters of "sex information" pictures, audiences read between the words.

In February 1929, as religious organizations issued demands for control, the General learned that press baron William Randolph Hearst would throw his considerable influence behind the movement for federal censorship. More bad news followed. In March, Iowa Senator Smith W. Brookhart introduced a bill to place the movie industry under the direct control of the Federal Trade Commission. Though Brookhart saw the mergers that swept Hollywood during the Depression as "a fight between two bunches of Jews," one "just about as bad as the other," he grabbed headlines with attacks on monopoly and morals in the industry.

Omens were everywhere. During the first six months of the year, state and municipal boards ordered a record number of deletions, over two thousand for crime and violence alone. "More than fifty percent of the United States, as far as attendance goes, is under censorship," Hays learned in April 1929. "More than sixty percent of the revenue derived from the sale of motion pictures comes from states and municipalities that have censor boards." Foreign censors were equally active. The British Board of Film Censors' cuts rendered an alarming number of prints almost incoherent, while the Australian and Canadian authorities banned 150 American pictures within a single two-month span. The central danger remained the Brookhart bill, a clangor on Wall Street and a standard for thousands of churchgoers, movie moralists, and professional do-gooders. Could the General halt them?

Hays was rescued by Martin Quigley, the publisher of *Motion*

Picture Herald. Quigley had married an heiress and constructed a power base on what one observer called "clever Irish politicking." A devout Catholic, he had been matchmaker for the Church and Hollywood when the 1926 Eucharistic Congress of Chicago was filmed; Hays' speech at that assembly "tied up the picture business for all time with the churches." Quigley wanted to harness the movies' power over American culture and morals. Though he had an iron conscience, he also understood that control over Hollywood could boost both the ad sales and influence of the *Herald*. Throughout the late 1920s, he scourged the West Coast producers and cultivated both the East Coast studio presidents and the Catholic hierarchy. And by 1929, when Hays chose euthanasia for the battered Don'ts and Be Carefuls, Quigley had convinced the industry that he was the moral barometer of the nation.

As the shadows of Hearst and Brookhart fell across Hollywood in summer 1929, Quigley conceived the notion of a code that would include not only rules and regulations but philosophy. Chicago censor board advisor Father FitzGeorge Dinneen pointed Quigley toward Father Daniel Lord, a St. Louis University professor who could write the document; but the Church stalled. Perhaps more "tied up" with the picture business than he wished—or aware of the backlash that a "Catholic code" could foster—Chicago prelate George Cardinal Mundelein saw controversy ahead and opposed the involvement of Father Lord or the Church. Quigley needed the Catholics; he feared that without pressure from them, the movie company presidents would not approve the code. Yet *too* close an association with a Catholic code could damage Quigley. He needed friends in both Rome and Hollywood to continue to walk the corridors of power. "I do not want the principal executives of the motion picture industry to feel that I am not giving major consideration to their interests," Quigley told Lord. "I feel that I can be most helpful generally by being left in the position of mediator and not advocate for either side." Quigley batted the problem around with Joe Breen, a good fellow Catholic who was then public relations man for Peabody Coal. As they sipped drinks, they talked "well into the mid-night" about "the gentleman on North State Street," Cardinal Mundelein. The bottom of the tumblers held the answer: when Quigley later assured Mundelein that the code would be an "industry code," one that would ban from pictures "things inimical to the Catholic Church," the Cardinal allowed Father Lord to proceed.

Basic to the Production Code Lord devised for Quigley were three working principles:

1. No picture should lower the moral standards of those who see it.
2. Law, natural or divine, must not be belittled, ridiculed, nor must a sentiment be created against it.
3. As far as possible, life should not be misrepresented, at least not in such a way as to place in the mind of youth false values on life.*

What followed elaborated the Quigley-Lord philosophy.

The Production Code termed movies "entertainment." Motion pictures could reshape "bodies and souls of human beings," and they could "affect spiritual or moral progress." But they were still entertainment. As such, those who produced them were bound to produce "correct entertainment" for the mass audience, "for the cultivated and the rude, the mature and the immature, the self-respecting and the criminal." Hollywood must not pander to that mass audience but honor the "moral responsibilities of the motion pictures."

Though the moral health of America seemed as ravaged as its economic health, Martin Quigley had a cure, and through the Christmas holidays he fussed over the Code. He not only made small changes in slant and diction, but plotted the route that the Code would travel from proposal to law. It was Quigley who understood how Hollywood worked, and Quigley who watched over the early January meeting between Cardinal Mundelein and Halsey, Stuart and Company, a Chicago investment banking firm with extensive interests in Hollywood. Lord called Stuart "the powerful man in the industry." Squeezed between God and mammon—Quigley thought—the producers would approve the Code.

Hays saw the Code in early 1930. "My eyes nearly popped out when I read it," he later wrote. "This was the very thing I had been looking for." The postmaster general who delivered the Committee on Public Relations and the Formula to America saw the Code as

---

* The complete text of the 1930 Production Code appears in the Appendix.

the way to silence Hearst and Brookhart, and soon he and Quigley were bound for Hollywood, where the signs would not read WEL-COME WILL HAYS!

Hollywood loved her dancing daughters. Throughout autumn 1929, studios like Universal had badgered Jason Joy to approve pictures like *Shanghai Gesture,* a controversial amalgam of illegitimacy, miscegenation, white slavery, and murder. A Universal production chief told Joy "that his company is pretty much in the 'red' and that they need a 'red-hot smash' to pull it out." That argument had become a chestnut around Hollywood, one that Hays roasted when he and Quigley brought Father Lord west to convince Universal and the other studios to accept the Production Code.

Listening to Father Lord and Elder Hays, immigrant producers probably felt a subtle pressure to assimilate, to nominally endorse the Judeo-Christian values of the Production Code and answer the prominent churchman whose censorship crusade had appealed to "Patriotic Gentile Americans." Morals alone could not win the producers' support, though. The predominantly Jewish men who ran Hollywood had little in common with the predominantly Christian reformers who opposed them. The former were rude frontiersmen, the latter fervent puritans. Accustomed to Hoosier bromides, the moguls assumed that the Production Code was razzmatazz for Washington and Wall Street. Another public relations gimmick. Another Formula.

The Code concerned morals; the *adoption* of the Code concerned money. Ever since Adolph Zukor had approached Kuhn, Loeb and Company for a loan to purchase theaters in 1919, the studios and the investment bankers had been partners, and in the late 1920s the banks poured dollars into Hollywood. The industry used the cash to absorb smaller competitors, monopolize first-run outlets, and convert both production facilities and theaters to sound. As long as Hollywood turned a profit, firms like Halsey, Stuart and Kuhn, Loeb showed no desire to control picture content. In the clouded atmosphere following the October 1929 Wall Street crash, however, public protests and congressional legislation threatened the bankers' investments. Along with distributors and theater managers, the money men called for restraint. In February 1930, the moguls approved the Code.

In March 1930, America learned about the Production Code

from *Variety*. That *Variety* scooped the *Motion Picture Herald* stung Quigley, who blamed Hays for the leak. Quigley was even more vexed when Hays formally announced the Production Code to the press. The newest code told producers to condemn criminality; to sanctify the marital vows and "not infer that low forms of sex relationship are the accepted or common thing"; to shun vulgarity, obscenity, and profanity; to clothe characters properly; to respect religion and national feelings; and to carefully treat "repellent subjects," including white slavery and brutal police interrogations. These "Particular Applications" of the Production Code, a Hays-doctored mishmash that bore a strong resemblance to the Don'ts and Be Carefuls, were *all* that Hays released to the press; he nowhere mentioned the philosophy behind them or the names of Father Lord and Quigley. Perhaps he wanted to hide the Catholic traces on the "General Principles," or wished to streamline a complex document for public consumption. Whatever the reason, the element of secrecy that would henceforth surround Production Code enforcement was already in place.

While Hays ballyhooed the Code as moral lodestar and industry triumph, his critics demurred. The *New Republic* compared the Code to the Don'ts and Be Carefuls, and predicted Hollywood business-as-usual. *Commonweal* accused Hays of attempting to "promote a nominal alliance with the church to camouflage an actual alliance with the devil." Others doubted that Hays or the producers would support the Production Code. "What with sound films making 'Damns,' clinking glasses, and machine-gun fire so obstreperously audible, Will H. Hays decided it was time to declare the motion picture industry moral again," commented a cynic in the *Outlook and Independent*. "With a few unctious phrases, he has glorified Will H. Hays and American wholesomeness, cleansed the silver screen, twitched away those thorns in his flesh, the church leaders, and reassured—whom?" No one. "The new code of film ethics, in our opinion, means exactly nothing."

The Code nonetheless promised some changes in Hollywood. Not only were the proscriptions more comprehensive than the Don'ts and Be Carefuls, but Colonel Joy would attempt real enforcement. For three years, Joy had forecast the censor boards' cuts and trims; he sent the predictions to the studios as suggestions, in dire cases warnings, but never demands. Now Hays had transformed Joy the consultant into Joy the gatekeeper: the new rules bound Joy to review each member-company picture and to approve only those that observed the rigid standards of the Code.

Joy feared the worst. Filmmakers who wished to challenge his rulings could appeal to a committee of three West Coast producers, the so-called Hollywood Jury. With members chosen in rotation, each juror recognized that one of his own pictures might soon be reviewed by a new panel, perhaps one containing the very producer whose work lay before him. A Hollywood Jury that favored self-protection and screen freedom would surely rule against the Studio Relations office. Should it not, the producer could still appeal the verdict to the Association in New York.

The early months of the Production Code and the Studio Relations office dispelled many such fears. The "entire office has developed into a beehive," one staff member wrote Hays, whose solemn appeals had turned some queen-bee producers into drones. Public criticism and demands for reform abated, and by October 1930, Quigley, whose role as Code author remained unknown, could commend the industry for its "serious and determined effort to maintain a wholesome screen." In the Association annual report, Hays noted that under the Code the studios had traded their "postwar preoccupation with morbidity and crime" for high-minded historical dramas and literary classics. The censor boards also remarked on the trend. "During the first six or seven months of this endeavor," Joy later observed, "the censors, with one or two exceptions . . . caught the spirit of the Code, and gave us the encouragement which had made it possible for us to keep the control of production under the Code." But many producers fidgeted. One complained that two-thirds of the stories he had under consideration "were based on 'Jack the Giant Killer' and the other third on 'Cinderella' "; the Code would permit nothing more sophisticated. Beyond the exaggeration lay many studios' concerns about the Code and the pledge to cooperate with Joy.

Whether the shotgun marriage between the Production Code and the producers could work depended on whether the Manhattan company presidents would control the Hollywood producers' tomcat urges. For some months, through a series of vigorous pronouncements about Code enforcement, the company presidents trained the gun on Hollywood. Toward the end of 1930, though, they relaxed their grip. With domestic attendance off almost ten percent and vital foreign markets burdened by new taxes and quota regulations, they suddenly ordered deep cuts in studio rosters and production costs. As *Variety* observed in December, "waste ceased being a mild misdemeanor and became a crime calling for capital punishment. And capital stepped in with a ruler."

The standard of measure was the box office. With unemployment approaching eight million, the producers could no longer take the automatic audience of the Jazz Age for granted. The lush days were over, and the mounting East Coast pressure sent Hollywood a message straight out of Darwin: those who produced runaway hits would keep their inflated salaries, swimming pools, and limousines; those who produced fizzles would join the soup lines. Hollywood had always been what writer Philip French called "a community torn by ruthless ambition and riddled with insecurity." In 1931, as attendance continued to slide, the cooperative spirit behind the initial success of the Code dissolved.

In October 1930, Hays had hired Joe Breen as public relations man for the Production Code. Breen commandeered some office space at Quigley Publications in Chicago, hired a clerk-stenographer, and strong-armed those who shaped opinion, from newspaper editors to Father Dinneen, whom Breen counted as "a great champion of the new Code." The Irishman could not always fathom Hollywood or—more important—Hays' reticence to clamp down on producers. The Association wanted to please everyone, from the censors to the producers. "I can understand the disposition to be charitable, and agreeable, and not offensive," Breen told one close pal, "but there are some things which crop up—and which have cropped up during the last eight or nine months, of which I have personal knowledge—which suggest to my mind that we ought to do a little fighting ourselves." Among the "we" were Hays and Joy, both of whom lacked the stomach for confrontation.

The studios bombarded movie houses with sex and violence. They believed that the more sensational the pictures were, the more competitive; the more competitive, the more profitable. In 1930–31, however, the New York censors alone made 468 cuts for indecency, 243 for inhuman acts, 1129 for incitements to crime, and 1165 for moral corruption. Other boards also scissored away, so much so that they lost the story. One censor admitted that his board had cut so much from *The Easiest Way* that on final viewing "we had to stop in the middle of it, because we thought we were looking at the wrong reels." Chicago censor Effie "Pinkie" Sigler made "wholesale" deletions in *Waterloo Bridge,* a 1931 Universal release about a bride turned prostitute, then told Joy that she had cut the picture merely to conform to the new Production Code.

Joy denounced such boards' "small, narrow, picayunish fault-finding attitudes," and occasionally sided with filmmakers; in particular, he devoted much time to protecting serious but controversial pictures from abusive cuts by local, state, and foreign censor boards. He found *All Quiet on the Western Front* full of "boldness and truthfulness" and helped Universal rally support for the film from such diverse sources as the Boy Scouts of America and (less successfully) various women's groups in Germany; he provided similar encouragement to Warners on *I Am a Fugitive from a Chain Gang.*

On such films as *Little Caesar,* which troubled the New York and British Columbia boards, Joy acted more as advocate than censor. When New York demanded extensive cuts that would eliminate much of *Caesar's* violence, Joy warned the censors that they threatened to "destroy the moral value of the picture" and that "the more ghastly, the more ruthless, the criminal acts, the stronger will be the audience reaction against men of this kind." Joy wore down New York board director James Wingate on *Little Caesar,* and the violence escalated with other hood operas.

Public Enemy was a 1931 Darryl F. Zanuck feature for Warners. Zanuck wanted sex and violence, and a young assistant hired to follow Zanuck around the Warner lot recording his instructions to subordinates was particularly impressed with the single-minded devotion accorded *Public Enemy.*

He was all hyped up about it, and kept repeating to [director] Willie Wellman and his crew that they mustn't let a drop of sentimentality seep into the action. 'Everyone in this movie is tough, tough, tough,' he kept saying. 'People are going to say the characters are immoral, but they're not because they don't *have* any morals. They steal, they kill, they lie, they hump each other because that's the way they're made, and if you allow a decent human feeling or a pang of conscience to come into their makeup, you've lost 'em and changed the kind of movie we're making.'

Released in April 1931, *Public Enemy* demonstrated that the gangster cycle was far from over. During its first week at the Strand Theater on Broadway, *Public Enemy* surpassed the record set there three months earlier by *Little Caesar.* Over twenty-five gangland epics were in production, most pale imitations of *Little Caesar* and *Public Enemy,* but each violent and sensational. Parents and church groups were outraged. With delinquency on the rise and Dillinger and the Lindbergh kidnappers on the loose, gangster movies became convenient scapegoats for a society apparently paralyzed by crime. Once the advocate of *Little Caesar,* Joy no longer pleaded with the censors for Hollywood clemency.

Locked factories, shuttered banks, and grim Hoovervilles became common across the urban landscape. Theater attendance declined, and Hollywood faced the full brunt of the Depression. The desperate Manhattan company presidents now let the producers call for the kimonos: for prostitutes and kept women, for sexual sin and secret fantasy, for *My Sin, Dishonored, Street Girl, Hot Stuff, Lady of the Pavements, The Purchase Price,* and *Tarnished Lady.* While the pictures delivered less than the titles, they nonetheless aroused those who supported federal regulation and censorship.

Joy understood that the odds against the Production Code were enormous: rowdy sex pictures could keep the wolf from studio doors. In search of rosy balance sheets—and blind to all but the wolf—hard-pressed executives would choose the hot stuff. With a debacle at hand and Joy under siege, Hays opened the Association armory and found almost nothing. Then he remembered that Irishman in Chicago, so "willing to work" that he would "*bite the legs*" off those who crossed him. Hoping for a small public relations miracle, the General sent Joe Breen west to face down the producers.

2

"You Can Be Had"

"THIS BURG IS probably the mad house of the universe," Breen wrote Hays from Hollywood in August 1931. Press relations were a shambles. Local reporters and free-lancers loved alcohol and hated work; they also "despise[d] the Producers." When the latter barred the press from the studios, the coverage turned worse. Breen wrote Hays: "The writing corps became over night a band of snoopers with spies and tipsters prowling everywhere—and reporting what they see and hear to the correspondents who are eager to print the stuff, come what may." The studios rolled out "blurb stuff" for reporters, who laughed it into the wastebasket. The situation had become impossible, Breen told Hays, and most producers had the "very definite suggestion that *you* 'must do something about it.' "

Breen could tell that the "picture people" would not do much for themselves. They had no decorum and no decency; they conducted their private lives in public, with no sense of audience, no sense of how offscreen mores could affect Hollywood press coverage and damage the industry. "For example," Breen wrote Hays,

a thoroughly competent and reliable correspondent told me the other night that one executive of a large studio gave a party to another executive of the same studio—a birthday party. The *name cards* at the dinner were *condrums* for the men and *cotex,* on which was a dash of ketchup, for the women. One very prominent lady star *told a group of correspondents who were interviewing her* that she is a lesbian. Down at the Los Angeles TIMES they told me the most amazing story of sexual perversion, sexual irregularities, etc., that I have ever heard. Recently, the head of a prominent studio was caught in bed fornicating with his neighbor's wife, by his own wife who came into the room, revolver in hand and failed to kill both of the bed-fellows simply because, in her excitement, she failed to quickly unfasten the lock on the pistol. A studio head whom you and I know *personally* very well is just now the laugh of the town because of his conspicuous and public liaison with a star' who is reputed to be the most notorious pervert in all Hollywood. And so it goes.

Whether true or false, such gossip affected the press's vision and would be hard to counter. Yet Breen told Hays that the "right stuff in the right man will form an amalgam that will surely crystalize into a huge achievement worthy of a real Crusader."

Who was the "real Crusader"? Breen wrote Hays an eight-page, single-spaced letter in August 1931, less a report than a hire-me pitch for Director of Hollywood Public Relations. The Association needed Breen the dynamo: a man prepared "to seriously take off his coat and go to work"; Breen the soldier: a man prepared to face "months of struggle to get a foothold, disappointments by the score, heart-breaking happenings that will upset all his plans and tend to nullify all his good work"; Breen the missionary: a man prepared to save "a great industry in which the lives and destinies, the hopes and the dreams of thousands of our people are inextricably involved"; and Breen the wonder-worker: "I have been able, I think, to get a first class, first hand, *lowdown* on the entire situation." Within months, Breen had become head of West Coast public relations.

As the winter snows melted, Main Street marquees from Ashland to Boston dripped with sleaze. Yet Breen appeared to have public relations for the Production Code, in his words, "thoroughly in hand." Despite the sex pictures, Breen wrote purple patches about Hollywood that may even have prompted the strong rejection of federal censorship that an association of women's clubs handed Hays in spring 1932. Once again Hays could boast—thanks in part to Breen—that the movies' program of self-regulation worked. "General indictments of the motion picture industry today come only from the uninformed, the malicious or those who earn a livelihood by derogation," Hays told America in 1932. "During the intervening year the trend in pictures has been away from sordidness and toward romance and clean comedy." Hollywood had the hootchy-cootchy in its blood, though, and even as Hays and Breen cranked out sunny press releases, a platinum blonde arrived in Los Angeles ready to mount an assault on Sweetness and Light.

Brooklyn-born Mae West had founded her career on *Sex.* Her boldly titled 1926 Broadway play challenged mores already battered by the decade and, according to the *New York Times,* won " 'ohs,' 'ahs' and partially restrained titters from its audience." Some theatergoers fled and some laughed, the *Herald Tribune* noted, but "the great majority remained in a state of stunned silence, wondering, no doubt, what was to be the next exhibition of complete frankness." Between 1926 and 1931, West authored two dramas about aberrant sexuality (*The Drag* and *Pleasure Man*), starred in a flapper melodrama that *Billboard* called "a set of pornographic pictures" (*The Wicked Age*), and adapted *The Constant Sinner* and *Diamond Lil* as lusty Broadway vehicles for herself. Joseph Wood Krutch concluded his *Constant Sinner* review with a commentary on the audience:

> It is difficult to imagine just where its members come from, but I have a theory. All the little boys who, in the early days of the movies, used to emit loud "smacks" when the hero kissed the heroine, must have grown up and gathered at the Royale just for the sake of being children again. They greet every suggestive line with giggles, gurgles, shrieks, and other strange noises not usually heard in civilized society. Their minds are so active that they discover fabulous indecencies even when there is none in sight. And they exhibit a sort of famished appetite for all references to sexual matters which is at once pitiful and alarming.

The Production Code had been adopted to assure the public that the movies would not pander to the common man's id. Had Breen read Krutch or Robert Littell, who wrote of the "degenerate shrieks from the balcony" at the premiere of *Pleasure Man,* he might have become unnerved by the prospect of Mae West in Hollywood. He would have understood that the actress kidded the vamp image, but the behavior of audiences would force the Hays Office to treat her as dead serious.

Audiences went crazy over *Diamond Lil.* The play opened on Broadway in spring 1928, toured well into summer 1929, and despite "vulgar dramatic situations" and "highly censorable dialogue" won over Hollywood. Universal production head "Junior" Laemmle needed some properties with sex appeal to balance his forthcoming prestige release, *All Quiet on the Western Front,* and by January 1930, he had contacted the Studio Relations Office about *Lil.* When Jason Joy answered that *no* company could make an acceptable picture from *Lil,* Universal countered that it might add Mae West to its writing staff, perhaps employing her to script short features. Joy knew where the back door led and naturally "discouraged the idea."

Aware that more such queries about *Diamond Lil* were forthcoming, Hays triggered an existing mechanism to blunt them. In fall 1927, he had urged the Authors' League to endorse Hollywood's pledge "to avoid the picturization of books or plays which can be produced only after such changes as would leave the producer subject to a charge of deception." While dramatists conceded that the movie industry could not produce censorable plays, they balked at the implications of the agreement. One possible scenario was clear-cut: Czar Hays would brand a drama "immoral," Hollywood would refuse to bid for the screen rights, and six months later Mammoth Studios would announce a picture that had appropriated the nub of the banned work. Authors' League resistance could not prevent Hays from maintaining a list of restricted plays, though, and in April 1930, he added *Diamond Lil* to it.

Like a duenna hovering about her charge, Hays used the "Index Expurgatorius" to keep Hollywood from Mae West for nearly two years. But the cordon that he had thrown around her increased her allure; fearful that another studio might grab her, Paramount invited the actress to southern California. So successful had Hays been, though, that even after the signing Paramount hesitated in casting her. "I sat around for twelve weeks drawing money and I never saw a script," West recalled. "This wasn't for me: either I worked or I wanted to get back on the stage. But they kept begging me and telling me they had a contract with me." She wanted to play Diamond Lil; instead, the studio finally gave her "a guest part."

Though Paramount scheduled the 1932 release *Night After Night* to groom George Raft as a matinee idol, Mae West salvaged the otherwise indifferent prohibition melodrama and tempted studio executives to feature the comedienne solo. Paramount certainly needed a "red-hot smash." Declining gross receipts conspired with enormous mortgage payments on Paramount-owned theaters to lead the company toward multimillion-dollar deficits. Despite administrative shake-ups in 1931 and massive layoffs in early 1932, the bleeding continued. These dismal conditions naturally ripened interest in Mae West and *Diamond Lil.* The story department told the front office that the playscript would make a poor picture: the Gay Nineties setting would alienate the core audience—college students, teenagers, and children. Assigned *Lil,* screenwriter John Bright found the play "a creaky, dated and absurd drama which Bwy audiences laughed *at* rather than *with*—while they were enjoying the ribald personality of the star." But management believed that the picture, shot quickly and thus inexpensively, might succeed. By fall 1932, *Diamond Lil* had been added to the tentative production schedule.

Hays learned of the decision to film *Lil* less than four weeks before the assigned startdate, less than a month after Jason Joy had resigned. Hays regretted both these events, but was not too surprised by either of them.

The announcement of *Diamond Lil* meant that Paramount had joined the Hollywood race to produce "sex pictures," a race begun when the Motion Picture Association board banned gang pictures in September 1931. Howard Hughes' spirited *Cock of the Air* served as front-runner. In one sequence, a prim Jane dressed in armor was chased by a randy Joe with a can opener; in another, a character remarked: "When Roger Hope [the hero] gets through with 'em, Don Juan himself couldn't make 'em." A Hollywood Jury supported Joy against Hughes—an independent producer outside the studio mainstream—and forced some cuts in *Cock of the Air.* But even the brutal reception that state and local censors accorded the picture could not turn Hollywood from sex.

Breen would help counter the reformers' howls over the sex pictures, but he could not battle alone. Only months before, he had told an East Coast associate that he expected Hays "to stand by me without any dodging or evasion or equivocation," a blunt plea that cast doubt on Hays' resolution. By spring 1932, Joy protégé Lamar Trotti had called for New York assistance: "Not since I have been here anyhow, have we had the variety of problems which have come up in the last two or three weeks—mostly involving sex situations—and I for one think the time has come to crack down as hard as we can somewhere."

Sound advice. But more and more when Joy played district attorney before the Hollywood Jury, the verdict favored the producer and undermined the authority of the Studio Relations office. Board members offered little consolation. By July, they seemed to chastise Joy more than they supported him. Some company presidents alleged bias, that Joy and Hays overlooked the smut in MGM releases yet attacked the salacious in other productions. The criticism was more than Joy could bear. When Fox Film offered him a post as story consultant in September 1932, he accepted.

The Studio Relations director should be flexible and combative, one Association executive told Hays; perhaps the General should make Trotti head and Breen "associate and bodyguard." But Hays wanted a *name,* someone with authority on the West Coast, someone whose experience and persona could cow the producers. The moguls were daunting. When Irving Thalberg learned that Trotti had called a scheduled MGM picture "utterly impossible," he hauled the young Georgia native "into a session which lasted literally far into the night." Meanwhile, Trotti told Hays, "my wife and his wife sat outside in the anteroom and starved. Thalberg, of course, is a man of persuasive powers and he used the usual high pressure salesmanship methods on me." Hays wanted someone with sales resistance. Perhaps someone from outside, someone immune to Hollywood glamour. Perhaps a professional censor, one who could rule the moguls and restore the integrity of the Code.

Hays settled on Colonel Joy's old nemesis, James Wingate. The former school superintendent and elementary-education specialist had been director of the New York board of film censors for five years; less tolerant than Joy but far more moderate than most industry critics, he seemed well chosen to revitalize the Studio Relations office. As one of their number, he could speak both to and for the nation's local censors, relating their concerns to Hollywood and Hollywood's to them. His credentials as an educator would also valorize Hays Office claims that films were healthy recreation for American youth. The General assured Doctor Wingate that the East Coast company presidents would support him, and confident that he could draw the moguls back to the Code, the stern educator moved west.

During the transition from Joy to Wingate, both men struggled with Paramount and *Diamond Lil.* The studio wilfully thwarted the Code. It had bought properties that Hays had personally banned, including the tangy *Virgins in Cellophane,* and ones that he had opposed, such as *A Farewell to Arms.* Paramount was "determined to put aside the conservative policy which has characterized the studio for years," Joy told Hays, "and to be as daring as possible." The plans for *Diamond Lil* added to the devilry. Corporate officials who ran the motion picture industry from New York had re-affirmed that *Lil* should not be produced, and when an irritated Harry Warner learned that Paramount had scheduled the picture, he wrote Hays to ask "whether I can believe my ears." Was Warner the conservative moralist or—sensing a bias toward Paramount—the jealous competitor? Hays needed no answer. He leaned on Paramount in Hollywood, then assured Warner that the project would not go forward.

The woman who sparked the furor had set up housekeeping at the Ravenswood Apartments in the old Wilshire District of Los Angeles, about one mile from the Paramount studios. Her meetings with the press suggested a narrow distance between Mae West and her theatrical persona. "Out here we're artistic," she told one news-paperman, "but more restrained. I like restraint if it doesn't go too far." Visitors found white furniture, gold trim, and mirrors every-where, including one on the ceiling over her eighteenth-century canopied bed; she would later tell reporters that she liked to see how she was doing. The wisdom pouring out of the Ravenswood made Hays' ears burn. "I think that the pictures are all wrong in the way they feature starved ingenues. You know, the flat-chested girls you see on the screen," West said. "Pained faces, sharp shoulders, knobby knees, terrible spaces between their legs. So flat you can't tell which way they're going." The connoisseur of sex and the former postmaster general seemed destined to clash.

In November 1932, not long after telling Hays that it would drop *Lil,* Paramount asked the Studio Relations Office to review an adaptation of the drama and note objectionable items. Down the hall, Breen shuddered: star, script, and director would constitute a lethal package that could destroy much that Breen had accomplished. Already those on the outskirts of the industry were disaffected: Martin Quigley now called the Production Code a "wash-out," while Alice Ames Winter, Hays Office liaison for the General Federation of Women's Clubs, had resigned from the Studio Relations Office. The trade journal *Harrison Forecaster* hinted that because sex pictures offended community standards, local exhibitors should pay bottom dollar for them. Breen could predict what editor Peter Harrison would say about the "constant sinner."

The Mae West screenplay for *Diamond Lil* centered on Mae, "one of the finest women [who] ever walked the streets." Although she sings for and presumably lives with saloonkeeper Gus Jordan, she maintains a certain distance from his white slavery operation and counterfeit ring; she even befriends a young fallen woman named Sally who wanders into the saloon and attempts suicide. "When women go wrong," Mae assures Sally, "men go right after them." Mae develops a yen for a Salvation Army mission worker named "Captain Cummings." "Why don't you come up sometime, see me?" she asks Cummings, in reality an undercover federal agent. The complications quickly multiply. Former lover Chick Clark pursues Mae, white slaver Russian Rita dies accidentally in a quarrel involving Mae, and Cummings lays traps for them all. A tepid antidote to all the crime and licentiousness, the script ends with arrests of the Jordan gang survivors.

Producers could weaken the censors' resistance to such material by stocking the credits with old-line Hollywood names. According to Lamar Trotti, the selection of Frank Borzage as director and Helen Hayes as star alleviated some concerns about the *Farewell to Arms* screenplay; John Cromwell and Irene Dunne performed the same service for the controversial *Ann Vickers.* Directed by Norman

Taurog and starring Constance Bennett, *Diamond Lil* might have walked past the local boards. But Lowell Sherman would direct and Mae West would star—volatile chemistry. Once a handsome leading man, Sherman had a reputation for casual dress and rough living. He had been at the infamous party hosted by Fatty Arbuckle a decade before and saw starlet Virgina Rappe "tearing off her clothes, clutching at her stomach and evidently in pain, groaning." He did nothing and said to himself, knowing that everyone had been drinking, "I guess that little girl has a bun on her and has indigestion." Rather than tame Mae West, the easy Sherman seemed one to play along. Wingate, not quite settled in his Hollywood office, sought advice from Hays; so sensitive was the matter that he communicated by cryptogram. Hays again went to Paramount, again received assurances that the company would drop *Lil*. Harry Warner knew better; he had already ordered a story outline for *Baby Face,* a sex-and-seduction tale calculated to raise the ante on rival Paramount. Twice burned, Hays ordered *Diamond Lil* "watched most carefully."

Meanwhile, Mae West, John Bright, and other screenwriters worked on what became *She Done Him Wrong,* a story that wove Bowery politics and Gay Nineties sex, with a colorful dramatis personae stolen from the play. *She Done Him Wrong* she was called, *Diamond Lil* she was. "Ah," Lil told the undercover agent at one point, "you can be had." So perhaps could James Wingate and Will Hays.

The stocky Wingate had confidence and moral certitude, but the Hollywood job also demanded compromise, a quality he notably lacked. As Doctor of Pedagogy from the New York State College of Teachers, Wingate had been the autocrat of the classroom; as New York Cato, the autocrat of the screening room. Wingate did not plead for changes in films, he demanded them. He had never been concerned for the artistic integrity or financial success of the picture before him. Lamar Trotti showed producers how to trim problem scenes and forestall deep censorship cuts. Faced with a problem scene, Doctor Wingate offered no healing advice that might enhance the patient's box office life. He recommended surgery—or else. Joy and Trotti attempted to arm pictures against those hatchet men, the local and state boards, but Wingate attempted to censor, to protect the public from Hollywood, not the reverse. Hollywood soon learned that because he was "set in his ways," he had no peripheral vision and no follow-through. He could indeed be had.

In November 1932, with the Joy-Wingate transition still in progress, the Studio Relations Office scanned *She Done Him Wrong,* noted the *Diamond Lil* stencil marks, then forwarded the script to New York. "By all means this ought to be stopped as it is a direct violation by Paramount of its most solemn agreement," Hays told Adolph Zukor. "You realize, as I do, the serious effect this will have on the other companies."

But Zukor had other concerns. With Paramount on the threshold of bankruptcy, Zukor had tabled all "solemn agreements." As the producer chose the supporting actors and the carpenters drove the nails into the set for *She Done Him Wrong,* the Studio Relations Office learned that Paramount had bought *Sanctuary.* Southern gentleman Trotti had read the William Faulkner novel two years before and found it "sickening . . . utterly unthinkable as a motion picture." Having purchased a book centered on a corncob rape, why would Paramount even hesitate to produce a Mae West picture? Breen could smell the flames, Hays could sense his ebbing influence. Paramount would proceed with *She Done Him Wrong* barely mindful of the Code. Hollywood executives would protest, then copycat *She Done Him Wrong.* Hays hoped that with his board behind him, though, he could halt the inevitable. At the November meeting, he brought into play his talents as an Indiana country lawyer: the broad smile, the stooped but calculated posture, the index finger soaring into the air and dive-bombing the lapel of a nearby spectator. Booming like a tent-camp evangelist, he asked board members to block the production of a picture on the "Banned List," one certain to open the floodgates.

Adolph Zukor countered that the screenwriters intended to use only "suitable material" from *Diamond Lil* and that Paramount would neither exploit nor mention *Lil* in its promotion and advertising; he did not need to add that the future of his troubled company rode on *She Done Him Wrong* and similar pictures. Sensitive to unspoken arguments involving dollars and aware that the film was in production already, the board permitted *She Done Him Wrong* to go forward.

Hays delegated the supervision of *She Done Him Wrong* to Wingate and Geoffrey Shurlock, Lamar Trotti's successor. Doctor Wingate told Paramount to remove all references to white slavery, kept women, and the Salvation Army (whose uniform the undercover agent wore); he also warned that Mae West's curtain line—"I always knew you could be had"—would lead not only to censorship troubles but to accusations that Hays had allowed the studio to make the banned *Diamond Lil*. He urged Paramount to highlight the Gay Nineties flavor and the comedy in order to move the drama as far as possible from "sordid realism." Paramount agreed "to go even further than we suggest in cleaning this story up," Wingate told Hays, but the General had heard promises before and reined in his optimism.

Not long after Thanksgiving, Paramount sent Wingate the lyrics to the Mae West songs in *She Done Him Wrong:* "Frankie and Johnnie," "Mazie," "Haven't Got No Peace of Mind," "Easy Rider," and "A Guy What Takes His Time." West had "no use for fancy drivin' " but loved "a guy arrivin' in low . . . a guy what takes his time." Double entendres and all, the song evoked the West *beau ideal*. Anonymous. Subordinate to women. Willing to engage in foreplay, perhaps indefinitely. Wingate warned Paramount to avoid the "suggestive and vulgar," especially in "atmosphere or accompanying action," then heard nothing more from the studio for over a month.

By early January 1933, when Paramount completed *She Done Him Wrong*, Hollywood and the Hays Office were still under siege. The 1932 presidential election had removed the last vestiges of Republican strength from Washington, and with the reign of the Grand Old Party over, the contacts whom Hays had nurtured over the years went home. New York boardrooms—Republican to the core—had reason to question the General's value in a Democratic federal government. Despite rumors of Hays' demise, though, fear and uncertainty may have saved the Hoosier evangelist.

The "lame-duck" winter was bleak. Fourteen million people—twenty-five percent of the American work force—were unemployed, and another quarter suffered diminished income from wage or hours cutbacks. Industrial production and farm prices reached all-time lows, foreclosures and bankruptcies all-time highs; the banking system virtually collapsed. Rumors that the new administration would scrub the gold standard caused depositors to panic and withdraw funds. Less than three weeks after Louisiana declared a special bank holiday to end the run, twenty-two states followed suit. Charitable agencies, their resources exhausted by ever-growing lines of the newly poor, closed their doors in despair. The political system seemed knotted. A leper to both congressmen and voters, President Hoover could do little. President-elect Franklin Roosevelt exuded confidence and promised a New Deal, but avoided specific commitments.

As the nation drifted toward calamity, so did Hollywood. Theater attendance had declined gradually through 1930 and 1931, then fallen sharply in 1932. By Christmas 1932, weekly attendance figures were off forty percent from 1929, and nearly twenty percent of the nation's movie houses had closed their doors. By the end of January, Paramount and RKO had entered receivership; Universal and Fox stood on the brink. Columbia, Warners, MGM, and United Artists remained solvent, but rumors of studio shutdowns and massive layoffs abounded. No one had a secure job.

What authority Wingate had soon evaporated. Hard-pressed New York executives cared no more for the Code than they had for the Don'ts and Be Carefuls. Again, the West Coast moguls pursued sex-and-spice, and they brooked no opposition from Joe Breen or the Studio Relations Office. When Wingate denied *Farewell to Arms* a certificate because it violated the Code, Paramount appealed and won a unanimous decision from a Hollywood Jury.

The "fairy sweet flower of sex" blossomed throughout Hollywood. Paramount had *She Done Him Wrong* and *Sanctuary;* MGM, *Red Dust* and *Red Headed Woman;* Sam Goldwyn, *Nana;* and RKO, *Ann Vickers*—all controversial pictures with sexual themes. While *She Done Him Wrong* at least had the saving grace of comedy, Warners' *Baby Face* was relentlessly sober. In November 1932, screenwriter Howard Smith conferred with Zanuck and Barbara Stanwyck about the picture; his sketchy notes preserved their suggestions:

The idea of Baby Face's father forcing the girl to dance at stag parties and to have affairs with the different men at the start of the story. The one definite situation where the girl's father beats her and forces her into a room where he knows a guy is waiting to spend the night with her—forces her into the room and turns the key in the lock after her. . . . How her father forces her to dance in the almost nude for the few shekels, which the men give her. . . .

Reformers who shunned the theater could read the inflammatory advertisements in the newspapers. *Thunder Below:* "A throbbing, vibrant story of a love-torn woman in a lonely colony of white men. She trades honor for 'love'." *Glamorous:* "Footloose beauty seeking men and money amid frenzied pent-house parties." *Forgotten Commandments:* "She's yours! She's beautiful, fiery, white-skinned, red-blooded! All she wants is love! Take her! Forget her husband! A rubber stamp gave her to him—a rubber stamp will give her to you. Any woman for any man. . . ." The combination of the pictures, the advertisements, and the reformers translated into a loaded gun. Mae West and the Code would determine whether Hollywood shot itself in the foot or the head.

In January 1933, Paramount invited James Wingate to a preview of the Mae West picture. The studio had thinly disguised the white slavery, changed "Lil" to "Lou," and converted the celebrated swan bed of the play into a more demure chaise lounge. Otherwise, *She Done Him Wrong* echoed *Diamond Lil*. Laying the groundwork for a defense of his own efforts, Wingate wrote Hays that Paramount had toned down the picture; he also soft-pedaled the audience reaction, "one of hearty, if somewhat rowdy amusement." He predicted that the picture and its songs would offend only "the more stringent censors." For the record, he urged Paramount once more to alter the ending and have undercover agent Cummings clear Lou with the authorities; he also suggested that the studio delete one of their last dialogue exchanges:

> Lou: Are those [handcuffs] absolutely necessary? You know, I wasn't born with 'em.
> Cummings: No. A lot of men would've been safer if you had.
> Lou: Oh, I don't know. Hands ain't everything.

The line would remain, though Paramount would at least have Cummings marry Lou. Wingate, perhaps influenced by the financial woes of the studio, demanded nothing more. In all innocence, he played out the role that Hays may have written for him: scape-

goat. Should Mae West and *She Done Him Wrong* tumble the Production Code house of cards, Hays could blame Hollywood and
hire a new administrator to deal with the moguls.

Paramount tinkered with *She Done Him Wrong* throughout January. Then, having made no substantive changes, it sent Mae West to
Manhattan to open the picture in early February 1933. During
premiere week at the Paramount Theater, as West appeared on stage
to sing songs and perform skits, audiences and several critics welcomed the return of two legends: Mae West and *Diamond Lil*. The
New York Times referred to the Paramount release as "a cinematization of 'Diamond Lil' " and even entitled its review "Diamond Lil."
Variety, which had faint praise for *She Done Him Wrong,* told the
industry that Paramount had remade *Diamond Lil:* "Nothing much
changed except the title, but don't tell that to Will Hays." While
New Outlook hailed *Lil* for "slipping undetected past chipmunky
Tsar Hays and his ban," *Vanity Fair* worried that the picture would
inspire vulgar imitations; producers would dismiss the "beery poi-
gnancy" of the original, accentuate the bawdy elements, and force
Hays to condemn West along with her smutty carbon copies.

Once *She Done Him Wrong* entered American theaters with the
Hays imprimatur, the General fielded the protests. Father Daniel
Lord, who had drafted much of the Production Code, turned livid
over *She Done Him Wrong,* "which everybody knows is the filthy
Diamond Lil slipping by under a new name." He acknowledged
that some pictures adapted from plays or novels had been only
"somewhat dirty"; he also acknowledged that filth was profitable,
whether the traffic was opium, cocaine, whores, or motion pictures. But he warned that producers who decided to "shoot the
works" would face a "day of reckoning." Perhaps the states would
take control of the movies, perhaps even the Church would.
The "motion picture industry will be very unwise to incur the
militant enmity of the Catholic Hierarchy," Lord told Hays. "It
has come perilously close to this with the type of thing produced of late."

Moved by fear, shame, or jealousy of the Paramount product,
even some of the moguls condemned *She Done Him Wrong*. Fox
Film president Sidney Kent wrote to Hays less than a day after
viewing "the worst picture" he had ever seen:

It was the real story of *Diamond Lil* and they got away with it. They promised that that story would not be made. I believe it is worse than *Red Headed Woman* from the standpoint of the industry—it is far more suggestive in word and what is not said is suggested in action. I cannot understand how your people on the Coast could let this get by. There is very little that any of us can do now. I think the place to have done anything was at the source.

Kent had branded Wingate as the goat. One solution seemed a stronger West Coast administrator, perhaps someone more palatable to Hollywood executives. Geoff Shurlock thought Wingate anti-Semitic; such an attitude would partially explain the wariness that existed between Wingate and the predominantly Jewish producers. Beneath the personality differences, though, lay knotty institutional problems. The distributors and exhibitors with whom the former New York State censor had dealt called movies "product"; they rarely opposed cuts because they watched the box office, not the screen. But producers called movies "pictures," resisted outside interference, and unlike their cross-country counterparts, would argue points with the censor. Wingate had no temperament for confrontation; moreover, once the Association board—including Kent—bucked Hays on *She Done Him Wrong,* he had no encouragement to rough up Mae West. Paramount likewise had no motivation to censor itself. The company desperately needed a hit and believed that West would deliver one; as lightning rod of the film industry, earning a handsome six-figure salary, Hays could absorb the jolts.

Hays was probably ambivalent about how the churches, the editorial writers, and the censor boards would respond to *She Done Him Wrong.* While he wished Paramount success, he knew that condemnation of the picture would not only vindicate his original stand on *Diamond Lil* but perhaps strengthen Production Code enforcement. State and municipal censors indeed took action. Their objections touched on characterization, situation, dialogue, and song. Though each board had different rules and often demanded different changes, the censors were so united on *She Done Him Wrong* that Adolph Zukor voluntarily trimmed a hundred feet of "A Guy What Takes His Time" from prints already in circulation. Leaving a scar on the picture, the cut was embarrassing and costly.

Hays gloated about the incident, though, and advised studio heads that they should take his advice in the beginning, not ex post facto.

Despite the censors' actions on *She Done Him Wrong*, Paramount moved ahead on *Sanctuary*. Hays told Wingate to exercise "the strictest supervision" over the production, for what Hays read and heard suggested that Faulkner heroine Temple Drake would shame even Diamond Lil. *Variety* and the *Hollywood Reporter* had condemned the novel, the *Memphis Evening Appeal* predicted that the screen version would offend "every sense of decency," and George Raft had refused a role in the picture because of the "unsavoury subject matter." Though later Hays learned that a contract dispute—not scruple—had come between Raft and *Sanctuary,* he remained convinced that the picture would damage Paramount and the Association. Hays wrote Wingate that with the New York office swamped, the East Coast would rely on the West to defend the industry: Wingate would oversee *Sanctuary* and, more important, the second Mae West vehicle. Meanwhile Joe Breen would monitor the publicity, the only contact that many reformers would have with the picture. With two scapegoats in place—a nanny professor and an Irish buck with fast legs and sharp horns—Hays left *Sanctuary* and Mae West to Hollywood.

3

Welcome Joe Breen!

JOSEPH IGNATIUS BREEN "spoke Hollywood." Tough and brash and larger than life, he was "just dumb enough," one associate recalled, and could see clear through the tinsel of the Tinseltown moguls.

Sons of immigrants, the Breen men were reared on the streets of Philadelphia. One brother graduated from St. Joseph's College and maintained a long association with the Jesuit campus; another became a priest. Joe had attended St. Joseph's but had dropped out by 1908 to learn the newspaper trade. Rather like the moguls who inflated studio vitae to complement their new status, however, Breen always called himself a college graduate.

Breen worked for several hometown papers in Philadelphia, traveled overseas as foreign correspondent, then moved to Chicago. There he directed press relations for the 1926 Eucharistic Congress and later for the World's Fair and the Peabody Coal Company. He had pals in the newspaper business, the censor boards, and the Church, and he could read them all. Breen knew when to josh and when to genuflect: he addressed the Right Reverend Monsignor Joseph M. Corrigan as "my dear Bozo" and Chicago censor board maven Father Dinneen as "Father." Breen also knew when to gladhand and when to backstab. He understood and respected power but would not be cowed.

No less than Hannibal, Breen loved war. He had survived "the confusion we had in England and Belgium during the Grand Fracas of 1914–1918 (I saw no service in France) and the chaos that followed in Germany, Poland, Austria et al, in 1919." Though peace was good, war was better. War compelled devotion to cause. It demanded what Hemingway called grace under pressure. Europe in the teens, however, was "nothing to compare" to Hollywood in the early thirties. The moguls owned the battlefield in 1933, and they controlled more loose women than General Hooker. Could Doctor Wingate, a stump from the groves of academe, rout them alone?

Breen thought not. As early as September 1931, when Chicago censor Pinkie Sigler rampaged through *Waterloo Bridge,* Breen had run interference for Universal and the Studio Relations Office. Breen approached Father Dinneen, whom he knew through Quigley, and convinced the priest to speak with the Chicago board. Breen performed other such services throughout 1931, and within nine months of the *Waterloo* affair was regularly screening pictures in Hollywood. By December 1932, with Joy en route to Fox and Wingate mired in controversy, Breen found himself meeting with the Hollywood Jury that examined—and approved—*A Farewell to Arms.* He soon understood that handling Hays Office public relations was much like janitorial work: better to control the moguls than clean up after them. He also understood that the Association needed Production Code enforcement, and that *real* Production Code enforcement would call for a *real* Production Code chief, perhaps someone whose exploits during the Grand Fracas would steel him for the inevitable Production Code wars.

Breen may or may not have ruled the college basketball court at St. Joseph's (as he often claimed), but he had the hardness and drive of a power forward. During early moments of the Hollywood game, Breen ran downcourt but let Martin Quigley take the shots. Two Catholic power brokers, Breen and Quigley respected yet never wholly trusted each other. Breen called Quigley "Pops." The nickname irritated Quigley, less because he was the younger man than because he was the more important and the name debased him. Hollywood producers made pictures and read *Variety,* bankers and film company presidents made money and read the *Motion Picture*

Herald; Quigley published the latter. Though the *Herald* concentrated on exhibition and distribution, Quigley made the Production Code his hobbyhorse. He frequently reported and editorialized against Production Code violations, for he knew that *Herald* readers in corporate suites could force stronger compliance. Perhaps more important, Quigley also knew that the mainstream American press raided the *Herald* for hints of rough-and-tumble Hollywood infighting and that studio heads feared the publicity and the embarrassment. Breen understood the delicate balance that existed between the movies and the media, especially when Martin Quigley controlled the scales. In early March 1933, Breen wrote to Will Hays that

> Q. is very much discouraged about the whole Code business. He feels that our folks here . . . continue to ignore it. . . . He feels that the staff which succeeded Col. Joy is not a good one. . . . I never saw him so down in the mouth about anything.

Breen drew no conclusion for the syllogism, but Hays would. And soon.

Breen gigged Wingate about the pictures then scheduled for production. *Ann Vickers* was "vile and offensive," *Sanctuary* "definitely incorrect morality to throw out from the screen," *Of Human Bondage* "the wrong kind of film—the kind of film which constantly gets us into hot water." Nothing changed, though. Hollywood in 1933 was run by the balance sheet, against which any Wingate initiative stood a poor chance. Even the most conservative company presidents yielded to pressures from Hollywood subordinates and aggressive sales departments. When Sidney Kent learned that the Fox studios planned to produce *The Power and the Glory*—the story of a railroad tycoon whose son fathered a child with his stepmother—he intervened immediately. "I think the quicker we get away from degenerates and fairies in our stories," Kent lectured Hollywood production chief Winfield Sheehan, "the better off we are going to be and I do not want any of them in Fox pictures." Audiences had flocked to *Cavalcade* and *State Fair*—"clean to the core"—and Kent wanted more such releases. But the salesmen who knocked on exhibitors' doors probably joined Sheehan and screenwriter Preston Sturges to protest a rigid diet of namby-pamby pictures; within weeks, Kent waffled and *The Power and the Glory* entered production. While other company presidents told Hays that they supported him, they conducted business as usual behind his back. Warners East Coast demanded that Warners West Coast reserve at least twenty percent of its schedule for "women's pictures." As production chief Zanuck explained to Wingate, "women's pictures" meant "sex pictures."

She Done Him Wrong demonstrated not only the box office power of "sex pictures" but the dilemma of company presidents. The Mae West production had cost Paramount less than a quarter million dollars to make and promised to return ten times that amount in North America alone. For the nationwide promotional campaign, publicist Arthur Mayer chose a photograph of "Lil" that prominently featured her bust. The copy read: "Hitting the High Spots of Lusty Entertainment." Mayer sent Zukor the publicity layout but heard nothing from him. After the art work had been executed and distributed, Zukor summoned Mayer to complain about the ads. Zukor's timing might seem puzzling, yet it followed a simple principle: having bound Paramount to uphold standards of good taste in advertising, Zukor needed to tell Hays, should the occasion arise, that he had not endorsed the promotion of "Lusty Entertainment."

Breen winced as exhibitors deemed the actress and the ad campaign a winner. A New York theater owner hailed *She Done Him Wrong* and maintained that his peers welcomed "sex in the luscious form of Mae West." The Victoria in Oklahoma City heralded "this hilariously ribald story of a gal whose intentions were strictly commercial"; as further enticement, the ads featured the picture's famous line, "You can be had." A theater just outside Atlanta (whose local censors had banned the film) did "a land-office business attracting capacity houses afternoons and evenings," while small towns played the comedy, then played it again. *She Done Him Wrong* enjoyed three thousand rebookings, more than the record-setting *Birth of a Nation*. Paramount released *She Done Him Wrong* abroad in the spring, and the English reviews suggested no cultural barrier: *The Times* of London praised West for an "amazing vitality and an air of self-conscious insolence which, in combination, are extremely effective."

On March 4, 1933, Roosevelt delivered his inaugural address, then—through the night—worked on a legislative assault on the Depression. The following day in Manhattan, Hays presided over a less visible but equally dramatic emergency session of the Motion Picture Association board. In January, *McCall's* had published an abbreviated version of a Payne Fund study of the movies; the data concerned the relationship between motion picture content and morality, behavior, attitudes, emotions, and health. Much of the focus had been on juveniles, and two of the social scientists who participated drew a none-too-conclusive conclusion: "That the movies exert an influence there can be no doubt. But it is our opinion that this influence is specific for a given child and a given movie." For the zealous, there were no "buts" about it. Beginning with the *McCall's* extracts, reformers shopped the nine separate volumes of Payne Studies for evidence that proved the movies detrimental. They intended to force Washington to do what Hollywood had not: ban smut. An associate wrote to Hays in October 1932 that "riding the movies is a profitable and tenable political position," and state legislators from Oregon to Georgia had moved into the saddle. For good reason, the Association called the Payne Studies the "Payneful Studies."

Throughout the all-night meeting on March 5, Hays lectured, cajoled, and pleaded. He told board members that his office could document over one hundred state proposals already introduced or drafted, and that the number could double by the end of the month. The Motion Picture Association must take positive action or face legislature that would dwarf all previous efforts at regulation. As dawn approached, the General persuaded board members that the "tendency toward confused thinking and the slackening of standards everywhere" demanded a return to "self-discipline in the motion picture industry." Paramount head Adolph Zukor joined his peers in signing "the Magna Charta of the industry," a document that pledged the moguls to reaffirm the Production Code.

Not long after April Fools' Day, the General went to Hollywood with the movies' New Deal. In a tumultuous meeting with West Coast executives, he claimed that the states had "upwards of one thousand bills" pending. Should the producers scorn the new Magna Charta—the sheet of paper that stood between them and state-by-state control of the screen—they would force him to lobby for federal censorship. The producers may have become even more hushed as he told them that Wingate had orders to enforce the Code. Period. "There is no use referring to pictures made by other companies," Hays warned, citing *She Done Him Wrong,* "and say, 'See what they got away with—we can do the same.'" The sex picture cycle must end.

In a grand gesture of compliance, Warner Bros. withdrew *Baby Face* from release and reedited the feature to suit Wingate. But other studios, too strapped to heed the General, tossed the Magna Charta into the dustbin. RKO finished *Ann Vickers* and *Of Human Bondage* with a wink and a nod for the Production Code and Doctor Wingate. Paramount was even worse. In *Bolero* one man urged another to visit Leona, hungry for love and not "fussy where she gets it." *Song of Songs* featured a sculptor palming the marble breasts of his creation; *Sanctuary,* a corncob rape scene that prompted the Production Code office to seek a "definite decision upon the Phallic symbol." Other studios threatened to make the run on sex pictures a stampede. In Warners' *Mandalay,* then in preproduction, Kay Francis stepped out of a bathtub and into Ricardo Cortez's arms. "For god's sake," producer Hal Wallis wrote director Michael Curtiz, "you have been making pictures long enough to know that it is impossible to show a man and a woman who are not married in a scene of this kind." Yet Wallis himself occasionally stepped over the line.

> We must put brassieres on Joan Blondell and make her cover up her breasts [Jack Warner cautioned Wallis on *Convention City*] because, otherwise, we are going to have these pictures stopped in a lot of places. I believe in showing their forms but, for Lord's sake, don't let those bulbs stick out.

Occasionally Hollywood tossed Wingate and company a crumb of hope. Through the grapevine the former censor heard that Sam Goldwyn had shut down production on a raunchy adaptation of Émile Zola's *Nana.* The short-lived celebration ended with a second rumor: writers were preparing a new screenplay that "may present even greater difficulties than did the original script."

Like Joan Blondell, Hollywood was busting out all over. In early

May, the hapless Wingate again complained to Hays that problems "continue to present themselves with amazing frequency." Two weeks later he wondered "why companies at this time, when we all desire to present pictures in conformity with the Code, continue to purchase and present for approval material which, even after a great deal of work has been done on it, must be close to the border line. The fact that some of these are even submitted to us . . . indicates a degeneration on the part of the person or company responsible."

Even as Wingate spoke, the *Magazine of Wall Street* recommended that those who owned film securities "at once write them off [their] personal ledger." Paramount meanwhile continued preproduction plans for yet another Mae West blockbuster. The studio sent Wingate the screenplay for *I'm No Angel* one week before the scheduled startdate. In the picture, Mae West would play a lion tamer and sideshow dancer named Tira. She achieves celebrity—and well-heeled male admirers—by ending her act on a courageous note: she places her head in the mouth of a lion. A millionaire pursues her, but his fiancée persuades an attorney (Cary Grant) to break them up. Though Tira falls for the lawyer and they become engaged, a former boyfriend and ex-convict shows up to prevent their wedding. Tira does not know that Slick has intervened, sues Grant for breach of promise, and acting as her own counsel wins the suit. In the last moments of the last reel, the lovers reunite, and she sings "I'm No Angel" to him. Paramount had obviously suspended "the Magna Charta of the industry": as she had in *She Done Him Wrong,* Mae would sing, rotate her hips, and dally with one man after another. Business—and pleasure—as usual.

"Mae couldn't sing a lullaby without making it sexy," *Variety* had noted, and Wingate sensed the impossibility of calculating the effect of each line of the script. The Production Code director sent Paramount a three-page letter detailing the potentially censorable material, including a reference to Tira as "the only girl who has satisfied more patrons than Chesterfields." But he concentrated on the songs, especially "No One Does It Like That Dallas Man" and "I'm No Angel." Though Paramount insisted that what the Dallas Man "did" was kiss and hug, studio officials agreed to change "Does It" to "Loves Me" and make the Dallas Man a wild-horse trainer who "tames 'em with a whip." James Wingate could only wonder whether Paramount had added sadism to sexuality. Several lines in the song "I'm No Angel" were equally dangerous. "Baby, I can warm you with this love of mine" and "Love me, honey, love me until I just don't care" suggested a naked libido; state and local censors would alter or delete the lines, Wingate warned Paramount.

The day after principal photography on *I'm No Angel* began, Wingate sent Paramount another three-page letter. He inveighed against certain lines and certain characterizations, then stated for the last time that until he saw the finished picture he could make no further recommendations. He expected the worst from the studio.

As the sum of her audiences' expectations, Mae West seemed to court sexual pleasure, but West herself—not Will Hays or James Wingate—blocked her female heroines from consummating their relationships. For West, readiness was all. Why else did she smooth her hair each time she invited a sexual advance? Why else did she design a corset for herself that served less as an enhancement of her figure than as a chastity belt? More than one Hollywood sage paired Mae West and Jean Harlow, whom Frank Nugent called "a two-woman campaign of sex-ridicule." But while moviegoers could imagine Harlow bedding Gable in *Red Dust,* could they picture West taking Grant in *She Done Him Wrong* or *I'm No Angel?* Pursuing sex without contact, West rubbed against the young Grant as a cat against a table leg. She even filmed the close-ups of intimate scenes without Grant on the set; she cooed into the lens until *Angel* director Wesley Ruggles cried "Cut," then adjourned to her dressing room while the crew shot Grant's matching close-ups. She wanted men, but not too close. As she told a magazine writer,

> I concentrate on myself most of the time; that's the only way a person can become a star in the true sense. I never wanted a love that meant the surrender of my self-possession. I saw what it did to other people when they loved another person the way I loved myself, and I didn't want that problem. I had to stay in command of my career.

Quite likely, the censors feared the independence and freedom of Mae West more than the sexual explicitness.

"I consider the situation hopeless," Alice Ames Winter told Hays in summer 1933. Months before, Hays had persuaded the silver-haired representative from the General Federation of Women's Clubs not to resign, for her recommendations on wholesome pictures (and there were always some) were a spoke in the public relations wheel. But now she saw no "will to righteousness" among the producers; the Code was "something to be 'got around.' " She again tendered her resignation from the West Coast office, and Hays again convinced her to withdraw it. When *I'm No Angel* opened, he and Breen would need her more than ever.

In September 1933, Paramount previewed *I'm No Angel*. Wingate found it better than expected and even believed "that the picture will meet with no undue criticism." An important Hays associate in New York not only called *Angel* "a knockout" but predicted that some of the dialogue would become famous. Perhaps he meant infamous. West first appeared on the midway poured into a gown with sequins encircling her breasts and tassels hanging from her nipples. She stood for marriage, she said, but only as a last resort; as she told one man: "When I'm good, I'm very good, but when I'm bad, I'm better." The Payne Fund studies had whetted the scissors; *I'm No Angel* would invite the censor boards to use them.

I'm No Angel opened in October 1933. The reviews were generally enthusiastic; the *New York Times* found the humor "shameless but thoroughly contagious," and *Newsweek* called the star the "world's best bad actress." *Variety* aptly noted that "the same plot mechanics and situations without Mae West wouldn't be a motion picture at all." That point was amply demonstrated by the turnout at the Paramount Theater, where "ushers were riding herd on a permanent corral of waitees in the lobby." Inside the theater, moviegoers roared. "Am I making myself clear?" Tira asked at one point; the audience laughter proved that she was. The picture had cost just under a quarter million dollars and, like *She Done Him Wrong,* promised to return ten times that amount. But at what price, Hays wondered.

In autumn 1933, Hays borrowed Colonel Joy from Fox. Joy would concentrate on "the general flavor of the pictures" and Wingate "the narrower considerations of the censor point of view." Hays then made Breen "Assistant to the President." The appointment not only demoted Wingate but allowed Breen to function as the de facto head of the West Coast operation.

With the New Deal in full swing and the National Recovery Administration parades whipping up enthusiasm for the Roosevelt agenda, shrewd moralists and film reformers attempted to bring censorship under the "Blue Eagle" banner. They used *I'm No Angel* and other sex pictures to argue for a rigorous NRA code for the movies. One week after *Angel* opened, *Christian Century* magazine invited readers to "turn to the movie ads. You find such items as this:

Mae Packs 'Em In. This 1933 'Don't Care' gal has PERSONALITY— swinging hips—bedroom eyes and the throaty growl of an amorous cat—she just doesn't give a damn!

Though Hays would finally persuade Roosevelt and the NRA to let Hollywood police itself, the Catholic Church wanted the amorous cat spayed. And unlike Roosevelt, the Church proved a formidable adversary.

Breen may have encouraged and even stage-managed the Catholic march on Hollywood. For several months in 1930, he had attempted to win Church support for the Production Code. "Much of this effort was devoted to contacting the Catholic press," Quigley recalled some years later, "getting the interest of the Catholic press in the work and getting their support for it." At that time, "we encountered nothing but an attitude of indifference. No member of the Hierarchy exhibited any interest in the work, and no aid was rendered from any Catholic source." But Breen never lost interest.

During summer 1933, as *Western Catholic* promoted movie boycotts, Breen met with Los Angeles's Bishop John Cantwell and saw "fire in his eyes." Breen fed the flames, less because he wanted to punish Hollywood than because he saw the phoenix that might rise. Wingate was Protestant, Hays Presbyterian, Shurlock Episcopalian, the moguls Jewish. Breen was Catholic, a professional Catholic at that, ready to interpret the Association for the Church, the Church for the Association. The opportunities for power and advancement seemed obvious. As *I'm No Angel* opened in October 1933, Breen read that Archbishop Amleto Cicognani, addressing the hierarchy, had condemned immoral motion pictures as crimes against innocent youth. "Catholics are called by God, the Pope, the Bishops and the priests to a united and vigorous campaign for the purification of the cinema," he said. In November 1933, Church leaders formed the Episcopal Committee on Motion Pictures. "Time can be taken to select with great care the members of this group," an Ohio archbishop noted. "A man like Mr. [John] Raskob [a Catholic tycoon] might be able to bring pressure to bear upon financial institutions like the Chase Bank of New York to prevent it from lending money to the producers of filthy pictures."

Hays called Breen to New York in late November 1933. Wingate had become dependent on Breen, and without him, Wingate said, he felt "pretty well swamped." Should the Catholics wage war on Hollywood, the former New York censor would become an early casualty; he lacked sound instincts (predicting that *I'm No Angel* would "meet with no undue criticism") and political savvy. Breen had both, in abundance. He had become the conscience, the spark plug, perhaps even the linchpin of the West Coast office. Because he had ties to the Church hierarchy, Hays questioned him not only about the Code and the moguls but also about Church policy and politics. Breen believed that Catholic agitation could benefit rather than destroy the industry—if someone could convince the studios to meet the churchmen halfway. Breen also believed himself the "someone," and Hays—physically and perhaps temperamentally too weak to dominate the producers—reasoned that whether Breen turned up savior or scapegoat, the Association could not lose. By December 1933, Hays had decided to confer on Breen the powers over the West Coast operation that he had already assumed.

To smooth the transition from Wingate to Breen, Hays went west in January. The towns the Hays train passed were almost more aware of the Payne Fund studies than of the movies they censured, for preachers, editors, and after-dinner speakers had turned the reports into brimstone. While Bishop Cantwell threatened to sermonize against "vile, filthy and dirty" pictures, the *Boston Sunday Post* told readers in bold headlines that Cardinal O'Connell had denounced the movies' "sinister effects."

When a sober Hays arrived in the City of the Angels, he found Breen more self-confident then ever. Producers would soon discover the tough negotiator behind the stage Irishman. RKO pro-

ducer Pandro Berman and director John Cromwell convinced
Breen that *Of Human Bondage* was "something of a classic." Though
Breen conceded the importance of the story, he nonetheless "reserved the right to reject certain scenes." Months before, after
Paramount and Warners had submitted the screenplays for *Bolero*
and *Heat Lightning,* two controversial sex pictures, Wingate had
recommended changes. Breen enforced them. He saw *Bolero* at a
studio preview but refused to approve the picture until Paramount
made cuts. On *Heat Lightning,* Warners had scoffed at Wingate for
recommending that three seduction scenes be trimmed to one.
Breen demanded changes on the release print, though, and he
wrote Hays that the studio complied "after considerable pressure
had been exerted on our part." By February 1934, Hays had raised
Breen's salary.

Despite Breen, some Hollywood leopards retained their spots.
Warners submitted an incomplete *Wonder Bar* but assured Production Code associates that the missing footage contained "nothing to
worry about." In one of the numbers later added to the release print
of the Al Jolson musical, an effeminate man approached a dancing
couple and tapped the man on the shoulder. "May I cut in?" he
asked, then the two men waltzed off together. Association counsel
Vincent Hart saw *Wonder Bar* in Manhattan and alerted Breen to
"one item which the audience did not seem to relish." Though
Breen wanted the bold cheek-to-cheek purged (the Particular Applications of the Production Code forbade "sex perversion or any
inference to it"), Jack Warner resisted. Breen wrote Warner about
Wonder Bar but heard nothing. He telephoned Warner but could not
reach him. "It is quite evident that the gentleman is giving me the
run-around," Breen told Hays. "He evidently thinks that this is the
smart thing to do." Unless Breen had more leverage, he would
never force Code compliance.

Breen needed absolute authority in Hollywood, and whatever
undermined that authority undermined the Code. He found the
Hollywood Jury especially subversive. One month after becoming
Production Code administrator, he had rejected *Queen Christina* and
MGM had appealed. According to director Rouben Mamoulian,
who later reminisced about the picture, Greta Garbo "strokes the
bedroom where she has been with her lover, so that she will remember every detail"; she "had to roll over a bed, and move around the

room in what was a kind of sonnet in action." More a dirty limerick, Breen contended, but the Hollywood Jury supported MGM.

Wingate thought that the jury system could serve a legislative function: Jury decisions, whether they favored Wingate or the producer, would create precedents that eased future Code enforcement. But the producers who decided each case were moviemakers, not trained jurists, and many of them had questionable films in production. Aware that stringent rulings could be used against their own pictures, the producer-jurors rarely supported the Code office. One trade paper reported that by May 1934 the studios had already successfully appealed four Breen rejections, and the Irishman felt his strength wane. Breen understood that a democracy demanded an appeals process. He also understood that democracy Hollywood-style not only smelled of cronyism but eroded the power of the Production Code and its administrator; on several occasions Breen had made concessions to the studios merely to avoid the potential rebuke of an appeal. "I have learned very much in the past two or three months," he wrote to New York in spring 1934. "One of the things I have learned is not to expect much help in the matter of clean pictures from a jury."

Prevention remained the key to enforcement, and prevention meant one-on-one with the moguls. Breen was unafraid of theatrical masks. Depending on the audience, he acted the proper gentleman, the shrewd horse trader, the informed college man, or the offended and outraged moralist. When Columbia announced *Red Square,* Breen became concerned. On arrival in Hollywood, he had arrayed his credentials before Columbia production chief Harry Cohn. "What's all this shit?" Cohn fired back. Breen reflected, then told Cohn that he regarded the question as a compliment: if "there's any expert in this town on shit—it's you," Breen said, so "if I have to be judged, I'm glad it's by professionals!" Breen and Cohn understood each other, perhaps one reason that Cohn dropped *Red Square,* a Lewis Milestone picture "glorifying a Communist and Communism."

Mae West posed a tougher challenge. As she later recalled:

When I knew that the censors were after my films and they had to come and okay everything, I wrote scenes for them to cut! These scenes were so rough that I'd never have used them. But they worked as a decoy. They cut them and left the stuff I wanted. I had these scenes in there about a man's fly and all that, and the censors would be sittin' in the projection room laughing themselves silly. Then they'd say 'Cut it' and not notice the rest. Then when the film came out and people laughed at it and the bluenoses were outraged, they came and said, 'Mae, you didn't show us that.' But I'd show them the scripts they had okayed themselves!

Though James Wingate, Geoff Shurlock, and other Breen lieutenants generally read the scripts, screened the pictures, and prepared the letters to producers that Breen signed, Breen himself closely supervised *Belle of the Nineties*. The third Mae West vehicle involved saloon singer Ruby Carter (West) and her love for two men, one of them an ex-convict; violent crime, prostitution, and narcotics shaded the background, and West herself doped a prizefighter and became accessory to murder and arson. The queen of the corsets had many of the best lines: "A man in the house is worth three on the street." And: "Don't try to get to heaven in one night." And: "It pays to be good—but it don't pay much." A March 1934 Production Code letter to Paramount contained not only four and a half pages of recommended deletions but a demand for "compensating moral values."

Neither as concept nor phrase had "compensating moral values" appeared in the Production Code, yet previous Code administrators had occasionally applied it to motion pictures. Three years before, Joy had censured *Common Law* because no character expressed moral outrage about the sexual activity of a young unmarried couple. While Joy and Wingate had merely flirted with the notion of "compensating moral values," Breen embraced it. "Compensating moral values" forced producers to balance all serious departures from the social norm with actions or voices that condemned them. Herman Mankiewicz translated the idea into words that his fellow screenwriters could understand. The hero and heroine must be virgins, he quipped. "The villain can lay anybody he wants, have as much fun as he wants cheating and stealing, getting rich and whipping the servants. But you have to shoot him in the end." Breen had sent characters to Death Row for crimes less grave than those of Ruby Carter in *Belle of the Nineties*. "You understand," he told Hays, "that if the picture is not in conformity with the Code, it will be promptly rejected." When early on Paramount threatened to appeal a rejection to a Hollywood Jury, Breen knew that the battle lines had been drawn.

The forthcoming struggle over *Belle of the Nineties* made Breen welcome the continued agitation of the Catholic Church. While some Catholics shunned the Hollywood crusade, the Episcopal Committee on Motion Pictures won support from important Catholics, including banker A. H. Giannini, who reportedly told Hays that he would tie Bank of America loans to clean pictures. "We need, I think, only four or five priests in the country as a National Committee," one Catholic advocate had told Bishop Cantwell in December 1933. "These men could make a lot of noise, and they could say things at times that perhaps we Bishops could not say." On April 11, the Episcopal Committee told the American Catholic bishops that it planned to recruit a "legion of decency" and wanted parishioners to pledge support for clean movies. The pledge would read:

I wish to join the Legion of Decency, which condemns vile and unwholesome moving pictures. I unite with all who protest against them as a grave menace to youth, to home life, to country and to religion.

I condemn absolutely those salacious motion pictures which, with other degrading agencies, are corrupting public morals and promoting a sex mania in our land.

I shall do all that I can to arouse public opinion against the portrayal of vice as a normal condition of affairs, and against depicting criminals of any class as heroes and heroines, presenting their filthy philosophy of life as something acceptable to decent men and women.

I unite with all who condemn the display of suggestive advertisements on bill-boards, at theatre entrances and the favorable notices given to immoral motion pictures.

Considering these evils, I hereby promise to remain away from all motion pictures except those which do not offend decency and Christian morality. I promise further to secure as many members as possible for the Legion of Decency.

I make this protest in a spirit of self-respect and with the conviction that the American public does not demand filthy pictures, but clean entertainment and educational features.

The movement soon gained momentum.

Some Catholics wanted to name names. "We say, 'Don't go,' " Father Lord told Quigley, "but we don't say *Where* they are not to go. And I think that is a definite weakness." Lord proposed that the Church classify films "Good, Bad, [and] Borderland." They would approve the "Good," disapprove the "Bad" "BEFORE THEY ARE REALLY STARTED," and send the "Borderland" to a committee composed of producers, representatives of the Association board, and members of the general public. The tough-minded Jesuit believed that he "could write the White List at present on the back of a postage stamp, and have room left over for the Declaration of Independence." Quigley, the servant of Rome and Hollywood, not only opposed Lord but persuaded the hierarchy against the notion of lists. The grass roots were another matter.

Monsignor Hunt of Detroit, whom the Hays Office considered an embittered opponent of Hollywood, ruled more than sixty pictures "unfit to be shown to the public" in spring 1934. The titles that appeared in the Catholic weekly *St. Leo* included *The Power and the Glory, George White's Scandals, Nana, Wonder Bar,* and *Design for Living,* the witty Noel Coward ménage à trois comedy. Though Catholic officials like Monsignor Hunt exerted only local influence, the possibility of concerted action and the appearance of an Index chilled the Association on both coasts. A Hays staffer sorted the sixty movie titles in numerous ways, the most compelling by company. Paramount and Warners had produced almost half the pictures on the list: twelve each. Even though Breen conceded that many reformers were " 'lunatic fringe' apologists" worthy of scant concern, he would not minimize the Catholics. As the hierarchy upgraded a "legion of decency" to "The Legion of Decency" and lent credence to rumors of boycotts, Breen warned Paramount that *Belle of the Nineties* was poor industry policy.

Meanwhile, principal photography on *Belle* continued. Breen hoped that the climate would encourage Paramount to observe the Code and avoid a confrontation. Almost daily he sent bulletins to Paramount and the other studios to warn of those marshalled for action against Hollywood. An odd blend of rumor and fact— acknowledged as such—the bulletins suggested the gathering storm and, more important, the way that Breen would ride it out. He promoted himself as the industry wallah, the Will Hays of the West Coast, and he used the bulletins to demonstrate his command over censorship matters. The implication: he could lead the producers out of danger. Breen referred to Catholics and other reformers as *our* critics and noted that *we* must clean up *our* pictures before *they* do it for *us*. At the same time, Catholics referred to Breen as *our* man. Father Lord wanted Hays to unleash the Production Code watchdogs, to add "those teeth about which he so loudly talked in times past" and have a "reliable man" make them bite. Joe Breen, whom Lord recommended, was ready. On May 12, Breen announced that the superintendent of Catholic schools in southern California had suggested that local club women "boycott unwholesome and immoral motion pictures." He would not allow *Belle of the Nineties* to become the prime target.

An indifferent Paramount had produced *Belle* to snare audiences that had flocked to *She Done Him Wrong* and *I'm No Angel*. In June 1934, with such former industry supporters as Father Dinneen mad at Hollywood, Breen drove to the Melrose Avenue studios to meet with Emanuel Cohen, William LeBaron, and three other Paramount officials. Mae West called the picture "not a good story because they [Breen and company] made me make it three times before I found out what they wanted." Despite the purported script changes, *Belle of the Nineties* remained an oily blend of sex, crime, and Mae West that Breen told the producers he could not and would not approve. Manny Cohen probably waved the Paramount receivership papers in Breen's face, argued that the company needed the box office bucks, and (since the sessions could turn thunderous) damned Breen and the Code to hell. Breen could insist that *Belle*—not he—posed the problem. He could also wave papers in Cohen's face, for one Rabbi Goldberg had recently "attacked Jewish movie producers who bring disgrace upon the Jewish people." Finally Cohen agreed to consider some cuts, then asked Breen to withhold a formal letter of rejection. The Production Code administrator forwarded such letters to Association board members in Manhattan, where the company presidents could point fingers and scold; the wily Cohen apparently wanted to elude East Coast control. Breen wrote to Hays:

> There is much 'under cover' work going on that smacks to me of a desire on the part of the studios definitely to outsmart and outwit the machinery of the Code. . . . The attitude we have found here with

regard to the public criticism which has become so widespread, is to belittle it all, to sneer at our critics and to continue to make pictures to suit ourselves. I am deeply concerned about it all.

Another scenario also seems possible. Should the contents of *Belle of the Nineties* have become known in Manhattan, Paramount could not have protected Zukor from the wrath of men like Sidney Kent. And equally important was that after cutting some of the more flagrant lines from the picture, Cohen probably hoped that Breen would negotiate on the rest. Once Breen had approved *Belle of the Nineties,* Cohen and Zukor could then blame the Production Code administrator for whatever controversy Mae West provoked.

But Breen decided to send the rejection letter to Paramount, carbon to New York. Two days later, Paramount agreed to make the cuts that Breen demanded, and the Production Code administrator approved the picture pending an acceptable final release print.

On *Belle of the Nineties,* tough guy Joe Breen made his bones. The censors and the Catholics had again proved instrumental, but while Breen scored points on *Belle,* he let Manny Cohen retain some questionable lines and incidents lest—pushed too far—Paramount appeal to the Hollywood Jury. West still appeared more the prostitute than the burlesque queen. She still hungered for "men and masculine charms," and she still turned phrases: as her maid walked away, West looked at her posterior and remarked, "I see it in your face." After Breen, *Belle of the Nineties* still had piquancy.

What happened next hurt Mae West more than Breen had. Darkening the shadow cast by the Legion of Decency, the New York censors objected to the theme, dialogue, and situations in *Belle of the Nineties* and rejected the picture. Board members were especially outraged by a happy ending that promised sex without marriage. "If they think it's too warm," West purred, "I'll cool it off." West and Paramount must have reasoned that other censors would follow the New York lead, for Manny Cohen suspended not only the New York but the national release of the picture until he could make the requested cuts. For the next month, Cohen worked on the picture; he even shot a new conclusion that showed the Tiger Kid and his inamorata exchanging wedding vows. *Variety* called the "benefit-of-clergy finale" an "obvious curtsey to Joe Breen." But although the New York censors—not Breen—had forced the change, the Production Code administrator had learned a lesson. Leniency was condemned, not rewarded. *Belle of the Nineties* would become the last Mae West picture to escape the full force of the Breen scissors. *

While Paramount snipped at *Belle of the Nineties,* Breen watched the Catholic furor mount. According to a midwestern newspaper, "the general sentiment against objectionable pictures has reached the point where intelligent theatre men [exhibitors] are beginning to take stock of the situation." Elsewhere, Father Lord blacklisted pictures for the Catholic periodical *Queen's Work,* and—ominously—the Archbishop of Cincinnati gathered information about the mortgage holders of theaters. Despite the pressures, some Catholics were not sanguine. In June 1934, Cardinal Mundelein wrote to Franklin Roosevelt about the bishops' campaign:

> We decided to use our own organization first in the endeavor to bring these picture people to a realization of the attitude of decent people of their own accord, before we would call on 'the strong arm' of the Government. Personally I doubt that we will have much success except in cutting down the box-office receipts. The background here is lacking. These people simply do not know different. Many of them have come up from the burlesque houses and they still cling to the standard they learned there. However, we will do our best. . . .

If Breen shared the doubts of Cardinal Mundelein, he never shared them with Hollywood. Breen and Quigley attended a bishops' conference in June 1934 and afterwards told Hays that although the war had been called off, the Catholics had not shouldered their muskets and marched home. The bishops soon met the moguls themselves. "Warner brothers not present," Father Lord wrote Quigley, "good excuses, but not there. Universal ditto. Otherwise

---

* Who killed Mae West? Not Breen alone. Toward the end of the decade, Barbara Stanwyck, Katharine Hepburn, and Jean Arthur were the new "fast-movin' gals"; Olivia de Havilland, Claudette Colbert, and Irene Dunne were intelligent and chic women. Mae West was Mae West, a throwback to Edwardian corsets, burlesque blue humor, and "Diamond Lil." Her *Go West, Young Man* (1936) brought Paramount a measly return, and *Every Day's A Holiday* (1938)—despite publicity generated by a "scandalous" radio skit with Charlie McCarthy—failed to make money.

much larger and much more representative crowd" than expected. Lord told the producers that the Catholics would henceforth demand Production Code enforcement.

> Not a comment by any of those present when I finished—except DeMille who said, "I guess silence gives consent." Today Joy tells me that there have been several calls and that [the meeting] caused a great deal of serious thinking and some considerable worrying. But nobody said, Tain't so. And that's something.

The editorials that poured into Hays' office—two hundred in five days—suggested the power of the Church.

Some Hays confidants encouraged the General to explore avenues of resistance. Scripps-Howard board chairman Roy Howard, who thought that the Association should oppose "church-dictated censorship," told Hays that he would not "run with the herd on this matter." Another Hays crony wanted the Association to mount a counteroffensive, one that could blossom into charges that the Church movement was anti-Semitic. Universal executive Robert Cochrane counseled against such a plan: "Laemmle and Harry Warner will be the only ones who will have guts enough to back us up. But Nick Schenck and Zukor and Sam Goldwyn will run like rabbits." Though box office revenue was still healthy, the loss of Catholic patronage would cripple Hollywood. Even *Variety* admitted that no business could thwart the Church, especially "when the latter's purpose is well founded." Breen told Hays that the time for concession had arrived. Hays agreed. In June 1934, as boycotts loomed and blacklists spread, he changed the Studio Relations office to the Production Code Administration and appointed Breen Production Code administrator.

When Hays converted the Studio Relations office into the Production Code Administration, he altered more than the name. He ordered member studios to submit all treatments and scripts to Breen; to direct all appeals not to a Hollywood Jury—now defunct—but to the Association board in New York; and to pay a $25,000 fine for releasing a picture that violated the Code. More important, Association members would bar from their theaters all pictures that lacked the Production Code Seal. After 1934, no picture without the Seal could secure a decent theatrical release or profit.

Breen had wide support. Among Catholics, he was God. A Cincinnati woman close to Hays' secretary wrote that when Archbishop McNicholas's aide visited her, he "did praise your Mr. Breen to me, over my tea-cups!" Among public relations men, Breen was Moxie. Hays' pal Lupton Wilkinson told Breen in July 1934 that "you [have] continued in the way you began in Hollywood, making the magnates eat out of your hand and like it." Among producers, Breen was warden. But the producers found they rather liked him. A raconteur par excellence, Breen may or may not have been sentenced to death by Hungarian Bolsheviks. He also may or may not have been deported by the British for involvement with the Irish Rebellion. He nonetheless swore that both had happened. What finally mattered was that Breen could manipulate narrative; he could hold an audience with a story. Producers liked Breen because he could help them thread plot and character through the Particular Applications of the Production Code. They also liked Breen because industry conditions offered them no choice.

"I am extremely happy the film industry has appointed a censor within its own ranks," Eleanor Roosevelt told America in her maiden radio broadcast. "This new announcement should do much to make these organizations feel that the film industry as a whole desires to cooperate and use its tremendous power for the improvement of the country." Audiences sometimes booed those who came between them and the screen; when Pasadena moviegoers saw the moralistic foreword that a California municipal censor added to *The Blue Angel,* they responded with "a terrific razzing." Now that such big boys as the Legion of Decency and the Production Code Administration had moved into the neighborhood, the Pasadena censor could return the insult with a broad Bronx cheer.

Back at the Ravenswood, in an apartment that one visitor called "superb late wedding cake," Mae West counted out her money. She had earned over a quarter of a million dollars in 1933 and would earn a third of a million in 1934. Once she became a millionaire, she would express contradictory attitudes toward censorship. To some journalists she would say that she favored censorship, that without it, "everything deteriorates." To others she would say that "the censors wouldn't even let me sit on a guy's lap, and I'd been on more laps than a napkin." And to still others she would say, "I believe in censorship. After all, I made a fortune out of it." Director Lowell Sherman called *She Done Him Wrong* "the great American wet dream." With the Production Code Administration and director Joe Breen would come the rude awakening.

THE
PRODUCTION
CODE
ADMINISTRATION
1934–1966

4

Dead End

"WE'RE OFF FOR Hollywood," Princess Tamara purred in *The Women,* "where dear Mr. Hays will protect me." The Princess Tamaras of the world assumed that it was Will Hays who had tamed the movies, but others—especially producers and industry observers—knew better. The English trade paper *Film Weekly* called Hays "a mere Hindenberg," reserving for Joseph Breen the title "the Hitler of Hollywood." By 1935, Breen had earned it.

Breen cut an imposing figure in Hollywood, a town where image mattered. His two-hundred-pound frame suggested authority, his personality exuded it. He cashiered properties, rewrote screenplays, supervised directors, and edited films. The moguls employed him (at least technically) but could not intimidate him. "The responsible heads of the studios are a cowardly lot. They are, too, an ignorant lot," he told Hays. Zanuck could threaten, Selznick could rant, Mayer could cry: once Breen drew his thin lips together and fixed his wide-set eyes, he would not move. With the powder-puff Hollywood Jury sent home and the Motion Picture Association board chastened by the Legion of Decency, Breen could issue authoritative decisions without fear of reversal. The Code was the Word, the gospel according to Breen.

"It is still a hell of a battle to keep [the producers] in line," one Breen associate told another. "If you could see some of the scripts in

Joe's office, you would not believe there had ever been any controversy at all." The Production Code director never let down. He not
only whipped the lions but attempted to make them like it. "I am
looking at pictures morning, noon, and night until I am almost
frantic," he wrote to an East Coast colleague in summer 1934. "So
far, so good. We have noted a disposition on the part of the studios
to do the right and proper thing. Our difficulty comes by way of
the task of convincing them that that which we seek to have them
do is the right and proper thing." For Breen, though, the job was
manageable.

When the stout Irishman traveled abroad later that summer, he
boasted that he and the Code had reformed Hollywood. Really
reformed Hollywood. No blarney. The screen would no longer
"leave the question of right or wrong in doubt or fogged." Or
"throw the sympathy of the audience with sin, crime, wrong doing, or evil." Or "present evil alluringly." Virgins in cellophane
were out of fashion; buttons would henceforth be buttoned, zippers
zipped. Those "nude and semi-nude beauties who have for so long
adorned Hollywood 'musicals,' " the Production Code director
told *Film Weekly,* "will be sent back to the dressing room to discard
their transparencies."

As Depression squalls turned to showers and sunshine, the nation
and Hollywood recovered their balance. Studio bookkeepers used
more black ink, theater attendance approached pre-Depression
levels, and the twin threats of federal regulation and Catholic boycotts faded away. With the clinking glasses—and the reformers—
silent, the press hailed the movies' self-control. A North Carolina
paper cheered the producers' movement from the "sensationalized
sex-madness" of the recent past to the current "level of cultural
achievement," while the *Rocky Mountain News* asked readers to
recall "the pictures you have seen during the past year" and the
"high percentage" that were "clean entertainment." Will Hays so
loved the encomiums that he reproduced six pages of them in the
Association annual report of March 1936.

Hays won two more blessings three months later. The Federal
Council of the Churches of Christ commended the work of the
Production Code Administration, and Pope Pius XI broadcast an
encyclical letter (probably authored by Martin Quigley) that noted

the improved moral content of American films. The Pope, who praised Catholic vigilance more than Hollywood control, used some telling qualifiers: "crime and vice are portrayed less frequently; sin no longer is so openly approved or acclaimed; false ideals of life no longer are presented in so flagrant a manner to the impressionable minds of youth." Hays overlooked the "less frequently" and "so flagrant," and tabbed the papal message a valentine. No less welcome were some love letters that soon arrived from the Legion of Decency. The Catholics rated pictures "A" (morally unobjectionable), "B" (morally objectionable), and "C" ("positively bad"). Though the specter of "C" for "Condemned" drove the Jewish moguls to shul, the number of pictures awarded "C" fell dramatically from 1934 to 1936.

The matter of rereleases showed that Breen aimed for straight "A"s. The studios could not make enough pictures to fill their theaters, and for years had rereleased old ones to take up the slack; the latter often had surprising box office appeal. When Hays created the Production Code Administration, Breen developed three categories for pictures produced under the Joy and Wingate regimes. In Class I were those withdrawn immediately, never to be rereleased. Class II included those pictures that would be allowed to complete extant contracts, then be permanently withdrawn; Class III comprised those that would be withdrawn, reedited to conform to the Code, then presented to the Production Code Administration. Along with *The Story of Temple Drake, George White's Scandals,* and *Baby Face, She Done Him Wrong* and *I'm No Angel* were dumped into Class I. When Paramount asked to rerelease the Mae West pictures in fall 1935, Hays was sympathetic but Breen was adamant. However conservative, Hays understood that the Paramount till could use the coins that Mae West could generate. Breen thought the rereleases "tragic" and told Hays that the Association board would have to choose between Paramount and Breen: "If an appeal is made, I hope the Board of Directors will turn down both of these pictures." Hays shunned confrontation and may have persuaded Paramount to withdraw its request before a meeting was held.

Paramount submitted numerous rereleases to Breen, most of them associated in the public's mind with the robust pre-Code era.

Breen passed few of them. He would not certify *Design for Living, Song of Songs,* or *The Blue Angel.* Joy had admired *The Blue Angel,* whose "Censor's Foreword" Pasadena audiences had razzed, but Breen would not approve the Dietrich picture (which Paramount distributed in America), with or without the preface. "It is a sordid story based on [an] illicit sex relationship between the two leading characters and contains a great deal of offensive suggestiveness in its portrayal throughout," he judged.

Breen rejected nine pictures submitted by Fox, five by Warners, and two produced by Howard Hughes, *Scarface* and *Cock of the Air,* the latter "because of its gross vulgarity and obscenity." He damned *George White's Scandals* (Fox) principally because a little girl had sung "Oh, You Nasty Man" and danced "a hootch dance"; he bounced *Topaze* (RKO) because the loose relationship of Reginald Mason and Myrna Loy lacked "compensating moral values." The National Board of Review, a civic organization that encouraged wholesome pictures, had deemed *Topaze* one of the best American features of 1933, an award that made Breen appear hard-nosed two years later. Yet Breen shut out pre-1934 pictures because he feared that their rerelease would trigger memories—and reform activities—of the Mae West era.

Where Diamond Lil was concerned, Breen showed no mercy. Mae West's *Klondike Annie,* more licentious than *Belle of the Nineties,* bordered on a travesty of religion and sex. Though Breen finally wrested enough concessions from Paramount to certify it, the studio later reneged. Breen immediately recognized that the preview print was "definitely *not* the picture which had been approved by this office," and he angrily withdrew the Production Code Seal. When Paramount executives sought clemency, he ordered the deletion of an entire sequence that connoted an "illicit sex affair." A memorandum for the files summarized the effect of the change:

> It eliminates all the so-called love talk and the talk about [Mae West's] beautiful white skin, etc. It also eliminates the scene of the two sailors in the chart room discussing the desirability of having a wife on a rainy night. Furthermore, it eliminates entirely the objectionable scene of Miss West sitting on the couch with [Victor] McLaglen—his appearance of fatigue; the business of the hair combing, and the final fade out with McLaglen kissing Miss West.

Paramount sheepishly complied, the Production Code triumphed.

The curb on sex pictures extended to the classics, whether foreign or domestic. *Ecstasy*, a 1932 Czechoslovakian release about sexual frustration, starred Hedwig Kreisler (later Hedy Lamarr), who swam nude in one scene and achieved orgasm in another. American distributors booked *Children of Loneliness, Love Life of a Gorilla, Ecstasy*, and other controversial imports into "art theatres" where pictures were exempt from Code approval. While the Catholics crusaded throughout the 1930s, *Ecstasy* played Washington, Newark, Los Angeles, and even Boston. After Jewel Productions exhausted the box office potential of the art theatres, it then appealed to Breen for a Code certificate as entree to the major companies' movie houses. Breen had cut the bare bosoms from Warners' *Untamed Africa* and Paramount's art theatre import, *Tabu;* the distributor of *Ecstasy* must have predicted that the nude swim would rock the boat and the orgasm swamp it. Breen sent two colleagues to the Kreisler picture and afterwards told Hays that it was "highly—even outrageously—indecent." Sensing a battle with the distributor, the General forced Motion Picture Association board members to screen *Ecstasy.* "The Directors were so bored with the first two or three reels that it was rather difficult to make them stay," Hays associate Francis Harmon told Breen. As Kreisler neared her climax, though, "they began to sit up and take notice." The implications alarmed board members, and Harmon told Breen that they would uphold his recommendation to deny the picture certification.

Domestic classics were no less problematic. In September 1934, MGM producer David Selznick asked the Production Code Administration to read the scenario from a silent *Anna Karenina* as well as a proposed new treatment. Well over a thousand such documents went through the office annually, processed by Breen staff members whom Hollywood called the Production Code boys. Karl Lischka drafted the response on *Anna,* then Breen made revisions. Lischka advised Metro to follow the script of the older version, "cleaner than the classic." If the studio treated adultery with restraint and the atmosphere with good taste, he concluded, the picture would escape criticism. The diplomatic Breen changed "cleaner" to "more acceptable." Fearful that Metro would translate a foot into a yard, he also deleted the conditional "if" and opened the conclusion with the stern words, "It is imperative that . . ."

More than other producers, Selznick constantly pressed Breen for concessions on Production Code enforcement. He pushed the story of *Anna Karenina* well beyond the limits, and when Breen saw the script that Selznick had in production, he demanded that MGM mute the treatment of adultery. Selznick drafted a combative letter of response.

In streams of consciousness, Selznick blustered that the Production Code director had reneged on earlier promises and thus left Metro with an impossible decision: to make "a completely vitiated and emasculated adaptation" of *Anna* or to scrap "a million dollar investment." Having raged, Selznick whined: Garbo would not be available for retakes (a common and sometimes convincing argument with Breen once pictures had gone too far). Having whined, Selznick threatened: he intimated that the purpose of the letter— with copies to MGM bosses Louis Mayer in Culver City and Nick Schenck in Manhattan—was the producer's "simply doing my duty to my employers in calling such reversals to their attention, so that they may decide what to do with the picture." And presumably what to do with Joe Breen.

Selznick and Breen compromised on *Anna Karenina*. Breen eliminated Anna's bastard child, yet despite his own and the British censors' opposition to suicide, he allowed Selznick to throw Anna beneath a train at the end. When the Chicago Legion of Decency later condemned *Anna,* Breen may have wondered whether he had made one concession too many. Yet compromise typified the self-regulation process.

Breen and the producers of sophisticated pictures almost invariably reached terms of agreement, sometimes even endearment. In Lubitsch's *Desire,* there were references to lost "virwility" (Dietrichspeak for "virility") as well as hand play beneath a dinner table and in Gary Cooper's pockets. In *The Awful Truth,* a screwball comedy of mutual suspicions between husband and wife, Irene Dunne goosed a pompous old woman, Cary Grant offered a racy double entendre on coal mines ("if you can sink a shaft in this north corner . . ."), and a nightclub performer showed off garter and panties during a dance. Just before "The End," Dunne snuggled under the covers and sent Grant, pajama-clad and standing in the doorway, a telepathic message. A close-up of a cuckoo clock suggested what happened next: The clock chimes midnight, and male and female figurines appear to mark the hour; instead of returning to his "house," however, the male follows the female into hers. Fadeout. In a cheaper picture, Breen would have bounced the dialogue, the stage business, and the racy close.

Val Lewton, who later handled censorship chores for Selznick International, thought that Breen barked more than he bit: the Production Code director always allowed "greater leeway" than his letters indicated. Even when he nipped, Breen could amuse. Lewton summarized for Selznick a conference with Breen on the oldest profession:

> Mr. Breen goes to the bathroom every morning. He does not deny that he does so or that there is such a place as the bathroom, but he feels that neither his actions nor the bathroom are fit subjects for screen entertainment. This is the essence of the Hays' office attitude toward prostitution, at least as Joe told it to me in somewhat cruder language.

Because both Breen and the producers with whom he worked were such tenacious men, their professional relationship sometimes became a personal one. Wounds healed, though. "We have tried to lean over backwards, keeping this within bounds," production assistant Gene Town told Breen about Walter Wanger's *Shanghai,* "but if there is anything that annoys you, sweetheart, let us know. Love and kisses. . . ."

The Hitler of Hollywood lived well. The Motion Picture Association soon paid him almost $60,000 annually—enough to employ two domestic servants—and tossed in both car and chauffeur as perquisites. At the Breens' home near the University of California campus, Joe was the autocrat of the breakfast table, the commander-in-chief of three sons, three daughters, and one wife. Mary Dervin Breen was the child of a Philadelphia saloon keeper, whom she later always called a restaurateur, and though she had borne Joe their six children, she clung to her own childhood. She wore her hair in blond ringlets, poured her matronly figure into sweet young frocks, and responded to her husband's jokes and barbs with high-pitched giggles. One Production Code associate intimated that her coloratura laugh alone might have prompted a less devout Catholic to rove, but in 1935, her only correspondent would have been the Production Code Administration.

After breakfast on weekdays and Saturdays, the chauffeur drove Breen to the Production Code offices or to the studios where he horse-traded on sin, crime, and evil. Breen was a superb administrator and negotiator, so efficient that as early as December 1934, Hollywood had heard rumors that a major movie company had offered him an executive position. But as Production Code director, Breen stood head-to-head with Mayer and Cohn and Warner. Why should he work under them?

En route to the office or the studio conference room, Breen scanned treatments, scripts, or staff-written letters pertaining to them. Sometimes he stared out the car window at the Beverly Hills mansions along Sunset Boulevard, the bungalows and manicured lawns of West Hollywood, and the art deco storefronts and opulent movie palaces near the scruffy Production Code Administration headquarters on Hollywood and Western. When the chauffeur passed a bus, Joe Breen could spot the Mexican cooks and Japanese gardeners, the pipe fitters and hod carriers, the mechanics and menials whose low wages and strong backs drove the southern California economy. Throughout the twenties, the studios had made hundreds of pictures about and for the working class, but only occasionally had an *auteur* challenged the American dream— Stroheim with *Greed,* Chaplin with *The Gold Rush,* Vidor with *The Crowd.* After the Depression silenced the optimism of the twenties, though, more and more films examined class tensions.

Hollywood never proposed a radical solution to social problems, a solution that would upend the New Deal, much less oppose capitalism. The studios had become too flush and too commodity-oriented by the late 1930s to bite the entrepreneurial hand that fed them. A picture that leaned too far left could alienate the middle-class women whose box office tastes sometimes determined profit or loss, and even liberal producers would not take that chance. When Selznick made *Anna Karenina,* he told the press that he "naturally eliminated most of the discussions about the agricultural and economic problems of Russia of the day, considering these of little interest to the large part of our audience who came to see Greta Garbo as Anna Karenina and Fredric March as Vronsky." Chaplin skewered factory labor in *Modern Times* yet made Electro Steel a spic-and-span model of American industry; even when he waved a red flag during a demonstration, the tramp championed humanity over industrialism, not communism over capitalism. American and international audiences expected Hollywood sheen.

When a producer drifted to the left, the picture that resulted concerned Breen because it concerned Hays because it concerned Manhattan distributors and theater owners, the locus of power within the industry. Filmmaker Richard de Rochemont called the average exhibitor a coward. He "wanted to hear only laughter— and none of that 'political' laughter either—and applause. A 'boo' would send him quavering to the booth to see what was being protested, and three complaints from patrons would make him talk of pulling out the reel." Escapism, however tame, continued to dominate the screen, but as Hollywood experienced labor troubles—with writers, actors, and technicians attempting to unionize—the number of social-problem films grew. Breen apparently had mixed feelings about them: the second-generation Irishman rooted for the underdog, the Production Code administrator condemned ugly stories of class warfare. Forever lecturing Hollywood, Martin Quigley warned Breen that the war against "Red propaganda" on-screen would make the battle for decency seem a skirmish:

> In many places in the industry, especially amongst our Semitic brethren, there seems to be growing an acceptance of the idea of radical propaganda on the screen. . . . [Hays] has been sidestepping and pussyfooting. Knowing him as I do, I feel that he doesn't want to see this happen, but at the same time he has no intention of carrying the banner.

Despite their earlier association and Quigley's firm support of the Code, Breen resented anyone who presumed to tell him what he should know or how he should run Hollywood. But since pictures that might be construed as radical propaganda could damage the general welfare of the industry, Breen approached them gingerly. Few challenged his political skills or his intellectual commitment more than *Dead End*.

When the opening-night curtain rose on Sidney Kingsley's *Dead End,* only three days before Halloween 1935, Manhattan theatergoers applauded. Set designer Norman Bel Geddes had re-created a dead-end street, complete with an elegant apartment house that abutted an East River tenement slum. The orchestra pit represented the river, and throughout the evening the Dead End Kids—Angel, Spit, Tommy, and the others—actually jumped in (onto the padded floor) while stagehands provided appropriate splashing noises and glints of water and light.

Dead End dramatized economic and social inequity through setting. With the unseen main entrance of the apartment building closed by construction work, the rich are forced to use a rear entrance and brush against the poor. The Dead End Kids added spice to the encounters and to the familiar melodramatic plot: Gimpty, a crippled architect, loves Kay. When gangster Baby Face Martin returns to the slum that spawned him, Gimpty reports him and collects the reward. Government agents kill Martin. Gimpty wants to marry Kay and save her from prostitution, but she refuses: "This isn't the miracle we were looking for." She departs with Jack Hilton, whose mistress she has been and who has promised to marry her. Meanwhile, during a street brawl, Tommy has wounded Griswald, a wealthy tenant, and faces prosecution. Gimpty decides to use the reward money to hire an attorney for Tommy, then exits with Tommy's sister, Drina. A cycle of poverty and crime intact, the final curtain falls on the raucous Dead End Kids at play.

An environmental determinism haunts *Dead End*. Even slum clearance and human tolerance, obvious solutions to acute social problems, seem mere Band-Aids. In another play, the death of Baby Face Martin would have resolved the narrative; in *Dead End,* it produces a hydra. Kingsley leaves no doubt that the Dead End Kids could become Baby Face Martins. They taunt, brawl, and steal; they smoke "Marywanna"; they curse. A children's benevolent society stalled the premiere for thirty minutes, but the street language remained. "Ah, ta' hell wid ya," the drama opened, and thereafter the Kids' lines astonished even calloused newspapermen. Robert Coleman told *Daily Mirror* readers that much of the coarseness "could have been eliminated without lessening the verity of the characters"; *Literary Digest* reported that sensitive theatergoers "winced, and perceptibly." According to *Variety,* the dialogue would generate adverse comment and dampen the matinee business. As the *Times* observed, though, the "salty street jargon" probably boosted ticket sales more than did the serious theme. And whither the dollars, whither Hollywood.

A Motion Picture Association staff member who attended the premiere found *Dead End* so gripping and "so sincere and ruthless a document that it is certain to be considered seriously by picture companies." The mix of poverty and social discord would worry the Association, however, for Hays and the corporate bosses believed that the cinema should not only affirm traditional values but mitigate or solve all problems at the final reel. *She Done Him Wrong* contained prostitutes, killings, and salty street jargon—no picture postcard of the American Way—but the comedy weakened the threat to national mores. *Dead End* contained a diseased prostitute, a brutal killing, adolescent profanity, and nothing to temper the grim stage picture at the final curtain. Unless Hollywood revised the adaptation, *Dead End* would offer moviegoers no panaceas.

The references to labor organization in *Dead End* would also have made Hays and the East Coast company presidents gloomy. Roosevelt had signed the National Labor Relations Act only months before, and militant union activity had already increased; tuned to the spirit of the era, Drina participated in an offstage strike for better wages and improved working conditions. Class struggles touched a nerve: the company presidents wanted the box office dimes that dramas of social unrest produced, but they feared the dramas' contempt for law and order. Censor boards were also skittish about these dramas, even when the studios made individuals—not political systems—both cause and solution of the unrest.

Staunch capitalists everywhere were apprehensive about an aroused mass. The *Los Angeles Times* had called the 1934 San Francisco General Strike "an insurrection, a Communist-inspired and led revolt." From Sullivan, Indiana, Hinkle Hays warned brother Will about Socialist "monkey business" among faculty at their sons' school, Wabash College. Even Hollywood feared more than fear itself. As May Day 1934 approached, Los Angeles police cautioned the moguls to secure their property rooms and arsenals lest agitators raid them for explosives, firearms, and especially machine guns. A "liberal with left-wing tendencies" (the epithet that Sidney Kingsley reserved for himself) was hardly the studio presidents' darling; neither was the drama of irremediable social injustice.

Kingsley and social-problem drama were somewhat more welcome on the West Coast than the East, not only by some directors and producers but by Joe Breen. Hays had told the Production Code administrator to discourage pictures that condemned American industry or preached rebellion; Breen had generally complied. But while he opposed double-bill fodder like Columbia's *I'll Fix It,* a story of schoolteachers versus corrupt administrators, he sometimes proved an advocate for tough-minded exposés. An anxious Hays could recall how Joe Breen had treated *Black Fury.*

Abem Finkel and Carl Erickson wrote Warners' *Black Fury* in summer 1934. The screenplay centered on immigrant coal miner Joe Radek, who lives by a simple philosophy: "Work and shut up." When Radek leads a breakaway movement from the Federation of Mine Workers, he loses all that he loves, from his girlfriend, Anna, to his buddy Mike. The distraught Joe finally barricades himself inside a mine until the company agrees to the workers' demands. Based on a true story, *Black Fury* pulled some punches. Finkel and Erickson made the loss of Anna—rather than social conscience— the reason that Joe opposes the Federation; they also displaced blame from management to outside agitators. Still, *Black Fury* painted a bleak picture of coal miners' lives. The industry refused to pay workers for laying tracks into the mines or to guarantee their safety on the job. In scenes borrowed from the headlines, Finkel and Erickson showed placard-bearing strikers on the march, schoolchildren taunting scabs, and rough industrial police. Throughout, they depicted the workers as noble and human. While *Black Fury* neither preached rebellion nor indicted the coal industry, it unquestionably threw sympathy toward labor and away from management.

Breen had only minor quibbles with *Black Fury,* and approved the story. It contained enough positive elements, he told Hays, "to permit its consideration for picture purposes." Hays seemed doubtful. As script revisions continued, he sought assurance from Warners New York that Warners Hollywood would "not produce a picture unfair to another industry," and told Breen to shadow the project. But the Production Code director would not heel. He suggested that the writers add some lines that established "that working conditions in the bituminous coal industry have greatly improved," and reminded Warners that the picture should not contribute to the climate of "industrial unrest" throughout the country. But he tacitly approved references to the gloom of coal miners' existence—the low pay, the inadequate safety precautions, the picket lines and condemnation of scabs.

As *Black Fury* went before the cameras with the extraordinary Paul Muni as Joe Radek, a coal industry spokesman complained to Hays about the film. What the owners did not need was more ammunition and public sympathy for John L. Lewis and his United Mine Workers. The casting—Hays must have known—meant that Warners would ballyhoo the picture for press and audiences alike. Breen again assured Hays that the coal companies and their supervisors would not be played as heavies but (like the miners themselves) as victims of "the dishonest intrigue of the racketeers." *Black Fury* made an important social point, and Paul Muni gave Joe Radek a dignity and humanity that other labor heroes could not command. For these and other reasons, Breen felt that the melodrama deserved more latitude. When Warners showed *Black Fury* to the Production Code office, Breen and company unanimously approved it.

Hays saw the picture in Manhattan and wondered whether he and the Production Code boys had screened the same print. He believed that *Black Fury* violated Code regulations on criminal behavior and asked Breen to take another look. Breen defended the original decision. While Joe Radek may have committed a criminal act, he was not a criminal; furthermore, Breen wrote Hays, *Black Fury* was "a fine social document" and "distinguished artistic achievement." The praise would have obvious implications for *Dead End.*

In November 1935, both Twentieth Century–Fox and RKO

asked the Production Code office to review a synopsis of the Kingsley play. Jason Joy, now the Production Code liaison at Fox, assured Breen that the studio would reject "the unimportant syphilitic angle and one or two obnoxious items." RKO seemed just as eager for a favorable answer.

Breen had more than a professional interest in *Dead End*. Despite his own salty street jargon and hail-fellow manner, he had pretensions to intellect. He wanted to be considered a man of discernment, a man well-read. The Pulitzer Prize conferred on Kingsley two years before predisposed Breen to back the play. He also wanted to reassure Hollywood—as Wingate had not—that the Production Code Administration could work with the studios on a controversial property. Despite the risk, he again proved an advocate of a social-problem story.

Breen knew that the syphilitic prostitute as well as the kept woman would demand attention; he also thought that the portrayal of the Kids as petty criminals would lead to objections from the censor boards. As he told RKO and Fox, though, *Dead End* was an "important social document" whose theme should allay concerns about children and crime and censors. Breen had taken a progressive stand. Hollywood could clean up what *Literary Digest* had called the "gutter-urchin epithets," but it could not faithfully adapt *Dead End* without exposing what *Theatre Arts* had called "immovable forces of social slavery, ill health, bad food, damp rooms." Still, despite the Production Code benediction, neither RKO nor Fox purchased the drama. Price and politics were sound enough reasons for any studio to drop the play, yet some outsiders thought that Breen had iced the project. More than once he shouldered blame for the moguls' and their East Coast superiors' timidity in matters political and social.

Then, in February 1936, independent producer Samuel Goldwyn made plans to adapt *Dead End* for the screen. As Joe Breen knew, Goldwyn would assure a high-quality production. The Goldwyn-isms that reporters prized marked a self-educated motion picture producer, not an intellectual. When Goldwyn made *The Children's Hour,* released as *These Three* in March 1936, an assistant worried that the censors would ban the picture because its central characters were lesbians. "So what's the problem?" Goldwyn asked. "Make them Albanians." The malapropisms made good Sunday supplement copy, but they misrepresented the taste and touch of the man. Goldwyn thought that strong stories about ordinary characters were the stuff of cinema. "If it pleases me," he said of each project he chose, "I feel there is a good chance it will please others. But it has to please me first." *Dead End* somehow pleased him.

In April 1937 Goldwyn sent Breen a long, unvarnished treatment of *Dead End,* one that raised far more of the work's problems than the short RKO and Fox synopses had. Although he knew that Breen would object to certain language and situations, he wanted to discover the boundaries of Production Code enforcement and avoid a too-rigorous self-censorship. Goldwyn must have hoped for an indication that Breen would relax all standards on the "gutter-urchin" elements of *Dead End,* especially since the censor boards sometimes followed the Production Code lead. So Goldwyn lobbed the ball into Breen's court. The sharp return of serve came more from reflex than scruple. Breen told Goldwyn that, while sympathetic to the theme of *Dead End,* the Production Code office would not bend the rules for social-problem pictures. In a seven-page letter focused on detail, Breen worked with pick and shovel. He ordered a number of words cut, principally because domestic and British censor boards invariably deleted them: "punk" and "louse"; "stinking" and "go to ———"; "bag," "bum," and "bushwah." He reminded Goldwyn that the character nicknamed Spit should not expectorate and that none of the boys should swim without tights or other clothing.

Then Breen treated venereal disease and death. Baby Face Martin had returned to the East River slum to find his girl Francey suffering from syphilis. Though Goldwyn hoped to handle the matter through euphemism, Breen ordered the producer not only to inflict another disease but to "*affirmatively* establish the disease from which Francey is suffering." He suggested tuberculosis. He also ordered that the death of Baby Face Martin not turn into a sideshow: no bullets pumped into the body, no more than two bullets, no shots of the dead body twitching. Finally, Breen recommended that Goldwyn

be less emphatic throughout, in the photographing of this script, in showing the contrast between conditions of the poor in tenements and those of the rich in apartment houses. Specifically, we recommend you do not show, at any time, or at least you do not emphasize, the presence of filth, or smelly garbage cans, or garbage floating in the river, into which the boys jump for a swim. This recommendation is made under the general head of good and welfare, because our reaction is that such scenes are likely to give offense.

Several days after Breen sent Goldwyn the seven-page letter, the two men met to hash out their differences. Breen had been a reporter, Goldwyn a glove salesman; both had once smelled of cheap cigars and rough humor, yet both were committed to the amenities. They agreed that Spit could spit, but not insensitively; they also agreed that "tramp" would substitute for the offensive "bum" in British release prints. While Goldwyn insisted that the Kingsley story demanded a strong contrast between rich and poor, he assured Breen that he understood "the need for the utmost care." Aware of the luster that enveloped a Goldwyn picture, Breen could drop the point and rely on the Goldwyn touch to protect American moviegoers from an exposé of life along the poverty line. Finally, producer and Production Code director reached an odd but, for Breen, not atypical compromise on Francey: her past and her dialogue would imply venereal disease, her cough would signify tuberculosis. Seasoned audiences could decode and resolve the apparent contradiction, while a straight-faced Breen could boast that he had made the communicable disease of *Dead End* socially acceptable.

What Breen demanded on *Dead End* obscures what he allowed. Though he forced Goldwyn to compromise on the treatment of children and sex, he let stand the management-labor strife that crowded the edges of the drama. A minor character in Kingsley's play, Drina here provided the romantic interest for the crippled architect; Goldwyn retained both her and her union activity. Off-screen, Drina picketed for social equality, for better wages and better living. On-screen, in a pivotal scene with a law-enforcement officer, she pulled back the hair that covered her forehead and exposed the wound put there by "one of you dirty cops." Breen not only refused to silence Drina, he also promised Goldwyn that "upon completion of this picture, we will communicate with London [where censorship problems were expected] and endeavor to impress upon them the seriousness of this play and its importance as a social document." Breen also agreed to rally support from women's groups and other organizations. Liberals had condemned Breen for the homogenized political and sexual content of American movies, yet on *Dead End* he had shown Goldwyn that the Production Code office could accommodate and even advocate social-protest pictures.

Bolstered by Production Code approval, Goldwyn launched *Dead End*. He cast Joel McCrea as the architect, Sylvia Sydney as the unionist, and Humphrey Bogart as the gangster Baby Face Martin; fresh from the stage and screen portrayal of mobster Duke Mantee in *The Petrified Forest,* Bogart would blend conviction with menace as the hood. Yet the stars would be the Dead End Kids, also fresh from Broadway and an antidote to the sweetness, dimples, and curls of Little Miss Shirley Temple. They included Billy Halop (Tommy), Huntz Hall (Dippy), Bobby Jordan (Angel), Leo Gorcey (Spit), Gabriel Dell (T. B.), and Bernard Punsley (Milty). Pert and rowdy, they called Goldwyn "Pop" and shared opinions on everything—especially moviemaking. "It's easy," Huntz Hall said. "You sit around and don't do nothing and get paid." Planning to apprentice himself to a plumber, Leo Gorcey disagreed: "This business is no good," he told the *New York Times*. "Now, you take my racket. There is always something new in it. And it's something you can see and be proud of. You put in a sink or a bathtub and you can see it and you know it'll last."

The Kids were quick studies. They were "marvelous," recalled a dialogue director who had worked with them on the East Coast, " 'cause they could pick up stuff very easily." Descending on Hollywood with countless performances of the drama still in memory, they frustrated Goldwyn and director William Wyler by occasionally substituting Kingsley's or their own lines for the laundered language of the screenplay. When they were good, though, they were very, very good, so good that Wyler barred them from the evening rushes lest they become self-conscious. While the adults watched the daily footage, the Kids cruised southern California in their Model T—at least until Leo Gorcey smashed the automobile into a telephone pole.

For *Dead End,* Goldwyn and Wyler wanted an authenticity that would exceed that of the Broadway production. Wyler hoped to shoot the picture in New York, "to juxtapose a block in the East Fifties with the Sutton Place elegance," but Goldwyn vetoed the idea. Instead, he had Richard Day create a set that would convey the same atmosphere. The complex of grimy apartment buildings, tiny alleyways, and seedy shops foregrounded by a large studio tank representing the East River became "the talk of the town." Not only scenery but prerecorded ambient sounds would enhance the effect, from the steam whistles of harbor craft to the sirens of ambulances and police cars.

Less easily resolved was the conflict over garbage. Goldwyn wanted nothing "that could be cheap or degrading in any manner," portrait photographer Bob Coburn recalled, whether the content pertained to Goldwyn's "studio or his stars or the type of picture he was making at the time." When Goldwyn visited the *Dead End* soundstage, he charged that Wyler had made the slum "dirty." Wyler bristled: the grime would compensate for the profanity and street slang that Breen and Goldwyn had removed from the Kingsley play. Wyler spit between his teeth as he spoke, and the more he argued, the more Goldwyn burned. According to *Dead End* screenwriter Lillian Hellman, Goldwyn stored his anger "in a properly blessed tin box, with a touch-spring top." Opposed, he turned stony, then stared, then breathed fire. When Goldwyn finally demanded that Wyler sweep the streets, the director quit. Hours later, the slum had been dusted and cleaned. Within twenty-four hours, the director had returned to the picture.

The "presence of filth" remained at issue. Though Breen had cautioned Goldwyn against "garbage floating in the river," both Goldwyn and Wyler had apparently agreed on dirty water. But a concern for hygiene dictated that they provide "clean" refuse. One *Dead End* news release celebrated the property man who halved the fresh, firm grapefruit, washed the carrot greens, and scrubbed the assorted debris that the Kids shared the water with. The boys loved the swim scenes despite the floating garbage, but Goldwyn ripped the story from the press file. As the *New York Times* reported, to "associate garbage, even of an aristocratic nature, with a Goldwyn epic was unthinkable." Goldwyn had not laundered the trash to charm Production Code associates; the genteel poverty of *Dead End* mirrored the Goldwyn—and Hollywood—aesthetic of realism edged with tinsel.

Wyler concluded principal photography on *Dead End* by spring 1937. With *Dead End* cut and scored, Goldwyn sent the release print to the Production Code office. Wyler had opened the picture with a movement through Manhattan to the East River slum, from freedom to confinement. Gregg Toland, the cinematographer who would shoot *The Grapes of Wrath* and *Citizen Kane,* had underscored the confinement with strong vertical and horizontal lines and compositions that were rich in tension and shadow. Caught between realism and expressionism, the style seemed to mirror the themes of frustration and desire. The actors were excellent, especially Humphrey Bogart. Baby Face Martin had some of the neuroticism of Duke Mantee, and what might have been a routine character (and performance) breathed fury. The Dead End Kids added spontaneity and authenticity; their vibrance contrasted with the grimness of their surroundings and made all the more poignant the "dead end." At the end of the picture, the camera reversed the opening movement and left the characters behind, alone and unchanged.

Breen watched *Dead End* on July 20, then told the producer that much in it would nettle the censor boards, including the moment when one of the Kids brandished a knife. Goldwyn persuaded him that the narrative demanded the "dangerous scenes." Breen certified the picture—without cuts—but felt so tentative about the approval that he wrote Hays to rationalize it:

> The story, as you know, carries an important social and sociological message, and it may be true that, in order to properly dramatize the moral of the story, a portion, at least, of the criminal activities, and the results which follow in the social system, as a result of crime-breeding, may be necessary.

Years before, Jason Joy had argued the same point with state censors and gotten nowhere. The canny Breen had recommended to Goldwyn that the Production Code Administration work behind the scenes to accomplish the necessary approvals. Breen had earlier sent the affable Geoff Shurlock east on a goodwill mission for the agency, and the itinerary would logically include the censor boards.

Now Breen asked James Wingate to tell Irwin Esmond, the chief New York censor, that *Dead End* was an important social document that had been sanitized by producer and Production Code Administration and had already earned praise from civic groups opposed to slums.

While New York deliberated, the trade press screened *Dead End*. *Motion Picture Daily* conceded the entertainment value of the picture but peppered the notice with "but"s and "although"s. From the perspective of 1937, many would agree with *Motion Picture Daily* that *Dead End* preached a "potent sermon"; the text included disease, frustration, and dashed hopes. *Variety* saw only the "but"s. Audiences would seek out *Dead End* as a gangster saga, *Variety* predicted, and be disappointed. "The picture public which has little regard for propaganda and high respect for entertainment will find in it a reversal of popular values." The *Variety* notice suggests how political *Dead End* appeared to the trade press: "There is no hope promised for a better day, no humor, no fun. Just dull, depressing existence, accurately and minutely reproduced in its sickening physical phenomena." Contemporary audiences would perceive *Dead End* as no Disney version of slum life but a clear-eyed dramatization of contemporary American social problems.

The New York censors quarreled with only one line, which Goldwyn hastily cut: "All cats look alike in the dark." Armed with the approvals of the Production Code Administration and the New York board, *Dead End* passed Ohio, Kansas, and Massachusetts with no eliminations. "It is another notable example of brilliant PCA work," Hays associate Ken Clark told Breen, and other accolades followed. *Commonweal* seemed pleased that *Dead End* shunned "the vulgarisms voiced in the play," and the *New York Times* hailed the picture as "an arresting, inductive consideration of the slum problem, a prima facie case for a revision of the social system." According to the *New Republic, Dead End* would "raise the artistic level of films in general." Even Will Hays came to see the value of the picture. In his annual report on the industry, he placed *Dead End* and *The Life of Emile Zola* at the top of his list of recent films that had "widened the range of motion picture entertainment." For *Dead End* the accolades, for Breen the abuse. The *Saturday Evening Post* reprinted portions of a Production Code letter on *Dead End* that made him appear prim and mean. *Literary Digest* sympathized with Wyler, forced to pour the stark Kingsley play into "the Haysian mold." (Later, when *Dead End* allegedly inspired some schoolboys to knife a classmate, the *Digest* called the incident "a strong argument" for "general censorship.") Breen brushed off the criticism and continued to promote the picture with women's and civic organizations.

Historians who charge that American movies did not "deal with pressing political or social issues in an honest and truthful fashion" blame Breen. Hollywood was not an apolitical community. An anthropologist who examined the culture found people "openly 'left' and 'right.' " She was surprised, though, that politics mattered almost not at all in professional relationships and the pictures the movie colony produced. "In general," she concluded, "men of many different ideologies worked within the same social system, more or less accepting it because of the large financial rewards." Few producers had a stomach for unionism and class struggle, the headline stories of the 1930s, unless they could turn a profit. Jack Warner made the near-revolutionary *Black Fury* and the near-reactionary *Black Legion,* then flushed when he saw Paramount's *John Meade's Woman,* whose pro-labor sentiments Breen had allowed. "I think this picture carries one of the most deplorable attacks on law and order than anything I have seen in a long time," Warner told Will Hays. "It had the sting of Communism unless I am mistaken."

Who controlled Hollywood? Joe Breen? the studios? the Manhattan company presidents? the distributors and exhibitors? the banks and investment houses? A collaborative art form, movies were made by countless hands. And whether they addressed "issues" at all—much less in "honest and truthful fashion"—depended less on Breen than on the Association, the moguls, the balance sheet, the writers' or directors' perseverance, and on and on. Breen had no more resistance to "issues" than those who employed him. "Why is everything so dirty here?" shouted Goldwyn—not Breen—on the *Dead End* set.

Though Breen sometimes confused the Code with the Decalogue, he could herald pictures that raised "the artistic level of films in general" and that—with typical Hollywood reticence—questioned traditional values. At the fade-out of *Dead End,* the architect could not secure a job; the unionist still walked the picket line, and though she could triumph over management, her wages would not be enough to take her brother from the slum. Inequity endured, from first reel to last, and the Production Code Administration had approved. But when Breen accorded one producer a concession on one picture, ten producers wanted ten concessions on ten others. Aggressive rounds of bid-and-ask wore down both studios and Production Code associates, and in the years ahead, the more the studios pressed Breen for concessions, the more calcified he would become.

5

Gone With the Wind

ONCE UPON A time at a West Coast dinner party, a fortune-teller sat behind a screen and invited the stars to query him. He revealed all the "intimate details of their private lives," noted an observer, yet they "never learned that the 'palmist' really was Will Hays, the movie censor." While holding hands in Hollywood, the General not only told secrets but took pulses. Was RKO bleeding again? Had a Paramount executive moved from heavy drinking to alcoholism? Would too many rough pictures on the Warners schedule undermine the goodwill of the Association? The trade press, the boardroom, and the moguls' dens buzzed with gossip, and some of it promised a dead end for Joe Breen.

What Breen cut from pictures obscured what Breen allowed, always more than Hollywood acknowledged. But only the dark side of Breen sparked comment from press, public, and producers. In Ohio, where state censors had cut the shot of trouserless Fred MacMurray from *Hands Across the Table,* the Cleveland *Plain Dealer* called Hollywood censorship a vicious threat to the future of motion pictures. In New York, where censors had cut the word "cats" ("a derogatory reference to women") from the soundtrack of *Dead End,* the *New York Times* tacitly endorsed a plan to abolish the Hays Office; prominent theatre professor Sawyer Falk told the paper that he would rather sully the American mind than stultify it.

In an autumn 1938 counterattack, Hays distributed to the press an eighteen-page mimeographed collection entitled "Excerpts from Recent Comment on Motion Pictures." The florilegium contained a posy from "one of America's greatest men of letters," who confided that he went to the movies twice a week. "In times past," poet Carl Sandburg told Hays, "we may have felt concern for the picture industry, but not now. The quality of films has increased so greatly in recent years that their worth is unquestioned." For many, though, Breen remained the Film Butcher for the World, the censor who lived by one commandment: "*Thou shalt not offend.*" Louis de Rochemont, whose *March of Time* lay beyond the control of the Production Code, tarred Breen for the "ridiculous things" that he made Hollywood do. The man-on-the-street added feathers. "What strange passion drives the Hays board?" a *Life* magazine reader asked. "Isn't it just possible that the public is staying away from more and more movies because it is tired of moviedom's fairyland?"

In July 1938, the Justice Department charged the eight major motion picture companies with monopoly and restraining practices in violation of the Sherman Antitrust Act, and the suit (*United States v. Paramount Pictures*) demanded that producers and the Production Code Administration be more circumspect than ever. When the *Saturday Evening Post* requested an interview in autumn 1938, Breen may have acceded out of both vanity and self-defense. J. P. McEvoy would author "The Back of Me Hand to You" for the December 24 issue; he had known Breen over the years, even dined with the Breen family, which probably led the Production Code director to expect tinsel and ribbon. Yet McEvoy proved more Scrooge than Santa. "You've heard a lot about the Hollywood Yes Man," the article began. "Now meet Hollywood's No. 1 No Man." Beneath the anecdotes and the thumbnail history of movie censorship, McEvoy had a serious point: the screenwriter spent too much time "pulling punches." Breen was apologetic:

> Women's organizations are always complaining to me that women smoke and drink too much in pictures, but if I try to cut it out, the writers object, saying women do smoke and do drink, and, besides, they can't be writing scenes with people just sitting around doing nothing but talk. You see, everybody's right.

The *Saturday Evening Post* feature occasioned more heat. Those who pulled the punches charged that "timidity and bad taste" had fathered the Production Code. The young Screen Writers Guild blamed the Code for the movies' failure "to deal with the everyday scene of life around us." Independent producer Walter Wanger agreed: "Under this Code it was—and is—almost impossible to face and deal with the modern world."

Though the Particular Applications of the Production Code were more stringent as written than as applied, the many Association board members who saw the Code as a bulwark against federal censorship were wary of change. Anathema in Hollywood, Senator M. M. Neely had drafted a bill to regulate distribution practices, but the hidden agenda concerned motion picture content. In April 1939, when Hays associates went to Capitol Hill to defend the industry, counsel Charles Pettijohn pleaded the movies' case with such "seductive argumentation" that the West Virginia senator planned to "emulate the example set by Ulysses and his companions when they were about to sail between Cylla and Charybdis—metaphorically I put cotton in my ears and urge my colleagues to lash themselves to the nearest logical mast." The testimony not only failed to impress the senator but provided ammunition for Code opponents. One Hays lobbyist told the Neely hearings that in four years Breen had demanded well over a hundred thousand changes from producers; several months later, that same number ricocheted on Hays stand-in Arthur DeBra when he addressed a Manhattan conference on censorship whose participants included civil libertarian Morris Ernst and socialist Norman Thomas. Many within the audience of three hundred heckled DeBra.

As the European war clouded the future of American pictures abroad and Hollywood competed more aggressively for domestic box office dollars, producers weakened their Production Code commitment. In late 1938, Breen had told Universal not to rerelease *All Quiet on the Western Front* until the company had trimmed a problematic love scene. Months later, he learned that Universal had distributed prints of the 1930 version—the love scene intact—throughout North America. Breen contacted the studio, but executives refused to corral and recut every print. Meanwhile, Hollywood resumed its search for controversial properties.

When an adaptation of John Steinbeck's *Of Mice and Men* opened on Broadway, Hays associate Vincent Hart attended. The "sex perversion" and the "vulgar, obscene and profane dialogue" that so astonished him prompted Breen to campaign against a Hollywood purchase. The box office success of *Of Mice and Men* was irresistible, though, and despite a $200,000 price tag on the motion picture rights, Warners nibbled. Independent producers Lewis Milestone and Gene Solow also expressed interest. They heard that Hays had blacklisted the drama, *Collier's* reported, "but they didn't let it bother them."

Producers could purchase an occasional blacklisted drama or overlook an occasional bit of Production Code wisdom. But they could not scorn Breen. Though story and stars may have been essential to motion pictures, money made them possible. And without Breen, there could be no money: until Breen offered the promise of a certificate, the banks would not approve production loans. When Milestone asked Floyd Odlum to finance *Of Mice and Men,* a middleman conferred with the Production Code's Issy Auster; the outcome, Auster noted, determined whether Odlum's agent "writes to New York with a 'go ahead' " or "tells Mr. Odlum to forget it." Producers, especially independent producers, bristled under the terms of their fealty to Breen, and as the decade neared its close, the relationship became more volatile.

Joe Breen and Hollywood respected and distrusted each other, resented and needed each other. They sniped and clawed, they even drew blood; but they understood that there could be no victor, that freedom and control, the *Plain Dealer*s and the M. M. Neelys, must forever contend. So Breen battled Hollywood. When he heard the love scene in a script called "a brief romantic interlude," he told the producer to cut the cant: "Listen friend, fucking's fucking. It's not a 'romantic interlude.' If you want to say it, why don't you say it?" And Hollywood battled Breen. On *Joy of Living,* the Irishman had preached temperance. The excessive drinking would offend audiences, he told producer Pan Berman, and cause other studios to ape the RKO model. Did Breen see the contradiction? Berman may have wondered. The producer ignored the advice, and the picture included what the *Hollywood Reporter* later called a "beer-drinking orgy."

Some producers attempted to manipulate Breen. The script for *Every Day's a Holiday* contained the usual double entendres and phallic wisecracks. "Yeah," Mae West would drawl, "I always carry it with me, and put down anything that comes up." When Breen tossed cold water on the gag, producer Manny Cohen seemed grateful. He intimated that West and others would heed the Production Code only if Breen wrote a tough letter on the picture. Breen must have been suspicious: Cohen could portray himself as the victim of an incorrigible West, produce a bawdy *Every Day*, and— through last-ditch negotiation with the Production Code Administration—hope to retain all but the most egregious lines. Breen wrote the producer a draconian one-and-a-half-page letter that conditioned the Seal on full compliance with the Code. Though stunned by the harsh language, Cohen had the last word. The cover of the press book for *Every Day* showed West lying atop a bed, her arm resting on a pillow, her head against a satin head-board. The artwork—and the dummy advertisements within— showed her prepared for "anything that comes up."

Producers Walter Wanger, Manny Cohen, and Hal Wallis could annoy Breen. Producer David Selznick could anger him. Selznick had been the wunderkind of RKO and MGM, where he produced *A Bill of Divorcement, Dinner at Eight, David Copperfield*, and many others. In 1935, he formed Selznick International. Since he gener-ated too few pictures to absorb an occasional box office fiasco, he demanded superior craftsmanship, from the screenplay to the final cut. With every production a major production, he ran the Culver City studio with two hands on the throttle. Inside the walls of Selznick International, he had authority and autonomy; outside, he had Joe Breen telling him what to do. Conflict was inevitable.

Though Lewis Selznick had been among the moviemen who hired Postmaster General Hays in 1922, his son David deplored the notion of an internal censorship agency. In that 1935 screed on *Anna Karenina*, Selznick had offered Breen "the back of me hand." Selz-nick had memorized *Anna* and "couldn't bear to leave out a felici-tous phrase," screenwriter S. N. Behrman recalled. But what Selznick wanted in, Breen sometimes wanted out. In a Selznick International booklet—a promotional gimmick called a "study guide"—the producer took revenge. He claimed that the Production Code Administration forced those who made "worthy pictures" to "suffer for the sins of those who had stooped to a tasteless commercialism." *Anna* had been plagued by "censorship questions," wrote Selznick, many so small-minded that they left English writer Clemence Dane "aghast." Selznick traced the "blows" that *Anna* endured, then concluded:

> There is no point in detailing the censorship problems beyond this. We had to eliminate everything that could even remotely be classified as a passionate love scene; and we had to make it perfectly clear that not merely did Anna suffer but that Vronsky suffered. But enough about censorship.

More than enough for Breen.

Six pictures later, Selznick again taunted Breen. To promote *The Adventures of Tom Sawyer,* Selznick International furnished materials for a Museum of Modern Art exhibit entitled "The Making of a Contemporary Film." The display cases housed not only screenplays, research data, set models, and costumes, but also an exchange of letters between the studio and Breen. Hollywood professionals would have called the Production Code letters routine: Breen cautioned Selznick to treat the village parson with respect, to have the schoolmaster refrain from corporal punishment, to remove the chains from the Negro slaves. Museum visitors unfamiliar with the Code may have been aghast. In one letter, Breen ordered Selznick to dress the boys at the swimming hole in trunks. The producer snorted, then refused to comply; he told Breen that camera distance and some well-placed foliage would protect American modesty. The MOMA exhibit caught Tom Sawyer *and* Joe Breen with their pants down.

In Hollywood, Selznick continued the ragging. While every company occasionally rushed last-minute script changes to the Production Code Administration—with shooting suspended until Breen telephoned his approval—Selznick International made the practice modus operandi. Production Code staffers had seen the pattern and understood the danger. Piecemeal opinions and approvals could lead the Breen agency to screening-room surprises, to scenes that, however harmless on paper, became censorable in the context of the finished picture. Selznick had pushed Breen to provisionally approve *Nothing Sacred* before the writers had completed the screenplay; he had sent *The Prisoner of Zenda* revisions to the Production Code office scene by scene only minutes before the cameras turned each day. Breen passed the pictures, but may have harbored the impression that behind Selznick's chronic tardiness lay a sly form of manipulation. The stakes had been small on *Nothing Sacred* and *The Prisoner of Zenda*. When Margaret Mitchell's story of the Old South entered production, though, Selznick raised the ante.

During the twenties, *Atlanta Journal* cub reporter Peggy Mitchell spent part of her $25 weekly salary on Griffith and De Mille and von Stroheim. Nourished by the eroticism and romance of the screen, along with the Civil War yarns she was reared on, Mitchell penned the epic that would make her and David Selznick American legends. The story of *Gone With the Wind* concerned Scarlett O'Hara—her yearning for Ashley Wilkes, her off-again, on-again affair with Rhett Butler, her sexual trials and tribulations. Mitchell's prose could be fervid. Scarlett was attacked in Shantytown by "a squat black negro with shoulders and chest like a gorilla"; he ripped open her basque and "fumbled between her breasts." Though Rhett Butler had better manners, he came home drunk one night and exorcised the ghost of Ashley Wilkes that haunted his marriage. He approached Scarlett with "hot" breath and hands that "went round her roughly, under the wrapper, against her bare skin." He became a mad stranger, a savage; he bruised her lips and "wiped out everything from her mind but the dark into which she was sinking and the lips on hers." What could Scarlett do? She abandoned herself to the "ecstasy of surrender." Mitchell had not been constrained by Don'ts and Be Carefuls, and had her novel gone to the screen when completed in 1929, these scenes and more could have scorched American theaters. Yet six years passed before the author of *Gone With the Wind* showed a Macmillan editor the manuscript. By then, the only hot breath in Hollywood belonged to Joe Breen.

As the *Gone With the Wind* galleys traversed New York, the movie's story consultants sensed the commercial potential of the material but expressed doubts. Aside from the weak box office prospects of Civil War dramas, the Mitchell story raised a host of censorship concerns, from the assault on Scarlett O'Hara to the black stereotypes, the brothel and childbirth sequences, and the gruesome scenes of battle and death. Selznick International's Kay Brown understood the minuses but also understood that *Gone With the Wind* suited the vision and temperament of her boss. Though less enthusiastic about the novel than Brown was, David Selznick agreed to show the Production Code Administration a treatment. The Breen response could warm or chill the project.

Production Code staffers met each morning to hear Breen discuss problems, make assignments, and tell a favorite anecdote or two. One winter morning, Issy Auster walked out of the "huddle room" with a précis of *Gone With the Wind* in hand. Breen considered the property no more important than any other, and although Selznick contended that the agency favored the major companies over the independents, Auster would treat *Gone With the Wind* according to standard agency policy: he would identify elements that could transgress the Production Code, offend the censor boards, or—most important—undermine the power of Joe Breen. The picturemakers could demand the censorable, Breen could rail against the innocuous; the process of negotiation brought both toward the center. While *Gone With the Wind* would have outraged only the most prim reader in 1936, Auster ferreted out numerous potential Code violations (many of them anticipated by the movie's story consultants) and produced a stack of bargaining chips for Breen.

An undaunted Selznick purchased *Gone With the Wind* in summer 1936 and named Sidney Howard screenwriter. The producer who adored "felicitous phrases" expected Howard to scale down the book, cut expendable narrative threads (such as Scarlett's marriage to Frank Kennedy), and dramatize the essential scenes. The Production Code made the last task formidable. Mitchell had shown Melanie in labor, her eyes "enormous with pain," her voice "like an animal dying in a trap," while beyond the window Atlanta burned with "pain and smell and noise." Because Hays and the Motion Picture Association had banned "scenes of actual childbirth," Selznick could not honor the Production Code without pulling the obstetrics from *Gone With the Wind*. He knew that Breen would also challenge the bloodshed, the prostitutes, and the ripped-open basques. A gambler, Selznick appreciated the odds against him. Mitchell's Rhett Butler had several "nights of love," Selznick wrote to Sidney Howard. "How the hell we can even use one is going to be a problem."

By 1937, Howard had drafted fifty pages of notes on *Gone With the Wind* and sent them to the Production Code office for an opinion. Though Auster questioned numerous plot points as well as some language, particularly the word "niggers" and the amorous phrase "I want you," he found the story generally acceptable. In a January memorandum to Breen, he summarized the problems, then offered solutions. Margaret Mitchell's "husbandly rape" had caused Scarlett to warm toward Rhett; could some unexpected tenderness from Captain Butler accomplish the same thing? And could the brothel become a saloon, the whores dancing girls? Despite concerns about sexual promiscuity and the childbirth scene, Auster predicted that the historical setting and "the character and personality" of Sidney Howard and David Selznick would minimize affronts to the Production Code. Breen may have suspected otherwise, but neither he nor Selznick would waste words over some notes.

As Macmillan posted record monthly sales figures on *Gone With the Wind,* Culver City drones indexed and cross-indexed the novel by sections, characters, and situations. Selznick hoped that the sweat would help assure the consonance of movie and book. The better the adaptation, though, the greater the potential for Production Code infractions. Selznick conferred often with Howard, both to supervise the writer and to keep more Mitchell than Breen in the scenario in progress. "Sidney and I have a terrific job on our hands," Selznick told director George Cukor, "as is apparent from our work today when we spent the whole morning up to one-thirty on nine pages of the script. I am weighing every word and every line most carefully."

More cerebral than dramatic, that pallid first draft captured the characters but not the sweep of the Mitchell novel; it nonetheless offered plenty for Breen to chew on. The Production Code director read the *Gone With the Wind* script, then met with Selznick, Howard, and Cukor on a Monday afternoon in October 1937. Though both Selznick and Breen moved toward entente, they covered their flanks. Selznick leaned on "character and personality." He could argue that the excellence of the novel and the good taste of the producer earned *Gone With the Wind* some latitude. Breen reminded Selznick that observance of the Production Code would keep the censor boards away from the picture.

Breen had a laundry list of warnings. He cautioned Selznick, Howard, and Cukor against the *"undue exposure"* of Scarlett during the dressing scenes, against the characters making the sign of the cross (a sore point with the British Board), against the close shots of the dead and dying. He told them to cool Rhett down; Captain Butler should not *want* Scarlett, he should *think more of her.* Likewise, however down-at-the-heels she became, Scarlett should not offer her body to Rhett in exchange for the money to restore Tara.

With Selznick on the ropes, Breen could have delivered the coup de grace. The Production Code chief had professional and personal concerns about the childbirth sequence and the "husbandly rape." The former told women that the pain of childbirth could surpass the joy, the latter that sex could mean not only procreation or even pleasure but wild abandon. Could a devout Irish Catholic condone either message? The father of six, Breen advised Selznick that the tears and blood of hard labor as well as the fist that gripped a towel tied to the bedpost would exceed the tolerance of moviegoers and censors. Scarlett could perhaps ask Melanie, "How do you feel?" She could not ask, "How *bad* do you feel?" (Mitchell had written, "Do you feel bad?" Despite later protests that he had faithfully reproduced the novel, Selznick altered many speeches and situations.) Ever the script doctor, Breen suggested that during the childbirth sequence Cukor focus on Scarlett or Prissy rather than Melanie. He also recommended that Rhett "take [Scarlett] in his arms, kiss her, and then gently start with her toward the bedroom. It is our thought that you should *not* go so far as to throw her on the bed." Much more accommodating than expected, Breen had bent on the childbirth sequence and the "husbandly rape." Perhaps the Pulitzer Prize awarded the novel had subdued him. Perhaps kudos from the just-released *Dead End,* another independent feature, convinced him that the picture would epitomize the Selznick International motto, "In the Tradition of Quality." Whatever the reason, Selznick and Cukor hailed the more liberal Production Code interpretation on *Gone With the Wind*.

In the aftermath of the meeting, Breen dictated some for-the-record comments on *Gone With the Wind*. "We recommend" and "we suggest" dominated the seven-page October 14 letter to Selznick International, yet "we ask" and "we urge" also appeared: "we" told Selznick to mute the childbirth scene, eliminate "*any suggestion of rape,*" and make an honest woman of Belle Watling. While Breen had not retreated from the oral concessions of several days before, Selznick thought that he had. The producer had "a peculiar kind of temper," his executive secretary Marcella Rabwin recalled, "very explosive and then very quiet." Production Code liaison Val Lewton assured the wrathful Selznick that "I can go down to [Breen's] office and, one by one, argue for those lines which you feel you don't want to lose. I think in many cases we can successfully overcome his objections." As Selznick cooled, he recalled that "Joe [was] most enthusiastic about the picture" and had even offered to protect a discreetly photographed childbirth scene from censorship cuts.

Should the property man order towels and hot water? Should the wardrobe mistress accent the décolletage? Should the carpenter build a brothel? A script approved by the Production Code Administration would have the answers. And because that script determined the casting, the assignment of craftspeople and crew members, and the design and construction of sets and costumes, many studios mailed revisions to the Production Code office scene by scene. Selznick believed that Lewton could handle censorship matters, though, and stalled Breen; he told Howard to proceed with the second draft. The producer expected to retain—undiluted—the "husbandly rape," the brothel, and other elements that had been challenged, for he bet that Breen would waffle, that the reputation of the popular novel would carry the film past the Production Code Administration and the local censor boards.

As Howard revised the script throughout January and February 1938, *Gone With the Wind* entered preproduction. The designs included the balcony that Rhett Butler and Belle Watling would share during the armory scene. There Belle would point out one of her debtors; Captain Butler would then recall his own unsettled account and hand Belle $100 in gold. Those who still doubted that Belle was a madam would be convinced by the rooms that Selznick had commissioned William Cameron Menzies to create for her. "Menzies' sketch of the interior of Belle's place is one of the funniest I've seen," *Gone With the Wind* technical advisor Wilbur Kurtz wrote. "The lily is not only gilded. It's embossed and set with rhinestones!" While Breen might rename the brothel a saloon, everyone would know what the boys in the back room could have.

Val Lewton feared a major confrontation with Breen; offered a *Gone With the Wind* with gross violations of the Production Code, the Irishman would toss Lewton and the screenplay out on Hollywood Boulevard. According to Lewton, only Selznick himself could wear down Breen:

> Believe me, I am not passing the buck. For the ordinary picture and the ordinary problem I feel I am adequate, but in this case where I know, for instance, that Breen would throw out the word "belch" and you might want to keep it in, I do think it best for you to see him.

Sidney Howard also found Selznick too proprietary about *Gone With the Wind*. When one actress turned down Scarlett O'Hara because she thought the love scenes repetitive and the "husbandly rape" watered down by "fear of censorship," she prompted Selznick to consider a rewrite. Howard bowed out for the pugnacious Jo Swerling, who bowed out for Oliver H. P. Garrett. "Honestly! What Garrett has done is leave the first half of the script just as long as ever," Georgia journalist Susan Myrick later wrote to Margaret Mitchell, "and shortened the last part to make it look as if somebody dies every few minutes. What the hell, of course." Selznick had meanwhile traded the *Gone With the Wind* distribution rights to Metro for Clark Gable, and since MGM would not release the picture until Selznick had earned the Production Code certificate, Breen—not Howard or Selznick or Garrett—would have the last word.

Selznick burned Atlanta in December 1938. With production under way, he could no longer stall Breen and in January 1939 sent him the first thirteen pages of the incomplete shooting script. Would the reputations of David Selznick, Margaret Mitchell, and *Gone With the Wind* sway Breen? Caught between the law of the Production Code and a tendency toward its more liberal interpretation, Breen could baffle producers. He scanned the first thirteen pages of the *Gone With the Wind* script and noted that the heroine had sounded an inappropriate note of distress in Scene 38. He told Selznick: "Omit the action of Scarlett belching."

The screenplay—which evolved during production—turned the entrance of Selznick International into a revolving door through which John Van Druten and F. Scott Fitzgerald as well as Oliver Garrett passed, each with small contributions to scenes and dialogue. By February 1939, Breen read what they and Selznick had written. Censorship matters on *Tom Sawyer* and *Anna Karenina* had become grist for the Selznick publicity mill, and Breen did not want a third turn on *Gone With the Wind;* besides the risk of personal embarrassment, he also wanted to be fair. So Breen tempered his response, part summer breeze and—because other producers would monitor *Gone With the Wind* for fissures in the Code—part tornado. In the latter mode he uprooted numerous elements deemed "unacceptable under the provisions of the Production Code": Belle Watling and Rhett Butler were portrayed as lovers, the Red Horse as a brothel, the "girls" as prostitutes. Promiscuity and censorable words, particularly "nigger" and "damn," dotted and marred the screenplay. No less contestable were the scenes of wounded and dying Confederate soldiers. Though Breen overlooked Scarlett's "accidental abortion" (her fall down the stairs), he noted that many other elements could not be approved.

Selznick proceeded as though all points were negotiable. As carpenters nailed together the interiors and exteriors of the Red Horse, tailors seamed the costumes for Belle Watling and her "girls," including one that Sue Myrick described as "a dark red velvet dress and a too-red hat trimmed with scarlet plumes." Casting also continued, with Tallulah Bankhead and Mae West both considered for Belle and both certain to turn Breen scarlet. (Ona Munson finally won the role.) Meanwhile, Selznick distracted Breen with the usual last-minute revisions of the shooting script.

Selznick thrived on chaos and pressure. Well into principal photography, carpenters and plasterers started constructing sets for
scenes that the producer intended to delete from the script. "I asked
if the front office ever told the rear office what it was doing,"
Wilbur Kurtz noted in a journal entry, "and both declared that was
never done." Indeed, the Selznick International research office had
never even been informed that the studio employed Kurtz as technical advisor. The pressures on Selznick were enormous, for he supervised everything, from wardrobe and color photography to the
completion of the script. In February, he replaced George Cukor
with Victor Fleming, a decision that crushed stars Vivien Leigh and
Olivia de Havilland. A month later, he replaced cinematographer
Lee Garmes with Ernest Haller. In April, Fleming collapsed and
Sam Wood took over. "Quite apart from the cost factor," Selznick
observed, "everybody's nerves are getting on the ragged edge, and
God only knows what will happen if we don't get this damn thing
finished." The production tired cast, crew, and Joe Breen.

Throughout the first six months of 1939, Lewton drove to the
Production Code office to argue for one concession after another,
not with Auster but Breen himself. During one meeting, the Production Code administrator accepted Belle as a prostitute. The
model would be *Stagecoach,* where the "Law and Order League"
had run Dallas (Claire Trevor) out of town for reasons understood
yet not spoken. If Selznick established Belle as a prostitute—
without elaboration or embellishment—the treatment of character
would be "perfectly permissible."

Breen had barely shut the door when Selznick told Lewton to
knock again. Could the picture show some hot times in the Red
Horse? Breen refused. Making prostitution attractive or pleasant
would "excite the lustful emotions of the young." Could Selznick
report some hot times in the Red Horse? Could he show how the
place aroused the curiosity of genteel Atlanta women? "Were you
really there?" Mrs. Meade would ask a man. "What did it look like?
Does she have cut-glass chandeliers and plush curtains and dozens
of mirrors?" Breen again refused.

Lewton scoured the Production Code for mention of brothels but
found none. The Production Code that Breen enforced lay in both
the Particular Applications and the "black books." The contents of

the latter were inspired by what one trade newspaper called the "influences of transient expediency and propinquity," while Section II of the former outlawed the justification of adultery and illicit sex and the treatment of "low forms" of sex relationships. Between the two, Breen had carte blanche on matters sexual. Another producer would have pulled the cathouse trappings from the Red Horse, yet Selznick was convinced that Breen would bend. Moreover, when the Production Code Administration focused on details rather than broad themes—especially after a picture had been shot—negotiations favored the producer. Breen understood that Hollywood demanded more "give" than "take" on million-dollar investments.

Though *Gone With the Wind* would lack the carnality of *Ecstasy,* with Hedy Lamarr in the delirium of orgasm, it would have more candor than routine big-budget releases of the 1930s. Breen had red-pencilled Scarlett pressing herself against Ashley, running her hands over her body, lying in bed with Rhett, and awakening with joyous memories of the "husbandly rape." Though Breen called the bedroom scene "enormously offensive," Selznick persuaded him to suspend judgment on all four sensitive points. Breen had also red-pencilled the cancan that Scarlett and Rhett watched in New Orleans. (The dance was another departure from Margaret Mitchell, who wrote only that Scarlett found New Orleans "the gayest place she had ever seen.") According to Lewton, the dance was anachronistic. According to Breen, it was indecent, an outrage to all who spotted the flesh between leotards and black stockings. When Selznick found no reference to the cancan in the Production Code, he reminded Breen that the Code office had approved the dance in Paramount's *Zaza* only months before. The scene in *Gone With the Wind* would stand.

Selznick dared the Production Code Administration on even more sensitive matters. Breen had approved a near-Victorian version of the "husbandly rape" sequence, and made Lewton a Production Code deputy. As one Selznick associate recalled,

Val Lewton, the contact man with the Hays office, was on the job all during the ravishment scene, impressing Victor [Fleming] with the fact that [Vivien Leigh] is not supposed to struggle against being carried away. 'But won't it look a lot worse, if I just go along without any protest?' she wanted to know. Val told her the Hays office must have overlooked that one and for gosh sakes to keep quiet or they might squelch the whole scene.

Selznick would continue the subversion. "There should be no cries from Scarlett," an alarmed Breen told the producer, "and we suggest that you fade out immediately that he *starts* to carry her up the stairs, rather than prolong the 'fade.'" The fade-out was a Hollywood marker for sexual intimacy, so well-established that when Breen objected to a love scene in the rereleased print of *A Farewell to Arms,* Paramount substituted a cut for the fade-out and won Production Code approval. Selznick would not only prolong the fade but would exceed the bounds of Breen on the morning-after episode. Scarlett would awaken utterly fulfilled. She would even sing to herself. During principal photography, word spread that Vivien Leigh needed a melody to hum, one that would pass the censors. Sue Myrick piped up, "It Ain't What'cha Do But The Way That You Do It."

When shooting ended in late June 1939, Selznick wired a celebratory message to Jock Whitney. "Sound the siren!" he wrote to his partner and backer. Whitney did, then Breen did. The Production Code administrator saw an early September preview of *Gone With the Wind* and blasted Selznick. The morning-after scene found Scarlett "figuratively licking her chops" and "yawning and stretching and snuggling under the covers," Breen said; local censors would object. Selznick countered that the preening illustrated an important story point: Scarlett had enjoyed the sexual encounter and, paradoxically, concluded that she had Rhett in thrall. Breen consulted Production Code associates Shurlock and Karl Lischka. Shurlock concurred with Selznick, Lischka did not. Breen remained troubled. Some protection footage existed, where Scarlett merely contemplated her chops, but Selznick hesitated to strike the original sequence. For one thing, the Breen office could relent. Lewton even thought that "I can show them that particular portion of film again, blandly assuring them that it had been cut and hoping that they will believe me." In addition, the protection footage had barter value. Selznick could perhaps trade Breen the stretching and yawning for permission to use the words "nigger" and "damn," two censorship matters still unresolved.

Margaret Mitchell thought the word "nigger" harmless. Sidney Howard had likewise hailed Mitchell's black characters as "the best written darkies . . . in all literature," wholly "uncolored by white patronising." Echoing the sectionalism of the novel, the Howard screenplay was a pastoral of docile and happy slaves. The Production Code Administration had prompted Howard to delete references to the Ku Klux Klan and to round out the black characters, yet the word "nigger" persisted through various script drafts. An anxious Breen could recall that when Lionel Barrymore uttered "nigger" in *Carolina,* blacks in Chicago, Washington, Baltimore, New York, and Los Angeles had thrown bricks at the screen. Would the more widely publicized *Gone With the Wind* become a cause célèbre?

The opportunity that *Gone With the Wind* offered underemployed black performers posed a dilemma for organized blacks, the Negro press, and the actors themselves. By February 1939, black publisher Leon Washington had circulated a petition among "colored maids" to boycott *Gone With the Wind;* a black clubwoman had also written to the Motion Picture Association to voice her concern. Such protests, along with the *Carolina* incident and the Negro press's howls over Paul Robeson's use of "nigger" in *Emperor Jones,* demonstrated why Hays wanted Breen to approach *Gone With the Wind* and "nigger" with caution. Blacks' concern for dignity was important; theater owners' concern for property was even more so.

Selznick was liberal by contemporary standards, and he persuaded Breen to allow the black characters—but not the white—to use the word "nigger." The black actors were upset. A tremor had rumbled through Selznick International in winter 1939, when some black actors threatened to leave the production unless the studio desegregated the lavatories. "I complained so much," Butterfly McQueen later recalled, that she was warned "Mr. Selznick would never give me another job." The word "nigger" hurt and offended her. Breen soon recanted and banned the word for all characters. With considerable reluctance, Selznick changed "nigger" to "darkie." Breen was no less grateful than the black actors. Had the Negro press fueled a controversy, both *Gone With the Wind* and Joe Breen could have been burned.

By summer 1939, the word "nigger" had produced an itch that Selznick wanted to scratch.

Increasingly I regret the loss of the better negroes being able to refer to themselves as niggers, and other uses of the word nigger by one negro talking about another. All the uses that I would have liked to have retained do nothing but glorify the negroes, and I can't believe that we were sound in having a blanket rule of this kind.

The producer scanned the novel for apposite references and found Uncle Peter telling Scarlett how the Yankees had called him "a nigger an' Ah ain' never been call a nigger by no w'ite folks, an' dey call me a ole pet an' say dat niggers ain' ter be trus'ed!" Later Big Sam told Scarlett that he "doan lib in Shantytown," home only to "trashy niggers." Selznick asked Val Lewton to search the novel for other "friendly-to-the-negroes" uses of the word, then challenge the ruling of the Production Code Administration. Breen had approved the word "wop" in *It's a Wonderful World,* he could approve "nigger" in *Gone With the Wind.*

Lewton prosecuted the case hesitantly. "I am not sure that you are aware of how resentful most negroes and negro societies are toward this book," he told Selznick. Moreover, in response to letters that the Production Code Administration and Selznick International had received from blacks, the studio had promised not to use the word "nigger." Breen encouraged Lewton to honor the commitment. He noted that the "intelligent negro" in the audience would understand how Uncle Peter and Big Sam used "nigger," but "the rank and file" would not. Would Selznick answer to theater owners who had had bricks tossed through their screens? Comfortable with his own benevolent attitude toward blacks, Selznick could not see the point. He anticipated a confrontation with Breen over Rhett Butler's tag line, though, and decided not to press on "nigger." The uncommonly short memorandum to Lewton read: "Okay, we'll forget it."

★   ★   ★

One censorship problem remained. In the last pages of the novel, Scarlett had pleaded with Rhett not to leave her. " 'Oh, my darling,' she cried, 'if you go, what shall I do?' " Rhett "drew a short breath and said lightly but softly: 'My dear, I don't give a damn.' " When Selznick transferred the line from page to screen, he expanded it by a "frankly." Jock Whitney deadpanned that "real old southern fidelity would not add the word 'frankly,' " but Breen eyed another word. He had routinely cut "damn" from pictures, and ordered it deleted from the *Gone With the Wind* screenplay as well.

Selznick believed that Breen would relent. The Irishman had "whipped himself up into a lather" about the moral values of *Intermezzo,* Lewton told Selznick, but the astute Geoff Shurlock had apparently persuaded him to certify the picture with minimal changes. Toward the end of the decade, Breen had passed both social-problem films like *Dead End* and piquant comedies like *Ninotchka* and *The Women.* The latter owed their tingle to the writers' craftsmanship and Breen's indulgence. "Well, girls," Crystal (Joan Crawford) told those who had gathered and undone her at the end of *The Women,* "looks like it's back to the perfume counter for me. By the way, there's a name for you ladies, but it isn't used in high society, outside of a kennel." The sword of *Belle of the Nineties* had become the butter knife of *The Women.*

When Selznick made a strong plea for "damn," Breen offered the producer a bargain: Selznick would drop "for God's sake" and certain other mild profanities borrowed from Margaret Mitchell, Breen would allow Rhett "damn." The munificent Breen even promised to fight any local censors who opposed "damn." Breen had made an extraordinary concession. While many censors had some fondness for Breen, they could make political hay of lapses in Production Code enforcement. Other filmmakers could also challenge an exception for Selznick. So, in winter 1939, Breen demanded a loophole. He told Selznick to cover the "damn" line with protection footage. Should Breen change his mind—or should the censor boards cut the profanity—Selznick would need the alternate take. In the Breen version, Rhett would tell Scarlett: "My dear, I don't care."

Then, in June, Breen opened the loophole and stepped through.

He confided to Lewton that he could not pass *Gone With the Wind* or any picture with "damn" because of "the hell that the Board of Directors would give [me] when trouble resulted." Why had the man who straight-armed Hollywood suddenly ducked behind board members' skirts? The sea change in Production Code enforcement had attracted far more notice than Breen wanted, perhaps more notice than he could bear. In a story headlined WILL HAYS OFFICE LETS DOWN BARS, the New York *World-Telegram* Hollywood correspondent would soon report that "there have been some pretty racy lines in some of the big pictures lately, and it's understood that an extra degree of latitude is to be granted moviemakers now that the war-hobbled industry needs more customers. (Of course, the Hays office itself never would make any such admission.)"

Producers' demands and Production Code absolutes held Breen in a vise. Reading constraint as bluff, however, Selznick threatened to carry "damn" to the Motion Picture Association board. Appeals to the company presidents were virtually unknown in the 1930s. Breen compromised, the producer compromised; both were aware that studio executives thought few censorship issues important enough to bother the East Coast moguls about. When Breen encouraged Selznick to appeal, the producer hesitated. He suspected that an appeal—a throwback to the days of the Hollywood Jury—could anger Breen and negatively affect the course of *Rebecca,* another Selznick picture then in production. Yet Breen *wanted* a board opinion; should board members support Selznick, they could formalize a more liberal application of the Production Code and perhaps ease the strain on the Production Code administrator.

Lewton advised Selznick to leave intact the protection footage ("My dear, I don't care") and screen *Gone With the Wind* for the Production Code Administration; after Breen had approved all but "damn," Selznick could then appeal to the board. Selznick consented. On a muggy Saturday night in September, Jock Whitney, Irene Selznick, Joe Breen, and a load of "Selznickers" motored to Riverside to preview the picture—without the "damn" tag line. The youthful audience had just sat through two hours of *Beau Geste,* but when "Margaret Mitchell" and "*Gone With the Wind*" appeared on-screen, the crowd stood and cheered. Four hours later, moviegoers stood again and applauded for more than five minutes.

Walking out, Joe Breen pulled Selznick aside and hailed *Gone With the Wind* as "without doubt the greatest motion picture ever filmed."

Selznick had been wise to leave the protection footage intact. The theater had been filled with teenagers, a more vocal audience than their parents. The cheers that greeted the titles could well have turned to huzzas and whistles had Rhett told Scarlett, "Frankly, my dear, I don't give a damn." Breen later grumbled about the Red Horse brothel and the morning-after scene, for neither had been cut to Production Code specifications. A strong reaction to the tag line could have added "damn" to the agenda of concerns and invited Breen to review the entire picture. Had the newspapers learned— and reported—that Rhett cursed, Breen could even have become vengeful. As it was, Lewton told Selznick, Breen anticipated "a hard fight on his hands with other producers who will say to him in the future, 'Well, you let David Selznick get away with it in 'Gone With the Wind.' '" Breen was nevertheless content to certify the picture on completion of retakes.

In September, as Europe went to war, Selznick could see "damn" everywhere. Already found in such popular magazines as *Liberty* and *Good Housekeeping,* "damn" was used by the *New York Times* and the Los Angeles *Examiner* in September editorials. Yet Breen remained steadfast: without the protection footage, he would not award *Gone With the Wind* a Seal. Chattering in early October about "the allegedly censorable scenes in 'GONE WITH THE WIND,' " the gossip columnist for the *Hollywood Reporter* made Breen even more resolute. With the premiere two months away, Selznick resigned himself to a confrontation with the board but hoped to avoid a formal appeal. He thought that some board members could convince Hays that the Association should not waste its time "on a silly point like this"; the General would then approve "damn" himself, without convening the Board of Directors. Meanwhile, Selznick cut the negative of *Gone With the Wind* so that it could later accommodate insertion of the "damn" footage.

In mid-October, Selznick took *Gone With the Wind,* protection footage and all, to Santa Barbara for another preview. Several persons who completed response cards commented on the ending, particularly the implication that Rhett would not return. One moviegoer, his acumen better than his spelling, noted that "Brett's leaving Scarlit at the last of the picture lacks a certain punch." Two days later, Selznick appealed to Will Hays that the "damn" line be inserted. The drama required the "forbidden word," he wrote Hays, and the public would not object; since "this dramatic word" would be used "in its rightfully dramatic place," it would not open the floodgates and cause a stampede of screen "damn"s. Selznick concluded that the protection footage gave "an impression of unfaithfulness after three hours and forty-five minutes of extreme fidelity to Miss Mitchell's work, which, as you know, has become an American Bible."

Breen proved an ally. He told Lewton in confidence that personally he believed the arguments sound. He could not publicly support Selznick, but he would encourage Hays to approve the line. "I have stated to David that I have no objections whatever to his taking the matter up with you," Breen wrote Hays, "and that we have no irritation or ill-feeling in the matter at all." Like Selznick, Breen thought that the General could rule on "damn" without a board meeting. Breen had made so many comparable decisions ex cathedra in the late 1930s that he probably expected Hays to follow suit. But Hays would not.

In late October, when Hays learned that Selznick planned to challenge Breen, he asked Francis Harmon to review the file on *Ecstasy*. The Association had been wary of a court battle on *Ecstasy* and prepared a brief on the case; it would follow the same procedure on *Gone With the Wind*. Hays fully appreciated—as perhaps Breen had not—that appeals could have legal consequences. Especially with Selznick involved. In a testy September 1939 memorandum to Jock Whitney, its content no secret among Hollywood insiders, Selznick wrote that *Gone With the Wind* offered "the ideal occasion to secure United Artists' support to telling the Hays Association that we want no part of them or their Code." The major companies would remain mum, afraid that any comment would affect the Justice Department case against the movies, and the guilds would support Selznick for an attack on "so insane and inane and outmoded a Code as that under which the industry is now struggling." Hays and Breen would have heard that argument before, but Selznick added a new twist: with the world on the threshold of war, Hollywood could no longer afford the luxury of self-regulation:

The whole damned Code becomes doubly onerous now that we are in danger of losing our foreign market. It was bad enough trying to make pictures that would break even when we had a world market to play to and with many of our best possibilities ruled out by the Code. But now, when we need at least to have something like the freedom that newspapers and magazines and book publishers and the legitimate stage have, when we need this freedom desperately, to have the industry itself strangle us is something which would be tolerated only by this short-sighted industry.

As an independent rather than a major producer, Selznick could have established a strong case against the Production Code Administration. "Damn the United States!" Philip Nolan had cried in *The Man Without a Country*. "I never want to hear that name again!" Why had Warner been allowed "damn" in a short subject and Selznick been refused in *Gone With the Wind?* "They cannot give the argument that this was historical since it is purely fictional," the revved-up producer told Whitney, "out of a book which holds no higher place in the affections of the American public certainly than does 'Gone With the Wind.' " Aware of the skittishness of the Hays Office, Selznick could use *The Man Without a Country* as trump card.

In the last week of October 1939, after Selznick filed the appeal, Harmon prepared a defense for Hays. The Production Code office sent Harmon copies of seventy-four letters or notes to Selznick and countless memoranda of record on *Gone With the Wind*. The documentation—which traced how much of the novel the producer had altered, from the childbirth sequence to the treatment of the Klan and the blacks—damaged the Selznick argument that an accurate translation of the book demanded the word "damn." Yet the shadow of the Justice Department and the need to exonerate the Production Code Administration from charges of discrimination made the Harmon assignment a more delicate task than Breen would admit. Federal antitrust statutes required the Production Code to meet the criteria of reasonableness and impartiality. Because censor boards routinely cut "damn" from imported pictures (those that never sought a Production Code Seal), Harmon could show that the profanity section was reasonable. He had more trouble with the second criterion.

Breen protested that he had snipped "damn" from numerous

recent pictures, including RKO's *Abe Lincoln in Illinois,* which, like
Gone With the Wind, had been based on a Pulitzer Prize winner; such
actions proved that major companies and independent producers
received equal treatment. What about *The Man Without a Country*?
"Damn" in *Gone With the Wind* was profane, Breen told Harmon,
"damn" in the Warners release was not. Yet Breen had allowed
social-problem pictures like *Dead End* and *The Man Without a Country* more leeway than straight entertainment pictures. The Association seemed vulnerable enough for Harmon to recommend that
Hays concede Production Code Administration error for the
"damn" in *The Man Without a Country* and reaffirm Section V of the
Code: "Pointed profanity . . . or every other profane or vulgar
expression however used, is forbidden." A damn was a damn was a
damn. To allow one "damn" in *Gone With the Wind* could release a
cascade of "damn"s in American motion pictures.

On October 25, Selznick flew east to plan the distribution of
Gone With the Wind and attend the Association board meeting.
MGM president Nick Schenck sat on the board that would hear the
"damn" appeal and, more conservative than Selznick, thought
"damn" less important than the producer of *Gone With the Wind*
made out; he had also shaved points from Selznick's profit participation in *Gone With the Wind.* Yet even had Selznick trusted
Schenck, the producer would have wanted to speak for himself.
Studio wags called Selznick "a gooser." Running on Benzedrine, he
ruled his studio less by threat or menace—the weapon of several
fellow moguls—than by the thoroughness and heat of his commitment. Both Harmon and Hays counsel Gabe Hess feared that Selznick and the dollars that rode on *Gone With the Wind* would persuade
the board to reverse Breen. Afterwards, board members would
have two courses: to waive the profanity rule for Selznick or
to amend the Code. The former might violate the federal law,
while the latter would not only remove "damn" from the roster of
forbidden words but confirm the rumors that Hays had loosened
his hold on Hollywood. Hays associates found neither decision
palatable.

The board met at four o'clock on October 27 to hear Selznick
and Harmon; it then reconvened in a "very stormy" executive
session. Hays told board members that he adamantly opposed both

the use of "damn" and a change in the Production Code. The presidents of Paramount, Universal, and Twentieth Century–Fox seconded Hays, Paramount's Barney Balaban doing so "in no uncertain terms." Others—including Schenck—supported Selznick. United Artists' Murray Silverstone lent the Selznick argument force and eloquence. He reminded colleagues that UA had been formed as a haven for independents, men who wanted to make their pictures, their way. The Association must foster—not hamper—moviemakers. As the dinner hour approached and the Silverstone corner filled, Hays weakened. He anticipated that the board would reverse Breen, and though he could veto a recommendation of the board, the board could overturn the veto with a two-thirds affirmative vote. More conciliator than czar, the General decided to suspend the meeting in order to consider how best to manage the outcome.

Selznick returned to the West Coast to lobby fellow independent producers for their support, but none proved eager to help. According to Selznick International legal counsel Dan O'Shea, producer Sol Lesser "carried [the] Bible on his back and [the] torch [of] 'righteousness' in his hand but I persuaded him." The wire that Lesser grudgingly sent Hays read: "Were I present at the meeting I would vote to permit the inclusion of the line in the picture." Hal Roach was Hays' good pal, and his telegram had no more juice than Lesser's: "To leave ["damn"] out would hurt the picture but to let it stay will not hurt the picture industry." Lesser and Roach wore two hats. As Hollywood producers, they were servants of Breen; as Manhattan board members, they were masters. Roach's *Of Mice and Men* lay before Breen during the period of the *Gone With the Wind* appeal; uncertain of where Breen stood on the Selznick picture, Roach may have chosen a middle path that would—without ostentation—encourage the more liberal tendencies of the Production Code administrator.

Selznick proved relentless. An expert on audiences, he framed an argument with considerable appeal to those who had entered the motion picture industry from amusement park operations and theater management. Britain, Germany, and France were already at war, Selznick told board members whom he could buttonhole, and when other countries followed, the industry could lose the lucrative

European market. More crucial than ever, domestic revenue would sustain Hollywood; the audience must have outstanding pictures, pictures different from the norm, pictures unhampered by a rigid Production Code. The punch that closed *Gone With the Wind* could translate into added box office dollars.

The Motion Picture Association board meeting resumed on November 1 at three o'clock. Though Hays wanted to screen the end of *Gone With the Wind*, both with and without the protection footage, Selznick had committed the negative to the lab. He sent board members the "give a damn" close, however, for he believed that once they saw the footage, they would overturn the Production Code Administration without debate. This time Hays had no dinner plans. "Trade practices and Hollywood conditions are now causing the greatest worry," lawyer Hays exhorted board members; solutions were possible, but an erosion of faith in the Production Code would jeopardize them. Turning history professor, Hays told board members that when the industry had attempted to shake the Depression blues with red-hot pictures, the cure had proved nearly fatal. The Association could not allow the economic pressure of shrinking foreign markets to loosen Production Code standards, not when the matter turned on one word in a one-thousand-page book.

But by the end of the afternoon, representatives of the major companies had joined independent producers to reverse Breen and let "damn" stand. Selznick had a multimillion-dollar investment in a spectacular motion picture; *Gunga Din, The Man Without a Country,* and other releases with questionable language or content suggested to board members that the public would accept "damn" in *Gone With the Wind*. After Hays warned that the decision could unleash the Justice Department bloodhounds on Hollywood, the Association devised what could be called the *Gone With the Wind* rule. The Production Code would henceforth ban the words "damn" and "hell" except when their use

> shall be essential and required for portrayal, in proper historical context, of any scene or dialogue based upon historical fact or folklore, or for the presentation in proper literary context of a Biblical, or other religious quotation, or a quotation from a literary work

provided that no such use shall be permitted which is intrinsically objectionable or offends good taste.

Legend persists that Hays fined Selznick $5,000 for using the word "damn." Yet board members passed the amendment to insure that Selznick and *Gone With the Wind* would honor—not breach—the Production Code. In mid-November, Breen approved the last retakes on the picture. "This ends the censorship on 'Gone With the Wind,' " Lewton told Selznick, and he was almost right.

The *Gone With the Wind* appeal illustrated that conservative exhibitors and distributors in Manhattan would listen to the more liberal picturemen from Hollywood, especially when the latter jingled box office bells. The results were immediately apparent. In Zanuck's *The Grapes of Wrath*, another instant classic, the Joads have a flat tire; Tommy mutters that Ma should get "the hell" off the bumper so he can mount the spare. Near the end of *Life With Father*, a policeman spots Mr. Day: "Going to the office?" "No," Father Day snaps, "I'm going to be baptized, dammit!"

While mainstream producers secured more license from the East Coast and the Production Code Administration, Breen continued to run the gauntlet of criticism, with moviemen like Selznick and Zanuck on one side, the specter of the Legion of Decency and assorted bluenoses on the other. The stress occasionally caused Breen to reverse himself. In *Destry Rides Again*, Marlene Dietrich used her bosom as her bank. Patting one deposit, she purred: "There's gold in them thar hills." Breen approved the line, but when he heard an audience howl with laughter, he filled out a withdrawal slip. "It was the best line in the picture," producer Joe Pasternak sighed. On controversial films, Breen and the producers shared a common risk. *Of Mice and Men*, which Breen had called "enormously dangerous," muted the profanity and obscenity of the Steinbeck original but retained the mercy killing and the hint of sexual perversion. Though Hays thought it a work of "very bad repute" and at the last minute wanted producer Hal Roach to change the title in order to dodge censure, Breen had admired and approved the picture. He nonetheless feared that releases like *Of Mice and Men*—along with the *Gone With the Wind* Production Code amendment—would inspire other producers of other "enormously dangerous" properties to storm the Hollywood Boulevard office to plead for still more concessions. Breen passed all donkeywork along to his associates; as more and more producers squeezed the Code, however, they increased the work Breen had to do personally. At Thanksgiving 1939, a Hays associate wrote Breen, "I sincerely hope that the atmosphere will clear appreciably within the next few weeks." It did not.

On Christmas Day, gossip columnist Jimmie Fidler broke the story of "damn." Hays Office "purists" had been shocked to read that "naughty, naughty word in the script," Fidler wrote, and Breen had rushed home from Manhattan to cut it; when Selznick attacked, Breen and Hays retreated. "The motion-picture industry has long since outgrown infancy. It's too old now to have its mouth washed with soap. Let our adult movies be their age!" The Christmas goose had barely cooled when Breen tore into Fidler. He called the "purists" charge not only "false but utterly ridiculous." For good reason he suspected that Selznick had leaked the account to Fidler, and according to Val Lewton, Breen telephoned Selznick International "wild about this." Breen could portray himself as the injured party. He had *encouraged* Selznick to move the Production Code from infancy to adolescence, to press an appeal that could reward both producer and Production Code administrator; Selznick had taken the olive branch and handed Breen the pits. Though Selznick probably tattled to Fidler, he attempted to placate Breen— chiefly because *Rebecca* remained on the Production Code Administration docket.

For Martin Quigley, "damn" meant that "damage will be done and ground lost after all the tedious and costly efforts of the industry to keep itself in line with American mores." Few agreed. As one critic quipped, the real shock was not that Rhett Butler cursed Scarlett but that he took so long to do so. Audiences loved the picture. After *Gone With the Wind* had been playing for several weeks at the United Artists theater in downtown Los Angeles, Val Lewton attended a screening.

In the second half the audience really went to work, especially on what we term the rape scene. They liked to have Gable compel Scarlett to sit in the chair and listen to him, and when he picked her up and ran up the stairs with her, the applause was almost equal to that extended to Babe Ruth when he made a home run. They enjoyed the bedroom scene on the following morning immensely . . . and when Rhett gave the tag line they applauded.

Audiences even liked the hospital sequences that Breen had once thought too strong. One reviewer noted that while Selznick did not show the operations, the shrieks stimulated the imagination. "Personally I'm not over keen on this gruesome stuff, but cinema proprietors tell me I'm in a minority. Most patrons enjoy it, particularly the women." The applause reaffirmed for Selznick the distance between the Production Code and the mores of filmgoers.

The government boards and the British censors passed *Gone With the Wind* with only minor cuts, while the Legion of Decency rated the picture "B," perverse evidence of Breen's "comparatively liberal attitude" toward the release. Yet Breen had no cause for celebration. In April 1940, Selznick finished *Rebecca* and temporarily retired from picturemaking; as envoi he told the *New York Times* that Hollywood needed a new "purity code." However well the Production Code had once served the industry, it had become obsolete. "Can you imagine how silly Rhett would have sounded if he had said to Scarlett, 'Frankly, I don't care,' " the producer asked. Over lunch with Selznick only three days before, Quigley had learned that "there is a campaign against the Code brewing among writers in Hollywood and New York." The co-author of the Production Code convinced Selznick not to hold "windy and, probably, fruitless sessions" that would foment a rebellion, but in the months following the *Gone With the Wind* premiere, Breen had mixed feelings about Production Code enforcement.

In reflective moments, Breen could almost admit that the Production Code had crippled Hollywood. "To satisfy everyone," an exasperated Breen told Q magazine in summer 1940, "every movie villain should be a native-born white American—with no college, no fraternal, no political affiliations. He must be a member of no church. He must belong to no lodge. He must have no profession. And no job." But when others criticized the Production Code Administration, Breen could turn flinty. After the British Board approved *Primrose Path* in May 1940, a Paramount executive told

Breen that the censors were apparently "letting down a little where morals are concerned." Breen read the comment as a veiled attack on Production Code enforcement. "Is it your thought that there is anything morally wrong with this picture?" he charged. "You may be interested in knowing that, except in New York, every censor board in the United States and Canada has passed the picture without a single elimination of any kind." The Production Code administrator was caught, as he had been throughout the decade, between the need to uphold the Code and the desire to relax its more unreasonable demands.

Torn by controversy, the censorship wars had become heated. Proponents of federal regulation turned vocal in the late 1930s, while new movies about Soviet Russia and the Spanish civil war prompted court battles between intellectuals and the state and local boards. Walter Wanger (not Breen) had diluted *Blockade,* the most prominent such release, but the aftermath affected the Production Code Administration. Because of *Blockade,* the Knights of Columbus announced that it would oppose the spread of "false, atheistic, and immoral doctrines." The International Alliance of Theatrical Stage Employees, the biggest Hollywood trade union, labeled *Blockade* propaganda and told union projectionists not to show it. Wanger's *Personal History* promised more of the same; Breen warned Hays that it contained anti-Nazi sentiments "and, less importantly perhaps, a flavor of pro-Loyalist sympathy in the Spanish War sequences."

Though some continued to attack Breen as the enemy of political cinema, he ground no personal ax. He frowned on political cinema—as he did on adultery, sexual perversion, divorce, and much else—because in one way or another the company presidents and sometimes even the Hollywood production chiefs told him they feared the repercussions. In any event, though he could caution, he could not ban. Rather like Carl Laemmle, who by 1939 was "glad [to be] out of the business," a crotchety Breen thought that too many "sacred cows" grazed in Hollywood. It was time for a change.

6

The Outlaw

AND

The Postman Always Rings Twice

IN MARCH 1941, "The Last Time I Saw Paris" captured the mood of the moment better than all the Gallup polls. Jerome Kern's haunting melody and Oscar Hammerstein's tender lyrics expressed Americans' yearning for a world seemingly lost forever. Only twelve months earlier, the war in Europe had threatened to expire from lack of interest. "Sitzkrieg" had replaced "blitzkrieg" as troops stared at each other for weeks on end across the front lines. Then, in April 1940, the Germans crossed the border into Denmark and launched a surprise air assault on Oslo. Within two months the map of Europe changed drastically. Panzer divisions slammed through Belgium and Holland, swept aside the British and French armies, and rolled into Paris unopposed.

By autumn, as London reeled under the blitz, Americans could sense the imminence of their own involvement. Many resisted. On Capitol Hill, members of the Congress of American Mothers strung up a coconut-headed effigy of the Florida senator who favored conscription, but the intimidation failed; Claude Pepper spoke out with even greater vigor, and Congress adopted the measure. On October 16, when seventeen million young men registered for the nation's first peacetime draft, the war in Europe arrived on America's front porch. At the end of the year, President Roosevelt called on the nation to cast off the shackles of naive neutrality and become "the great arsenal of democracy." More protests followed, but as Congress moved the Lend-Lease proposal through the legislative machinery, Americans could feel the world shrinking. They longed for that time only months earlier when Paris was free, her heart young and gay.

The morning after Roosevelt signed the Lend-Lease bill in March 1941, Joe Breen sat alone in his office pecking away at the Underwood in the corner. Normally he dictated official correspondence, but this letter required secrecy; neither Miss Taylore (his prim executive secretary) nor the boys down the hall could know its contents. The words came hard even for an old newspaperman accustomed to cranking out reams of pointed prose. "I have become definitely convinced that I should not continue with this work," he began. "The general difficulties, which seem inseparable from a job of this kind, coupled with the peculiar worries and demands and long and tedious hours . . . compel me to say, reluctantly, that I cannot continue to cope with this task." He thanked Will Hays for his "unfailing kindness" but assured him that the decision was final. Joe Breen would leave the Production Code Administration effective June 15, 1941.

At age fifty, Breen could feel his world closing in. "It is difficult to forecast just how long we can continue to keep our feet on the ground, in the midst of this confusion and confusing criticism," he had written Hays some months before, disturbed by recent attacks on such approved pictures as *Primrose Path* and *My Little Chickadee*. The job he so relished in 1934 had by June 1941 drained him; he longed for "some other work where the demands on me would not be so exacting and so difficult." That month alone, Breen and company had labored on 154 feature films and scripts, and while the staff handled many of them, an increasing number required those "long and tedious hours" that taxed his patience.

Worse still were the mounting frustrations. By August 1940, with American profits frozen in Britain and American features banned in Germany and the occupied territories, Hollywood rushed headlong for the domestic box office. Breen could understand the need to compensate for losses abroad during a war, but he could not allow commercial lust to ravage the Code. He had read this scenario before: while producers sold sensationalism, Production Code representatives winked at Code violations; the apocalypse had swallowed up Jason Joy and James Wingate. Now the portents were reappearing. In February 1941, Charles Pettijohn, Hays' longtime friend and chief lobbyist, had informed Breen of a pending "legislative *censorship* epidemic" in the Midwest. Bills had already been introduced in four states and at least five others seemed sure to follow. Nailing the point, Pettijohn relayed a question from a hard-boiled railroad attorney: "Doesn't Mr. Hays have any influence with the producers anymore, and has that fellow Breen out there killed himself or has he just been compelled to walk the gangplank?"

Those who drew sabers on Breen were not mutineers but the very studio heads who had welcomed him aboard just seven years before. In their quest for a larger market share, the moguls sent the company presidents below deck and raced to purchase sordid and salacious new properties that nudged the Code director ever nearer the water. Columbia sought clearance for *Tobacco Road;* Warners bought *Kings Row;* Metro submitted a treatment of *The Postman Always Rings Twice*. Breen delayed each but noted the threat to his authority. Soon the acquisition of such properties would generate new pressures to ease the rigid restraints of the Code.

As Breen composed his letter of resignation, he thought less about new studio acquisitions than another dilemma. On March 29, he outlined the problem for Hays: "In recent months we have noted a marked tendency on the part of the studios to more and more undrape women's breasts. In recent weeks the practice has become so prevalent as to make it necessary for us, almost every day, to hold up a picture." Breen often exaggerated: to Hays because he wanted strong board support for pending problems, to the moguls because he needed bargaining chips when negotiations began. In this case, though, Breen provided evidence. During the past two and a half weeks, he had sent ten pictures back to the studios for removal of "breast shots." Most, like Paramount's *Kiss the Boys Good-bye* and MGM's *Model Wife,* required only minor snips. But one seemed beyond redemption.

"In my more than ten years of critical examination of motion pictures," Breen wrote Hays,

> I have never seen anything quite so unacceptable as the shots of the breasts of the character of Rio. This is the young girl whom Mr.

Hughes recently picked up and who has never before, according to my information, appeared on the motion picture screen. Throughout almost half the picture the girl's breasts, which are quite large and prominent, are shockingly emphasized and, in almost every instance, are very substantially uncovered.

The endowed young girl was Jane Russell. The picture was *The Outlaw.*

After an absence of almost eight years, Howard Hughes had returned to Hollywood in 1939 with an idea for a new picture. The producer of *Cock of the Air* wanted to make "an important western," free of the traditional trappings and formula endings that characterized the genre, filled with earthy sex and violent shoot-outs to excite patrons as no other western ever had. The central players of *The Outlaw* would be two males whose wits and fast draws keep them alive in a violent, lawless world. Though they meet as foes, Doc Holliday and Billy the Kid share not only a code of honor but an eye for spirited women and good horses. They quarrel over Doc's horse (Red), then over Doc's girl (Rio). Both value horse over girl. A third triangle involves Doc's longtime friend, Sheriff Pat Garrett. Jealous of Billy, for whom Doc has much affection, Garrett seeks to kill the Kid. Doc saves Billy once, but later takes the fatal bullet that Garrett meant for the young outlaw. In the end, out of respect for Doc, Garrett allows Rio and Billy to ride off into the Western sunset.

At one of the several parties following the premiere of *Gone With the Wind,* Hughes approached publicity man Russell Birdwell and sketched the scenario. Both men were celebrities, Birdwell through his triumphant promotional campaign for *Wind,* Hughes through a record-breaking round-the-world flight in July 1938. Though Hughes had made the covers of *Life* and *Time,* Birdwell failed to recognize him; the lanky aviator wore an ill-fitting tie and tails, probably borrowed from a subordinate, and looked more like an unemployed actor than a man worth thirty million dollars. The more Hughes talked, however, the more interested Birdwell became. Birdwell may have doubted the wisdom of an epic based on the legend of Billy the Kid, but he had seen Hughes' *Scarface* and felt that the producer would deliver what he promised. For $1,500 a week, he signed on to promote the film.

Birdwell's chief task would be to attract publicity for the film's two unknown leads, Jack Buetel and Ernestine Jane Geraldine Russell. The twenty-three-year-old Buetel looked barely sixteen and fit Hughes' vision of a youthful killer, but Birdwell knew the slender, baby-faced Texan would be a hard sell as sex symbol. He concentrated on Russell. Hughes had selected the nineteen-year-old receptionist and part-time model from a stack of photographs. "Having spent most of my teens skinny," she later remembered, "I was just glad I'd filled out." So were Hughes and Birdwell.

While Birdwell mapped out his promotional campaign, Hughes concentrated on assembling a production team. Had Hughes the good sense to leave *The Outlaw* to professionals, the picture might have been the "important western" he intended. The production staffers whom he assembled in 1940 were industry standouts. Director Howard Hawks and screenwriter Ben Hecht had collaborated before, with excellent results, on *Scarface;* cameraman Gregg Toland had just completed innovative work on *Citizen Kane.* Thomas Mitchell (Garrett) and Walter Huston (Holliday) were veteran character actors who could flesh out the sketchy roles. But Hughes clashed with Hecht over the script and replaced him with Jules Furthman. He also pestered Hawks and Toland about the early rushes; Toland stayed but Hawks soon departed for Warners and *Sergeant York.* Rather than replace the director with another professional, Hughes took the helm. As interfering producer, Hughes frustrated the crew; as director, he wrought chaos. His frequent mood shifts perplexed and rubbed raw the actors. Told to prepare for a twenty-sixth take, Mitchell lashed out at the director, questioning both his skill and his sanity; Huston sulked and occasionally would not even speak to Hughes. Russell and Buetel followed orders, but with Hughes often away from the set pursuing war contracts and managing his far-flung empire, the production bogged down.

During one of those nagging delays, in early December 1940, Breen wrote an initial letter on *The Outlaw.* While he knew that Twentieth Century–Fox would distribute the picture and eventually require the Seal, he nevertheless wanted to know what the cock of the air was up to. Breen was polite, for he then had no reason to censure Hughes or even suspect major problems: "I 'see by the papers,' as Mr. Dooley used to say, that you have begun shooting on your picture and it occurs to me that you ought to let us have a copy of your shooting script." As an independent producer without Association membership, Hughes had no obligation to send Breen anything, yet he obliged.

Furthman's screenplay arrived the day after Christmas and Breen assigned it to veteran readers Geoff Shurlock and Al Lynch. Following typical office procedure, both men took copies home that evening, read it, and reported the problems at the ten o'clock "huddle" the next morning. That afternoon they composed a letter that traced the major Code difficulties: one scene of "illicit sex," several of "undue brutality and unnecessary killings," and an ending that allowed Billy to escape punishment for his crimes. To Shurlock and Lynch, the sex scene appeared the least troublesome. In the initial confrontation between Rio and Billy, she attacks him with a pitchfork, seeking revenge for his having gunned down her brother. He eludes the assault, forces her down on a mound of hay, and the two struggle. Furthman intended rape, but neither Shurlock nor Lynch read it that way. They warned against "questionable angles or postures" and the "exposure of Rio's person." They wanted the violence toned down and the characterization of Billy as a "cold-blooded murderer" changed. They wanted no glory for a criminal, and recommended that Furthman find some way to establish the fact that Billy had been wrongly accused of his crimes.

Four days later, Shurlock and Lynch visited *The Outlaw* set, where Furthman, acting as writer-director-producer during another of Hughes' long absences, promised to correct all items noted in the letter. Furthman must have sensed that the two lieutenants had missed the point of the hayloft scene because he asked them to view a rough cut. The thrust of the scene all too apparent, Shurlock and Lynch immediately advised some cuts to remove even the hint of rape. Furthman again promised to comply.

Several weeks later, Furthman telephoned Shurlock. Hughes had returned and directed a scene that could pose a minor problem. After a shoot-out, Billy suffers a near-fatal wound. Holliday lugs the outlaw to his shack, and orders Rio—his girl—to tend the wound. Unaware of the earlier hayloft encounter, Doc gallops off on Billy's horse. Rio ponders murder, but soon decides that she loves the young cowboy. The scene that bothered Furthman had Rio bending over the delirious Billy, where for an instant she exposed "a flash of her breasts." It sounded innocent enough to Shurlock. Unlike Breen, he normally trusted filmmakers to choose Code compliance over bad taste. Assuming that Rio's dress was modest and the "flash" offered no more than a breath of décolletage, he advised Furthman that the scene would probably pass, and the matter was dropped.

Days later, Hughes himself telephoned Shurlock. The producer wanted to add a new scene. Rio had originally attempted to combat Billy's chills by warming him with hot stones; Shurlock and Lynch had not wanted the stones placed "against Billy's thighs" but otherwise made no demur. Now Hughes wanted Rio to warm the outlaw with her body. Hughes promised that he would not suggest intercourse—despite the two adults in bed together—and sought an immediate ruling. Could Rio and Billy share a bed for medicinal purposes? Shurlock turned to Breen. Angling for another executive post in Hollywood, where he would perhaps have to become an advocate of bundling and other such sports, Breen offered as liberal an answer as he could make. The British censors automatically deleted bed scenes, but the Production Code Administration did not; if Hughes filmed the sequence with discretion, Rio could provide the body heat necessary to save the boy.

On the last Tuesday in March, the day after Breen drafted the letter of resignation to Hays, he talked with RKO executives about a future as a $104,000-a-year production chief with the company. On Wednesday, he had a minor skirmish with Hal Wallis. He had ordered a goosing gag removed from Warners' *Affectionately Yours* and Wallis protested. The producer had just viewed Twentieth Century–Fox's *That Night in Rio* and noticed a scene of Don Ameche backing into the foot of a statue and emitting a loud squeal. Wallis wanted to know what special Code provision allowed Ameche's reaction: "Is it that the goose was committed by an inanimate object, or that it was a Technicolor goose, or that the 'goosee' was male?" On Thursday, as Breen pondered the Warner question, a finished print of *The Outlaw* arrived at Production Code headquarters.

Just after lunch, Breen joined Shurlock and Lynch in the small screening room on Hollywood Boulevard. Shurlock nervously shuffled his notes, for previews meant uncertainty, especially when Breen sat in. What if Shurlock had missed something in the script? What if he had offered Furthman bad advice by phone? Breen would catch the error and taunt him forever. Though Breen would never publicly embarrass anyone who worked for him, *The Outlaw* was a Hughes-Shurlock-Lynch production, and Breen loved snafu stories, loved those little goofs that he could build into elaborate anecdotes and use over and over again, always with the butt of the humor uncomfortably present. Perhaps more than any other, that prospect kept his staff picky. Better to err on the side of caution than become the object of yet another Breen tale. As the early reels flickered across the screen, though, Shurlock relaxed. Furthman and Hughes had followed his instructions to the letter. Billy was not the cold-blooded killer of the script, but a young man whose personal code of honor would not allow him to run from a fight. He drew only in self-defense. The brutal fight scenes and shoot-outs had been toned down; even the hayloft encounter faded out precisely where Shurlock had suggested.

In reel five, Shurlock lost his composure. When Rio leaned over Billy's sickbed, her low-cut peasant blouse revealed an expanse of cleavage that showed just why Russell had been chosen for the role. Toland's lens zoomed in on the grand canyon, and Shurlock knew that he had been taken. The inadvertent "flash of breasts" that Furthman had asked him to authorize filled the screen. Then, before Shurlock could wipe the steam from his glasses, Rio knelt to remove her stockings and prepare for the bed-warming scene; more cleavage, this time accentuated with a lingering shot of Russell's exposed legs. Later reels were no better. Rio stooped before a mirror, reached out across an open campfire, and twisted in frustration while tied between two stakes. For that bondage scene, Hughes had designed a special brassiere to enhance the thrust of the breasts; Russell later claimed it was uncomfortable, so she inserted tissue to create the desired effect.

Beyond the Kleenex and the peep show, Hughes had retained

dialogue and situations that Shurlock had ejected from the script. Rio was obviously Doc's live-in companion before Billy arrived, and Rio and Billy obviously slept together in Doc's absence. Though Shurlock had warned that casual sex required "compensating moral values," Hughes had not only snubbed the Code rule but constructed much of the film's humor around casual sex. When Billy pulls Rio toward the bed, she attempts to discourage him and says, "You're not well enough for that." After Doc learns that Billy and Rio have fooled around, Billy says that he has only "borrowed" Doc's girl just as Doc has "borrowed" his horse. "Tit for tat," he tells Doc. Billy then offers the girl for the horse, but Doc declines; he has grown very fond of the animal. When Billy later repeats the offer, Doc responds with disdain: "Cattle don't graze after sheep."

"Miss Taylore!" shouted Joe Breen as he marched out of the screening room into his office. He dictated a terse note to Hughes: *The Outlaw* was "definitely and specifically in violation of our Production Code." He cited two fundamental problems, "the inescapable suggestion of an illicit relationship between the 'Doc' and Rio, and between Billy and Rio; and the countless shots of Rio, in which her breasts are not fully covered." The note was hand-delivered that afternoon, and at six o'clock, Hughes called to ask for an evening conference. The airman had promised Fox delivery of the feature by mid-March. Already beyond the contract deadline, he hoped to speed progress toward the Seal by meeting directly with the Production Code boys. Three hours later, Shurlock and Lynch politely dismissed Hughes' protest that his film was no worse than many other current releases and advised him either to abandon the feature or appeal the ruling to the Board of Directors. They told Hughes that while he might resolve the illicit sex with some added dialogue to show that Rio suffered, he could not hope to preserve the continuity of the picture once he removed the "breast shots." A rebellious Hughes asked for a second meeting, this time with Breen.

On Saturday, Breen reiterated what Shurlock and Lynch had told Hughes on Thursday evening. He also seemed to invite an appeal, a course of action he normally resisted. He apparently wanted a test case (as he had had on *Gone With the Wind*) that would force the Association to define the limits of acceptable breast exposure. With

Hollywood bent on bosoms, the Production Code Administration—as well as production chiefs at such studios as RKO—
needed help from New York, and *The Outlaw* could dramatize the
problem well. An appeal would further delay release of the picture,
so Hughes stalled. Aware that Hays had scheduled a Hollywood
trip the following week, he asked for a third hearing with the
General present. He again made little progress. At Hays' insistence,
though, Breen agreed to compile a list of required "breast shot
deletions" so that Hughes' staff could determine how best to remove the objectionable scenes. That evening, Breen, Shurlock, and
Lynch sat through the two-hour feature to record the needed alterations. They included virtually every scene involving Russell's
peasant blouse—thirty-seven specific shots. The list was hand-
delivered to Hughes headquarters the following morning. By afternoon, Hughes announced that he would appeal.

At the mid-May hearing, Russell Birdwell represented Hughes.
Birdwell's reputation for flesh peddling made him an ironic choice,
but he proved a capable advocate. As the company presidents
watched with their usual interest, Birdwell spread before them a
collection of cheesecake shots. The photos revealed the movies' love
affair with female breasts, Birdwell argued, and Hughes had simply observed an old and honorable Hollywood tradition. Birdwell
had selected the stills carefully: the stack that he circulated included
a photo from at least one current release of every major studio. Were
the board members who dozed through *Ecstasy* impressed? Perhaps, for they informed Birdwell that with some minor cuts, *The
Outlaw* could have a Seal. The deletions amounted to about sixty
seconds, much less than Breen had demanded.

The board's tolerance may have puzzled Breen, but he kept his
own counsel. With less than a month to serve as Code director, he
saw no point in futile protests. Besides, as RKO production head,
he might have breast shots of his own to preserve. Yet he must have
drawn satisfaction from the cuts required by state and municipal
censors. Despite the Seal, censor boards in Pennsylvania, Massachusetts, and Maryland demanded significant eliminations. Ohio
wanted all breast shots listed by the Code office scissored—and
more. While Hughes and the censors scrapped, Breen cleaned out
his desk.

Dubbed "Hollywood's current mystery," the pending departure of Joe Breen set rumor mills churning. Had Hays fallen out with him? Had the studios dumped him? *Newsweek* argued the latter, that "a recent pile-up of complaints" prompted the resignation. Protests had indeed mounted during his final months. A spring 1941 Breen injunction against "sweater shots" had so upset Hollywood that studio photographers wondered what was left on the clothesline. As columnist Lucie Neville observed:

> Nightgowns and frilly lingerie haven't been worn in an o.k.'d still in years. Strapless evening gowns have long been banned, unless the pose shows more gown than girl from the waist up. Negligees must be of firm material, or be unrevealing either in silhouetted shadow or in decolletage. . . . Bathing suits are o.k.—if the poses are modest, but they are classified as leg-art, and, besides, studios think it's a little corny to put their players in swim attire the year round. Sweaters have been the perfect substitute for stars who refuse to be photographed in bathing suits, and for pretty players whose gams wouldn't win beauty contests.

Jack Warner bristled when the Code office vetoed the initial script of *Kings Row* for its illicit sex, sadism, nymphomania, and a mercy killing, while Fox executives cried foul when Breen held up release of *Blood and Sand* because of a gruesome bullfight sequence. Louis Mayer was piqued over Breen's deletions from the final print of *Dr. Jekyll and Mr. Hyde,* from the opening montage ("all scenes having to do with the swan and the girl and the stallion and the girl") to the cabaret scene ("the crotch shot of the dancing girls"). But neither reporters' gibes nor studio gripes alone had prompted Breen's resignation. Tired of playing an offscreen voice, he wanted a major role. And RKO had promised top billing. The five-year contract that he signed in May 1941 guaranteed $1,700 per week plus $200 for entertainment and $100 for limousine and chauffeur. The shanty Irishman was moving up, and he had no regrets. Better still, he would no longer have to tangle with men like Howard Hughes.

The terms of the RKO contract show just what Hollywood thought of Joe Breen in the 1930s and early 1940s. He was neither Hollywood pariah nor (in a pejorative sense) Hollywood censor; he was an industry man, an administrator whom the Manhattan company presidents and the Hollywood executives respected. He was not the Production Code per se—as much as he revered it—but the Production Code Administration director. He was not the Kansas or Ohio censor, he was Hollywood's benevolent conscience, the studio good uncle, a member of a large family whose welfare concerned him. If Breen and the moguls fought, sometimes bitterly, what close families did not? None could deny that he had enforced the Production Code *they* had written or, perhaps more important, that he and they were one.

"Breen trouble" was producer shorthand for differences of opinion with the Production Code office. "Now Hollywood *really* has Breen trouble," *Liberty* announced in 1941, "and resembles a small boy who threatened to run away unless papa let him play with that nice sharp razor and suddenly papa took him up on it." The Manhattan corporate fathers had reason to fret. Could Hays find another Code man who could, when needed, face down Louis Mayer, Jack Warner, or Howard Hughes? Would the studio boys behave without the firm hand of Breen? Most thought not. Several had wanted RKO to withdraw its offer for the good of the industry; others wanted Breen to replace the aging Hays. Despite rumors, the move went as scheduled. Hays asked Shurlock to run the agency until a new permanent director could be hired, then ignored the problem, hoping that the mild-mannered Englishman would grow into the job. The arrangement proved unsatisfactory for all concerned.

"I was feeling uncertain every day of my life in those times," Shurlock later said. Reluctant to judge the creative decisions of others, the tentative Shurlock lacked authority. The board made matters worse in June 1941 when it announced a resolution to have "at least one picture in which no drinking is shown for each film in which there is drinking." Shurlock had too many rules and not enough license. Despite good intentions, he soon embroiled the agency in controversy. In MGM's *Two-Faced Woman,* Greta Garbo pretended to be her own unattached and slightly promiscuous twin sister, and seduced hubby Melvyn Douglas. Shurlock, who thought that director George Cukor had handled the material with a delicate touch, awarded the picture a Production Code Seal in October 1941. But the Legion of Decency saw an "immoral and un-Christian attitude toward marriage" in *Two-Faced Woman* and, for the first time since 1934, condemned a feature with the Seal. The board fretted, Hays fumed, and Shurlock feared for his job. When MGM quickly added a new scene to *Two-Faced Woman*—letting Douglas learn of the sister-switch before he consummates the affair—the Legion relented and dropped the "C." The flare-up passed and Shurlock survived, but neither he nor Hays forgot the experience.

On Sunday, December 7, the surprise attack on Pearl Harbor directed the concerns of American moralists to more urgent matters. Art director Lyle Wheeler recalled that "there was a lot of fear at that time that [the Japanese] might be planning an attack on California" and that hospitals and other areas would be evacuated. Howard Hughes was among those who caught the war fever. Laying aside negotiations with state censors, he poured his energy into war contracts and aviation. *The Outlaw* languished.

Meanwhile Breen's new hat started to pinch. He had accepted the RKO offer on the assumption that he would have total control over feature films, but studio president George J. Schaefer—not production chief Joseph I. Breen—had the final cut and the final say. Unaccustomed to constant supervision or complex budgets and frustrated by his inability to reverse RKO's sagging fortunes, Breen longed for his former post. In early spring 1942, with the blessing of the RKO board, he took an extended vacation in Mexico. On his return, he approached Hays and found the General with ears—and arms—spread wide. In May, Breen once again became director of the Production Code Administration.

Back at his desk, Breen glowed: he had returned home. He belonged in the executive suite of the Production Code office, in the center leather chair of the tiny screening room, in the limousine that whisked him home and to studio conferences. The Shurlock tenure had shown that perhaps Breen *was* Production Code, Production Code director, and Production Code Administration. Within the sometimes cruel and unusual bounds of that Code, Breen was an exceptional script doctor. He tended toward the literal, which both amused and enraged screenwriters, and he had a dollars-and-cents approach to the movies: they were more entertainment than art. But he loved motion pictures as much as the moguls did. Some directors and producers called Breen their friend, some their cross.

Most knew where they stood with him, though, and many found that his stone walls had a chink that let them pass through. Despite the tangles over screenplays and rough cuts that went on hour after hour in Production Code headquarters, Hollywood remained faithful to him.

While Breen, Shurlock, and Hays shuffled positions, Hollywood offered them a respite. The war years were among the least controversial in Production Code history. The Office of War Information monitored the movies' ideological message, a task that the studio front office usually controlled anyway, and Breen continued to focus on what he always had. "Herman Shumlin told me he had quite an argument with the Breen office over Paul Lukas's killing of the fascist in *Watch on the Rhine*," screenwriter Nunnally Johnson remarked. But Shumlin and Breen had not clashed over politics: "The code [office] didn't seem to like the way [Lukas] got away with it." The horror of total war made Hollywood's occasional moral lapses seem much less significant, and the studios' contribution to the war effort also discouraged bluenoses from baiting an old enemy.

Hollywood sold the war and made it pay. Motion pictures offered soldiers a "two-hour furlough"; they assured a country at war that all it was fighting for deserved preservation. When Roosevelt raised the tax on admissions, moviegoing became practically a patriotic act. Admissions jumped by one-third; freedom rang, and profits soared. Breen reveled in the commercial successes of the industry in the early 1940s, even more in the absence of serious criticism. With the Legion of Decency and its Protestant allies silent, he felt invigorated. Beneath the superficial calm, though, he sensed that the America around him was changing, that the Victorian, small-town morality that underlay the Code would become one of the many casualties of the war. The bosom mania of *The Outlaw* soon provided fresh evidence.

For eighteen months, *The Outlaw* had gathered dust in the Hughes warehouse. Unwilling to make the cuts required by state and local censors and preoccupied with war contracts and plans for an experimental plywood transport plane (later dubbed the Spruce Goose), Hughes slighted distribution of *The Outlaw*, and eventually so irritated Twentieth Century–Fox that its executives refused to handle the film. The maverick Hughes was nonetheless determined to place the orphaned *Outlaw.* For six months, his agents scoured the countryside for the perfect theater, one daring enough to handle the picture and strong enough to resist local censors. Meanwhile, Birdwell pumped up interest in the feature. His strategy was simple. He would ignore the two-dimensional *Outlaw* and sell the three-dimensional glamor of Jane Russell.

The task seemed daunting. Fan magazines, the publicist's standard vehicle for star-building, enforced an absolute ban on pictures of starlets who had not yet appeared on-screen. But Birdwell knew there were other, more attractive venues. During the final years of the 1930s, a national publishing craze—the picture magazine—emerged. *Life* appeared on American newsstands in November 1936, and by spring 1938, *Look, Pic,* and *Click* also vied for dominance of the new field. The competition opened virgin territory for the shrewd publicity man; good cheesecake boosted circulation, and Birdwell served all they could swallow. There were occasional snags. When he ordered photographs of Russell playing basketball in the "right kind of middy blouse," one designed to "show off her breast outline," his assistant, Dale Armstrong, called time-out. "Jane's breasts are still a problem," he reported. "Attempting to shoot her with a brassiere was very bad. When we took the brassiere off, they drooped considerably and did not make for the best possible pictures. However, after conferring with the dressmaker, we have decided to tape them, which seems to be the best solution."

The tape held. The photos of Russell's sultry stare and thirty-eight-inch bustline made for sensational picture-magazine art. "Her pictures attack the eye," *New Yorker* columnist Alva Johnston observed. "She has some curious power of jumping out of the magazine page like a bareback rider through a hoop." Birdwell soon found more hoops than he could handle. *Life* and *Look* photographers followed her to boat launchings and beauty contests; *Pic* and *Click* ran various poses, including several of the "breast shots" that Breen had snipped from the movie. When *Esquire* printed a two-page layout, circulation jumped 186,000 copies; then even the fan magazines lifted their ban. By 1942, Russell had become a star without ever having appeared in a motion picture. So startling was the phenomenon that one of the trade papers assigned a reporter to determine just how much publicity this newcomer was getting. He learned that in one three-week period, photos of Russell had decorated the covers of eleven national magazines, while stories about her had appeared in 532 dailies and 448 Sunday papers.

After months of delays, with Breen almost on holiday because of the few censorship concerns, Hughes finally settled on a February 5, 1943, premiere date at the Geary Theater in downtown San Francisco. He planned a gala affair, extravagant for a nation conditioned to wartime sacrifice. With the Office of Defense Transportation urging Americans to avoid unnecessary travel (the major leagues canceled spring training to comply with the government request), Birdwell brought two trainloads of reviewers from Hollywood to San Francisco. Though the community reserved its hotels for those with defense priorities, Birdwell booked the junketeers in the Mark Hopkins for three days of champagne and caviar. At the premiere, Mayor Angelo Rossi was supposed to honor Hughes for his war work, but Rossi developed "other commitments." Perhaps he had heard the rumors that onstage after the show, Jack Buetel and Jane Russell would reenact scenes cut from the movie. Or perhaps he had seen the ads. Birdwell blanketed the city with billboards of Jane recumbent on a mound of hay, a flimsy blouse loosely clinging to those ample breasts. Her sensual gaze promised more than the film would deliver, but it offended nonetheless. Local moralists descended on town hall with protests, and when threatened with arrest warrants and a possible theater closing, Hughes and Birdwell agreed to remove the signs.

At the premiere, the tame Russell and Buetel sketch was awkwardly performed but applauded. Not so the picture. The reviewer from *Time* called *The Outlaw* "a strong candidate for the flopperoo of all time," and noted the "incredulous stares" exchanged by more than fifty critics as they sat through a two-hour feature described as "corny, overdrawn, melodramatic." Others heard the audience laughter—frequently *at* rather than *with* the picture—and suggested that Hughes had intended to parody the Hollywood western. The dead-serious Hughes was upset by the response. Within days he began reediting the film, poring over the audience reports from the Geary and searching for new scene combinations to eliminate the unintended humor. The solution eluded him. By late March, that brief single-theater run had grossed $158,000; should that record figure snowball during a general release, Hughes could recover his $2.5 million investment by late summer. In April, though, the producer withdrew *The Outlaw* from exhibition.

The sudden disappearance of *The Outlaw* astonished the industry. Always secretive, Hughes never explained why he chose to abort the San Francisco run or why he passed up the opportunity to distribute the feature nationally. The Legion of Decency condemnation may have influenced him, but more likely he tired of the project and moved on to other, more important matters.

By summer 1943, the nation was ready to abandon the save-and-sacrifice ethic of 1942. Weary of shortages and rationing, of long hours in dingy factories, of curfews, car pools, and Victory Gardens, Americans pursued diversion to relieve the oppression of war. Liquor consumption jumped thirty percent, despite a government ban on alcohol production. Bootleggers returned, and good Canadian whiskey sold for $12 a pint. Youngsters who swelled the work force in huge numbers spent lavishly on comic books, records, and concerts; book sales, especially paperbacks, soared. Unknown in 1942, crooner Frank Sinatra filled auditoriums with such adoring and aggressive bobby-soxers that in 1943 he needed a police cordon to protect him. Burlesque and strip-tease shows also packed houses with demonstrative fans. In Portland, Oregon, war workers on the swing shift rioted when city officials enforced a midnight curfew against the all-night girlie galas near the factory.

The war years also bared the flesh. The War Production Board ordered cutbacks in the use of all fabrics, and the fashion world obeyed. Casualties included men's vests, wide lapels, and the second pair of suit trousers. The change was more drastic for women. Dubbed "patriotic chic" by Manhattan designers, the new styles included backless dresses, bare shoulders, short skirts, plunging necklines, and daring two-piece swimwear. The change had been spurred by more than the attempt to conserve cloth or to assert femininity at a time when so many women had adopted male roles. Female fashions suggested the war-inspired weakening of traditional moral values. The consequences of a war that had eroded the moorings of family, church, and community were frightening. In just four years, truancy and juvenile crime had increased by more than twenty percent, the divorce rate by more than sixty percent. "Victory girls" congregated near the gates of military posts, attaching themselves to young servicemen without benefit of clergy. The number of underage girls arrested for sex offenses more than doubled, while prostitution and venereal disease flourished.

Breen had always believed that the Production Code embodied fundamental principles of Christian morality. A Catholic of stern convictions, he knew those truths to be eternal and absolute, beyond the touch of momentary whims and passions, the permanent expressions of divine guidance. Yet he also recognized that the war had unleashed forces that Hollywood could not ignore. The 1930 proscriptions against violence and murder, and especially adultery and illicit sex, now seemed outmoded; the endless stream of movies about fearless warriors and faithful wives old-fashioned. Just beyond the door of the Production Code Administration on Hollywood Boulevard, sex was in the ozone. "Constancy is unknown out here," Tennessee Williams wrote to a friend in August 1943. At cocktails one evening, German actor Peter Van Eyck

came in wearing very sheer silky trousers and a pale green shirt unbuttoned to reveal his pale gold chest. Another girl, a houseguest, was there. Margo [Jones] and I both felt the atmosphere was charged with an almost hysterical sexuality and torment of jealousy and suspicion although there was much exchange of kisses and darlings all around. That is how things are in Hollywood all the time, no peace where sex is concerned, only continual frenzy and intrigue.

Breen wanted to hold the line as long as possible, but in the end he would have no choice; the frenzy would force him to ease up. With reservations, reluctance, and finally resignation and a sense of defeat, he would.

The slippage had begun even before *The Outlaw* played San Francisco. In *The Miracle of Morgan's Creek,* Preston Sturges constructed a smart comedy around the character of Trudy (Betty Hutton), a "Victory girl" who contributed to the war effort by dating young servicemen about to leave for the front. On one of these outings she becomes drunk, marries a soldier, and awakens the next morning unable to remember the affair or anything about the young man. The complications that follow include a pregnancy, confused identities, and the birth of sextuplets. Two years earlier, Breen might well have demanded that Sturges abandon the project or at least make wholesale changes to remove the "loose treatment of marriage." In early 1943, though, he quibbled over dialogue (for example, "How can I remember his name when I can't even remember his . . ."), then approved the feature. An amused James Agee later wrote: "The Hays office has been either hypnotized into a liberality for which it should be thanked, or has been raped in its sleep." In *For Whom the Bell Tolls,* Breen forced Paramount to ditch the sleeping bag and any reference to "the earth moving," but granted a Seal despite the obvious affair between Jordan and Maria. He also allowed independent producer Hunt Stromberg to adapt Gypsy Rose Lee's *The G-String Murders* (retitled *Lady of Burlesque*) with only the "Pickle Persuader" skit and the "diamond-studded zipper" deleted.

In September 1943, Breen took an even more dramatic step by sanctioning a treatment of *Double Indemnity.* Eight years before, the Code chief had warned studios away from the James M. Cain novella because of the adulterous relationship between the two leads, the explicit details of the murder of the heroine's husband, and the "low tone and sordid flavor" of the story. Although the Billy Wilder–Charles Brackett screenplay eliminated objectionable plot lines and some of the "sordid flavor," its chief protagonists still committed adultery and a vicious murder, yet Breen approved it with barely a murmur. Producers called the release of *Double Indemnity* "an emancipation for Hollywood writing" and flooded the Hays Office with murder and eros. Producers "have got hep to the fact that plenty of real crime takes place every day and that it makes a good movie," Cain told the press. "The public is fed up with the old-fashioned melodramatic type of hokum." Breen acceded to producers' wishes. In 1944, he certified *The Big Sleep* once Warners altered "certain phases of depravity"; he also approved *Mildred Pierce,* another James Cain book that he had lobbied against on the eve of its 1941 publication. While he still felt the story "sordid and repellent," Breen allowed Jerry Wald and Warners to proceed. He called *Forever Amber* "raw stuff, filled on almost every page with details of adultery, illicit sex, crime, perversion, abortion and God only knows what!" but approved a Twentieth Century–Fox adaptation. He even passed Selznick's *Duel in the Sun,* "a story of illicit sex and murder for revenge, without the full compensating moral values required by the Code." Martin Quigley called Breen soft; Raymond Chandler concurred. The Hays Office, Chandler told reporters, feared "antagonizing the remaining studios which support it." Chandler sensed what Breen must have known only too well: the sheer number of "sordid" pictures proposed had made Production Code enforcement more selective.

While sex and murder had been around Hollywood at least since D. W. Griffith, writers in the early forties, many of them in psychoanalysis, developed their characters and plots along Freudian lines. "Theft, robbery, safe-cracking, and dynamiting of trains, mines, buildings, etc., should not be detailed in method," the 1930 Production Code read. But where did the Code address crime with a psychopathological twist? Where did it address Carmen Sternwood, the emotionally disturbed young woman in *The Big Sleep* who sucked her thumb and posed for pornographic pictures? Or Walter Neff, the insurance agent in *Double Indemnity* who became obsessed with the desires of his female accomplice in murder? Almost a generation old, the Production Code addressed themes of psychopathology with neither assurance nor directness. And when the themes proliferated, Breen had to raise the floodgates to accommodate them.

The Postman Always Rings Twice nearly destroyed the dam. The third Cain novel to tax Breen's wartime tolerance had first landed on booksellers' shelves in 1934. The notices were powerful. "There are several disgusting scenes and the characters are scum," one reviewer wrote, "but that book is a work of art." Others compared Cain to Lardner, to Hemingway, to Caldwell; Cain seemed more daring than any of them. "This is strong men's meat," Herschel Brickell wrote, "and not for those who mind blood and raw lust."

The story: At the Papadakis roadhouse, hobo Frank Chambers and Cora Papadakis passionately make love and resolve to kill her husband, Nick. Though they betray each other during the ensuing investigation of the murder, a shrewd defense lawyer saves them from prison. Cora takes Frank swimming and offers him the opportunity to drown her; he refuses. But the affirmation of his love comes to nothing. Cora dies in an automobile accident, a jury convicts Frank—wrongly—of her murder, and the book ends with the unrepentant narrator on death row. Cain summed up *Postman* in words a studio executive could understand: "a couple of jerks who discover that a murder, though dreadful enough morally, can be a love story too, but then wake up to discover that once they've pulled the thing off, no two people can share this terrible secret and live on the same earth."

As Joe Breen could tell from the press clippings, *The Postman* seemed destined for the movies. Cain "would be an asset to the tabloids," one reviewer observed, "because he leaves lots of space for pictures." A British commentator noted that the effect of *The Postman* registered "more like that of a film than of literature." The sixteen chapters of the novel resembled a screenplay continuity, not only containing scenes but approximations of camera shots within scenes. The breathtaking pace also suggested the cinema: Frank and Cora met on page 5, copulated on 15, plotted murder on 23, and killed Nick by 67. The "American Dostoyevsky," film director Lewis Milestone called Cain, yet the Russian author concentrated on "why," the American on "what" and "how"—the elements of fiction that Hollywood so eagerly embraced.

It was understatement to say that *The Postman* violated the Production Code General Principles. The "sympathy of the audience should never be thrown to the side of crime, wrongdoing, evil or sin," the first Principle read; Frank Chambers, the lead character who also sympathetically narrated the story, was an adulterer and a murderer. The second said, "Correct standards of life, subject only to the requirements of drama and entertainment, shall be presented." Chambers drank and fornicated; like Cora, he lacked moral compunction, and as he faced death asked neither God nor man for forgiveness. "Law, natural or human, shall not be ridiculed." In the courtroom charade of the latter half of the novel, Cain introduced two characters, one more cynical than the other: the district attorney and the defense counsel.

Though *The Postman* contained neither profanity nor explicit

sexual sequences, the reader sensed the presence of both. As Cain
would later observe:

> People think I put stark things in my stories, or indulge in lush
> descriptions of the heroine's charms, but I don't. The situations, I
> dare say, are often sultry, and the reader has the illusion he is reading
> about sex. Actually, however, it gets very little footage.

From his experience with Mae West and *I'm No Angel,* Breen knew
all about illusion and sex. More to the point, he understood just
how potent the "little footage" in *The Postman* really was. When
Frank and Cora first make love, she moans, "Bite me! Bite me!" He
sinks his teeth into her lips and feels "the blood spurt into [his]
mouth." After they kill Nick and roll his automobile down the
slope, Frank tears Cora's blouse to prepare her for meeting the
police; sexually aroused, she cries, "Rip me! Rip me!" At the ocean,
the pregnant Cora tells Frank, "My breasts feel so big, and I want
you to kiss them. Pretty soon my belly is going to get big, and I'll
love that, and want everybody to see it. It's life."

The studios could never resist a potential blockbuster, much less
one that smelled of scandal. In October 1944, ten years after he had
purchased the screen rights, Louis Mayer sensed the wind shifting
in Hollywood and submitted a new story outline. Frank would
yearn for freedom and Cora for success; though their passionate
attraction would remain, Metro promised Breen that their lust
would be suggested rather than flagrantly expressed. Nick Papadakis, dubbed Nick Smith to insure distribution in Greece, not
only stands between them but becomes a coarse and cheap man
whom even a woman less venal than Cora would wish out of the
way. While Cora dreams of expanding the diner, Nick announces
that they might soon return to Canada so that Cora can nurse his
invalid sister. The murder thus seems motivated by fear and well-
earned hostility rather than mere lust. James Cain made *The Postman* a meditation on fate and reasonless doom, thematic elements
that the *film noir* supplied through chiaroscuro lighting and dy-
namic visuals; in deference to Breen, though, the *Postman* screenplay balanced the sexual passion of Frank and Cora with the
remorse that they (but especially Frank) feel for killing Nick.

Because of the hullabaloo that surrounded the release of Paramount's *Double Indemnity,* MGM still feared for the *Postman.* Yet Breen seemed amenable. Producer Carey Wilson met with the Production Code administrator, then reported to Cain:

> Breen says it can be done and he's tickled to death I'm going to try it. I wasn't there over twenty minutes, but you should have seen his face when I got up to go and hadn't said one word about "Double Indemnity." And as I held out my hand he said, "Well, what are you waiting for? Why don't you say 'What about "Double Indemnity"?' And I said: "Because I know you're just sitting there with your right all cocked ready to shoot it when I begin, and I'm not going to give you the chance because I'm not going to say it." So then he laughed about it and I had taken the wind right out of his sails and, believe me, we're not going to have any trouble.

Breen could joke, he could even be tickled to death. Certainly he was relieved that Metro and Carey Wilson—not a renegade studio or a loose horse like Howard Hughes—would adapt the novel.

By April 1945, Metro had a temporary script. Though screenwriters Harry Ruskin and Niven Busch had cut much of the anger and feeling out of the novel, Breen predicted that "the overall flavor of *lust*" would bring the censor boards down on *The Postman.* Wilson cajoled, and Breen bent. In a long talk with Wilson, Breen assured the producer that by cutting out "all scenes of physical contact—hugging and kissing—between Cora and Frank," the picture could win a Seal and avoid the state and local examiners' wrath. So the lovers tucked in their libidos, and to demonstrate the price of fornication, an imprisoned Frank became remorseful over Cora's accidental death.

Had director Tay Garnett shot *The Postman* in the brooding style of *film noir*—strong on shadows and spareness—he might well have put the wind back into the Breen sails. But the ambience of Metro-Goldwyn-Mayer hardly encouraged Garnett to produce a cold and harsh *Postman.* *Film noir* thrived on pinched budgets and intellectual commitment, neither of which characterized MGM. John Douglas Eames called the 1945 Metro production schedule "a cuisine liberally sprinkled with such cornflakes as musicals, moppets and animals." The past was *Red Dust* and *Red Headed Woman,* the present

Van Johnson and Esther Williams, all sunshine and splash. Some MGM executives could not stomach *The Postman*. Offered *Past All Dishonor,* the novel that Cain wrote as Garnett started *The Postman,* a Metro official argued that Cain and his fiction disgraced the studio and the industry. Garnett knew how *The Postman* should look to please not only Joseph Breen but Louis Mayer. When the picture entered principal photography in summer 1945, he bathed the sets in light and diffused the fatality of the story.

Producer Carey Wilson saw the picture as a "study in white." An MGM press release stated that Lana Turner (Cora) would wear forty-one different costumes, each one white. According to screen-writer Harry Ruskin, "Turner dressed in white so that the public understood that the girl's pure. She may be playing around with the guy, but she's not taking her pants off for him." The cut of a wardrobe concerned Breen more than the color: would breasts nestle behind sweaters or spill from halter tops? The Production Code administrator never cautioned Metro about costume or cleav-age, though, perhaps because he understood how Metro would package Turner. Anne Baxter (*Guest in the House*), Gene Tierney (*Leave Her to Heaven*), and Turner all played vixens that season. Only Turner had vulgar edges. In a "B" picture at another studio, she might have been played cheap; in an "A" production at MGM, Metro artists coiffed her hair, shadowed her eyes, powdered her face, and draped her body until she resembled a socialite setting out for a charity tennis match.

John Garfield (Frank) provided whatever grit the adulterous cou-ple had, and here and there Garnett worked against MGM refine-ment. The MAN WANTED sign prominent in the Smiths' window had the force of a sexual come-on. Almost perversely, though, it moved the drama further away from the theme of fate: the desire for work—not blind chance—seemed to carry Frank Chambers into the diner. The Breen recommendation to cut out "all scenes of physical contact" prompted Garnett to communicate their passion in movie shorthand. When Cora sees Frank, she tends hamburgers on the grill; Garnett used the sizzling meat, like the perennial crashing waves, to telegraph sexual arousal. The director also filmed Chambers' affair with an animal trainer. "They had this girl's cat act in the [first cut of the] picture," Cain remarked, "leopards and pumas and lions and everything rolling around with each other." Garnett probably hoped that the beasts would serve as symbols for the hugging and kissing that Breen had discouraged.

"Is this girl shacking this guy into bed?" Ruskin had asked Carey Wilson before finishing the script. "I know we don't put it on the screen, but *I* have to know." The producer could not decide. "He didn't know then and he doesn't know *now,*" Ruskin told Cain. "That's why the central part of the thing is so fuzzy and shaky and squashy." Garnett knew the answer but lacked consistent control. He planned to shoot the bathing sequences at Laguna Beach, but day after day, heavy fog rolled in. The crew moved south to San Clemente. The fog followed. As days became weeks, the front office leaned on Garnett. "That's when Tay fell off the wagon," Turner later wrote. Though he had quit alcohol three years before, the anxiety and the criticism sent him to the bottle. "He was a roaring, mean, furniture-smashing drunk. The girl friend he'd brought along stayed for a while, then gave up. The studio sent nurses, but even they couldn't help." The fog soon cleared, film production resumed, but *The Postman* suffered.

The beach footage that drove Garnett to drink also created problems for Breen. As part of the early promotional campaign, *Life* published a picture story of the evening swim in an August 1945 issue. "Love at Laguna Beach" featured six photographs of Garfield and Turner, Garfield in bathing trunks and Turner in two-piece swimsuit, white naturally. In one shot, Turner wrapped her arm around the prone Garfield; in another, moodily lit from behind, they were mouth to mouth: "A torrid kiss by moonlight seals the couple's reconciliation," *Life* panted. Even by postwar magazine standards, the photographs were not inflammatory, but their connection with *The Postman Always Rings Twice* caused sparks.

The long conversations with Carey Wilson, a responsible industry producer, had assured Breen that Metro would not thumb its nose at the Code. The promotional campaign for *The Postman* would create expectations, though, and Breen wanted Wilson to understand their effect. Breen had banned *The Postman* ten years before because of the "illusion of sex"; he now feared that social critics and censors would form judgments about the picture based on either their memories of the novel or—worse still—the publicity stills of "torrid kisses by moonlight." For their mutual protection, Breen dropped Wilson a note of warning.

> From the type of publicity which your studio has been handing out, these people [public interest groups and censors] will get the impression that there is some dirty work at the cross-roads! This will result in your picture being viewed, in many places, with a very critical eye by those with a predisposition to be agin ye! And, the Censor Boards may lay for your picture and, with a prejudiced mind, begin to hack h—— out of it when it is presented for their examination.

Breen must have been ambivalent. The censor boards' approval of *The Postman* would vindicate the work of the Production Code Administration, while their disapproval would argue for a stricter application of the Code. That Breen could hope for the latter again demonstrated how much eros and murder had shaken the Code in the mid-forties.

By early 1946, Wilson and Garnett had completed principal photography, edited the picture (cutting out the "leopards and pumas and lions" sequence), and held a press screening. "THE POSTMAN" EMERGES AS TORRID MOVIE, the Hollywood *Citizen News* reported. Correspondent Virginia MacPherson had overlooked the "compensating moral values," the punishment of Cora and Frank, and the dozen telling alterations that Breen had demanded; she had seen the "illusion of sex." *Hollywood Reporter* publisher Billy Wilkerson—a poker-playing crony of Louis Mayer—predicted that the release of *The Postman* "will cause a storm of controversy, the like of which the industry hasn't seen in years."

But what more could Breen do? He had blocked an adaptation of *The Postman* for ten years, long enough to diffuse the notoriety that attended its 1934 publication. Despite the many changes in the screenplay—and Breen had demanded enough to insure that MGM observe the letter of the Production Code—eros and murder remained the core of the finished picture. The General Principles were forever sullied: the lovers earned some audience sympathy; Chambers drank and fornicated (though with less gusto); and the behavior of the district and defense attorneys tended toward mockery of the law and the legal profession. The Seal on *The Postman* would close the parenthesis on an era of Code enforcement; it would tell Hollywood to purchase the most salacious books and anticipate Production Code certification.

Another parenthesis closed in September 1945. Two weeks after the Japanese surrender in Yokohama Harbor, Will Hays stepped down as President of the Motion Picture Producers and Distributors of America. For twenty-three years he had served the studios well; he had preached the gospel of self-regulation and soothed the politicians and professional moralists. But now the moguls wanted the "Presbyterian pope of Hollywood" to abdicate. They had tired of Main Street homilies; they doubted his continued vitality, and they questioned his ability to solve the postwar problems facing the industry. With the Justice Department resuming its antitrust suit, the studio unions demanding major wage hikes, and a war-devastated Europe desperate for American films but incapable of paying for them, the Association needed fresh ideas and new blood. At first Hays resisted, but when the board offered him a five-year contract as an advisor at $100,000 per year, the General relented. "It looked like it might be difficult," one producer cracked, "but all we had to do was give him half a million in severance pay."

Over a year earlier, the board had decided on a successor, Eric Allen Johnston, president of the Chamber of Commerce and the "darling of U.S. free enterprise." A handsome and "smooth-mannered super-salesman," Johnston tackled the job with the aggressiveness of a street-corner huckster. He immediately announced his intention to streamline Hays Office operations, then flew to Hollywood to negotiate an end to labor violence. By the end of the year, he had trimmed the name of the Motion Picture Producers and Distributors of America to the Motion Picture Association of America, established a Washington base, and offered ex-War Production Board official Julius A. Krug a new position as executive vice-president in charge of Association affairs on the West Coast.

In Hollywood, Breen's antennae quivered. He had always run the Production Code office without New York interference, yet had counted on Hays for assistance where needed. The new regime brought doubts. Johnston quickly criticized the Code Office, suggesting that the growing complaints about movie morality resulted "from human fallibility in applying code rules, rather than from the rules themselves." In January 1946, with *Variety* predicting a board-inspired crackdown on "films with questionable moral themes," Breen wondered whether the naming of Krug might not also have been meant to push the Irishman out the door with the General.

Release of *The Postman* that spring magnified these concerns. "Within the limits of the movie medium," *Newsweek* reported, "the film is as explicit as it can be." *Life* called the picture a "catalog of the seven deadly sins" and recommended that "the fainthearted" stay away. Protesting too much, *Time* may have caused a box-office swell. The "hideous story" of *The Postman* featured "reptilian bits of legal chicanery," characters "as amoral as zoo exhibits," and dialogue "paced and keyed like an erotic discussion between a couple of cats." With Hollywood ablaze—or so the headlines in the Hollywood *Citizen News* and *Hollywood Reporter* screamed—Breen turned on the hose. In April, he forced Samuel Goldwyn to revise scenes that condoned divorce or touched "on the sacred intimacies of married life" in *The Best Years of Our Lives,* and he blocked four new stories from Paramount (*The Great Gatsby, Horizontal Man, Vixen,* and *Wayfarer*) because they dealt "with sordidness, drunkenness, illicit sex, adultery, bastardy, seduction, suicide, gangster activities, etc.,—just the kind of material which, we think, is responsible for the widespread criticism which is now being visited upon this industry."

Through the spring, as the press put heat on Hollywood, Breen continued to oblige producers who exercised wit and imagination. In one of several chats about plumbing in Ernst Lubitsch's *Cluny Brown,* Cluny tells the hero that she loves "unloosening the joint" and "banging" away. In *The Ghost and Mrs. Muir,* a prim stenographer balks at one word her salty sea captain boss has dictated. He demands she type it, though, and director Joe Mankiewicz had her "hit the keys, reluctantly, exactly four times." Rather than *Cluny, The Ghost, The Postman,* or any of the other risky features that Breen had approved in the final war years, though, the second release of *The Outlaw* caused the tallest flames. To promote the western, Howard Hughes loosed one of the most vulgar advertising campaigns in motion picture history. From billboards, magazines, newspapers, and radio came the compelling questions: "What Are the Two Great Reasons for Jane Russell's Rise to Stardom?" and "How Would You Like to Tussle with Russell?" Over Los Angeles, a skywriter spelled out *The Outlaw* followed by two huge circles, each carefully dotted in the center; in New York, the marquee of the Radio City Music Hall—before the war years a bastion of family entertainment—proclaimed in its largest letters: THE MUSIC HALL GETS THE BIG ONES!

Box office soared. Long lines of patrons awaited the opening at four Los Angeles movie theaters; elsewhere *The Outlaw* packed houses. With billboards promising NOT A SCENE CUT—EXACTLY AS FILMED, active imaginations and "pectoral curiosity" drew the crowds. Once inside, audiences reacted "with sounds more appropriate to smoking room literature than a public theater." The effect was instantaneous. Industry leaders condemned the lurid ads and demanded their withdrawal; *Variety* predicted a new wave of state and local censorship; Johnston and his staff were inundated with letters demanding to know how such a salacious and degrading film could have received the Code Seal. Darryl Zanuck expressed his personal outrage to Breen: "When an ad like this appears in the paper . . . I have a hell of a job keeping my boys in line. The whole campaign for this picture is a disgrace to the industry." Zanuck intended no criticism of Breen; in fact, he refrained from a public blast at Hughes lest he damage the Code office. Like Breen, though, he sensed that the Hughes campaign would eventually harm the agency. The most vocal critics would never view *The Outlaw;* they would judge the film based on the ads, not on the movie, and the Breen office would bear the onus.

Johnston acted decisively. Less than a week after the picture opened, he charged Hughes with having "openly and repeatedly" violated the Association's advertising code, and after a brief hearing on April 23, the board voted to remove the Seal from *The Outlaw.* The following day, Hughes filed suit in federal district court for a temporary restraining order to block the Association. The case presented the first significant challenge to the legality of the Code Administration. Hughes alleged that members of the Motion Picture Association had engaged "in a conspiracy to suppress competition," had used the Seal to coerce the producer to submit script, picture, and ads for Association approval, and through their actions, had deprived Hughes of both profits and "rights guaranteed by the First Amendment." He asked the court to prevent the Association from withdrawing its Seal and to award him $5 million in damages.

Whatever the substance of the First Amendment claim, Judge John Bright dismissed the suit on much narrower grounds. He treated Breen and Hughes as the consenting parties of a simple contract; Hughes had submitted his film voluntarily, and had accepted—then breached—the terms of the Seal. While Hughes had the right to advertise his picture as he chose, the Association had the right, even the obligation, to remove its Seal whenever the ads proved offensive. Bright rejected conspiracy claims as groundless, the First Amendment claim as irrelevant. Convinced that Hughes had launched the suit as another of his publicity stunts, the judge refused to rule "in favor of one whose sole object is a selfish one." Johnston, Breen, and the company presidents rejoiced. Bright had upheld the principle of film decency and confirmed the legality of the Production Code Administration. To insure that the word reached every corner of the industry, Johnston ordered that extracts of the ruling be reprinted in a special news release, and insisted that copies be sent to all production companies, distributors, and exhibitors.

Despite the Hollywood outrage over Hughes and his ads, many independents shared the airman's belief that the Motion Picture Association discriminated against them. Not long after the trial, Mary Pickford expressed their frustration. "As things stand now," she told *Variety,* "the Big Five [Paramount, RKO, Loew's, Fox, and Warners] are both Congress and the Supreme Court. They not only make the rules, but they sit in judgment on the operation of them, so that an independent has no recourse." Foreign producers concurred. Chasing after a share of the postwar American market, British filmmakers suspected that Breen erected special barriers against them. The charge only added to Breen's mounting problems. If he tore through an import like *Wicked Lady,* the British would view the attack on "built up" and exposed Restoration bosoms as "part of the American conspiracy" to deny them Stateside play-dates; the backlash could prompt new parliamentary legislation against Hollywood features. If he looked away from Production Code violations, Breen told Eric Johnston, "the American producing companies hereabouts would raise a howl that would reecho throughout the industry." Only after much haggling did he convince the *Wicked* picturemakers to shoot expensive retakes.

Back in Hollywood from a goodwill tour of England, Breen issued formal instructions that the Code Seal be struck from all prints of *The Outlaw.* The action, delayed first by an unsuccessful appeal of Judge Bright's ruling, then by Hughes' air crash on July 7, caused an estimated eighty-five percent of the nation's theaters to shut out *The Outlaw.* Once recovered, though, the hard-headed Hughes pressed on, booking the picture for long runs in independent houses. The lurid ads and censorship problems continued. Ohio and Maryland banned the feature entirely. A Baltimore judge upheld the ban, claiming that Russell's breasts "hung over the picture like a thunderstorm spread out over a landscape," while Pennsylvania and several municipal censors demanded extensive alterations. New York City officials threatened to void the license of any theater owner who booked *The Outlaw,* and in San Francisco, police arrested an exhibitor on obscenity charges. Church groups, inspired by the Legion of Decency, protested local showings throughout the country. In Philadelphia, Harrisburg, Galveston, and St. Paul, religious pressure caused exhibitors to drop the feature. Wherever *The Outlaw* played, though, it attracted remarkable crowds. It outdrew *Gone With the Wind* in Atlanta, broke theater records in conservative cities like Louisville and St. Louis, and reportedly grossed over $3 million.

In the midst of the controversy, *Variety* observed that the "move toward liberalization of censorship, both inside and outside the industry, has been pretty well shelved by the current ruckus over *The Outlaw.*" Breen could sense the irony. In the tolerant atmosphere of the war, risking his own reputation, he had accommodated Hollywood. The motion picture that best symbolized his wartime leniency, *The Postman Always Rings Twice,* had been a fire that blazed, then flickered out. Despite some reviewers' *tsk*s, there were no Legion boycotts, no nasty letters from outraged patrons, no cuts by censor boards. Yet Howard Hughes and *The Outlaw* had brought the Code and Breen full circle. Religious pickets dinning the ears of theater owners, state legislators threatening stringent measures, local censors snipping away with renewed vigor—it all resembled the chaos of March 1941, when Breen had drafted his resignation.

Breen was not personally responsible for the furor over *The Outlaw*. The board had granted the Seal; the New York staff had reviewed the ads. Few beyond the industry knew that, though, and Breen could almost predict that the postman—his pouch filled with murder and eros, bosoms and "screen realism"—would soon approach the door and ring again.

As the World War became the Cold War, some new independents—many of them from abroad—would send Breen a passel of letter bombs. European directors had little in common with the moguls, the pictures little in common with Hollywood product. The Italian neorealists had new ideas, new values, and new approaches to screen drama. They would inspire American writers and directors, and puzzle American producers and American studios. More than ever, they would test Joe Breen and the Particular Applications of the Production Code Administration.

7

The Bicycle Thief

WHEN AMERICAN GI Rod Geiger returned from Italy in 1945, his barracks bag contained an unusual war trophy: a print of Roberto Rossellini's *Open City.* Geiger had purchased exclusive United States rights to the film for $13,000; over the next seven years it grossed more than $3 million in American theaters. From such profits revolutions are made. *Open City* stirred filmmakers across Europe into a frenzy of activity; Italy alone produced 822 features between 1945 and 1953, most aimed at expanding the beachhead created by *Open City.* France followed close behind. In the vanguard of this foreign invasion was a small group of Italian filmmakers, quickly dubbed "the neorealists."

Led by Rossellini, Luchino Visconti, and Vittorio De Sica, the neorealists displayed a grasp of the human condition that made Hollywood pictures seem slick and stylized. The new Italian films were uncompromising; they were filled with harsh detail, from garbage-laden streets to crumbling plaster, dilapidated furniture, and frayed clothing. They showed ordinary lives twisted by events and social forces beyond their control. The characters prompted thought and reaction about man's plight, and when the lights came up, moviegoers could analyze and argue about the picture much as they could a work of serious fiction. This intellectual element captivated audiences and critics; the neorealists' painful, almost documentary approach seemed to make enlightenment rather than entertainment the principal measure of excellence. The Italians won over even coiffed and perfumed Hollywood stars. "If you need a Swedish actress," Ingrid Bergman wrote to Rossellini, whose work on *Open City* had inspired her, "I am ready to come and make a film with you."

Some were less rapt than Bergman. Viennese-born director Billy Wilder attributed the gritty atmosphere of Italian cinema to a dearth of money and technical sophistication. While filming *Sunset Boulevard,* Wilder yelled to cameraman Johnny Seitz: "Johnny, keep it out of focus. I want to win the foreign picture award!" But for many serious filmmakers, truthful pictures like *Open City, Shoeshine,* and *The Bicycle Thief* illustrated the long-ignored artistic and intellectual potential of the medium. Attuned to the shifting moral climate, spurred by the success of austere postwar features like *Scarlet Street* and *Crossfire,* Stanley Kramer, Elia Kazan, and others wanted to move the American screen toward a new maturity. They advocated a more honest, less cautious cinema, one built on a simple, unaffected realism and aimed at providing the audience with food for thought. At Warners in 1947, producer Jerry Wald wanted *Flamingo Road* to become a distillate of Italian movies. "I have always believed that a good picture is a success because it is an honest portrayal of the life it deals with," he told director Michael Curtiz, and "that the best films are made when you take a chance—when you lead with your chin." Wald instructed Curtiz to make *Flamingo Road* "a blast of realism, which we hope will make people sit up in their complacency." The screen was no pulpit, he added, "but you still can do something that is important and constructive in people's lives and make it entertainment that will sell at the box-office."

Thanks to Breen, *Flamingo Road* provided a blast of Hollywood fluff. Breen found the values of postwar America and American movies increasingly at odds with his own, and he had discouraged an adaptation of Robert Wilder's seamy novel of political corruption almost from the moment Warners submitted it. He hated the "sordidness" of the book; the characters were either "crooked" or "engaged in adultery or illicit sex." The heroine was "an inmate of a brothel who becomes the mistress of a politician," Breen observed, and she ended up "by murdering the villainous sheriff who is the political boss of the state." Wald sought to condemn bossism and voter apathy—to warn the public that "unless the good keep their eyes open there will always be some son-of-a-bitch trying to step in and usurp its rights and privileges." Breen feared that by "emphasizing the complete corruption of politics in the State of Florida," *Flamingo Road* would prompt calls for new censorship in the South. And eventually the studio acceded to Breen's demands. Warners moved the story to an unnamed state in the 1920s to avoid the indictment of contemporary Southern politics; it turned the brothel into a "high-class roadhouse and speakeasy," wed the heroine (Joan Crawford) to her rising politico, and made the killing accidental. The alterations sapped much of the power and most of the message. "Contrary to expectations, there's no political significance to the plot," *Variety* reported. "Instead, it's a satisfying drama of a woman who finds romance despite becoming involved in a dirty political fight between state party leaders."

Most "message movies" never reached Joe Breen; because of their obvious commercial risks, the studios nipped them in the Story Department. In May 1950, Fox story analyst George Byron Sage hailed the "humanitarian view" of a drama about displaced persons but added that "from a commercial standpoint it is necessary to be a little cold blooded." A company man, Sage turned down the submission. When message movies went forward, the studios "thought not in ideological terms but about what would woo an audience." Accordingly, Breen greeted some of the message movies he *did* see with an open hand. "We don't pass on subject matter," he told columnist Ezra Goodman in a rare interview. "We pass only on treatment. If a subject is controversial—say a *Gentleman's Agreement, Home of the Brave* or a picture on slum clearance—that is none of our business."

Such comments were sincere, but they masked behind-the-scenes battles. When Breen read the screenplay for *Gentleman's Agreement,* he urged Darryl Zanuck not to make the heroine "a divorced woman." With a divorcee as lead, the story contained a "flavor of acceptance and even tacit justification of divorce." After the war, as the American divorce rate soared, Breen turned rigid; his Catholic convictions and the Production Code emphasis on the sanctity of marriage made him extraordinarily sensitive and prompted him to block any hint that divorce could solve domestic problems. Except "when it was obtained against the wishes, and generally over the objections, of the sympathetic lead," divorce was taboo. On *Gentleman's Agreement,* he asked Zanuck not to refer to Kathy's former marriage and ordered him to eliminate her key line: "I was right not to settle for second-best—I was right to keep hoping—because it's all come true." Zanuck refused to comply. On a picture of less merit, Breen might have pushed harder, but he passed *Gentleman's Agreement* without further comment.

Still, Breen was not letting up. He felt that a few message movies were good for the industry, and on some topics he would make allowances. "Our job is to see that reasonable decency and good taste prevail in films," Breen said. But the Code's extensive list of taboos, along with Breen's definition of "decency and good taste," could turn the open hand into a fist. On *Pinky,* Breen urged Zanuck to "avoid physical contact between Negroes and Whites" lest it offend Southern audiences and provoke new censorship in the region. In Richard Brooks' novel *The Brick Foxhole,* a homosexual was the focus of the killer's blind hate; in *Crossfire,* the dark and gripping *film noir* based on the book, the homosexual had become a Jew. While anti-Semitism was acceptable on-screen, "sexual perversion" was not.

Many young picturemakers in the late forties thought that the Code barred cinematic realism. "Hollywood is gutless. You can't make an honest, forceful picture here," Mark Hellinger complained. "The code under which we now operate is highly restrictive. *Open City,* about which many people are shouting, could never have been made here under any circumstances." Only months before, in a long memorandum to Warners executive Steve Trilling, Jerry Wald had voiced almost identical sentiments:

Frankly Steve, I am depressed and distressed. . . . No wonder the industry is continually being ridiculed—no wonder it has to continually apologize for itself. . . . This piling up of continuous censorship is what is making our pictures empty, and running along with a competent mediocrity. We could never have made *Odd Man Out* in this country, or *Shoeshine,* or *Open City.* . . . You've got to help us. This is serious.

Neither Hellinger nor Wald advocated scrapping the Code. But like the Hollywood professionals who gathered for *Life*'s "Round Table on the Movies" in May 1949, they did want the document modernized; they did want Breen's firm hand relaxed so that they could treat serious subject matter more realistically. The world and the screen audience had changed dramatically since 1930. As Robert Rossen, one of the Round Table participants, observed: "We have a new audience, an audience that has grown up out of the war and been in contact with greater realities." That audience expected the screen to reflect the values and morality of the early 1950s, not the early 1930s. In the two decades since the Code was adopted, American attitudes toward divorce, infidelity, premarital sex, prostitution, and other former sins had become more liberal. The war's brief encounters, casual sex, and quickie marriages pointed to that fact; the Kinsey Report confirmed it.

"When these people talk about realism," Joe Breen sneered, "they usually talk about filth." Confronted with Round Table liberals, Breen became even more rigid. The flexibility he displayed on *Black Fury* and *Dead End* gave way to an almost obsessive nitpicking that inflamed some filmmakers. When Breen reviewed the screenplay of Warners' *Glass Menagerie* in March 1949, he found the script acceptable but wanted two of Tom's lines changed because they suggested "an incestuous attraction toward his sister." The studio complied, removing the following lines: "Then all at once my sister touches my shoulder. I turn around and look into her eyes. . . . Oh, Laura, Laura! I tried to leave you behind me. But I am more faithful than I intended to be." An outraged Tennessee Williams called the speech "the best, most lyric lines in the entire narration." He could not "understand acquiescence to this sort of foulminded and utterly stupid tyranny" and tabbed the charges "insulting to me, to my family, and an effrontery to the entire motion picture industry!" The Irishman nonetheless rolled over Tennessee and the *Menagerie,* then continued the quest for screen decency and good taste.

The waning months of 1949 were among the most difficult in Breen's career. Studio executives, squeezed by dwindling foreign markets and the persistent slide in domestic attendance, reverted to older, pre-Code patterns. Each script seemed to contain more objectionable material than the last. The wave of brutality, violence, adultery, and illicit sex taxed Breen's skills and energy; persistent efforts to inject abortion, narcotics addiction, and other taboo subjects pushed him to the brink of despair. At the end of November, Breen expressed his frustrations to Martin Quigley: "We are really having a desperate time of it. During the past month, at least, more than half of the material submitted here has had to be rejected. We have had nothing like this situation since the early days of 1934." The difficulties left Breen highly suspicious, even paranoid. He suspected a plot, an insurgence led by younger filmmakers that would cause the studios "to fight the Code, and to kick over the traces." The threat to his authority was not accidental. "There is some sinister force at work hereabouts. I just cannot put my finger on it, but I am satisfied in my own mind that this condition, which has come about in recent months, did not just 'happen.' There is an African in the woodpile!"

Conspiratorial visions were all too common in a nation beset by startling revelations. The Communist victory in China, the Soviet detonation of a nuclear bomb, and the protracted trial of Alger Hiss had conditioned Americans to accept a world of sinister forces and evil cabals. Breen's vision targeted a much smaller plot, but one equally threatening to his world. And it was this vision, this exaggerated fear of a conspiracy to undermine the Code, that shaped his response to Vittorio De Sica's *The Bicycle Thief.*

Set in the poverty and bleakness of postwar Rome, *The Bicycle Thief* tells a simple though elegant story about a man's desperate search for his stolen bicycle. The unemployed laborer, Antonio, has secured a job as a billboard plasterer, a post that requires a bicycle. His wife reluctantly pawns the family's only remaining possessions of value, six bridal sheets, to get her husband's bicycle out of hock, but almost immediately one of Rome's many petty thieves snatches it. The remainder of the picture traces the frantic efforts of Antonio and his ten-year-old son, Bruno, to locate the thief and recover the precious bike. The frustrations and disappointments of the search bewilder, then begin to diminish the man. At one point Antonio turns on Bruno; out of pure despair, he slaps him, and the two continue their pursuit on opposite sides of the street. When eventually Antonio spots and corners the thief, he finds him desperately poor, no better off than his victim. The police cannot locate the bicycle among the thief's meager possessions, so Antonio must accept defeat. Utterly distraught, he attempts to steal a bicycle, but its owner's angry friends catch and beat him; only Bruno's anguished pleading saves Antonio from further humiliation. Though father and son are finally reconciled, the quest has ended. Hand in hand, Antonio and Bruno disappear into the vast Roman landscape to face an uncertain future.

While the plot of *The Bicycle Thief* might "not deserve two lines in a stray dog column," De Sica's images present "the perfect aesthetic illusion of reality." They lead the viewer into the shabby, bleak world of Antonio and Bruno almost without effort, giving the appearance of a sequence of small human events photographed totally unposed and uncontrived. The director's hand is omnipresent, though, shaping what seems a series of fortuitous episodes into "a carefully orchestrated tour through the various social hells of urban Italy."

A journalist described Vittorio De Sica as "an exceedingly handsome man, standing about six feet tall, with dark eyes and a thick, wavy, immaculately groomed head of graying hair. . . . There is about him the air of unabashed patrician elegance that often characterizes the well-turned-out Italian male." Matinee idol, international celebrity, a notorious ladies' man who once bragged that "brides left their husbands on their wedding nights to pursue me," the public De Sica connoted neither personal depth nor drive. Behind the camera, though, another De Sica emerged—determined, uncompromising, occasionally brutal, yet ever-calculating. At one point during the filming of *The Bicycle Thief,* he pressed his untutored star, Lamberto Maggiorani, beyond the poor man's limits. The simple steelworker from Breda turned on the director, pummeled him with a series of blows, then collapsed in tears. Almost at once De Sica started the camera and captured the emotional realism he had been seeking.

The same determination and commitment to realistic cinema kept De Sica from Hollywood. In 1946, almost two years before *The Bicycle Thief,* he produced *Shoeshine* and established his credentials as a rival of Roberto Rossellini. Lucrative offers from California followed. David Selznick wanted to back *The Bicycle Thief*, but De Sica rejected the bid because it would have required pepping up the film to Yankee standards and casting Cary Grant in the role of Antonio. Planning to dedicate his film to the poor of Rome, De Sica could find no place for Grant's urbane sophistication and polished appearance. He toyed with casting either Henry Fonda or Barry Fitzgerald, but when Selznick showed interest in neither, the Italian "poet of poverty" struck out on his own. He put his own money in the film, raised additional lire from three wealthy Milanese friends, and made the picture his way.

Released in 1948, *The Bicycle Thief* won acclaim throughout Europe. Critics called it "brilliant and devastating," a "powerful image-poem (*New York Times*), a "superlative exercise in screen realism" (*Sight and Sound*), and simply "the best film since the war" (*Film Quarterly*). The cinéastes honored it with five Silver Ribbons (the Oscars of Italy), the British Academy Award for Best Picture, and the grand prize at both the Brussels and Locarno Film Festivals. It was without doubt the most universally praised feature of the postwar decade. After its United States premiere in December 1949, *The Bicycle Thief* earned new honors from the National Board of Review, the New York critics' association, and the Motion Picture Academy. Foreign language pictures usually traveled the art theatre circuit, an agglomeration of fewer than three hundred cinemas specializing in imports, documentaries, and offbeat independent productions. While another three to four hundred theaters occasionally booked exceptional films without the Code Seal, even the most sanguine importer hoped for only a tiny percentage of the vast American market. With *The Bicycle Thief*, however, distributor Joseph Burstyn thought that he could break out of the confines of the art houses and into the much more lucrative first-run theaters of the Motion Picture Association.

Polish immigrant Joe Burstyn's lively smile and frail figure belied a shrewd intensity. Starting out as press agent for New York's Yiddish theater, he had a flair for promotion. He quickly displayed a remarkable grasp of the European movie market and what would sell in the emerging metropolitan art theatres. By 1936, he had formed a company with ex-Paramount publicist Arthur Mayer. Over the next decade the two men struggled with mixed success to broaden Americans' cinematic appetite.

Even for a foreign distributor with the best track record in America, *The Bicycle Thief* would be a hard sell. Yet Burstyn had experience and persistence. In 1945, he and Mayer had bought Geiger's print of *Open City*—largely on Burstyn's hunch—and opened the film in New York's World Theater. When practically no one but the critics came, Burstyn remembered that one of the company's most successful films of the 1930s, *Club de Femmes,* had been promoted by exhibitors as "a spicy lesbian tale." He decided to follow a time-honored Hollywood adage, one that Breen had long rued: sell the sizzle, not the steak. Breen soon felt the splatters. Burstyn altered a quotation from *Life* and advertised *Open City* as "sexier than Hollywood ever dared to be." Once moviegoers read the blurb and saw the new promotional stills—one showed some women in a tender embrace, the other a man being flogged ("to tap the sadist trade")—long lines formed at the ticket window. Mayer and Burstyn later sold Rossellini's *Paisan* with an ad that pictured a slightly disheveled young woman and a recumbent, obviously relaxed male enjoying a cigarette. Patrons quickly grasped the coded message, and *Paisan* surpassed *Open City* at the box office. The race was on. Over the next three years, Mayer and Burstyn competed with other importers like Ilya Lopert and Irving Shapiro to garner and promote the best of the Italian renaissance. By the end of the decade, though, interest died. Tired of waiting for what the ad promised and the film never delivered, moviegoers stayed home to watch Milton Berle or professional wrestling. Excellent neorealist pictures like De Sica's *Shoeshine,* Visconti's *The Earth Will Shake,* and Rossellini's *Germany, Year Zero* flopped miserably.

Arthur Mayer read the disheartening figures, decided that American audiences wanted "more Victor Matures rather than more mature pictures," and in September 1949 sold out to Burstyn. The stubborn Burstyn refused to give up. Ever the optimist, he sensed that with the right film and the right promotional campaign he could break the economic bonds of the art theatre market. The following month he secured distribution rights to *The Bicycle Thief.* The film opened to critical acclaim at the World Theater on December 12, and over the next five weeks provided the largest gross of any foreign-language feature to play the house. Warners quickly contacted Burstyn about running the picture in selected urban theaters nationwide. Since such engagements would require a Code Seal, Burstyn forwarded a print to Breen in late January.

Joe Breen could hardly be considered a serious student of motion pictures, but he seemed to recognize the importance of *The Bicycle Thief.* Less enamored than the critics, he apparently liked the film and felt that with minor changes it could earn his approval. Breen found only two scenes troublesome. The first was a brief, slightly poignant episode in the midst of the frantic daylong search for the stolen bicycle. Antonio's son pauses beside a Roman wall, apparently to relieve himself. His back is to the camera and before he can begin, his father compels him to abandon the call of nature and continue the chase. The second problem, more important to the plot, involved Antonio's pursuit of the thief into a "house of tolerance." The run through the bordello showed nothing even remotely sensual. The women were clothed, unattractive, and occupied only with their Sunday morning meal. Neither scene was likely to offend or lower the moral standards of the audience, and technically neither violated the Code. Yet Breen found both unacceptable. He informed Burstyn that before the Production Code Administration could issue a Seal, the distributor must remove the two scenes.

Joe Breen ran the Production Code Administration on the rule of precedent, and while neither moment in *The Bicycle Thief* violated the Code per se, both countered a long line of prior decisions duly recorded in the agency's "black books." Bruno's pause by the wall ran afoul of the Breen dictum that "toilet humor" must never appear on the American screen. The Production Code included no mention of toilet humor, but it did warn that the "treatment of low, disgusting, unpleasant, though not necessarily evil, subjects should be subject always to the dictates of good taste." For Breen, toilet humor of any kind—perhaps especially when a wall became a toilet—exceeded the bounds of "good taste." Breen personally delighted in such humor, yet the jokes that he swapped with the Production Code boys were not alluded to on-screen. Quite simply, Breen believed that the Hollywood creative community lacked decorum, and that if he ever allowed even the most innocent of toilet gags, unscrupulous producers would flood the screen with them.

Since 1934, Breen had worked to cure the movies of incontinence. He had banned wet beds, wet diapers, and wetting dolls, and routed obvious toilet gags. Occasionally his attention lapsed. He allowed the dog to foul the Chancery Court floor in *The Awful Truth* and the Joad kids to flush in *The Grapes of Wrath;* he also looked away in *Cheaper by the Dozen* so that Clifton Webb could stop the car in the country and let the kids "visit Mrs. Murphy." Otherwise, Breen missed little. He ordered a scene cut from *The Paradine Case* because it showed a commode in a jail cell, another from *The Best Years of Our Lives* because a dog wet on the floor. "You pass stuff like that," he told his colleague Jack Vizzard, "and the next thing you know you have a scene of a dapper young fellow in Paris standing at a pissoir, leaking away with a smile on his face. And then, along comes Marilyn Monroe . . . and our boy turns around, and does a big tip of his straw hat, and says 'Bon jour, mademoiselle.' " Such an attitude toward toilet humor—supported by numerous precedents—made Breen rule that Bruno button up.

The house of tolerance scene likewise countered a long-enforced taboo against screen bordellos. While the Code was silent on brothels, the Breen-enforced taboo was drawn from a logical reading of the rule on locations: "Certain places are so closely and thoroughly associated with sexual life or with sexual sin that their use must be carefully limited." For Breen, that provision meant that bedroom scenes must be carefully regulated and brothel scenes entirely forbidden. Since 1934, Breen had ordered that directors and producers delete from their scripts any brothel scenes. The studios normally relocated the sequence to a saloon or gambling house (sometimes, as in *Gone With the Wind,* none too convincingly), and the problem was solved. In *The Bicycle Thief* that option was not available. The scene was already in the final cut and, with the cast long since dispersed, De Sica could hardly be asked to reshoot it. The only remedy was to edit the sequence and—while retaining the essential confrontation between the hero and the thief—hope to eliminate any indication that Antonio had entered a brothel. From experience, Breen suspected that the cut would not pose serious continuity problems, so he saw nothing wrong with rejecting *The Bicycle Thief* until Burstyn altered the picture.

Denying the Seal was dangerous. That such an important film

might be excluded from the nation's major theaters because of two brief and innocuous scenes would enflame Code opponents and leave Breen and company open to the increasingly frequent charge of "sniggering censorship." That *The Bicycle Thief* was a foreign film would add to the embarrassment. The producers of *Wicked Lady* and a number of other European films thought that the Association had used the Seal to exclude foreign competition from American theaters, a charge that disturbed Motion Picture Association president Eric Johnston. For four years Johnston had sought ways to improve the climate for American pictures abroad. Now, with European governments attempting to expand their own film industries and reduce the cash drain caused by the popularity of American movies, Johnston was hardly eager to convey the impression that the Production Code blocked access to the American market. Over one-third of United States film revenues came from foreign rentals, and the industry, burdened by quotas, taxes, and other regulations, wanted no new excuses for further retaliatory laws.

Breen could never afford to slight the broader concerns of the company presidents; still, he elevated Code integrity over mere external considerations. When proper enforcement and other industry goals clashed, Breen instinctively sided with the Code, even at the risk of offending Johnston. Only months earlier, the French government had asked the Association to rescind the ban on *Devil in the Flesh*, Claude Autant-Lara's bold study of an openly adulterous relationship between a French schoolboy and the lonely wife of a soldier. The picture had attracted both acclaim and controversy. Boycotted by French and Belgian bluenoses, principally because of an explicit scene that showed the young couple on the verge of intercourse, *Devil* set box office records throughout Europe and Latin America. The producer cut the questionable scene before shipment to the States, but Breen still banned the film because of "gross illicit sex and adultery." Pressure from the French government made the State Department intervene on behalf of Autant-Lara. A more sympathetic attitude toward *Devil* and other French imports, a Department official told Eric Johnston, might both improve Franco-American relations and help induce the French to release impounded profits from American film rentals. Johnston

then asked Breen to reconsider the ban. The case-hardened Irishman was wholly unsympathetic. He supported all attempts to
avoid threatened boycotts and to shake American dollars from
continental exhibitors, but these had nothing to do with the Code.
If Johnston and the Association board wanted to change the Code
or grant a special waiver for *Devil in the Flesh* or all foreign films,
that was their concern, not his. Breen would enforce the Code he
was given; he could not and would not be influenced by "extraneous matters." Johnston withdrew, and the *Devil* ban stood.

Breen saw *Devil in the Flesh* and *The Bicycle Thief* as one. The
Italians might fuss and critics would certainly protest, but Bruno's
pause and the bordello had to go. Breen did not seek conflict. He
obviously hoped, perhaps even expected, that Burstyn and De Sica
would quietly cut the offensive frames and resubmit the film for
approval. Four years earlier, when Breen had initially denied
Rossellini's *Open City* a Seal because of a brief scene showing a child
sitting on a chamber pot, Burstyn, after consulting the director,
had trimmed the sequence to gain Code approval. The case of *The
Bicycle Thief* was different: its director would brook no interference
with his picture. An astounded De Sica wired Burstyn that *The
Bicycle Thief* had circulated uncut throughout Europe, and that
Americans should judge for themselves the merits and morals of the
entire film.

Caught between his preference for the Seal and his desire to
honor De Sica, Burstyn undertook a press campaign to have the
Association overrule Breen. His determination to circumvent
Breen stemmed less from pique than from cleverness: he sensed that
Breen's response offered him a new opportunity to promote the
film as forbidden fruit. The same month that Breen rejected *The
Bicycle Thief,* Howard Hughes rereleased *The Outlaw*—along with
the provocative poster of Jane Russell in the barn—for yet another
run through the nation's theaters. Despite cuts made to soothe
Breen and the Catholics, *The Outlaw* still bore the tantalizing
stigma of a banned film and broke attendance records wherever it
opened.

Joe Burstyn knew what that meant. Breen could propel *The
Bicycle Thief* well beyond the narrow clientele for art films, and
Burstyn was determined to seize the moment. The film's reputa-

tion, combined with the inoffensiveness of the two scenes, was bound to draw the attention of critics and civil libertarians alike. Burstyn would merely alert the press and pose as the defender of freedom and cinematic integrity. He damned the Breen action as "a subtle form of sabotage," and trumpeted his intention to appeal the ruling to the Motion Picture Association Board of Directors.

The cards fell as Burstyn predicted. Critics and civil libertarians rushed to the defense of *The Bicycle Thief.* The National Council on Freedom From Censorship, an American Civil Liberties Union affiliate, denounced the Production Code ruling as "a shocking demonstration of censorship," a "violation of free thought and expression," and a disgrace to the industry, especially at a time when the Motion Picture Association itself was fighting legal battles against the censor boards. The *New York Times'* Bosley Crowther, always hard on the Code, suggested that the cuts illustrated how the Breen office had lost touch with reality, how the staff had "put their minds in deep freeze." *Life* referred to the film as "one of the finest ever made" and called Breen's demands "ridiculous." In no way sexy, *The Bicycle Thief* appealed "to the mind, not the glands." Then *Life*'s editor recanted, remembering one "sexy moment" in which Antonio pastes "a lush and extremely suggestive portrait of Rita Hayworth on a wall." The poster, he concluded, "offers a piquant commentary on Hollywood sensuality versus the dignity and propriety of *The Bicycle Thief.* Maybe Hollywood just couldn't stand the implied criticism."

Worse still for Breen, the Production Code Administration suffered three additional embarrassments just before the hearing on *The Bicycle Thief.* First, the Legion of Decency rated *The Bicycle Thief* "B" rather than "Condemned." In the past, the Catholics had almost always condemned pictures that Breen turned down, so the break with tradition not only won press coverage but added to Burstyn's argument that the Production Code Administration had acted unreasonably. Early in March, the Motion Picture Association's own "Estimates of Current Pictures," a collection of puffs on contemporary movies, recommended *The Bicycle Thief* as "a picture for everyone," a film that "transcends the barrier of language and speaks directly to the mind and heart." Breen reddened over the obvious snafu by the New York office, but he could not undo the damage. Finally, just five days before its late-March board hearing, *The Bicycle Thief* won the Oscar for Best Foreign Film.

In another time, Breen might have welcomed Burstyn's appeal as an opportunity to clarify Code interpretation. Board rulings created the strongest precedents and normally enhanced the authority of the Code administrator. Combined with the Academy Award, however, the critics' support of Burstyn and De Sica caused Breen to view *The Bicycle Thief* as something more than a simple challenge. Some weeks before the board hearing, he sensed that Burstyn's appeal might be part of a larger Hollywood plot to weaken the Code. His exaggerated fears were fed by screenwriter Fred Niblo, Jr., an occasional Breen confidant. "In my opinion, *The Bicycle Thief* is a trial-balloon rather than a case in its own right," Niblo wrote Breen. "Evidently it has the backing or blessing of some people in the studios who have lent themselves, consciously or stupidly, to the role of boring from within. It may well be that this is only the first round of a bigger fight."

Breen's fears stemmed from persistent speculation that had circulated throughout the film colony since the Supreme Court's divorcement decree in 1948. As a result of *United States* v. *Paramount Pictures,* the major studios were being forced to sell their theaters, thus nullifying a crucial element in the Code system. The affiliated theaters—those large chains owned by RKO, Fox, Loew's, Paramount, and Warners—were vital to Code enforcement because they dominated the film rental business. As long as the theaters refused to screen pictures without Seals, major producers had little incentive to bypass the Breen office. Divorcement freed these chains from any corporate supervision and thereby increased the likelihood that they might ignore the Code altogether.

In January 1950, with the process of divorcement just under way, even *Variety* speculated about the demise of the Breen office. While noting that most exhibitors and producers would continue to honor the Code, Herb Golden, veteran Hollywood reporter, predicted that in the wake of divorcement "if a picture comes along which exhibs feel will be highly profitable and not cause them too much trouble, there will be a lot more chance of selling it without a seal than there has been in the past." This potential could lure producers to the "beckoning field" beyond the Code, to the "exploration of husband-wife-lover relationships, divorce, drugs and murder-without-retribution material." Such speculation tended to intensify Breen's paranoia.

If Niblo was right, if *The Bicycle Thief* was the first round rather than the bout itself, Breen wanted to stop the challenger then and there. He ignored a recurrent lung ailment and announced travel plans to New York, where he would make the case an issue of his personal leadership. No less clever than Burstyn, he knew that most board members respected his judgment and, even more, his long service to the industry. To strengthen his position, though, Breen rummaged through office files for precedents, instances in which similar scenes had been removed at the agency's urging. The evidence would demonstrate why he and his associates had demanded the cuts and why Burstyn's appeal was unreasonable. Breen incorporated the precedents into a carefully prepared six-page statement for delivery at the hearing.

On the afternoon of March 28, fifteen of the Association presidents met at the Columbia boardroom in New York City. Some of these industry graybeards saw the Code as sacrosanct; they were certain that Breen's vigorous enforcement had saved Hollywood from near-calamity in the 1930s and protected it in the years since. Aloof from the specifics of motion picture production, they were not the conspirators Breen feared; they never experienced and thus never resented the sting of the Code's broad constraints or Breen's sometimes petty rulings. They were the industry's ever-conservative money men. Perhaps more important, they regarded any challenge—especially from an outsider—with suspicion.

Recent events served only to amplify their caution. Just two weeks earlier, Senator Edwin C. Johnson, Chairman of the Committee on Interstate and Foreign Commerce, had proclaimed his intention to leash "the mad dogs of the industry." He proposed legislation that would require all actors, directors, and producers to have a government license to ply their trades, essentially a federal permit that could be revoked whenever their conduct violated the law or contemporary moral standards. Distributors would also need a permit for every picture released, with licensing officials told to bar any feature that encouraged "contempt for public or private morality" or starred "persons of ill repute." Although the proposal seemed preposterous and had little active support in Congress, it startled industry leaders.

Johnson had been stirred by the infamous Bergman-Rossellini affair. Ingrid Bergman had astonished an entire generation of film-goers when she abandoned her husband and child to join Rossellini in Italy; shock turned to anger when the couple announced her pregnancy. Letters and petitions to the Motion Picture Association demanded that the company presidents ban Bergman pictures. Worse still, within days of the prenatal announcement, RKO (then owned by Howard Hughes) launched a high-powered publicity campaign for *Stromboli,* Rossellini's new feature with Bergman as star. *Variety* called the picture "a 20 minute travelog of Stromboli [an island off Sicily] in an 89 minute film." *Stromboli* was not salacious; Breen had approved it without comment, and RKO managers fretted that the tame picture would leave audiences cold. Even the advertisements, which the New York office combed for traces of tussle-with-Russell, were not provocative. But that was before the pregnancy. Now phrases like "Bergman Under the Inspired Direction of Rossellini" and shots of Stromboli's volcano spurting lava assumed new meaning. Hughes exploited the opportunity. Rushing through an order for multiple prints, he booked 125 theaters in greater New York for an unprecedented saturation release and mounted a promotional blitz. By late February, *Variety* claimed that no picture in history had received "even 10% of the space and radio time racked up by *Stromboli*." A frustrated Gordon White, director of the Motion Picture Association advertising code, again complained about "the unrelenting pressure which Mr. Hughes brings to bear on us whenever he chooses to take a personal interest in an advertising campaign."

Another volcano heated up in Washington. Only weeks earlier, an unknown Wisconsin junior senator had claimed to have a list of 205 card-carrying Communists in the State Department; that notorious Wheeling, West Virginia, speech had turned Joseph McCarthy from bit player to star almost overnight. Watching McCarthy's rise from obscurity, Senator Johnson wondered whether an assault on Hollywood morals could do the same for him. The ex-cowboy from Colorado launched the government licensing bill with extravagant oratory, easily quotable and designed for the headlines. He condemned the "nauseating commercial opportunism" of RKO for its "shameless exploitation" of the Bergman affair and denounced the "vile and unspeakable" Rossellini as a "narcotics addict, Nazi collaborator and black market operator." Ingrid Bergman, he told the Senate, had been his favorite actress until this "common love thief" had stolen her affections; now she was "a powerful force for evil." Lumped with Rita Hayworth, whose hasty marriage to Prince Aly Shah Khan had also shocked filmgoers, Bergman had become one of "Hollywood's two current apostles of degradation."

The movie colony could not quite fathom "Big Ed" Johnson. *Variety* speculated that his outburst was political folderol, intended to bolster sagging popularity at home and undercut the appeal of a potential opponent from Denver who was president of Fox Inter-Mountain Theatres. The Motion Picture Association denounced his measure as a "police state bill" that would create a "commissar" of American morals. While the law seemed unlikely to pass, the film community shuddered at the prospect of public hearings. Industry leaders blamed much of the sharp attendance decline of late 1947 on the famous "Hollywood Ten" investigation, and a new congressional inquiry into filmdom morality could dig up some dirt that might turn away still more patrons.

With the Johnson hearings looming, the Motion Picture Association board settled into the plush seats of the Columbia screening room to view *The Bicycle Thief.* Since most had already seen the film at local theaters, Eric Johnston showed only the two scenes in question. Breen then read his six-page statement. His tone fluctuated between that of the confident barrister citing precedents before an appellate tribunal and that of the young prosecutor seeking to sway a jury with impassioned rhetoric. He referred to "hundreds of cases" in which toilet gags had been removed from American pictures, and demanded the same treatment for *The Bicycle Thief.* While admitting that Bruno's pause might "appear to be 'realistic' or 'humorous' or 'cute' to certain sophisticated audiences, it is in bad taste." The brothel scene was even more dangerous "because such locales inescapably suggest commercialized vice and human depravity, and arouse unwholesome interest and curiosity on the part of youth." But the cornerstone of the argument involved the dangerous precedent that the board would set by approving the scenes: "If, for any reason whatsoever, such scenes are to be appraised as acceptable, such approval may be properly deemed to set a precedent for all future motion pictures," Breen thundered, and soon "the motion picture screen will be flooded with similar scenes."

The presentation was earnest but not candid. Board members could have endorsed the picture *and* preserved screen morality. Bruno and the bordello would have offended only the most squeamish viewer and—despite the Breen fervor—would hardly have caused a Hollywood revolution. The studios were not adventurous, and even had they pushed toilet humor or brothel scenes beyond the bounds of contemporary standards, Breen could always set new guidelines. If board members feared a precedent, they could address the problem without ordering cuts in *The Bicycle Thief.* They could grant a special exemption—without precedent—for this film, or, as in the case of "damn" in *Gone With the Wind,* they could amend the Code and allow such scenes in all films but only under carefully prescribed circumstances. Though Breen understood the alternatives, he was mum. For him, the appeal was a matter of both personal principle and Code survival. Burstyn must give way.

Burstyn had little comment. Perhaps he felt that the critical praise and recent Academy Award for *The Bicycle Thief* rendered further argument unnecessary; more likely, he thought the appeal a charade. Recognizing board members' support for Breen, the distributor sensed that he could not alter the outcome. He offered a few comments about the awards for the film, its unqualified and uncensored acceptance abroad, and the tasteful handling of the two scenes in question. He did challenge Breen's assertion that the scenes could be eliminated without damaging continuity—the cuts would entail gouging hundreds of additional feet to cover the absent sections, he argued—but when finished he retired quietly to an anteroom to await the board's decision.

The outcome was foregone. Shaken by the Bergman-Rossellini affair and the pending Johnson hearings, the Association upheld Breen and ordered Burstyn to cut the offending frames. He refused, and without the Seal *The Bicycle Thief* continued its run in art houses and independent theaters.

It was to be a Pyrrhic victory, however, for the case of *The Bicycle*

Thief sparked intense criticism of the Production Code Administration. In a two-column *New York Times* story called "Unkindest Cut," Bosley Crowther termed the outcome of the appeal "the sort of resistance to liberalization or change that widely and perilously oppresses the whole industry today." ACLU staff counsel Herbert Levy denounced it as "ill-advised super-prudishness," and others pointed to its narrow parochialism. Burstyn grabbed a placard and joined the demonstration. In a series of press releases, he accused Breen of applying petty standards that the vast majority of Americans had long since rejected; after all, he said, censors in New York, Pennsylvania, and Ohio had approved *The Bicycle Thief* without cuts. Burstyn also hammered at the theme of Code office discrimination against foreign pictures, claiming that Breen acted in concert with the major studios to exclude competition from abroad.

Breen might have ignored Burstyn's first charge; after all, he was accustomed to press attacks on agency rulings. But it was no small matter—especially after the unpleasantness with Eric Johnston over *Devil in the Flesh* and *Wicked Lady*—when he and his colleagues were accused of plotting against the import of foreign films. Breaking a fifteen-year tradition of Code office silence and showing how testy the times had made him, Breen lashed out. He called Burstyn's claims "utterly false" and listed over fifty pictures produced abroad that had earned the agency Seal in 1949. Breen also denied that his ruling represented either censorship or a ban on *The Bicycle Thief.* Rehearsing what had happened on the *Outlaw* suit, he explained that the Code system was voluntary. Like other producers and distributors, Burstyn could market his film and theaters could show his film with or without the Seal. Burstyn had submitted *The Bicycle Thief* voluntarily; he had refused to make the two minor cuts necessary for Code compliance; his problems were his own. "Censorship" was uninvolved.

The Breen manifesto boosted the appeal of the picture. By mid-April, *The Bicycle Thief* was running in forty-six independent theaters and was outdrawing *Open City* and *Paisan* in each. Burstyn fully exploited the Seal he never had. One of his ads featured a shot of Bruno at the wall, with the caption "Please come and see me before they cut me out. . . . *The Bicycle Thief,* the uncensored version."

De Sica's film performed well throughout the major art houses on both coasts but, as often the case with foreign features, sold few tickets in the heartland. The slippage caused Burstyn, ever persistent in the search for new bookings, to reopen the Seal question. Again he tried subterfuge. Rather than approach the Code office directly, he induced De Sica to employ Count Graziadei, an Italian lawyer, to handle the matter so that Burstyn would not appear personally involved. Graziadei suggested a compromise: De Sica would eliminate the brothel scene, Breen would let Bruno unbutton. Angered over Burstyn's ads and his gloating to the press, Breen refused. In a letter to the New York office at the close of these final negotiations, Breen expressed his frustration with "people like Burstyn, who give us an immense amount of trouble, and refuse to accept the judgment of our Board, capitalize on the whole matter in their advertising, and then—after they have sucked their limited market dry—come around looking for our seal."

Breen blocked one blow only to take another in the stomach. Three of the Association's five theater chains suddenly announced plans to show *The Bicycle Thief.* For the first time since 1934, major theater organizations had booked a picture that lacked the Code Seal. Breen's exaggerated fears no longer seemed exaggerated. The circuit bookings for *The Bicycle Thief* represented the first serious "chink in the Code's armor." It meant that the exhibitors' pledge—the fundamental link in the movies' system of voluntary Code compliance—had finally been broken.

The immediate consequences of the breach were unclear. Only two weeks after Breen moved to Dart Square, the Production Code boys' new headquarters at the corner of Beverly and La Cienega, *Variety* suggested that the actions of the circuit presidents meant "the code ban has collapsed." Others were less certain. Was the rupture permanent? Or were a handful of exhibitors merely exercising their postdivorcement independence? Would they have booked *The Bicycle Thief* had the Legion of Decency condemned it? Had the Legion become the power behind Breen's throne?

As the speculation whirled in Hollywood, Breen was forced to take stock. He knew that he had blundered. His blind adherence to the Production Code had threatened the very existence of the operation he had worked so hard to preserve. Burstyn and De Sica had not only defied the Code and won but had pried open a door that Breen wanted barred. What stood behind Burstyn and De Sica could knock down that door once and for all—and Breen with it.

8

Detective Story

AND

A Streetcar Named Desire

IT WAS THE stormiest meeting in the history of the Screen Directors Guild. For six and a half hours on the evening of October 22, 1950, Guild members hurled accusations at one another across the ballroom of the Beverly Hills Hotel. Then Cecil B. De Mille, a founding member and Hollywood's most successful money-director, denounced his subversive opponents and began to recite their names in a strange German-Yiddish accent that drew attention to their foreign origins—"Mr. Villy Vyler," "Mr. Fred S-s-s-ini-mon"—until boos and catcalls from the audience interrupted the performance. George Stevens rose to demand that the De Mille–dominated board of directors resign, and even such longtime conservatives as John Ford and Fritz Lang supported the move. De Mille sat down, defeated. The victor that Sunday evening was Guild president Joseph Mankiewicz. De Mille and his right-wing allies, mostly studio oldtimers, sought the implementation of a Guild loyalty oath, and Mankiewicz and his liberal supporters (William Wyler, Fred Zinnemann, John Huston, Billy Wilder, and twenty-one other directors) called the meeting to prevent De Mille's aging cabal from taking control. "We saved the guild that night," Mankiewicz remembered. But at what price? To insure that their motives were not questioned, all twenty-five liberals signed an oath affirming that none was a member of the Communist party or supported any organization that advocated the violent overthrow of the government. It was a loyalty oath to fight a loyalty oath.

And it was a sign of the times. Ever since the Hollywood hearings of October 1947 and the Waldorf-Astoria declaration the following December (pledging the studios to dismiss any employee who failed to cooperate with the House Un-American Activities Committee), the film community had nervously awaited the sound of that second shoe. By autumn 1950, even the most naive sensed the imminence of a jolting thump. In April, the Supreme Court had rejected the final appeal of the Hollywood Ten, leaving future Committee witnesses with the unenviable choice of taking the Fifth or naming names. In June, the North Koreans had invaded South Korea, the Senate debated Joe McCarthy's charges of Communist infiltration of the State Department, and the Justice Department predicted victory in the Rosenberg case. The anti-Communist compulsion had taken hold of American politics. How long would it be before the House Un-American Activities Committee booked a return engagement in southern California? How long before that second shoe heralded a blacklist?

Hollywood liberals like Elia Kazan saw their enemies "regrouping in the shadows." (Kazan chose not to attend the Guild meeting on October 22 because he feared that his past membership in the Communist party would be used by De Mille to defeat Mankiewicz.) Fearful and helpless, the liberals reminded one reporter of "marooned sailors on a flat desert island watching the approach of a tidal wave." Their instincts told them to seek cover where they could find it. Some who had flirted with communism in their youth looked for lawyers and "fixers" who could arrange clearance for past sins. Others weighed the costs of abject surrender and naming names. Still others sought the security of loyalty oaths. Four days after putting down De Mille's putsch, Mankiewicz sent a letter to all Guild members advising them to set aside personal reservations about the organization's loyalty oath and "sign it now!" What Dalton Trumbo called the "time of the toad" had arrived in Hollywood.

More than Washington witch-hunts and blacklists frightened Hollywood that fall. The movie industry faced its most severe economic crisis since 1933. Over the preceding four years, the net profits recorded by the major studios had declined by almost sixty percent. Production costs had nearly doubled, the divorcement decree had forced the studios to sell off their lucrative theater chains, and worst of all, domestic attendance had plummeted. From early in the war through 1946, American movie theaters sold between eighty and ninety million tickets per week. The sharp decline began in 1947, and by mid-1950, average sales had slipped to fifty-six million. During the first six months of that year, six hundred theaters permanently closed their doors. Industry analysts blamed the decline on everything from the growth of night baseball to the lack of disposable income. They noted the GI Bill that drew veterans to college, the soaring birth rate that kept young couples home, the migration to the suburbs that distanced regular patrons from theaters, and the dramatic increase in spending on houses, cars, and appliances that drained the pockets of consumers. But Hollywood's problems also stemmed from the shifting preferences of the fickle public; while movie attendance nose-dived, revenues from bowling alleys, racetracks, and museums soared. Friday night audiences ignored the local cinema in favor of high school football and basketball games; do-it-yourselfers stayed home to convert the attic into yet another bedroom or construct a brick barbecue in the backyard. At the beginning of 1950, fewer than one million homes contained television sets. By Christmas, the number had quadrupled, and competition from the electronic hearth would soon provide Hollywood with its stiffest challenge yet.

With desperate studio executives looking vainly for properties that could lure Americans back to the theaters, Joe Breen, like Kazan and the Hollywood liberals, continued to sense his enemies "regrouping in the shadows." The outcome of his battle against *The Bicycle Thief* that spring had revealed the dangers of excessive rigidity. The mockery in the press, the calls for Code reform, the defiance of theater owners in booking De Sica's picture without a Seal, all pointed toward a major new assault on the Production Code. In October, just two weeks before the riotous Directors Guild meeting, Breen learned that yet another large theater chain, the Skouras circuit in New York, had booked *The Bicycle Thief,* an event *Variety* called "the most significant break yet" in the Code system. The fact that Spyros Skouras, president of Twentieth Century–Fox, held a financial interest in the chain prompted new speculation about the commitment of the studios to the Code and caused Breen to anticipate "a terrific explosion hereabouts some day in the not-too-distant future." To defuse the situation, Breen, like the Hollywood liberals, fashioned a strategic withdrawal. His first small step backward came that same October when, confronted with two stubborn directors supported by two powerful studios, he eased off and in the process opened the Code to mature movies.

Though they were both over forty years old, William Wyler and Elia Kazan were in the vanguard of that new breed of Hollywood filmmakers—the American cousins of Rossellini and De Sica— who had long worried Breen. Independent, uncompromising, and fiercely committed to cinema as art form, Wyler and Kazan resented the Code-based impediments to moviemaking for adult audiences. "It's not the business of the motion picture industry to be the guardians of children," Wyler told *Variety*. "That's the job for parents." In summer 1950, as American forces rushed across the Pacific to hold the tiny perimeter at the southern tip of Korea, Wyler and Kazan sought to bring two compelling Broadway dramas, *Detective Story* and *A Streetcar Named Desire,* to the screen. Both tried to preserve the integrity and realism of the original sources and both ran headlong into Joe Breen. Like the dogfaces in Korea, though, Kazan and Wyler fought the adversary to a standstill. And while neither triumphed, both won enough concessions to claim partial victory.

The stage version of Sidney Kingsley's *Detective Story* opened in 1949 to strong reviews. Described as "grim and grotesque, touching and horrifying," it chronicled a busy eight-hour shift at a Lower Manhattan precinct house. Kingsley's thorough research (two years in a New York squad room), combined with the same "genius for detail" evident in his earlier *Dead End,* gave the play a "remarkably realistic" tone; the station house was dreary and dilapidated, the detectives sweated, grumbled about court delays, and grew frustrated with the "wacky complainants and befuddled minor offenders" who plagued their existence. Yet Kingsley had more in mind than a simple slice-of-life cop drama. He intended *Detective*

Story as commentary on "the danger inherent in men who are so convinced that their ends are just that they are troubled by no scruples and moved to no mercy." The central character, Detective James McLeod, can "smell evil," and his psychopathic righteousness, his inability to understand or forgive the failings of others, ultimately destroys him.

Detective Story included two Production Code taboos: abortion and the murder of a police officer. The primary target of McLeod's hatred is an abortionist whose illicit operations have killed several women. Despite McLeod's dogged pursuit, Dr. Kurt Schneider has consistently avoided prosecution through slick legal maneuvers and the bribery of key witnesses. As the play opens, McLeod seems finally to have compiled unshakable evidence based on the testimony of a disenchanted nurse and a girl hospitalized through Schneider's incompetence. But the girl dies, the nurse is bought off with a fur coat, and the case collapses. McLeod's uncontrollable hatred erupts in the back of a paddy wagon, where he beats Schneider senseless. The investigation of the outburst reveals that McLeod's wife had engaged in a premarital romp with a gangster that ended in an abortion by the very same doctor. McLeod knew nothing of the affair or the abortion, and the revelation sends him over the edge. Though he tries, he cannot forgive his wife. His all-consuming hatred turns on her, and she leaves him. With both his marriage and career destroyed, McLeod ponders the wages of hate. Kingsley ultimately saves his hero (and the audience) from excessive introspection through a sudden but artificial conclusion. In the final scenes, a desperately unbalanced four-time loser grabs a police revolver, holds the precinct hostage, and threatens to kill anyone who moves toward him. McLeod sees this as an opportunity almost heaven-sent, a way around his suffering and disgrace. In an obvious act of self-destruction, he walks directly into the prisoner's gun and his death.

Paramount acquired the rights to Kingsley's play shortly after it opened, and turned the property over to William Wyler, who had directed *Dead End*. Except for deafness in one ear, a painful souvenir of Navy service in World War II, Wyler had changed little since the earlier film. The small and fiercely driven director still abhorred compromise. As George Stevens observed, "Willy has this little demon inside him. It keeps telling him he has to be the very best there is." In 1950, Wyler could afford lofty ambitions. Though actresses like Olivia de Havilland found him "somber" and "painful" to work with, they loved the performances he somehow shaped. From *Dead End* through *Jezebel, The Little Foxes, Mrs. Miniver,* and *The Best Years of Our Lives,* his pictures won critical praise, large audiences, and two Oscars for best direction. In 1946, to gain greater control over his material, he and fellow veterans Stevens and Frank Capra formed Liberty Films, an independent production company. The experiment lasted only two years, but when Paramount bought Liberty, the deal guaranteed the three filmmakers much of their hard-won freedom.

Wyler selected *Detective Story* from among several properties the studio offered, partly because of his success with *Dead End,* partly because of the play's grit. Like many of his colleagues, he found Italian cinema fascinating and occasionally entertained guests at home with screenings of the most recent imports. *Detective Story* lacked the subtlety of *Open City* or *The Bicycle Thief,* yet the soiled and smoky atmosphere of the squad room, the curious collection of minor characters trapped in a claustrophobic environment, and most of all, the downbeat ending appealed to Wyler's instinct for realism. He had altered the ending of *The Best Years of Our Lives* to suit Goldwyn, changing what would have been an ambiguous close—with Dana Andrews, frustrated and disillusioned, wandering among the relics at the airfield—to a more positive finish with Andrews finding love and new hope. Wyler always felt the former ending superior, more true-to-life, but Goldwyn liked to see people smiling as they left the theater. As his own producer at Paramount, Wyler hoped to avoid such compromises.

Like the "bad cops" who had appealed to Nicholas Ray and Otto Preminger, whose *On Dangerous Ground* and *Where the Sidewalk Ends* had entered production, Detective McLeod also attracted Wyler. "He thinks he's all-knowing," Wyler told journalist Richard Dyer MacCann, "that's what's the matter with him. People ought to watch out when they start thinking they're all-knowing, especially people in authority." McLeod's blind self-righteousness, his compulsive lust to punish even the most minor offenders, smacked of the attitude of the right-wing red-hunters then plaguing the film community. An outspoken liberal, Wyler detested the House Un-American Activities Committee and in 1947 had joined with John Huston and others in forming the Committee for the First Amendment to fight the witch-hunts. But doing so left him vulnerable. Fortunately Paramount production head Y. Frank Freeman, a vigorous anti-Communist himself, always supported his prize-winning director. He told Wyler that when anyone called for his scalp, "I tell them you're just a bleeding heart, a do-gooder, a peace monger, in short a damn fool, but no commie." Though Wyler resented the defense, it seemed to work. Unlike many of his Hollywood friends, Wyler never encountered problems with the blacklisters.

Originally Wyler planned to compress Kingsley's play to heighten its realism. He hired Dashiell Hammett, known for his crisp flint-hard dialogue, to rewrite the drama, but the master of detective fiction quickly abandoned the project and Wyler turned it over to Robert Wyler (his brother) and Philip Yordan. The two eventually convinced the director to film the play with only minor alterations. Several long speeches in which Kingsley commented on the dangers of a police state were trimmed, but otherwise *Detective Story* went to Breen in June 1950 much as it was performed on Broadway.

Breen made it clear from the beginning that the central problem with the play was the element of abortion. Until Wyler resolved that matter, Breen would not even discuss the forbidden cop-killing at the end of the script. In a sense the arrangement of priorities was ironic. The murder of a police officer was specifically prohibited by the Code; abortion was not. That a 1930 document on film morals drafted by a Catholic lay leader and a priest would include no specific reference to abortion seems odd, but Quigley and Lord wrote only the philosophic rationale for movie censorship. Hays had not included abortion among the Particular Applications of the Production Code because abortion had not earned censorial attention in the 1920s. The absence of an abortion taboo caused Breen almost no problems during his initial decade as Code administrator. A topic so hush-hush attracted few producers, and on those few occasions when abortion appeared in a script—as it had in *Campus Wives, Rebecca, Kitty Foyle, Foundation Stone, Marriage Is a Private*

Affair, and *The World Is Ours*—Breen simply red-pencilled the reference, and without a ripple of protest the studio removed or glossed over it.

By the late 1940s, though, Breen swam in choppy waters. The softening of moral standards during the war and the rapid increase in illegitimate births that followed took some of the stigma from abortion, and the topic began to creep into popular magazines and public discussion. In this changed atmosphere Breen met increasing resistance. In April 1949, when he denied script approval to MGM's *The Doctor and the Girl,* the studio challenged the abortion taboo. Appealing directly to Eric Johnston, MGM claimed that since the Code failed to mention abortion, the topic should be classed with other "repellent subjects" like hangings, electrocutions, and surgical operations, subjects that were allowed if "treated within the careful limits of good taste." Breen fired a hurried letter to Johnston defending his position with arguments similar to those used nine months later against *The Bicycle Thief.* "We must strive for a uniform interpretation of the Code," he argued. Even though MGM might handle abortion tastefully, allowing the topic would create a precedent and complicate "our work in other pictures in which the same subject matter, *per se,* may be *questionable* or *unacceptable.*" Breen predicted that if Johnston approved the reference to abortion in *The Doctor and the Girl,* "within the next year—if only because the subject matter is 'new' and 'fresh'—we will have the subject of abortion injected into fifty pictures presented for our approval."

Johnston never felt comfortable with Joe Breen, never quite trusted this glad-handing Irishman on the West Coast. To Johnston, Breen was a holdover from the Hays regime and a bit too independent to be a good team player. In 1947, Johnston had attempted to ease Breen into retirement, sending a Quigley nominee, New York juvenile court judge Stephen S. Jackson, to join the Code staff as heir apparent. When Breen departed for an extended vacation in Jamaica, Jackson floundered and the studios rebelled, demanding the former Code director's return. Breen came back, stronger and louder than ever. After that, Johnston avoided Hollywood and treated the Code office as an appendix, an organ he could do without. Unwilling to dirty his hands with *The Doctor and the Girl,*

Johnston instructed Breen to work out the problem with the studio, and the result was a compromise in which MGM traded dialogue references to abortion for indirect hints that an illegal operation had been performed. The abortion element in *The Doctor and the Girl* attracted little comment when the film appeared in September 1949. The picture was "an exploitation natural" because of the topic, but while several reviewers noted the veiled reference to abortion, MGM resisted temptation and avoided advertising "the unforgivable sin."

The month following *The Doctor* compromise, Breen had applied the same standard to *Beyond the Forest*. Again, specific use of the word "abortion" was removed, but Bette Davis's trip to a "psychological counselor" told all but the kids in the front row that she intended to abort. The Warners release caught the full wrath of the Legion of Decency. Weak reviews combined with unseemly content made exhibitors skittish, and the Legion's "C" offered them an excuse to cancel contracts. "Every hour the 'C' rating stood," a studio executive told the Breen office, "Warners was losing playdates by the gross." Desperate studio executives asked Breen for help, so he dispatched Code staff member Jack Vizzard to act as intermediary with the Catholic fathers. Trained for the priesthood, Vizzard seemed an ideal agent, but he found the mood at Legion headquarters in New York one of "suppressed anger."

Executive director Father Patrick Masterson was miffed at Warners for producing this "sordid story" and equally distressed at Breen for having approved it. While the Legion objected to the "unrelieved evil" of the plot, it reserved its wrath for the abortion. Masterson was adamant: abortion should never be suggested on the screen. As with sex perversion and dope addiction (both specifically prohibited in the Code), any reference to the topic would "incite a morbid and dangerous curiosity which might very well lead to the desire for imitation." In other words, the Legion wanted the Code amended to prohibit any reference to abortion. In the meantime, Vizzard negotiated a series of deletions that changed the "psychological counselor" to an attorney, removed the suggestion of abortion, and lifted the Legion rating to a "B."

Breen had one eye that drooped. "He had a kind of leer eye," one associate recalled, "one wicked eye and one bright eye." The

wicked eye flashed whenever the Legion condemned a movie that he
had previously approved. While Breen resented the implicit criticism of his judgment, he also understood that motion picture self-
regulation worked best when the Legion and the Production Code
Administration applied the same standards. In this case, since he
agreed with the Legion's standard and had only modified a previously inflexible policy to suit his boss in New York, Breen could
find some comfort in the result. Seven months later, when the script
for *Detective Story* arrived on his desk, Breen offered no compromise. Paramount would not only have to strike all references to Dr.
Schneider's profession but, in addition, clearly identify his illegal
activities as something other than abortion.

Resentful of the "many rules in the code that prevented the
making of adult films," Wyler argued that Schneider's profession
and the wife's abortion were essential to Kingsley's play and could
not be cut without destroying the story. With no abortion, how
could McLeod's hatred of the criminal be transferred to his wife?
Breen understood the dilemma, and in the script conference that
followed offered a solution. Schneider could traffic in black market
babies; in dialogue Wyler could show that Schneider's illicit "baby
farm" was poorly run, and that several newborns had died as a
result of his negligence, among these Mary McLeod's illegitimate
child. Sixteen years of doctoring scripts to retain basic story elements yet eliminate Code violations left Breen supremely confident. He felt certain that his idea would be sufficient to carry the
story. (That "baby farms" could rationalize abortions apparently
escaped him.) A less assertive and independent director might have
accepted the proposal without demur, but not Willy Wyler. Distressed by Breen's inflexibility, he argued that *Detective Story* treated
a sensitive subject in a responsible manner. The screenplay neither
condoned nor justified abortion; it portrayed the abortionist as
utterly despicable, and consistently condemned his crime.
McLeod's wife, because she had turned to Schneider, endured
shame, lost her ability to bear children, and suffered the destruction
of her marriage. What could be more moral?

Breen never questioned Wyler's assertions. In fact, he agreed that
the presentation of abortion in *Detective Story* would be proper if the
Code allowed the presentation of abortion. But he also maintained

that some topics were so dangerous and so offensive they belonged
forever offscreen. It was simply a matter of protecting the impressionable members of the audience. "The evil of the abortion type of
murder is so heinous in its very nature," he told Johnston, hoping
for East Coast support, "that we best serve our audiences, especially the young and the adolescent, by making certain not to call it
to their attention."

With the abortion taboo threatening the integrity of the Kingsley
play, Wyler's frustrations spilled over in an interview with Thomas
Brady of the *New York Times*: "Certain subjects can't even be
discussed; it's as if they didn't exist. The play forcefully condemns
abortion and it is proper to insist on condemnation of crime in
films. But apparently we are not even to be permitted to condemn
in *Detective Story*. This is ludicrous." Wyler concluded his comments with a statement that might well have been voiced by any of
a dozen young Hollywood filmmakers tied to Breen's apron
strings: "The Code is old fashioned. It is fifteen years old, but
the company heads won't hear of amendments. Why not discuss
reality?"

Like Wyler, whose sentiments he shared, Elia Kazan was caught in
a frustrating standoff with Breen. The issue was rape. Tennessee
Williams' *A Streetcar Named Desire* opened on Broadway in December 1947, but despite critical praise, standing-room-only audiences, and a Pulitzer Prize, Hollywood showed little interest.
Fearful of a property with artistic pretensions and censorable content, the studios shied away until August 1949, when Wyler convinced Paramount to consider the play as a vehicle for Bette Davis.
Breen discouraged the project and Wyler moved on to *Detective
Story,* but the following month Charles Feldman, a successful talent
agent with higher aspirations, purchased the screen rights to *Streetcar* for a reported $350,000. Feldman and Williams then sought to
convince a reluctant Kazan, who had directed the play, to undertake
the screen version.

At forty-one, Kazan regarded himself as "the leading progressive
in the performing arts." Three years of coastal commuting had
brought him virtually every prize Broadway and Hollywood could

offer. *All My Sons, Death of a Salesman,* and *Streetcar* made him the most sought-after director in New York; a string of box office successes—*A Tree Grows in Brooklyn, Panic in the Streets, Gentleman's Agreement,* and *Pinky* (the second top-grossing film of 1949)—left studios bidding for his services. His two-year flirtation with communism in the mid-thirties was still secret, and his future seemed limitless. "I'd never be that high again," he later recalled. With John Steinbeck and Arthur Miller both preparing screenplays for him, Kazan first rejected Feldman's offer. He also lacked enthusiasm for the project. "It would be like marrying the same woman twice," he told Williams. "I don't think I can get it up for *Streetcar* again." But Williams needed that second wedding. In 1947, he had accused Irene Selznick (who produced *Streetcar* for the stage) of attempting to "[clean] up the play to protect the movie rights." Some weeks later, during a *Streetcar* tryout in New Haven, he had heard Louis Mayer recommend a new ending to insure "the audience would believe that the young couple would live happily ever after." Without a principled screen director behind the adaptation, Williams feared that the Hollywood barbarians would prostitute his *Streetcar,* would soften and simplify its complex message in order to appeal to a mass audience.

Visions of Stanley and Stella happily-ever-aftering in some blissful screen version of *Streetcar* brought Williams back to Kazan. He knew the director could be tough (Kazan sent his clothes out to be "cleaned and rumpled," Vivien Leigh said), and that toughness would protect his fragile play. Eventually Kazan signed, partly out of friendship for Williams, partly because of the $175,000 offer. Feldman then sold the entire package to Warners, which agreed to furnish half the purchase price and lease its facilities in return for distribution rights and a share of the profits, an arrangement that would soon be standard between the major studios and independent producers. As with most later agreements, the contract between Feldman and Warners required the producer to deliver a picture "entitled to receive a Production Code certificate."

Like Wyler on *Detective Story,* Kazan finally decided to "just shoot the play." He drew most of his actors from the Broadway cast and planned to adhere with few exceptions to Williams' powerful drama. Committed to screen realism, Kazan wanted to portray—

without compromise—the slow moral and mental collapse of Blanche DuBois. He also recognized that hard-boiled sex sold tickets. With *Streetcar,* art and sex could make a potent combination. As he informed Jack Warner later in the year, the drama contained two elements that would draw patrons: "1/ It is about the three Fs. 2/ It has class." And, he added, "What made it a Pulitzer Prize winner—the poetry—must be kept in, untouched so that it will appeal to those who don't want to admit that they are interested in the moist seat department. (Everybody, of course, is!)"

Williams' screenplay offered few concessions to the Production Code. While eliminating some of the drama's harsh language, it retained three elements that Breen found unacceptable: "an inference of sex perversion" (Blanche's husband, a homosexual and a suicide), "an inference of a type of nymphomania" (Blanche's fondness for young boys), and a rape "both justified and unpunished."

At the end of April 1950, Warner executives and Charles Feldman met with Jack Vizzard and Geoff Shurlock to consider solutions. The first two problems were resolved with dispatch. References to the young husband would be altered to remove all hints of homosexuality, while Blanche's promiscuity, which contained "an erotic flavor that seems to verge on perversion," would be explained as a product of her search "for romance and security, and not for gross sex." The rape proved more difficult. To Williams, Stanley's rape of Blanche contained the "pivotal, integral truth in the play." Without it, he later told Breen, "the play loses its meaning, which is the ravishment of the tender, the sensitive, the delicate, by the savage and brutal forces of modern society." Knowing how Williams felt, Feldman defended the rape, but Shurlock and Vizzard rejected his plea. After several hours the conferees settled on three possible options. In the first, which Feldman preferred, the violent confrontation remained; in a subsequent scene, when Blanche accused Stanley of rape, he denied it and successfully proved his innocence. In the second, the confrontation was dropped, and a demented Blanche only imagined that she had been raped. In the third, favored by Shurlock and Vizzard, Stanley contemplated rape but backed off when he saw that Blanche had lost touch with reality.

Kazan accepted the first two parts of the compromise. In fact, he later concluded that eliminating the homosexuality actually strengthened the story. Or so he told Breen. "I wouldn't put the homosexuality back in the picture if the code had been revised last night and it was now permissible. I don't want it. I prefer debility and weakness over any kind of suggestion of perversion." He was also pleased by the leeway allowed on Blanche's promiscuity. While the Breen boys had demanded minor editing to soften the portrait, Kazan was surprised they required no more. Later he would praise the Code staff for helping work out the problem of how to mask Blanche's past from children yet show adult moviegoers that she "was acquainted with every traveling salesman from Tallahassee to Texarkana."

Kazan was not happy about the Breen office slant on the rape, though. Stanley and Blanche—and Kazan—had had that "date" (as Stanley called it) "from the beginning." It provided the climactic confrontation that destroyed Blanche, and without it, the play lost direction and meaning. Kazan demanded a face-to-face meeting with Joe Breen.

In late May, Kazan, Feldman, Breen, and Jack Warner hashed out the rape in Warner's lush trophy room. Unlike many Code meetings, this one contained no levity. Breen and Kazan were dead serious. And as he listened to Kazan, Breen had an unpleasant sense of déjà vu. Kazan was obviously sincere about artistic integrity, the need for screen realism, and so on; he was also deeply committed to a faithful translation of the play. The Code was the Code, however. Breen was polite but firm: there would be no rape.

No less principled, Kazan announced his withdrawal from the project. Feldman paled: "You mean to say that if the 'rape' is not in, you will not do the picture?" Kazan nodded, so Feldman and Warner worked on Breen. Both knew that if Kazan left, so would Williams; without either, no *Streetcar*. Eventually Breen relented. Though Kazan's talent and Feldman's desperation contributed to his decision, he was probably more motivated by the fear that Warners would make the film without a Seal, market it as an American classic, and lure even more theater chains than *The Bicycle Thief* had. Kazan could keep the rape if "done by suggestion and delicacy." In return the director would change the ending to provide retribution and "compensating moral values"; that meant

"Stanley would be 'punished' and that punishment would be in terms of the loss of his wife's love."

Williams' play had ended with Blanche taken away to an asylum and Stanley and Stella reunited on the porch steps. She "sobs with inhuman abandon" at the loss of her sister. He kneels beside her and soothes her while "his fingers find the opening of her blouse." The fondle had been cut from an early screenplay draft; now Kazan and Williams had to find a realistic and powerful alternative to the reunion. Williams eventually added just two lines. The sobbing Stella looks down at her baby and whispers: "We're not going back in there. Not this time. We're never going back. Never, never. . . ." The screenplay ends with Stanley calling after his wife as she mounts the stairs toward a friend's apartment. This was the kind of strong ambiguity that Breen office pressure sometimes inspired, an ambiguity that allowed careful viewers to see that Stella's "was just an emotional outburst of the moment."

But the late-May accord soon broke down. Either Breen had second thoughts or Kazan misread the original understanding, because when Feldman submitted a revised script in July, Breen once again insisted that the producer cut the rape. Feldman quickly sought a new compromise. Instead of the rape, Stanley might hit Blanche, and thus cause her mental collapse. Breen liked the idea; Kazan vetoed it. By late August, the two sides were still at an impasse. Williams interceded with a long letter to Breen that pleaded for retention of the rape and rehearsed the "great concessions" Kazan and the playwright had already made "to attitudes which we thought were narrow." They had cooperated with Breen on every occasion, had even shown deference when they thought his judgment unwise. "But now we are fighting for what we think is the heart of the play, and when we have our backs against the wall—if we are forced into that position—none of us is going to throw in the towel!"

Kazan shared Williams' determination but chose not to press Breen, at least not yet. In May, he had gained the measure of the man. He knew that if he forced the issue, Breen might harden. But if he stalled, Breen might yet be finessed. Throughout, Kazan was confident that he could shoot the scene with the "suggestion and delicacy" he had promised in May and that Breen would come around. In other words, Kazan practiced discreet avoidance. He ignored Breen's demands for script changes and acted as though no problem existed.

The strategy worked. As Kazan explained to the *Los Angeles Times,* he shot the scene "in such a way that grownups will know what happened," while children would sense only that Stanley "did the woman some wrong." Breen approved the scene without comment, but still had reservations. Kazan told Warners the following month that Breen "begged me to see to it . . . . that your exploitation people kept the ads within the bounds of good taste. I think Joe felt that he was letting us down very easy as far as the seal requirements went, and didn't want to be put further on the spot by the ads which might . . . be selling the rape scene."

Breen did let Kazan down easy. With the Code system breached by *The Bicycle Thief* and filmmakers desperately searching for new subjects to reawaken audience interest, Breen could not afford to provoke a major studio. Had he rejected *Streetcar,* Warners would probably have appealed the ruling to the Association board. A new and more intense round of Code bashing in Hollywood would ensue. Kazan's subtle handling of the rape gave Breen an out. He could approve screen content that he had absolutely forbidden only weeks before and avoid what he feared would be a major Code confrontation.

Streetcar marked a turning point. Geoffrey Shurlock, Breen's second-in-command, later observed: "For the first time we were confronted with a picture that was obviously not family entertainment. Before then we had considered *Anna Karenina* a big deal. *Streetcar* broke the barrier." The crack in the Code ultimately proved wide enough to allow *Detective Story* through as well.

William Wyler had a reputation in the industry as a "lousy perfectionist!" His "Do it one more time," repeated again and again, brought many performers to the edge of exasperation. After nineteen takes of a scene in *Wuthering Heights,* Laurence Olivier exploded, "Good God, man, what do you want?" The tiny director replied: "I want you to be better." Behind the relentless demands, though, lay a quiet savvy and a sense of when to yield. Wyler had been angered by Breen's unwillingness to allow the element of abortion in *Detective Story*. Initially, he sought Paramount's support for an appeal to the Association board, but when the studio refused, Wyler reworked the screenplay. He was determined to convey as much of Kingsley's realistic detail as possible, but he agreed to play Breen's game. By October, he too had adopted a strategy. He would follow the pattern of *The Doctor and the Girl* and hope that Breen would demand no more. Removing all use of the words "abortion" and "abortionist" from the script, he added a single line of dialogue that referred to Schneider's "baby-farm grist mill." The screenplay would hint that Schneider had performed illegal operations, but Wyler hoped that the addition of the "baby-farm" element would sufficiently blur the doctor's occupation to satisfy— and perhaps even flatter—Breen, who had made the suggestion months before.

Remarkably, Breen was content. When he read the script in early November, just after having approved the rape scene in *Streetcar*, he chose to ignore veiled references to Schneider's earlier operations as well as McLeod's gory description of the doctor's kitchen: "It looks like a place where they slaughter chickens." Breen instructed Wyler to remove one line indicating that McLeod's wife had been rendered infertile by Schneider, but otherwise allowed the changes to stand.

Breen's willingness to make concessions extended into *Detective Story*'s remaining problem, the cop-killing. In 1936, as part of an effort to discourage gangland shoot-out scenes, Breen had personally written the Code amendment that forbade cop-killing. But McLeod's death was entirely different, and Breen wanted to "save it." He informed Luigi Luraschi, Production Code liaison at Paramount, that the murder of McLeod at the end of the play violated the "letter of the Code," but not its "spirit or intent," and he promised to "present a special appeal" to the board asking for "specific authorization" to approve the death scene. Since the board resisted special exemptions, the East Coast staff advised Breen to draft a Code amendment that would give him authority to determine when the murder of a police officer should or should not be allowed. Breen quickly settled on adding a simple clause to the statement prohibiting the murder of law-enforcement officials: "unless such scenes are absolutely necessary to the plot."

Former Postmaster General
Will H. Hays (1926).

Will Hays and the founders of the Motion Picture Producers and Distributors of
America (*from left*): E. W. Hammons, J. D. Williams, Winfield Sheehan, Cortland
Smith, Carl Laemmle, Rufus Cole, William E. Atkinson, Hays, Robert H.
Cochrane, Samuel Goldwyn, Marcus Loew, Adolph Zukor, William Fox, Lewis
Selznick, Myron Selznick.

Before Production Code enforcement, pictures such as *Red Dust* (1932) posed enormous problems. The prostitute Vantine (Jean Harlow) wore kimonos that showed more than they covered, and told the plantation boys (Tully Marshall, Donald Crisp, Clark Gable) she was "not used to sleeping nights."

"Lust Trapped Me"; "Desire Ruined Me"; "I'm a Shame-Drenched Sinner"—screamed the ads for *The Story of Temple Drake,* one of a number of films made in 1933 that led to Production Code enforcement. *From left:* Florence Eldridge, Miriam Hopkins, and Jack La Rue.

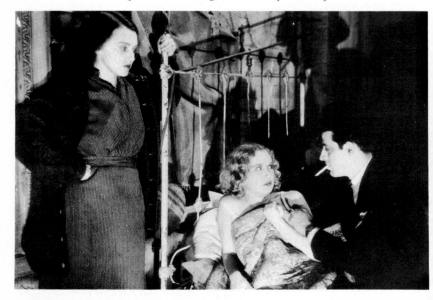

Cary Grant and Mae West in *She Done Him Wrong*.
CUMMINGS: Haven't you ever met a man that could make you happy?
LADY LOU: Sure. Lots o' times.

Russell Hopton and Mae
West in *I'm No Angel*. The
Barker introduces Tira the
Incomparable, "the girl
who discovered you don't
have to have feet to be a
dancer."

When he read the *Dead End* treatment and noted the East River swim scenes, Production Code director Joe Breen ordered Samuel Goldwyn to dress the kids in pants and to underplay the "garbage floating in the river, into which the boys jump for a swim." Goldwyn fought for swimsuits but volunteered to launder the trash. According to the *New York Times,* to "associate garbage, even of an aristocratic nature, with a Goldwyn epic was unthinkable."

Director William Wyler (*seated*) with Humphrey Bogart, Claire Trevor, and Allen Jenkins on the set of *Dead End.* Although censors in Finland, Czechoslovakia, and Greece rejected the picture, Breen used contacts abroad to help Goldwyn ease *Dead End* past major European censor boards.

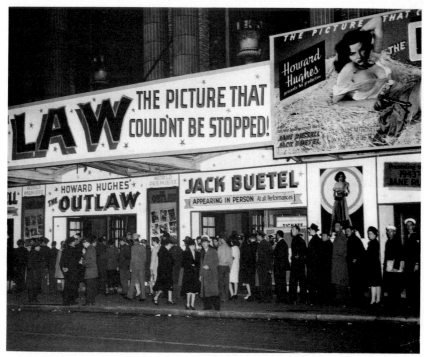

The premiere of *The Outlaw,* San Francisco, February 1943. This billboard and others like it throughout the city prompted local police to prepare warrants for the arrest of both Howard Hughes and publicity chief Russell Birdwell. Hughes ordered the billboards removed.

"How would you like to tussle with Russell?"

"It is not unlikely that we will have considerable difficulty with Metro if and when they put [*The Postman Always Rings Twice*] into production," Breen wrote Hays in 1934, "and we may need your help in the battle which is sure to ensue." MGM made the picture eleven years later, starring John Garfield and Lana Turner, in the more liberal postwar era.

Joe Breen had one face for the camera, another for the moguls, "a cowardly lot" who needed someone to "raise hell with them."

In 1950 Breen still wore a vest with chain and keys suspended from the pocket. Less old-fashioned, especially about movie mores, was Breen's successor, the urbane Geoff Shurlock (*left*).

The gates of the bordello, where Antonio (Lamberto Maggiorani, *left center*) confronts the pathetic bicycle thief.

Detective McLeod (Kirk Douglas) learns the truth about his wife's (Eleanor Parker) premarital affair and abortion.

The murder/suicide in *Detective Story* prompted Breen to press for the Code amendment that erased a twelve-year ban of cop-killing on screen. *From left:* William Bendix, Kirk Douglas, Joseph Wiseman.

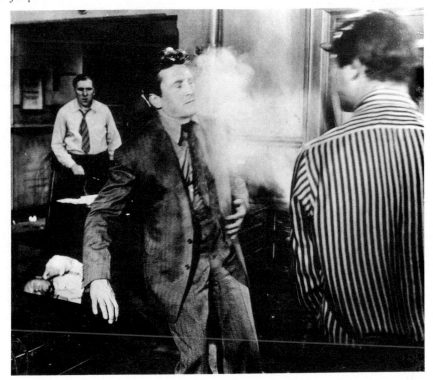

"Ravishment of the tender." Marlon Brando as predator, Vivien Leigh as victim in *A Streetcar Named Desire*.

"Will you try to seduce me?" Maggie McNamara asks William Holden in *The Moon Is Blue*, as Gregory Ratoff drives imperturbably on.

Maggie McNamara and Otto Preminger on the set of *The Moon Is Blue*.

Jane Russell "Looking for Trouble" in *The French Line*. The costumes and certain "indecent movements" in the dance numbers earned this Howard Hughes picture a Production Code office ban.

Seated in the Beverly Boulevard projection room (circa 1957) are Production Code staff members Al Van Schmus and Harry Zehner (*front row*); Milton Hodenfield, PCA Director Geoff Shurlock, and Morris Murphy (*second row*); Eugene Dougherty, Jack Vizzard, and M. A. J. Healy (*back row*). Laura Greenhouse (*seated at the desk*) charted the number of kisses and killings, lawyers and doctors, bedroom scenes and mental diseases in the three features she screened each day.

The Catholic Legion of Decency demanded an "over 18" tag line in the advertisements for *Lolita*, but many exhibitors admitted youths to theaters.

Once Professor Humbert (James Mason) settles down with Lolita (Sue Lyon) and enrolls her in school, he tells her to shun "nasty-minded boys."

Who's Afraid of Virginia Woolf violated Section V of the Production Code: "Pointed profanity . . . or every other profane or vulgar expression however used, is forbidden." Screenwriter Ernest Lehman used "gah damn" and "for cry sake" in early drafts, then, along with Jack Warner and director Mike Nichols, removed the gloves and challenged the Production Code Administration. *From left:* George Segal, Elizabeth Taylor, and Richard Burton.

GEORGE: "Who's afraid of Virginia Woolf?"
MARTHA: I am, George. I am.

The enormous success of such films as *Bonnie and Clyde* and *The Graduate* led the American press to speak of a "film generation," one whose tolerance for screen violence and screen sex helped speed the death of Production Code mores. *From left:* Michael J. Pollard, Faye Dunaway, and Warren Beatty in *Bonnie and Clyde*.

Anne Bancroft and Dustin Hoffman in *The Graduate*.

"It invades intimacies. It transgresses common candor," Production Code staff members told *Blow Up* director Michelangelo Antonioni. Here, Thomas, the fashion photographer (David Hemmings), straddles model Verushka.

Over the years, the "R" (Restricted) rating expanded to admit content once deemed taboo. "If this is an R," *Variety* wrote of 1980's *Cruising* (starring Al Pacino, *center*), "then the only X left is actual hardcore."

The amendment was to be presented to the board on March 27, 1951, along with two other proposed changes: one added abortion to the list of forbidden subjects, and a second, requested by the Federal Narcotics Bureau, banned the depiction of drug use or drug traffic. Breen also wanted a fourth amendment to clarify the Code section on suicide. In script negotiations on *Detective Story,* he had chosen not to raise the fact that McLeod's final self-destructive act could easily be read as a suicide. Nonetheless, the implication was obvious and it brought Breen's attention to the "hazy and indefinite" wording of an important 1938 Code revision: "suicide, as a solution of problems occurring in the development of screen drama, is to be discouraged as morally questionable and as bad theatre." Breen opted to consider McLeod's death a murder. Yet the prospect of similar scenes in the future caused him to seek an amendment noting that suicide "should never be justified, glorified, or used to defeat the due processes of law."

Breen's efforts to "save" *Detective Story* illustrate how far he had moved since *The Bicycle Thief.* Less than a year before, his adherence to precedent and fear of Code conspirators had led him to deny the Seal to a film classic over two innocuous scenes. Now he was pressing the Association board for two significant amendments to the Code. His conversion was far from complete: Breen would never become an advocate of screen realism or adult movies. But he had learned an important lesson in 1950. With Hollywood's audience vanishing, studio executives hungry, and exhibitors willing to screen *The Bicycle Thief* even without the Seal, Breen was forced to see the virtue of pliancy.

The four amendments sailed unopposed through the March 1951 board meeting, and with the absolute ban on cop-killing lifted, Breen granted final script approval for *Detective Story.* As Wyler began rehearsals, Kazan sampled the audience reaction cards from the first previews of *Streetcar.* Most were positive, but to appease Warner executives who felt the picture dragged, he reedited, gained Breen's approval of the final print, and went to Mexico to start his next project, Twentieth Century–Fox's *Viva Zapata!*

Meanwhile, the mood in Hollywood turned ugly. On March 21, the House Un-American Activities Committee opened its hearings on Communist infiltration of the motion picture industry, and plunged the movie colony in fear. Actors Howard Da Silva and Gale Sondergaard took the Fifth at the opening session; Larry Parks, star of *The Jolson Story,* admitted past membership in the Communist Party and, in a vain effort to save his reputation and career, named his comrades. As the parade of witnesses continued, Hollywood watering holes buzzed with speculation about what names would appear on the Committee's next list of subpoenas. Even worse, the first-quarter profit figures had just been released. At Fox, profits were down fifty percent and studio executives were being asked to accept drastic pay cuts. Zanuck was furious (he would soon resign over the flap), and Kazan worried that *Zapata* might be scrapped.

On his first day back from Mexico, lunching with Jason Joy and Geoff Shurlock in the Fox commissary, Kazan picked up another bit of unsettling news—*Streetcar* was in trouble. The Legion of Decency had threatened to condemn the feature and Warners had postponed its opening. For days Kazan sought an audience with Jack Warner to find out what was happening, only to be met with delays and evasions. Then he learned that the studio had secretly dispatched *Streetcar*'s editor, David Weisbart, to New York. That meant cuts. "I am more disturbed than I can possibly tell you," he wrote Warner's chief assistant. "I don't want any meddling by these people into the guts of my picture." Kazan was doubly distressed that the studio had once again borrowed Jack Vizzard to act as go-between. "He is certainly the most conservative and squeamish of Joe Breen's people," he complained. "The person representing us with the Legion of Decency should have a hearty respect for our picture. In a personal conversation with me, Vizzard characterized *Streetcar* as 'sordid and morbid.' I would say that he was not the best person to defend it."

Kazan knew that by sending Weisbart and Vizzard to New York, the studio had announced its willingness "to do anything necessary to knuckle under" to the Legion. Having invested $1.8 million in a feature of questionable audience appeal, Warners could hardly ignore a Legion "C." The Church had only recently demonstrated its considerable powers. In December 1950, when the Paris Theatre in New York showed Rossellini's *The Miracle* (another Burstyn import), the Legion had responded instantly. Catholic staffers circulated a three-page memorandum calling the film "a blasphemous and sacrilegious mockery of a most sacred event, the conception and birth of Jesus Christ." When Francis Cardinal Spellman demanded a boycott, the Catholic War Veterans organized a rotating force of one thousand pickets to parade in front of the theater, and local priests stood prominently in the lobby to discourage wayward parishioners. City officials also heeded the prelate's call. Commissioner Edward T. McCaffrey revoked the theater's license; when Burstyn obtained a court injunction to allow continued screenings, the fire department suddenly found the Paris in violation of safety codes. The intimidation, which included two bomb scares, eventually spread to Queens, where the Knights of Columbus established a picket line at an independent theater showing *The Bicycle Thief.* Though the local commander justified the action on the grounds that De Sica's film "glorified a thief," the obvious target was Burstyn. New York film critics also felt the Church's sting. Having selected *Ways of Love* (the trilogy that included *The Miracle*) as best foreign film of 1950, they planned an elaborate awards ceremony at Radio City, but when the theater manager received a phone call threatening a Catholic boycott, the critics were forced to move the gala elsewhere.

In the summer of 1951, as Burstyn struggled to show *The Miracle,* Hollywood could see only the awesome consequences of defying the Church. The fear of the pulpit brought timid Warners officials and Jack Vizzard to Manhattan to negotiate cuts in *A Streetcar Named Desire.* They found the Legion in no mood for compromise. Father Masterson had already concluded that simple alterations could never raise *Streetcar* out of the "Condemned" slot. "From the moment the word 'DESIRE' is seen on the streetcar," he told a Warners representative, "the entire tone of the picture is 'desire' (physical desire)." When Vizzard's arguments failed to move Masterson, the studio turned in desperation to a second intermediary, Martin Quigley.

Vizzard accompanied Quigley when the latter first viewed *Streetcar* and described his reaction as they left the projection room.

His face wore the ashen look of a man who had seen IT. He flicked his dull agate eyes at me and painfully drew a cigarette from a silver case, while he let words and emotions roll through his mind. When he had finally fitted the cigarette into a long holder, he lit it, inhaled with slow deliberation, and uttered his verdict. 'Jack,' he declared, 'I tell you, this fellow Kazan is the type who will one day blow his brains out.'

Having promised Warners every effort to clear *Streetcar,* however, Quigley pressed on. After several additional screenings and Legion conferences, he settled on a dozen cuts that could induce the Catholics to rate the picture "B." One required elimination of close-ups of Stella's face as, after a quarrel, she descends a stairway toward Stanley. Kazan had alternated close and medium shots "to show Stella's conflicting revulsion and attraction to her husband," but Quigley and the Legion concluded that the shots made their relationship "too carnal." Another removed Stanley's line just before the attack on Blanche: "You know, you might not be bad to interfere with." Apparently designed to lessen the suggestion of rape, the cut particularly irritated Kazan because it eliminated "the clear implication that only here, for the first time, does Stanley have any idea of harming the girl. This obviously changes the interpretation of the character, but how it serves the cause of morality is obscure to me."

Kazan attempted to convince Quigley, and then Warners, that the cuts were wrong-headed and weakened the film, but to no avail. "The plain fact was—and I had to recognize it—the picture had been taken away from me, secretly, skillfully, without a raised voice." The film he had "worked like a demon" on, and fought Breen so hard to preserve, had been devoured "by the gluttonous Pope of Fiftieth Street," and there had been nothing he could do to prevent it. An embittered Kazan later told the *New York Times'* Murray Schumach:

Warners just wanted a seal. They didn't give a damn about the beauty or artistic value of the picture. To them it was just a piece of entertainment. It was business, not art. They wanted to get the entire family to see the picture. They didn't want anything in the picture that might keep *any one* away. At the same time they wanted it to be dirty enough to pull people in. The whole business was rather an outrage.

A Streetcar Named Desire and *Detective Story* opened later that fall. Critics found both impressive, both triumphs of adult drama. Many classed the two with George Stevens' *A Place in the Sun* and Billy Wilder's *Sunset Boulevard* as heralding a new era of mature entertainment at the movies; a few even directed praise at the Production Code agency. "Joseph Breen has eased up to give film audiences a truer picture of life via the screen," Boston *Evening American* observed. *Holiday* praised *Streetcar*'s "high quality and unabashed honesty," and expressed surprise that "the nympho-maniac had not been changed into an alcoholic or a shoplifter [and that] the crucial rape incident retains its importance." However disappointed Breen was that most reviewers of *Detective Story* still referred to Dr. Schneider as an abortionist, he had to be pleased with the general reception accorded both films. He had let down the barriers slightly and the response was positive.

Even the Young Turks, the Mankiewicz crew, seemed happy with the more liberal Breen. When Kazan went public with the story of Quigley and the Legion of Decency, he cast Breen as the filmmaker's friend. In an interview shortly after the Legion con-frontation, he called Breen "a hell of an understanding, decent guy," and told Philip Scheuer of the *Los Angeles Times* that "I'm just tickled he's in the business." Wyler also praised Breen and admitted that *Detective Story* could never have been made had the Code been applied blindly. The two directors would meet Breen on their next pictures, which made them especially eager to reinforce his toler-ance and court his goodwill. While flattery may have been part of the intent, Kazan and Wyler—and Hollywood—recognized that Breen had taken an important step. Despite the climate of fear in the movie capital, despite an emerging blacklist and congressional red-hunts, Breen had quietly loosened the Code. He might have chosen this moment to come down hard on Hollywood liberals. Their social realism often conveyed a powerful indictment of American society that was decidedly unwelcome in the early years of the Cold War. To send such images abroad may have irked Breen, but, as Stanley Kramer recalled, "everything—as long as it was inter-pretation—was negotiable." Even Jack Warner, who had suspected Breen of using Code rules to "cloak the real arguments" against *To the Victor* and *Key Largo,* two late-forties pictures with political implications, could not charge Breen as an ideologue. When approached by an FBI representative about Hollywood anticommunism, Breen was "courteous" but insistent that "he had nothing to do with the situation and further that the motion picture studio executives were the ones who directed the policies of the Association of Motion Picture Producers, Incorporated."

Breen welcomed the praise from Kazan and Wyler. But between such aggressive directors constantly urging greater latitude and the Legion of Decency peering ever more intently over his shoulder, he was aging fast. The weakening of Code compliance on *The Bicycle Thief,* as well as the struggles over *Detective Story* and *Streetcar,* had sapped his vitality and carried his thoughts to retirement. Barely a month before Kazan's comments, Ivan Spear had suggested in *Box Office* that Breen had relaxed Code taboos to preserve the Production Code Administration's "lush honorariums." Normally such a charge would have brought a scorching response, but in this case Breen simply clipped the item from the paper and filed it. In November, he felt better and decided that Christmas in Spain might restore his energy. The trip was cut short when his health failed again. Rushed back to Presbyterian Hospital in Los Angeles, Breen underwent surgery that removed a large section of lung. He bounced back rapidly but thereafter conserved his energy for only the toughest cases, two of them just ahead.

9

The Moon Is Blue

AND

The French Line

THE 1956 CHRISTMAS issue of *Life* featured a portrait of the ideal American woman. A thirty-two-year-old suburban housewife and mother of four, she cooked well, cleaned house better, and was "pretty and popular." Her weekly round of activities included club and PTA meetings, ceramics classes, choir practice, and church on Sunday. She dieted and exercised "to keep her size 12 figure," and she dressed conservatively; in public, she always wore a girdle. She was all that was wholesome in that most wholesome of decades.

The *Life* ideal expressed the desire for feminine domesticity and family togetherness that helped define the American 1950s. After reaching a peak in 1946, the divorce rate tumbled; marriage and birthrates soared. "Going steady" replaced "playing the field" as teenagers searched for the perfect relationships they found at home. To be single—especially to be single and happy—brought wary glances. *Modern Woman: The Lost Sex,* a 1947 best-seller by two psychologists, suggested that "bachelors of more than thirty, unless deficient, should be encouraged to undergo psychotherapy," and spinsters should be barred from teaching because of "emotional incompetence." Marriage was man and woman's natural state, the only condition that allowed for personal fulfillment and social harmony.

"Fitting in" was the leitmotif of the fifties, a decade of joining.

"The family that prays together, stays together" became so famous an expression that it was parodied in *Francis Goes to West Point*: "Among us mules," Francis drawls, "a family that stays together—brays together." (Breen predicted that audiences would be offended, but let the mule speak.) The rewards of domesticity were all that Depression America had longed for: the ranch-style home in the suburbs, the station wagon to haul the kids, television, air conditioning, frozen foods, Little League baseball, chlorophyll toothpaste. Concurrently, however, another vision of American womanhood was being created in the erotica of the 1950s. The nude calendars on the back wall of the corner gas station, partially hidden behind the greasy hoists and oil barrels; the French postcards and dog-eared copies of *I, the Jury*; the flickering "stag movies"—each provided a rush of excitement, whether from sexual arousal or contact with the forbidden.

In December 1953, Hugh Hefner introduced America to yet another image of womanhood. The *Playboy* "Sweetheart of the Month" (soon to be called "Playmate") was Marilyn Monroe. Nude on a red velvet drape, she conveyed an honest and near-innocent sexuality absent from the *Life* portrait. Marilyn was not the Norman Rockwell woman but the Norman Mailer woman, the "sweet angel of sex," the symbol of "prurience that tweaked America in those more innocent times." *Playboy* tamed the erotica of the Texaco station and the lumberyard, made it glossy, sophisticated, almost respectable—only a jot more evocative than the sexy come-ons used to sell toothpaste and after-shave in the *Saturday Evening Post*. One person was not buying, though, and his sales resistance made 1953 yet another year of turmoil and challenge.

BREEN OFFICE LOSING POWER, *Variety* shouted. The lead paragraph below the March 1953 headline made an even more startling comment: "After 19 years of rigid self-regulation, the film industry apparently is ready to drop the Production Code Authority. No announcement has been made . . . but there are definite signs that the industry feels the Code has outlived its usefulness." The fact that Otto Preminger planned to release *The Moon Is Blue* with or without the Seal had prompted the story. *Variety* reporter Mike Kaplan called the challenge to Breen a major "turning point" in Hollywood history; should *Moon Is Blue* prosper without the Code

Seal, others would adopt the Preminger model and the Breen office might "not live to see its official 20th birthday, July 15, 1954."

While the story may have soured the morning coffee for Breen, it was hardly news. The weathered Irishman understood better than anyone in the industry just how vulnerable the Code system had become. Less than a year earlier, in the famous *Miracle* case, Joe Burstyn and his lawyer, Ephraim London, had convinced the Supreme Court that motion pictures had earned the same protections as other media under the First and Fourteenth Amendments. While the Court stopped short of prohibiting state censorship altogether, the ruling nonetheless curbed the authority of the local boards. Hollywood producers hailed the decision as triumph, as long-overdue recognition of the movies as a form of communication. The view from Production Code headquarters on Beverly Boulevard was less sunny. Calling the case "Burstyn's latest attempt to stir up trouble," Breen predicted that it would revitalize local censors and complicate Production Code enforcement.

Even worse from Breen's perspective, the 1948 *Paramount* ruling that divorced production from distribution and exhibition now neared completion. RKO, Twentieth Century–Fox, Paramount, and Warners had finally—and grudgingly—complied with the decree; only Loew's continued to resist selling its theaters. The newly independent chains owned over seventy-five percent of the nation's downtown first-run theaters; these ornate movie palaces generated over forty percent of all domestic film rentals and, because smaller chains and locally owned neighborhood theaters counted on the publicity splash from the larger theaters, also shaped the booking choices of all other exhibitors. So powerful were the chains that unless an independent filmmaker could guarantee access to one of them, he could not easily secure production front money.

The circuits had been free to show unapproved features since 1942, when, thanks to Justice Department pressure, the Motion Picture Association had relaxed the binding provisions of the Code. The change was hardly noticeable, though. The Association swapped the official sanctions for a "gentleman's agreement," and the theaters continued to run Code-approved features exclusively. The *Paramount* ruling not only canceled the sweetheart deal but eliminated all studio coercion in the selection of films. Breen fretted about the consequences. Inertia, the looming presence of the Legion of Decency, and the memory of outraged pickets and boycotts caused most exhibitors to avoid pictures that ventured beyond the manners and mores of the Code. Yet the circuit bookings of *The Bicycle Thief,* which had wounded Production Code enforcement and shaken Breen, could not be dismissed as an aberrance. To protect the Code, Breen would have to meet the producers more than halfway.

In early 1953, Breen appeared almost confident about the future. He had approved such serious adult drama as *Carrie, Moulin Rouge,* and *Come Back, Little Sheba,* and despite a candor that the "compensating moral values" could not blunt, the puritan watchdogs had never barked. Perhaps they were lying catatonic before the television screen or clipping backyard barbecue recipes from *Sunset.* Even *From Here to Eternity* escaped censure. James Jones' sensational novel contained so much potentially censorable material that few in the industry believed it could ever become a motion picture. Aside from the extensive profanity, it included excessive brutality, an adulterous relationship between the two principal leads, and a love affair between a soldier and a brothel prostitute. Screenwriter Daniel Taradash was a seasoned veteran of the Production Code wars. Aware that Breen had been charged to insure the balance of freedom and control, Taradash retained much of Jones' gritty dialogue but tossed away the profanity and muted the brutality. He made Jones' brothel (the "New Congress Club") "a sort of primitive U.S.O." and the prostitute a "B-Girl." The adultery between Sergeant Warden and the Captain's wife challenged both the Production Code office and Taradash. Breen demanded "a strong voice for morality by which their immoral relationship can be denounced," but when Taradash modified the script to emphasize the Captain's cruelty and infidelity, the Code director softened his stand. He settled for the addition of one line: in the parting scene, the wife expresses regret for their adultery.

It took six months to work through the problems on *From Here to Eternity,* and much of the power and honesty of the novel were lost in the attempt to please both Joe Breen and the United States Army, which also expected virtue to triumph. But the effort rewarded Columbia, Taradash, and Joe Breen. The reviews praised the studio for daring to film the novel, Taradash for capturing its spirit, and the Code office for passing the picture. Even Martin Quigley cheered. In a signed editorial entitled "Well Done," he cited *Eternity* as proof "that given sufficient ability and good will, a producer is able to bring to the screen the best in the available material without outraging the sense of decency of an audience."

Producers who exploited sex on-screen knew enough to placate both Breen and the Catholics. Of the almost one hundred films on the Legion of Decency "Condemned" list in February 1953, none had been produced or distributed by a Hollywood studio. As one filmmaker told *Variety,* "We've found the way to get across an interesting idea involving Marilyn Monroe or Jane Russell, but without being boldly indecent about it." But the Legion figure alone told Breen that the pressures were building, that with the independents and the foreign directors producing "C" pictures, the period of calm was only temporary. Weekly film attendance had dropped nearly fifty percent from the halcyon days of 1946, and it was just a matter of time before someone decided to produce a "boldly indecent" feature and bypass the Production Code.

Otto Preminger looked more the Viennese aristocrat than the Hollywood rebel. Six feet tall and solid, Preminger saw the world through sad, passive eyes that were weary beyond his forty-eight years. He had played character roles—the Nazis of *The Pied Piper, Margin for Error,* and *Stalag 17* seemed his forte—but the movie colony knew him as the autocrat of the set. A favored director at Twentieth Century–Fox, he could "mangle the muse for the sake of a shooting schedule," and he could terrorize young actors. "He shouts even louder than Goldwyn," David Niven remembered, "and can be very sarcastic." He was also astute. Sensing that divorcement created broad new opportunities for independent production, Preminger renegotiated his five-year contract with Fox in 1951, accepting half pay in return for six months' annual freedom to follow other interests. That same year he coproduced and directed a curious little comedy on Broadway called *The Moon Is Blue.*

Critics tabbed F. Hugh Herbert's play humorous but lacking in substance; audiences made it the surprise hit of the season, "the perfect example of successful mental comedy," in which witty dialogue triumphs over "plot, character, and problems . . . almost as naive as those in a musical show." As *The Moon Is Blue* opens, a struggling television actress meets a successful and slightly jaded young architect at the Empire State Building. After some hesitation, she accepts his invitation to dine at the Stork Club. During the cab ride, he suggests stopping at his flat to replace a missing button. The dialogue provides a flavor of what is to come.

DON: You don't mind waiting, do you?

PATTY: I'm not so sure. Will you try to seduce me?

DON: I don't know; probably, why?

PATTY: Why? A girl wants to know.

DON: A girl is supposed to be intuitive about those things. You don't go around bluntly asking people such questions.

PATTY: I do. I always do.

DON: And what happens if they say yes, they're going to try to seduce you?

PATTY: I generally believe them and then I'm out one dinner.

DON: And if they say their intentions are honorable?

PATTY: I generally believe them, but you get fooled sometimes. I hate men like that. After all, there are lots of girls who don't mind being seduced. Why pick on those who do?

The plot unfolds in Don Gresham's elegant apartment, where the third central character appears, an upstairs neighbor. Wealthy, cynical, and comfortably decadent, David Slater approaches sex with few concessions to traditional morality, yet he, like Don, finds the aggressively virtuous Patty fascinating. Both men view her as a challenge, a test of their seductive charms, and both pursue her. After a series of complications and misunderstandings, she emerges with her chastity intact and Gresham in tow. Love and virtue triumph. Yet by pitting the youthful innocence of Patty against the middle-aged cynicism of Slater, playwright Hugh Herbert turned a stale comedy of manners into a delightfully droll commentary on the topic of seduction. The humor came principally from the "shock lines," from Patty ("Men are usually bored with virgins") or Slater ("steak, liquor and sex, in that order"). Such casual sex-talk sold Broadway tickets for two years.

Joe Breen liked steaks and liquor. The father of three sons and three daughters, he probably also liked sex. But he did not much like *The Moon Is Blue*. According to Hollywood lore, *The Moon* encountered Code resistance because of its "blue language," specifically because of words like "virgin" and "seduce" sprinkled liberally throughout the text. That story, which Preminger broadcast to ballyhoo the picture, distorted the truth. Breen rejected *The Moon Is Blue* not because of dialogue, but because of perspective. To Breen, *The Moon Is Blue* had an unacceptably cavalier approach toward seduction and illicit sex. Moreover, the Production Code not only forbade the use of seduction as a "subject for comedy" but ordered that pictures not show "that low forms of sex relationship [including sex outside marriage] are the accepted or common thing." Both Breen and Jack Vizzard, who later assumed much of the burden of defending the Code office, considered the second clause "one of the most important provisions in the entire Code." Throughout the stage version of *The Moon Is Blue*—despite Patty's eventual triumph—characters ridicule her sexual innocence constantly; she seems the oddball for clinging to a set of standards that sophisticated women have long since rejected. As Vizzard observed, the story made free love "a matter of moral indifference."

Breen's rejection of the screenplay did not shock Preminger. The script submitted in December 1952 included virtually every line of Herbert's play, which the Code office had already twice turned down. On both occasions, Breen had been so blunt that Paramount and later Warners had abandoned interest in the property. But Preminger would not oblige. He intended to produce *The Moon* as his first independent production—during the six months that belonged to him, not Fox—and he would virtually dare Breen to ban it.

In autumn 1952, Preminger and Herbert had formed a small production company, with *The Moon* as their sole asset. They asked David Niven, whose career had slumped, to play the cynical Slater and selected an unknown actress from the Chicago stage company, Maggie McNamara, for the role of Patty. Yet they knew that success depended on finding a "bankable" star, someone equally willing to challenge the Code, whose name would lend credibility to their project. Preminger approached William Holden. A conservative dresser who voted Republican, Holden seemed the perfect Holly-wood citizen. When Preminger met the quiet actor on *Stalag 17,* though, he noticed a streak of rebellion just beneath the junior-corporate-executive surface. Others sensed it too. "Holden is in constant revolt against authority," Billy Wilder remarked. But un-like more conspicuous Hollywood rebels, he shunned moody out-bursts, moldy sweatshirts, and method acting. "It's an odd quality these days," Wilder noted. "He does not bite women's thighs. He does not ride a motorcycle. He would like to. He is a hot-rodder at heart." Holden the Republican saw independent production as an open sesame to tax-sheltered income; Holden the hot-rodder saw it as the chance to work under Preminger, a souped-up Hollywood *auteur.* When he not only joined *The Moon* company but agreed to share the risk by accepting a percentage in lieu of salary, United Artists offered Preminger and Herbert a contract.

Holden, Herbert, and Preminger seemed almost gleeful in their assault on Hollywood tradition. Like three young boys flipping the bird at the cop on the corner, they sought the excitement of inno-cent rebellion. When Preminger lunched with Code associates Vizzard and Shurlock in early January, he projected calm defiance. As a token concession, he offered to add dialogue at the end of the picture condemning the "immoral philosophy of life" expressed by Slater; beyond that, he would not budge. He would shoot the film "pretty much as per the script . . . submitted," he told the Breen boys, with or without Code office sanction.

A "small roundish man of staccato speech and modest manner," Geoff Shurlock had graduated from Dartmouth with a Phi Beta Kappa key. He had a dry wit, a quiet skepticism, and—though he lacked the actorish flair of Joe Breen—a passion for the theater. Shurlock had been Breen's counterbalance for nearly two decades. Cultured and well-read, he often differed with the coach, but as a team member, he never questioned—and always carried through on—the plays Breen called. On *The Moon Is Blue,* though, Shur-lock did not share his colleagues' concerns. Unlike Breen and Vizzard, he had attended a local production of *The Moon* and found it "swell. A lot of fun." In staff discussions, he tried to convince Breen and Vizzard that the plot elements and dialogue that they found so offensive were actually tame in performance. He also believed that the Code prohibition against the comedic treatment of seduction was "idiotic" and ought to be either amended or ignored. Though Breen overruled him, Shurlock took these assumptions into the conference with Preminger. The director blustered on, then Shurlock unexpectedly turned reasonable. He even expressed confidence that a *Moon* made with good taste could earn the Seal.

Vizzard was no less puzzled than Preminger, but he seconded Shurlock at the luncheon. He would later accuse his associate of "drawing a long bow," of cozying up to Preminger at the expense of Code consistency. The fact was, however, that Shurlock thought *The Moon* could be made to suit Joe Breen. He knew that good direction could soften the impact of objectionable dialogue and that humor could ease filmmakers into territory forbidden to serious drama. Only the week before, Breen had approved the *From Here to Eternity* screenplay; to bless a near-scandalous novel one week and curse a harmless comedy of manners the next seemed not only irony but hypocrisy. So Shurlock ended the luncheon on the upbeat: the director promised to review the original Breen letter, adopt changes that would not destroy the play's humor, and submit the completed picture for final judgment.

Otto Preminger was calmed, United Artists executives were not. They knew that Joe Breen, not Geoff Shurlock, would determine whether or not *The Moon* won the Code Seal. United Artists perhaps thought that, as the co-author and staunch defender of the Production Code, Martin Quigley could influence Breen, for UA president Arthur Krim chose Quigley as lobbyist. After a conversation with Preminger, Krim and Quigley concluded that the objections to *The Moon* were minor, but Breen was not amenable to compromise. He was distressed with Preminger's "cold and definite rebuff," and, as one staff member recalled, he "would not be pushed around by anybody, including his own Church." He was determined to block *The Moon*: "If Krim feels that this story can be worked out," he wrote Quigley, "I'm afraid he is going to be in for a great surprise. It will require a drastic rewriting of the story as it now stands, to bring it within the provisions of the Code."

The future of *The Moon Is Blue* fell on Krim and his partner, Robert S. Benjamin. The forty-one-year-old show business lawyers had turned red ink to black less than a year after coming to United

Artists in February 1951. To protect the company reputation for quality movies, they had lured independents back to UA. A strategy dubbed "creative autonomy" offered the producer front money, distribution guarantees, and near-absolute freedom; after Krim and Benjamin approved the original package, usually a story idea or rough script plus the stars and budget, the producer could make the film without interference. In an industry "where the writer has long been regarded as a lazy cur, the director as a dangerous spendthrift, and the actor as a charming but alarming child," this plan "seemed worse than heresy," said Murray Teigh Bloom in *Harper's*. But "creative autonomy" enabled the two Manhattan lawyers to attract such men as Otto Preminger.

At the end of January 1953, Krim and Benjamin weighed the dilemma of *The Moon Is Blue*. Even though United Artists was not a current member of the Motion Picture Association, neither partner was anxious to market a picture without the Code Seal. An Italian import could prosper in scattered independent theaters and chains, but according to industry pundits a mainstream feature could not. Canceling Preminger's contract would damage UA's reputation, however, especially in the eyes of those it most wanted to court. Besides, Krim and Benjamin liked long shots. With less than a quarter-million invested in *The Moon*, the odds seemed worth the risk. At the end of the month, they deleted a clause that required delivery of a Code-approved *Moon*, negotiated a production loan from the Chemical Bank of New York, and committed United Artists to a frontal assault on Joseph I. Breen.

When Preminger sent Breen the finished picture in April, complete with the "immoral philosophy of life" codicil, the Production Code director responded with a terse note that denied certification because of the film's "unacceptably light attitude toward seduction, illicit sex, chastity and virginity." Preminger seemed honestly shocked. Between his token concessions and UA's promise to release the picture with or without Production Code approval, he thought that he had hemmed in Breen. In a long and passionate letter to the Code commandant, he claimed to have "leaned over backward in making revisions" for the Code office and expressed amazement over the Seal turndown. The centerpiece of the letter was a long defense of the morality of *The Moon:*

Our picture does *not* have a light attitude towards 'seduction, illicit sex, chastity and virginity.' On the contrary it is a harmless story of a very virtuous girl, who works for her living, who neither smokes nor drinks, who is completely honest and outspoken, who resists temptation and whose one aim in life is to get married and have children. . . . There are no scenes of passion in our picture, no scenes of crime or vice. We concede that there is a discussion of sex—a topic of somewhat universal interest—but we are both deeply convinced that it is handled in such a way that it cannot conceivably harm those whom the Code was created to protect.

Though Preminger may have been posturing, the tone of the letter hints that he had had second thoughts about sending *The Moon* into the marketplace without the Seal. An informal *Variety* survey of exhibitors in April suggested that no major chain would book his feature without Production Code approval. But Preminger had no visible impact on Joe Breen, who told him to appeal the agency ruling to the Association board. Two weeks later, United Artists obliged Breen.

The Moon appeal would become Breen's last stand. Though he and the Production Code would forever be twined, he and the Production Code Administration had almost parted company. He rarely attended story conferences or read scripts; since 1951, he had been de jure the director but de facto the consultant. Geoffrey Shurlock and Jack Vizzard provided the agency leadership. They took the phone calls, doctored the scripts, and arranged the compromises that shaped and reshaped the Code from month to month. It was Vizzard who stood helmet-to-helmet with Stanley Kramer on *The Wild One,* telling the producer that it was "terribly un-American to justify the motorcyclists" and to retain the "fury, violence, lawlessness, the destruction of property, brutality, drunkenness and callousness and contempt of society with which the script abounded." It was Shurlock who confronted John Huston on *Moulin Rouge,* insuring that the "sordid and immoral relationship" between Lautrec and the prostitute Marie would not offend the censor or patron.

While Vizzard and Shurlock ran the Beverly Boulevard office in tandem, it was the flexible Shurlock, not the more conservative Vizzard, who represented the future of the Production Code. Shur-

lock understood adult cinema. Breen had championed *Dead End,*
tolerated *The Postman Always Rings Twice,* and conciliated on *A
Streetcar Named Desire* and *Detective Story,* yet he viewed adult pictures with one drooped eye. Shurlock had a more catholic outlook.
Despite his virtual control, though, he could not always be as
liberal as he wished. The Breen name was on the door, the Breen
signature on letters to producers. And should those producers push
too hard or too far, they would draw the scarred old lion from his
den. In spring 1953, Otto Preminger had done precisely that.

At the May 1953 board hearing, the case for *The Moon* was
presented by New York attorney Samuel Rosenman, who seven
years before had served Eric Johnston as counsel when Howard
Hughes sued the Motion Picture Association over the withdrawn
Seal for *The Outlaw.* Rosenman could have reminded the company
presidents that in four days the industry would celebrate the first
anniversary of the *Miracle* decision; he could also have told them
that they represented the past, Preminger the future. But the board
needed no goading, and he merely elaborated the arguments of the
Preminger letter to Breen: in plot and theme, *The Moon Is Blue* was
a moral picture.

Gordon White mounted the case for the Production Code Administration. Though Breen was vitally interested in the appeal,
the timing was impossible. He had promised his wife a European
trip, and had scheduled meetings with censors and producers overseas; he could not dally at home. He nonetheless stopped over in
Manhattan, where he drilled White. Breen told White to stress not
only the Code violations but several key points that would rouse
board members who were fathers or grandfathers of young
women. White followed orders. The presentation contended that
The Moon would be "highly offensive to many parents to whom
virginity of their daughters is still a matter of greatest concern, and
who do not consider this a matter to be laughed at." He further
stated that the film contained "a very strong element of suggestion
to the young and immature, and especially to those already rebellious against parental restraint, that it is a reasonable and safe
thing—a socially desirable thing—for a young girl to visit in a
bachelor's apartment at night, and that this may be done without
danger and with probably quite agreeable results."

Whom would the company presidents choose to represent Hollywood, the *Life* ideal woman or the *Playboy* sweetheart? The board divided sharply. A narrow majority seemed inclined to overrule Breen and grant Preminger the coveted Seal. Chastened by the abuse they took on *The Bicycle Thief* and aware that United Artists would market the picture no matter what, these board members reasoned that denying the Seal to a harmless comedy could maim the Code. Despite board disapproval, exhibitors faced with a shortage of good pictures would be sorely tempted to book *The Moon,* while the Seal on the picture would, at worst, stretch the boundaries of Production Code rules. Also, Eric Johnston had been courting United Artists for two years in hopes that Krim and Benjamin would return to the Association. To deny *The Moon* a Seal— Johnston could argue—would push the distributors farther away and invite future confrontation.

Loew's president Nicholas Schenck turned obdurate, and as the board's elder statesman, he had much influence. Twenty-six years in the boardroom had taught Schenck caution; unlike others at the hearing, he recalled how seemingly innocuous little comedies had once infuriated Catholic and Protestant reformers. He may also have been moved by Gordon White. The "damn" on *Gone With the Wind* (for which he may have offered lip service) was one matter, the behavior of young women in the *Playboy* era another. As the final vote approached, Schenck made a "passionate appeal" to his fellow directors: "I wouldn't let my daughter see it. It's true that the girl is not seduced in the time she spends with the boy, but other girls in a similar situation might get closer to the flame. I vote no." The statement made the difference. The board refused *The Moon Is Blue* the Seal.

Krim and Benjamin may have been disappointed, but they were contractually obligated to release the film. *The Moon Is Blue* would now require special handling. Over the weekend following the hearing, the United Artists partners met with New York staffers and decided to prerelease *The Moon* at carefully selected downtown theaters in Chicago, New York, Los Angeles, and San Francisco. They hoped that strong box office in these relatively liberal communities might convince not only independent theaters but the major chains to book the film. The early signs looked good. A special screening for New York exhibitors and members of the trade press went reasonably well. The audience enjoyed the movie, laughing "so hard as to drown out some lines." While one observer noted that between the outbursts of laughter, many "squirmed in embarrassment," most theater owners in the audience later expressed their desire to play the film despite the Association ruling.

In the meantime, Max Youngstein geared up the United Artists publicity department for a campaign to exploit a notorious banned movie. A pupil of the Howard Hughes school of film promotion, he hitched *The Moon* ads to a seminude female moon watcher. Preminger was "outraged." Youngstein was all wrong. *Moon* heroine Maggie McNamara lacked the Gemini endowments of Jane Russell; she was more fragile than fulsome. Called an "odd looking little bird," she would not attract audiences in search of décolletage. More important, Preminger feared that such an approach might scare away potential exhibitors. While Youngstein assumed that only the most courageous independent theater owners would book a picture without the Seal and that lurid ads would be needed to offset the limited rentals, Preminger believed that *The Moon* could do better. He hoped that the picture could attract a much wider clientele, specifically those exhibitors who usually ran only Code-approved features. To reach them, United Artists must sell *The Moon* as a light comedy touched by the risqué. Preminger won out, and Artemis surrendered her place to two pigeons perched on a windowsill peering beneath a partially closed blind.

Preminger may not have wanted *The Moon* sensationalized, but he took every advantage of the Association ban. In the weeks prior to release, he promoted *The Moon* as an extreme challenge to the Production Code. At one press conference after another, he denounced Breen's "hypocritical interpretation of an antiquated Code," and dared the public to become judge and jury on the moral merits of his picture. Some early reviews followed the Preminger lead; they devoted more lines to the absence of the Seal than to the movie, and many of them described the forthcoming release as an historic event, the first test of Code strength since *The Bicycle Thief.* Other reviews were curiously divided. Many applauded the courage of Preminger and United Artists but found *The Moon* less than worthy of the effort. Bosley Crowther called it "speciously risqué" and "tedious," and rued the fact that "such a middling and harmless little thing" could generate such a fuss. For James D. Ivers, of the *Motion Picture Herald, The Moon* was "a clever, brilliantly written, flawlessly acted and directed bedroom comedy"; Ivers nonetheless condemned Preminger for targeting the film toward those "who like to think themselves sophisticated" and for his "astonishing contempt for audiences of the innumerable Main Streets that lie importantly between Broadway and Hollywood and Vine."

The chief defenders of Main Street morals resided not far from Broadway, in the New York offices of the Catholic Legion of Decency. One week after *The Moon* appeal, just as Preminger started his promotional campaign, Monsignor Patrick Masterson led a delegation of ten cohorts to another special screening of the picture. The Legion group found *The Moon* more humorous than harmful and advised rating it "B." That move would have represented a triumph for Preminger and United Artists. In 1953, the Legion of Decency placed eighty-nine films—fully a quarter of those reviewed—in the "B" category; the label bore no stigma by the 1950s, and exhibitors booked "B" pictures with almost no fear of community protest. But Masterson and his chief assistant, Monsignor Thomas Little, overruled the tolerant evaluators. In a memorandum stamped PRIVATE AND CONFIDENTIAL, Masterson and Little explained to the Legion's diocesan directors that *The Moon*'s commercial success "would be used to destroy the Code operation." Unless the Legion condemned the picture, they concluded, the Breen office could not remain "the first bastion of strength in preserving proper moral standards in motion pictures."

Masterson and Little were uncomfortable as Breen cheerleaders, perhaps because the "Condemned" assigned *The Moon* was more policy decision than comment on the merits or morals of the picture. To avoid a confrontation, they withheld public announcement of the "C" rating and asked the ever-available Martin Quigley to intercede with Krim and Benjamin; maybe an elder statesman could convince the United Artists wunderkinder that they could damage the welfare of the entire industry. But Quigley as Legion rather than UA emissary frightened Preminger. The director recalled that when he had last faced the Legion of Decency in 1947, Fox president Spyros Skouras had become "so frantic" to remove the "C" on *Forever Amber* that he knelt before the Legion representative, "kissed his hand," begged for help, and "actually began to cry." The Catholics relented—but only after Skouras forced Preminger to turn down the steam on the movie. A twice-told tale from the Hollywood sagas, the story of the mogul and the priest no longer had much snap. In 1947, when the Catholics could send the industry Richter scale to eight-point-five, Fox had had almost six million dollars in *Amber;* that sum was perhaps worth a kneel and a sob. In 1953, United Artists had less than half a million dollars in *Moon.* Krim and Benjamin "behaved very well," Preminger said. "Though they were nervous, they supported me." Quigley went away, and the "C" stuck.

By mid-June 1953, the combat lines were drawn. Masterson died suddenly, but Monsignor Little stepped in. He fired off special messages to diocesan directors in each of the four cities where *The Moon* would have prerelease engagements and reminded them of the boycott clause in the Legion's famous pledge. He urged "wholehearted cooperation in putting into motion the policies under which the Legion has operated so effectively in the past." Diocesan newspapers carried editorials that blasted United Artists and Preminger for sabotaging the Code, and both Francis Cardinal Spellman of New York and James Francis Cardinal McIntyre of Los Angeles labeled attendance "an occasion of sin." Yet the pulpit exhortations and the pickets they spawned—so effective two decades before—could not overcome public curiosity. Despite mediocre reviews, *The Moon Is Blue* played to excellent crowds at each prerelease screening. Its maiden week at the Woods Theatre in Chicago netted $40,000, the best weekly showing at that house since 1951. Two weeks later, the movie smashed records at the Four Star Theater in Los Angeles and performed almost as well in New York and San Francisco.

The real breakthrough came during the first week in July, when three of the industry's five recently divorced theater chains booked the film. In rapid succession, United Paramount, Stanley Warner, and National Theatres announced that they would play *The Moon* throughout the country. These circuits controlled over 2,400 theaters, including many of the largest in the trade. Their endorsement virtually guaranteed *The Moon*'s success and at the same time dimmed the future of the Production Code Administration.

In general release on July 15, *The Moon Is Blue* raced to fourth among the top five box office smashes of the week. While Hollywood touts swapped rumors that the company presidents were studying major Production Code revisions and that Breen faced "rough sailing ahead," the Motion Picture Association hurriedly attempted to end speculation and shore up the sagging Production Code. The Association staff focused on what Hollywood did best: the manufacture of illusion. In Hollywood, with Breen abroad, acting director Shurlock canvassed major producers and trumpeted that "without exception" they had "reaffirmed their support of the Code and its principles." He had of course sought out gentlemen like Y. Frank Freeman and shunned the likes of Otto Preminger. On the East Coast, Eric Johnston called on the Association Board of Directors to endorse the Code. At a carefully staged press conference, Johnston—with Shurlock and several corporate bosses beside him—declared the system of voluntary compliance stronger than ever. "Reports that producers were weakening in their support of the Code are pure and utter nonsense," he asserted. The Code was a "living and vibrant document" whose principles of morality and taste "are ageless." Though Johnston also wrangled statements from the General Federation of Women's Clubs and the Conference of Roman Catholic Bishops, he could not enlist theater owners' support. For some years they had resisted an Association plan that would commit them to show only Code-approved features, a "pledge" that would have the force of moral law. In autumn 1953, with *The Moon Is Blue* moving toward its sixteenth consecutive week on the *Variety* top ten, they would not rally round the Code.

At the end of June, when the guns had fallen silent in Korea, the rapid cancellation of defense contracts had brought a downturn in both the economy and theater attendance. Hollywood responded by cutting back on production, and by late September the studios resembled Hadleyville at five minutes to High Noon. At MGM things were so slow that Joan Crawford, then working on *Torch Song,* had full use of three personal dressing rooms. Sending home all its gardeners, Paramount invited secretaries to uproot plants and flowers from the studio grounds. Twentieth Century–Fox planned to shut down production for an entire month, and extended a program of layoffs that insiders estimated would reach thirty to fifty percent of the work force by November.

Faced with both smaller audiences and product shortage, theater owners showed little interest in narrowed booking options. Johnston pressured an association of smaller exhibitors to issue a general statement that reaffirmed support for the Code, but the group added a rider: "It does seem a pity that in times like these, the so-called art theatres should be the sole beneficiaries of high grossing pictures that could be exhibited to adult audiences in the regular theatres without hurting anyone." The Theatre Owners of America, representing larger chains, also resisted Association appeals. Its executives chose not to issue any statement on the Code until convention time in November, and even then offered the Johnston office "rather grudging" support for the Code. The two groups' pallid resolutions did not bind individual exhibitors, who could book unapproved features whenever they chose. But for the moment, Johnston and Breen had achieved at least an illusion of unity.

While the Motion Picture Association dredged up public statements and pledges, Catholic leaders across the country responded to the Legion of Decency call to arms. The Conference of Catholic Bishops advised theater owners who eyed *The Moon* to "bear in mind the potential loss of Catholic patronage not only for that attraction but others which follow it in the same theatre." Parish newspapers labeled *The Moon* "sophisticated smut," and local chapters of the Catholic Daughters of America, the Knights of Columbus, and the Catholic War Veterans manned picket lines and leaned on community officials to ban the feature. In Poughkeepsie, Monsignor Michael P. O'Shea confronted the city council with a petition bearing over four thousand signatures and demanded an ordinance blocking "immoral shows and motion pictures." Responding to similar pressure, officials in Seattle, Milwaukee, Minneapolis, and St. Paul delayed *The Moon*'s opening; the Jersey City public safety director ordered police to seize all prints of the film and jail the manager of the Journal Square Theatre for exhibiting an "obscene, indecent" movie.

The attempt to block exhibition often intensified public curiosity. Despite dire warnings by the Omaha Archbishop and a picket line manned by the Knights of Columbus, *The Moon* drew block-long crowds to the ticket windows at two suburban houses. When Memphis censor Lloyd Binford banned local showings, the

United Artists branch manager moved the film across the river to West Memphis, where it played to standing-room-only crowds. At the same time, Catholic pressure did limit bookings. Forced to choose between a potentially lucrative single run and the long-term wrath of local moralists, many theater owners passed on *The Moon Is Blue*. The picture also suffered rough treatment by state censors. Total bans in Ohio, Maryland, and Kansas cut deeply into potential profits and required costly litigation. Preminger, Krim, and Benjamin could nonetheless occupy a front table at Romanoff's without fear of embarrassment. Extended runs of *The Moon* in 1,100 large theaters, many of them urban houses, partially offset the limited play-dates and state bans. Holding its own against such notable competition as *Shane* and *Gentlemen Prefer Blondes, The Moon* grossed nearly $3.5 million, enough to reach fifteenth on the 1953 *Variety* top fifty.

To outsiders, especially those who had exhorted Hollywood to abandon self-regulation, *The Moon Is Blue* sounded the death rattle of the Legion of Decency and the Production Code. The film was "totally innocuous," one prominent Catholic later observed; Catholics who saw it puzzled over the "Condemned" rating, and the dialogue that followed seriously undermined the Legion. Along with the *Miracle* decision the year before, the Preminger challenge seemed to open the American screen to adult drama. It seemed to demonstrate that the mighty Production Code Administration and Legion of Decency had withered, that courageous filmmakers could now afford to probe once-taboo subjects without concessions to Breen and the Catholic fathers.

Just as the crisis over *The Moon Is Blue* subsided, an associate handed Breen a page ripped from the St. Louis *Post-Dispatch,* an ad that announced the forthcoming premiere of the new Jane Russell picture, *The French Line*. In a simple two-by-four-inch teaser, it read: "J. R. in 3-D. It'll knock BOTH your eyes out!" The Hollywood outlaw was again on the loose.

Howard Hughes' *The French Line* was designed to bolster the sagging fortunes of RKO. Under Hughes' inept management, the studio lost over $20 million in five years, $6 million in 1952 alone.

In September of that year, with stockholders crying for relief, the enigmatic Texan tried to sell his shares in the studio to a five-man Chicago syndicate, but the deal collapsed when rumors linked the new owners to the Chicago underworld. Hughes resumed control in February 1953, and the following month forwarded the *French Line* script to the Breen office. The screenplay appeared tame. The corny story concerned a Texas oil heiress (Jane Russell) so rich that no young man will court her. To find true love, she takes an extended voyage to France pretending to be a poor model and predictably discovers a suitor (Gilbert Roland with French accent) worthy of her affections. In an attempt to expand Russell's success in *Gentlemen Prefer Blondes,* Hughes added nine song-and-dance numbers. The script contained little hint of the controversy that would follow, yet the combination of Hughes, Russell, and three-dimensional projection made Breen nervous. Visions of cleavage spilling into the orchestra section of American movie houses led him to include the boilerplate he always used when he feared suggestive costuming: "Specifically, the breasts of women must be fully covered at all times." Because Hughes was the producer, Breen also added: "Any compromise with this regulation will compel us to withhold approval."

During script negotiations, Hughes complied with all of Breen's instructions. He removed a running gag involving a "professor of love" who seemed to be "teaching the fundamentals of seduction," a joke based on the Kinsey report, and a character portrayed as a "pansy." He also deleted several double entendres ("Already I have spread myself thin") and other minor quips ("You're lucky you found one who likes you with your clothes on"). Pained by the struggle over *The Moon Is Blue,* Breen applauded RKO's attitude. Yet the Production Code director knew that even a wholesome screenplay could offend when translated to film, that evocative costumes and camera angles could turn an innocent dance number into a torrid bump-and-grind. Most of all, he knew that he could not trust Hughes. In September, with *The Moon* still on the *Variety* top ten, an RKO executive asked the Association what sanctions could be used against a member company that violated Code regulations. The bland query told Breen that Hughes planned to follow the path blazed by Preminger. When he screened *The French Line* in November, he knew why.

Not since *The Outlaw* had Breen seen such a display of décolletage. The picture opened with a tame striptease (Russell ducks
behind furniture as she disrobes) and progressed to the far more
offensive "Looking for Trouble" number in which the camera and
the cleavage danced in tandem. A Production Code associate told
Breen that the costumes had been "intentionally designed to give a
bosom peep-show." Jane Russell concurred. "I fought and beefed
and argued," she later claimed. "I had an awful time with some of
the dance costumes they wanted me to wear. They were really
bad—hardly anything at all." Hughes loved the costumes, loved
the dances, loved the Russell torso, all enhanced by gestures and
glances. A male character referred to Russell's "big brown . . . [his
hands forming the outline of breasts] eyes"; staring at the alluring
hope chest of Jane Russell, Gilbert Roland spoke of its "peculiar or
particular riches." Other characters called Jane by her nickname,
"Chesty."

Breen viewed the picture twice, then forced the Production Code
staff through three additional screenings before he rendered a verdict. This time the staff was united: Hughes had gone too far. Breen
informed RKO that *The French Line* could not be approved without
drastic alterations.

Though *The French Line* exceeded the Production Code limits on
breast exposure, Howard Hughes was not alone as a female-flesh
peddler. In December 1953, as Hugh Hefner undressed Marilyn
Monroe in the maiden issue of *Playboy,* starlet Terry Moore toured
Korea for the USO; her white ermine bathing suit and "strip-tease
Santa" left the boys from Peoria panting. St. Nick brought Las
Vegas crapshooters another present. For her show Marlene Dietrich
wore a gown that "did not have a low-cut top. It had no top at all,
save for a transparent film of net on which rhinestones were sprinkled at real random." *Ecstasy,* the Hedy Lamarr vehicle that Breen
had nixed in the 1930s because of the nude swim and the orgasm,
played college campuses, while *Striporama* set records at art houses
on both coasts. In Hollywood, the stars came out. "Joan Fontaine
used to always pull this stuff," Paramount Production Code liaison
Luigi Luraschi recalled. Her repeated attempts to show more cleavage than Breen allowed at last brought Luraschi to the soundstage.
"I said to her, 'Look, Joan, you want to pull it down, pull it down.
You know what'll happen? When we edit the picture, your closeup

won't be there, we'll be on somebody else.' " The tug of war ended, yet the sudden scorn for modesty suggested more than random titillation.

Beneath the ironclad girdles and calf-length skirts, beneath the pleated trousers and loose-fitting sport coats was an America that yearned to cast off the rigid sexual bonds of the early 1950s. Though GIs who returned from the war with high expectations savored the educational benefits and suburban homes, many were somehow discontent. Four years of pin-ups and promises should have led to more than Melamine dinnerware and a Buick sedan. The malaise produced curious contradictions—Norman Vincent Peale and Mickey Spillane, Billy Graham and Marilyn Monroe, Mary Worth and *Mad* magazine. It also produced a growing market for the sexy. *The French Line* seemed to capture the new spirit of undress, and Howard Hughes could not let Breen dampen it. Ignoring the Production Code, he scheduled the film for a December 29 premiere at the five-thousand-seat Fox Theater in St. Louis and filled the newspapers with more ads. "J.R. in 3-D. That's all, brother!" "Jane Russell in 3 Dimension—and What Dimensions!"

The French Line represented a much more serious threat to the Production Code system than *The Moon Is Blue*. Unlike United Artists, RKO belonged to the Motion Picture Association, and its defection would break the industry's solid front. No member company had released a picture without the Seal since the original Production Code agreement in 1934. "What was at stake," Vizzard later recalled, "was the survival of the whole system, and even the whole concept, of achieving decency in the movies. A successful breakthrough by Hughes, exploiting the bulge created by Preminger, would spell eventual doom for the entire experiment."

The only formal penalty available for use against an errant member of the Association was the $25,000 fine, which Breen immediately took the necessary steps to assess. The Association tied the penalty to a legal finding—a determination that the film released was the version denied the Seal—so Breen sent Vizzard to the St. Louis premiere. While $25,000 would have been inconsequential to Hughes, the Vizzard mission had a larger purpose. Breen suggested that while in St. Louis, Vizzard should drop in on Archbishop Joseph E. Ritter. A "soft-spoken but fearless German,"

Ritter welcomed the chance to help enforce the Breen office ban. In the prelate's office, Vizzard and Ritter fashioned a "special emergency" letter to be read in all diocesan churches two days before the premiere. Attributed to the Council of Catholic Men of St. Louis, it warned parishioners that *The French Line* violated both industry and Legion of Decency standards and that good Catholics should avoid attendance. Ritter also issued a second letter to be read at all New Year's Masses: any of St. Louis's 473,000 Catholics who attended *The French Line* would fall "under penalty of mortal sin." Vizzard supported the action but sensed the irony: "The thought that there might be an enormous disproportion here had to be suppressed. That the eternal fate of a human being should have to be connected to Jane Russell's mammaries, no matter how heroic, was a bit much."

The French Line opened to overflow crowds and played before a record sixty thousand in the first five days. Could all of the seat holders have been non-Catholics? Almost without exception, the critics disliked *The French Line*. But neither bad reviews nor rumors that a police morals squad would raid the theater could thin the queues for what *Variety* called "a front box seat for a burley show."

With *The French Line* and *The Moon Is Blue* on the front burner, Breen was barely able to manage. Then he spotted Sam Goldwyn—match in hand—over the back burner. The day before *The French Line* opened, Goldwyn demanded "modernization" of the Code. A signer of the original 1934 agreement and veteran producer of recognized taste, Goldwyn could not be dismissed as a frustrated fast-buck artist. In an industry where reputation counted nearly as much as image, Goldwyn had clout, and his public outburst, along with the continuing success of *The Moon Is Blue* and reports of standing-room-only crowds for *The French Line,* created an "open season on the Production Code."

Variety rushed to poll leading exhibitors and found them lukewarm toward the Code. "Almost unanimously," they resisted "being 'pledged' blind to observance of Code edicts," and many expressed doubts as to the wisdom of Breen office decisions. Trans-Lux Theatres president Richard Brandt and several others thought that the industry should dissolve the Production Code Administration; like Goldwyn, many others wanted modernization. Over the next six weeks, the trade papers chronicled an intense debate. The powerful Theatre Owners of America, as well as smaller associations representing independent producers and distributors, quickly issued statements favoring a Code update; the Screen Writers Guild also joined the chorus with *Moon* author and new Guild president F. Hugh Herbert, gleefully offering his personal assistance for the rewrite. Perched on the fence, Eric Johnston advised caution and asked for specific suggestions in writing. Behind the scenes, Martin Quigley urged the Catholics to raise the Legion ratings to the "dignity, force, and obligation of Church law." He then railed against the "continuing cabal of clamor against the Code," and accused those who wanted revision of trying to reduce the document to "a sham and a pretense."

As usual, Breen avoided public comment. But not all was grim on Beverly Boulevard. Breen could still read the Hollywood signs, and they had started to favor him. Despite all the din and debate, all the abuse of Production Code enforcement and calls for revision, he sensed one simple fact missed by the industry seers: Howard Hughes and *The French Line* could save the Production Code.

From the beginning, the film community tolerated the Production Code and its often abrasive director exactly because of people like Hughes. It was not the sophisticated comedy of a *Moon Is Blue* or the earthy realism of a *Streetcar Named Desire* that threatened the industry's delicate relationship with the guardians of American morality; it was the rank opportunism of a *French Line*. And Breen knew the industry was not yet ready to stake its future on a "bosom peep-show." Throughout all the noise over the Production Code in January, not one spokesman defended either Hughes or his film, and *Variety* reported that "screen freedom liberals" and trade executives on both coasts were voicing strong resentment toward the Texas airman. One unnamed vice-president expressed the common sentiment:

The Code has been defied before . . . but for the most part there was some 'principle' involved. In the Hughes matter I fail to see how 'principle' enters into it. I don't quarrel with nonconformists generally but in this case Hughes is trying to make a buck with his picture at the cost of tremendous industry prestige and at the risk of bringing new censorships upon us far more burdensome than we've ever had before.

Breen knew that both industry solons and even some of the wolves at his heels would soon link Code reform and *The French Line;* they would see the Hughes movie as "the thin edge of the wedge" that would open the screen to a parade of even more salacious films. By mid-January 1954, some in the industry were beginning to make that association. Alfred Daff, a Universal executive, spoke out against any serious Code tampering, lest "the fly-by-nighters and producers of sex exploitation films . . . take advantage of the situation and make it so much harder for the rest of the industry."

Hughes misread the industry. Thinking that calls for reform had weakened Breen, the unpredictable Texan suddenly ended the St. Louis run. Attendance had tapered off, and the Legion of Decency was about to condemn the picture; it was time to send *The French Line* to the Production Code office for a second review. Again Breen's staff sat through multiple screenings, and despite the 3-D goggles took detailed scene-by-scene notes. RKO president James R. Grainger (Hughes was chairman of the board) attended the last screening to lobby for a favorable response, but Breen was adamant. *The French Line* was "definitely and specifically in violation of the Production Code," Breen told Grainger, and would have to undergo major cuts.

Hughes was not yet willing to comply. Confident that hard-pressed exhibitors would okay "J.R. in 3-D," he scheduled *The French Line* for general release in late February. The ensuing weeks went badly for Hughes and the picture. State censors in New York, Pennsylvania, Kansas, and Ohio banned *The French Line;* the Legion of Decency and Catholic hierarchy targeted it for a new round of pickets and protests. Worse still, major exhibitors turned cold.

As Breen predicted, *The French Line* led many in the industry back to the Code. National Theatres' Charles P. Skouras, who had booked *The Moon Is Blue,* now called on fellow exhibitors "to respect the principles of the Motion Picture Producers Association Production Code." American Theatres' Sam Pinanski warned that any serious tampering with the document "would be ruinous" for exhibitors, and Leonard Goldenson, president of the mammoth

United-Paramount chain, called the Code "sound in principle" and advised his affiliates to reject all unapproved pictures. As if to confirm the voice of the theatermen, the Association board formally denied that "changes or revisions" in the Code were necessary or anticipated. Individually signed by the president of every member company except RKO, the statement told the world that "the fundamental principles of the Production Code are not subject to change with the passage of time" and that "nothing in the Code has ever prevented the making of superlative, artistic and dramatic entertainment." The board thus served official notice that continued agitation for a Code rewrite was futile.

The emerging industry consensus closed down the path blazed by Preminger. In rapid succession the major chains rejected *The French Line;* even the RKO Theatres—divorced from RKO Pictures—refused to book it. Smaller chains and independents whom Hughes had counted on to ignore the ban also shunned him. Many who had played *The Moon Is Blue* found *The French Line* far too risky. According to *Variety,* they calculated that running the Hughes feature would "result in a major migraine in the form of public and church antagonism." By February, a hard-pressed RKO had lined up theaters in only three cities.

The Hughes Tool Company made nothing that could bore through an industry brick wall. But Hughes would not surrender. He dispatched personal confidant and legal advisor Noah Dietrich to plead for one more review. Dietrich told Breen that Hughes had misjudged the public temper and would now make substantial changes. Would Breen specify the needed cuts? Breen went to the file, pulled out a "List of Unacceptable Items," and wished Dietrich well. He warned, though, that even if Hughes cut every unacceptable item, the altered picture would still require a final review for the Seal. As Dietrich left, full of good cheer and better intentions, Breen must have been elated. Hughes seemed to be knuckling under, an action that could send a strong message to the film community. The New York office was equally pleased. A Johnston associate wrote Breen praising his efforts to bring the maverick into line and calling the Hughes capitulation "a tremendous thing all around, especially for us." The whole affair would serve as "a lesson," he predicted, "heeded even by some of the thickest skulls."

It would "be a long time before another serious break developed in Hollywood against the Code."

The champagne and caviar were premature. Despite distribution headaches, the stubborn RKO chairman would not alter *The French Line*, at least not as Joe Breen wanted. Hughes may have reasoned that with Hollywood production down over twenty percent in early 1954, exhibitors would soon become desperate for new titles. Theatermen needed frequent marquee changes to lure the dwindling number of regular patrons, and *The French Line* could prove one answer to the product shortage. But Hughes' defiance was far from complete. Though he would not oblige the Production Code Administration, he authorized deep cuts for the state censors, and in several cases eliminated more footage than Breen had required. He could thus retain the enticing stigma of a banned film yet remove a major barrier to exhibition. The tactic did nothing for Hughes' balance sheet. While a number of smaller independents booked the feature, the big chains did not. Even worse, the state censors chopped out the film's primary assets. Released for general distribution in May, with bosoms no longer ablossom, *The French Line* earned terrible reviews. "There's no use pretending about this picture," Bosley Crowther wrote. "It's a cheap exhibitionist thing in which even the elaboration of the feminine figure eventually becomes grotesque." *Newsweek* thought that America should not censor *The French Line* but pity it.

In February 1954, the sixty-year-old Breen had told Johnston that in autumn he would resign. Weakened by the lung operation in 1951 and a recurrent back ailment, Breen had contemplated retirement for over two years, but had remained to battle the succession of Production Code challenges. A street fighter to the end, he could not abandon the reins during an assault; it would look too much like a resignation under fire, and Breen was determined that neither Preminger nor Hughes would have that satisfaction. Once the theater chains and the Association board had reaffirmed their commitment to the Production Code, however, Hughes' final act of defiance no longer seemed to matter. The public announcement of the retirement would come in summer, for Breen wanted no one in the industry to link his departure with *The French Line*.

On the evening of March 25, 1954, one year after *Variety* had predicted the demise of the Code, Joe Breen strode onstage to collect a special Oscar for service to the industry. It was a night to remember. *From Here to Eternity,* a film that had taxed his tolerance but bore the Seal, won eight awards, including Best Picture; *The Moon Is Blue,* nominated for three Oscars, gained none. The golden statue that Breen gripped as he thanked the Academy carried the inscription "To Joseph I. Breen, for his conscientious, open-minded and dignified management of the Production Code Administration." For some in the audience, especially those who yearned for the freedom of the novel or the theatre, an Oscar for the "Hollywood censor" was out of place, even embarrassing. But for those who could remember 1934, when fears of mass boycotts and federal regulation had threatened the future of a depression-ridden industry, Breen had earned the long overdue tribute.

In twenty years, Joe Breen had become as much a Hollywood institution as Oscar itself. Like the powerful moguls who had voted him the Academy Award, he could be crude, arrogant, and dogmatic; his petty rulings could frustrate intelligent writers and insult able directors. Few doubted that he was sincerely committed to the Production Code and the welfare of the industry, though. Breen and those in Manhattan who supported him thought that the movies could not survive as an independent form of entertainment unless they respected the moral sensibilities of mainstream audiences. Unchecked, producers would resort to shady plots and exposed flesh, they would court public outrage and federal regulation. Breen had protected the film community from its own natural impulses.

If Breen played a key role in the evolution of a popular art form, he also overstayed his welcome. For two decades he had shaped that special universe that appeared on American screens. During his tenure the threat of mass boycotts and federal censorship disappeared, the power of local censors dissipated. But Breen never quite grasped that the cure could be as damaging as the disease, that rigid Code enforcement, which seemed so necessary in 1934, could separate Hollywood from the world around it. *From Here to Eternity* and *A Streetcar Named Desire* were great films but should have been greater, and by 1954 more producers than ever thought that the artificially genteel view of life that Breen imposed on them had retarded the emergence of a unique art form.

Though Howard Hughes and *The French Line* reminded Hollywood why Joe Breen and the Code existed, the lesson was soon forgotten. Television, divorcement, the vanishing audience, the fall of the studio system, the rise of the independents, the success of *The Moon Is Blue,* and, symbolically, the death of Will Hays in spring 1954 all pointed toward a new relationship between the industry and its Production Code. It was time for Joe Breen to step down. And it was a perilous time for Geoffrey M. Shurlock to succeed him.

10

Lolita

As Joe Breen cashed his first retirement checks, a boy with sensual lips and light-brown sideburns cut a disc for a Tennessee record company. The potential of the voice promised attention, but jobs were scarce for poor kids with spotty educations, so the boy continued to drive a truck for a living. Weekends another boy played hillbilly music at a West Texas roller rink. Though the kids skated to songs made popular by Hank Williams and Bob Wills, the boy on the bandstand sometimes broke away from Western swing to produce a different sound, one so propulsive that it made his steel-rimmed glasses dance down the end of his nose. Yet another young man with country roots pumped out song after song for honky-tonk beer-drinkers along the Louisiana Gulf Coast. Like the boys from Memphis and Lubbock, he had heard the lean, earth-hard rhythms of Negro blues bands and integrated them into his playing. Elvis Presley, Buddy Holly, Jerry Lee Lewis, and others had no name for what they pioneered (ministers tabbed it "jungle music"), but someone called it rock 'n' roll—a slang term for copulation. By the end of the decade, rock 'n' roll had become an industry that virtually dominated AM radio and the popular music business. It had become an anthem for restless youth, a war cry for the rebellious. The croon-spoon-tune of *The Moon Is Blue* and even the Rubenesque displays of Jane Russell seemed tame when compared to the throb of slapped bass fiddles. Goodness gracious, great balls of fire, indeed.

Rock 'n' roll caught the turbulence beneath the surface of American life in the 1950s. Despite the outward calm, the later Eisenhower years witnessed a renaissance of rebellion, much of it "rooted in the tremendous disaffection of the young." While their parents enjoyed the good life in suburbia, adolescents often found those "faceless dormitories of the middle class" confining and sterile. They questioned the unabashed materialism, the transparent morality, the stifling conformity of American culture; they applauded the cynicism of the beatniks, and worshiped at the shrine of James Dean. These causeless rebels expressed their discontent through minimal acts—beer blasts and joyrides, jeans worn low on the hips and T-shirts with packs of Camels rolled in the sleeves, ducktail haircuts, crude slang, and occasional outbursts of vandalism.

Cultural confusion affected their elders as well. Anti-integration riots in Little Rock, Arkansas, shattered a veneer of racial harmony; Sputnik demonstrated Soviet superiority in the space race and triggered a national debate over the quality of American education. Voters grew cynical. Ike's chief-of-staff was dismissed for taking bribes; his vice-president, Richard Nixon, was jostled and jeered in Latin America. The economy slid into recession. The sale of tranquilizers mushroomed, dress styles began to cross gender lines— pink shirts for men, pedal pushers for women—and button-down males turned from puritanism to Playmates of the Month. Bunny-herd Hugh Hefner went to court over *Playboy* numerous times, but readers provided the most eloquent defense: by 1958, they were five million strong. Though the nation may not have been more sexually active, it had become more sexually curious, sexually aware, and sexually preoccupied.

The contretemps between the Production Code Administration and the picturemakers over *The Moon Is Blue* and *The French Line* demonstrated that not everyone was comfortable with the new candor, yet Geoff Shurlock balanced Ike and Hef, the conservative grandfather and the prince of sexual expression. Despite appreciation of what Breen stood for, a Selznick International executive had called Shurlock's appointment as acting director in the 1940s "a great relief to us all"; Stanley Kramer termed his 1954 appointment as permanent director "a godsend." Over the years, Shurlock would attempt to accommodate the producers, while also attempting to persuade the Association board that only more liberal decisions could insure the survival of the Production Code Administration. The Englishman had no honeymoon, though. Efforts to loosen the Production Code—including a 1954 Code amendment that erased taboos on miscegenation, liquor, and some profane words—were called "not enough" by independent producers, "too much" by the Legion of Decency. Shurlock could do no right. He refused Preminger the Seal on *The Man With the Golden Arm,* but the Legion granted the story of heroin addict Frankie Machine a "B." He approved Kazan's *Baby Doll,* the heavy-breather about a Southern bigot and his underage bride, which the Legion then stamped "C." The controversy over both features made Shurlock envy his predecessor.

The second director of the Production Code Administration was no Joseph Breen. He had no beach house, no Hollywood clique, no family. He tossed no memorable New Year's Eve parties where Hoot Gibson (as he had one December 31 at the Breens) drew his pistol and fired six rounds into the ceiling. No movie star, he drove used cars and usually ate in the office commissary. He had been married to the eccentric Ella Shurlock, but they lived in separate flats of a duplex until her death in 1953. He later moved into the La Brea Apartments, near the Production Code office where he worked. Not long after Ella died, he found himself in downtown Los Angeles and outside one of the last remaining taxi dance halls. He told an associate that he entered the hall "to broaden his education." There he met Mabel, who had come from the Pacific Northwest when her husband had deserted her and her baby. Shurlock responded to her—perhaps out of loneliness, perhaps sympathy, perhaps affection, no one could tell—and soon they were seen together at the Hollywood premieres and awards ceremonies that Shurlock occasionally attended and enjoyed. Mabel was as coarse as Shurlock was refined, "really a 'dese-and-dozer,' " the associate recalled. Yet as Hollywood couples went, even Hollywood couples of disparate ages, they were unremarkable, especially when compared to a celebrated nymphet and her swain.

In 1947, novelist Vladimir Nabokov had begun what he called "a short novel about a man who liked little girls." A Russian émigré and Cambridge graduate, Nabokov turned *The Kingdom by the Sea* into a short story, then back into a novel set in his adopted homeland, America. In *Lolita,* thirteen-year-old Humbert Humbert falls in love with young Annabel Leigh and, forever after, becomes obsessed by near-pubescent girls. Recovered from a failed marriage and nervous breakdown, he settles in Ramsdale and falls for the daughter of his landlady. "It was love at first sight, at last sight, at ever and ever sight." To be close to Lolita, the narrator of the book (now Professor Humbert) marries her mother, the widowed Charlotte Haze. He continues to rhapsodize about "the nymphet" in a diary. One day Charlotte finds the journal but dies accidentally before she can expose Humbert. Without telling Lolita what happened to her mother or returning to Ramsdale, Humbert removes her from summer camp. And later, at an inn called the Enchanted Hunters, Lolita seduces Humbert.

Lolita never again offers herself to Humbert. Motoring across America with the nymphet as hostage, Humbert warns her that if she tells what they have done, she will be institutionalized. They stop long enough in a small Eastern town for Lolita to enter a girls' school and take part in a school play, *The Enchanted Hunters.* But when Humbert suspects that his stepdaughter has a lover, he uproots her for another cross-country trek. In Elphinstone, Lolita escapes. Humbert soon realizes that he and Lolita's lover—playwright Clare Quilty, the author of *The Enchanted Hunters*—resemble each other: "He mimed and mocked me. His allusions were definitely highbrow. He was well-read. He knew French. He was versed in logodaedaly and logomancy. He was an amateur of sex lore." Three years pass. Despite a relationship with a childlike woman named Rita, Humbert pines for the nymphet. They finally meet again, but Lolita refuses to leave her new husband for Humbert. The frustrated professor murders Clare Quilty, then concludes the novel from a cell.

Lolita was at once nightmare and dream, a satire of American life and American mores. Lending the gamy content an academic perspective, Humbert noted that "Dante fell madly in love with his Beatrice when she was nine." Both Lolita and Beatrice were moral

and emotional innocents, but only Lolita was sexually experienced.
More important, while Dante and Beatrice were close in age,
twenty-five years separated the professor of desire from the pre-
pubescent Lolita. Beneath the crust of the novel lay an innately
American concern: the professor and the nymphet had conspired to
slay innocence, and though by the end Prisoner Humbert understood the consequences of what he had done, the loss remained.
The crust meanwhile exuded an odor of pornography. What better
proof than the fact that *she* seduced *him?* Whether prospective
publishers would read long enough to uncover the moral epiphany
was one question. Whether Americans would accept the notion of
the child as mens rea was another.

More than popular literature, the movies had promoted an image
of children as innocents. From Jackie Coogan and the Gish sisters in
the teens to Shirley Temple and Jane Withers in the thirties and
Mickey Rooney and Margaret O'Brien in the forties, children were
tender innocents; nurture—not nature—produced wild boys of the
road. Casting directors could have told an ugly behind-the-scenes
tale of the child stars, one that Hedda Hopper alluded to when she
described them as "a flock of hungry beasts driven by the gale
winds of their pushing, prompting, ruthless mothers." But aside
from curmudgeons (Graham Greene compared the "precocious"
and "voluptuous" Shirley Temple to Dietrich), audiences doted on
screen children. They were fix-it kids, boys and girls who used
innocence to do good. After World War II, the permissiveness of
Dr. Benjamin Spock's *Common Sense Book of Baby and Child Care*
(1946) affirmed that children remained naturally innocent. But the
aromatic sexuality of rock 'n' roll, along with the juvenile delin-
quent pictures of the 1950s, announced a change.

Hotter than "Rock Around the Clock," the manuscript of *Lolita*
crisscrossed New York throughout 1954. Some publishers found
the novel controversial, others pornographic, in the early 1950s two
strikes against acceptance. American courts had traditionally excluded the "lewd and obscene" from the protections afforded by the
First Amendment, so a manuscript thought truly pornographic had
little chance of publication. *Lolita* nonetheless continued to kick
around New York. Mary McCarthy read a bootleg copy in November 1954, then passed it along to Philip Rahv via the concierge

of the Chelsea Hotel; Rahv scanned it but declined to publish an excerpt in *Partisan Review*. Others nibbled—including publisher Roger Straus, who lost interest when Nabokov suggested that the novel appear under a nom de plume—but at least four major publishers rejected it. A disappointed Nabokov sent *Lolita* to Paris, where in 1955 Olympia Press published an English-language edition for the expatriate trade. For better or worse, the book *looked* pornographic. Not long after an American ordered a copy from France, a UNESCO envelope arrived; inside was a "two-volume, sewer-green-covered" edition with "quick-rot, slime binding" and a "heavy pollution of typos." So mean was the reputation of *Lolita* that when publisher Nigel Nicolson took on the book in England, his parents scolded him and the voters of Bournemouth turned him out of Parliament.

The year after excerpts appeared in a 1957 issue of *Anchor Review*, an American finally published *Lolita*. The notices were all that G. P. Putnam's could wish for. Abusive, complimentary, and controversial, they helped make the book news, and they boosted sales. "*Lolita* is pornography, and we do not plan to review it," snapped the Chicago *Tribune* Magazine of Books in an announcement that may have jingled cash registers. The *New York Times'* Orville Prescott called *Lolita* "dull" and "repulsive," while Leslie Hanscom of the New York *World-Telegram* wanted to "land a Babbitt's righteous punch on the super-civilized nose of the author." The *New Republic* editorialized against *Lolita,* an "obscene chronicle of murder and a child's destruction." *America* condemned the book.

Playwright Clare Quilty had a "passion for tantalization." So had *Lolita,* and Hollywood could not resist. By September 1958, within weeks of the appearance of *Lolita* in bookstores, Stanley Kubrick and James B. Harris had optioned the novel and contacted Shurlock. The independents' submission of an "obscene chronicle" to the Production Code Administration became yet another sign of Hollywood at the crossroads.

That the industry was in transition seemed obvious. Louis Mayer had died in 1957, Harry Cohn in 1958. Though he would later return, Zanuck had stepped down at Twentieth Century–Fox in 1956. After *A Farewell to Arms* in 1957 and *Porgy and Bess* in 1959, Selznick and Goldwyn retired; their best work had been behind

them for more than a decade. The studios also changed. In the late
fifties, when the box office bottomed at a record low of thirty-five
million tickets a week, Universal and RKO were sold to television
production companies, while Fox and Metro welcomed to the lot
independent director-producers like George Stevens and Alfred
Hitchcock who could help soak up overhead. The corporations
sacrificed corporate identities for cash infusions.

The Code changed as well. In 1956, pressured by the independents who wanted screen freedom, the Association undertook a
major Production Code rewrite that lifted all remaining taboos
except nudity, sexual perversion, and venereal disease. When
"treated within the careful limits of good taste," drug addiction,
prostitution, and childbirth were suddenly acceptable subjects. The
changes were less important than the signal they carried: from now
on, Shurlock told Hollywood, "it's the treatment that counts." The
treatment had always counted; what could be treated had drastically changed, however, and some saw the revision as a board-
sanctioned notice that—despite the rally *The French Line* had once
inspired—the 1930 Production Code was moribund.

Though *Lolita* had the potential to lend a knockout punch to the
Production Code, Shurlock may have been surprised that producers Kubrick and Harris had approached him about the novel.
An adaptation seemed ideal for the art theatres, those houses that
welcomed pictures without the Seal. "We pride ourselves that our
audience is above average in intellect," exhibitor Walter Reade
noted; "we think our audience is well aware of the subject matter of
the film prior to entering the theatre; we find it impossible to
believe that our patrons stumble into the theatre and are shocked to
behold what they see and what they hear." A low-budget *Lolita*,
faithful to Nabokov and scornful of the Production Code, would
probably have been the darling of the art house circuit.

The thirty-year-old Kubrick had made two low-budget pictures,
then formed a company with James Harris and produced three
acclaimed works: *The Killing, Paths of Glory,* and *Spartacus.* He
wanted something more than the cult fame of *The Killing* and *Paths
of Glory,* though, and few doubted that he had the drive to accomplish it. "He'll be a fine director some day," Kirk Douglas remarked, "if he falls flat on his face just once." No Roman holiday

for the star or the director, *Spartacus* had nevertheless shown Kubrick the power of big budgets. The literary or cinematic merits of the Nabokov novel were not unimportant, but Kubrick and Harris saw *Lolita* as a property that could expand their independent production company. Royalties from American and foreign publications of *Lolita* would soon free Nabokov from the professorial duties that had supported him for years; perhaps with luck, the screen adaptation could perform another miracle for Kubrick and Harris. All hinged on financing, which could hinge on the approval of the Production Code Administration. The September 1958 meeting with Shurlock was key.

The East Coast scandal about *Lolita* had apparently not reached the West Coast, for Shurlock had heard nothing about the novel. Assuming the worst, Kubrick and Harris had changed one story point even before calling on the Production Code Administration: they had made father and stepdaughter husband and wife. The plot points that they retained roused suspicion enough on Beverly Boulevard. The producers insisted that they would treat the sexual relationship inoffensively, though, and draw innocent humor from the conflict between a mature man and a gum-snapping adolescent. They promised Shurlock that they would make *Lolita,* not a sequel to *Baby Doll.* A Kentucky marriage license would deodorize the story of a preteen and an older man, Shurlock conceded, yet he cautioned Kubrick and Harris that a twelve-year-old bride who looked twelve years old could block a Seal. Armed with a warning ticket, not a citation, the producers announced to the trade press that they would film a *Lolita* that Shurlock could certify. Now they could cruise Hollywood for a distributor.

Men on-screen had been debased by passion before: Emil Jannings by cabaret singer Marlene Dietrich in *The Blue Angel,* aristocrat Leslie Howard by waitress Bette Davis in *Of Human Bondage.* In the Paramount comedy *Houseboat,* a twelve-year-old fell for Sophia Loren; "never having read 'Lolita,' " the screenwriters quipped, "he thinks his aim is unattainable." Aware that Hollywood loved such tales (*Blue Angel* was remade in 1959, *Of Human Bondage* in 1964) and confident that the aura of scandal attached to the novel would sell the project, Kubrick and Harris had enormous expectations. And when they turned to United Artists—a haven for independents, especially those whose pictures challenged the Production Code—they were certain of backing. After all, UA vice-president Max Youngstein broadcast that he could "outsmart the Code." But UA gave Kubrick the comeuppance that Kirk Douglas thought he deserved. According to UA West Coast representative Robert Blumofe, the producers made "one of the most presumptuous and arrogant demands for a deal that we have ever had, particularly when it comes from a couple of youngsters like these." UA passed on *Lolita*.

Kubrick and Harris had not purchased the *Lolita* screen rights, which seemed unmarketable without a distribution deal. Shurlock naturally hoped that the partners would abandon the project, for the theme of the novel seemed to promise that even the most innocent adaptation would draw protests. In March 1959, though, the producers shredded the Kentucky marriage license, aged the now-unwed heroine three years, and drove to Burbank. They told Warners that the picture would concern a no-good fifteen-year-old and the older man whose life she ruined. Company executives turned to Shurlock, who urged them to consider the "possible adverse reactions to the simple announcement that Warner Bros. was going to make a movie based on this novel." Whether because of Production Code resistance, the producers' demands for final cut, or other reasons, Warners also passed on *Lolita*.

Kubrick turned to Columbia. The company had recently distributed *And God Created Woman* (with Brigitte Bardot in the buff) through its art film subsidiary, Kingsley-International, and foresaw another boon with *Lolita*. The subsidiaries were an improvised—and cheesy—construct that had further shaken the foundations of the Production Code; they were exempt from the rules imposed on Motion Picture Association member companies, and thus allowed the studios to distribute pictures that could not pass the Shurlock office. For a Columbia-financed rather than Columbia-imported picture, though, the company wanted the Seal to guarantee the widest possible distribution. Columbia browbeat Shurlock: should he not allow a thirteen-year-old unwed Lolita, the company would appeal to the Board of Directors. Shurlock greeted the bluff with British cool and, perhaps afraid that the Production Code administrator would not bend, Columbia also passed on *Lolita*.

Kubrick was piqued. "The Code has become the loose suspenders that hold up the baggy pants of the circus clown," he told *Look* in summer 1959. "It allows the pants to slip dangerously, but never to fall." From hours spent hunched over a chessboard, Kubrick might have learned more restraint. But Code bashing had become common. That same year, Shurlock rejected *Happy Anniversary*, a comedy about a honeymoon that precedes a wedding. Producer Ralph Fields appealed, and the board passed the picture with the addition of only one line for the husband: "I was wrong. I never should have taken Alice to that hotel room before we were married. What could I have been thinking of?" Fields gloated in the *New York Times* and *Herald Tribune* that the Association had snubbed the Production Code Administration. Shooting *Sons and Lovers* in England, producer Jack Cardiff told reporters that he had dismissed the "infantile" counsel of Code officials. In late 1959, with the wounds of the *Lolita* negotiations apparently fresh, Kubrick struck again. The Code "did not make much difference any more," he told Hollywood reporter Bob Thomas, then told Shurlock that he had been misquoted.

Over at Twentieth Century–Fox, while Kubrick and Harris continued to scratch around Hollywood for a palatable distribution arrangement, a gaffer threw a spot against a black curtain. Marilyn Monroe came out, announced that her name was "Lolita," and cooed that she was not allowed to play . . . with boys . . . because her heart belonged to daddy. *Let's Make Love* would promote *Lolita*—if only Kubrick and Harris could make the picture. Seven Arts offered them the chance. With the expanding television production company putting up the money, Kubrick purchased the Nabokov novel for a reported $125,000.

After a valedictory entitled "On Censorship," Nabokov left Cornell University for Los Angeles in early 1960 to author the *Lolita* screenplay. The Russian author enjoyed southern California. He dined with such celebrities as John Wayne or Gina Lollobrigida and, near home, prowled a "blooming canyon full of good butterflies." Though Kubrick maintained some distance, he told Nabokov that the linchpin as far as Production Code Administration approval went was Lolita's age. She could be younger (and a wife) or older (and a concubine), but not twelve and unwed. Kubrick wanted wide distribution, and he wanted the Seal. When Kubrick met Nabokov, he suggested some Hollywood flimflam, ten reels of license followed by one reel of morality. Lolita and Humbert would carry on throughout the picture, but in a late scene the audience would learn that they had been secretly married all along. With the issue suspended and a promise that Kubrick would "heed my whims more closely than those of the censor," Nabokov started writing.

Nabokov worked throughout summer 1960, producing a four-hundred-page manuscript. Kubrick, meanwhile, was preoccupied with casting. From the standpoint of narrative integrity and Production Code approval, the director found Lolita the most complex role to fill. He tested numerous women, including Tuesday Weld: "I didn't have to play it," noted Weld. "I *was* Lolita." By late summer, thirteen-year-old Sue Lyon, a blond model with television experience, had won the role. Kubrick showed Nabokov her photograph and confidently added that she could be made "younger and grubbier." Months before, Errol Flynn had proposed himself for Humbert, and his young mistress Beverly Aadland for Lolita, but Kubrick may have thought the handsome actor (once charged with statutory rape) too on-the-nose. He cast the smooth James Mason as the professor and Peter Sellers as the dramatist Clare Quilty.

The plan to shoot *Lolita* near London would allow the producers to earn a British subsidy, expand the budget, and elude the eyes of the Production Code Administration. Kubrick followed a pattern that had become common even for directors who worked in Hollywood: he conferred with Shurlock to secure the necessary conditional approvals, then—without further discussion—set out to produce the work far from Shurlock's supervision.

By the time Seven Arts financed *Lolita,* Shurlock could sense that the Production Code Administration had entered the twilight years. The signs were everywhere. The major companies were major in name only; they were distributors—not producers—of pictures. A pattern of European production and Hollywood distribution had become common: during the first six months of 1960, the major studios *made* only fourteen of the ninety-eight pictures they released. Though the rise of the independents as well as a Writers Guild strike had trimmed American studio production, the dispute could not account for the fact that Italy, France, and England had eighty features in production in June 1960, Hollywood only nineteen.

A feature story on Shurlock in the *Los Angeles Times* concluded with a rhetorical question. "Know what Geoff does on weekends? Goes to see foreign films. 'I've got to know what THEY are doing.'" A decade before, Shurlock would have screened the pictures at his Beverly Boulevard office, but in the late 1950s and early 1960s, most foreign-film importers bypassed the Production Code Administration. One distributor told Congress that because the Seal cost a minimum of $500, fewer than five percent of the independents sought one. "We do not play the major circuits and we just don't need it, there is no reason for it and we don't go ask for it." Know what Hollywood producers and directors like Kubrick did on weekends, though? They went to see what THEY were doing, then pestered Shurlock for Production Code concessions.

Though Shurlock wanted American producers to have the same freedom of expression that Europeans enjoyed, he feared the consequences of abandoning the Production Code. Many American producers agreed. During the period when Kubrick worked on *Lolita*, Jerry Wald argued that the Code shielded America from "an orgy of sin, smut, and sensationalism." Yet Wald also produced *Peyton Place, Return to Peyton Place,* and the celebrated *Best of Everything,* which he boasted contained "every kind of sexual relationship you can think of." Others attempted to outdo Wald.

In *Man-Trap,* suburban couples fired martini water guns at one another and played rounds of "Braille," a game where blindfolded husbands must identify their wives by touch. *Oscar Wilde* (and two months later *The Trials of Oscar Wilde*) probed the secrets of a notorious "sodomite," and *The Last Sunset* fell on a gunslinger drawn to the daughter of his former lover. Billy Wilder cracked that the times were almost right for "a movie about a young man who has a passionate love affair with his mother. At the end he learns that she is not his mother and he commits suicide." Years before, actors would have shunned such roles. Now Jeffrey Hunter (fresh from Christ in *King of Kings*) portrayed the suburban husband in *Man-Trap* and Kirk Douglas the father with latent incestuous desires in *The Last Sunset.* Almost de rigueur, the Leslie Caron of *Gigi* and *Lili* lost her "cumbersome virginity" in *The L-Shaped Room.*

The Last Sunset and the Oscar Wilde stories challenged the Pro-

duction Code ban on "sex perversion or any inference to it."
Throughout the period, Shurlock had been pressured to bend the
rule, especially where it concerned homosexuality. The movies
usually mocked "the third sex," which had been on-screen at least
since *Different from the Others,* a 1919 German drama starring Con-
rad Veidt. Some veteran producers as well as Breen and Shurlock
thought serious treatment of homosexuality improper. On *Tea and
Sympathy* (about a prep school youngster who overcomes impotence and fears of latent homosexuality through the tender sexual
intervention of his housemaster's wife), Deborah Kerr found the
Production Code Administration "very difficult about the homosexual angle, which is, I understand, their objection. Adultery is
OK, impotence is OK, but perversion is their bête noire." Breen
had vetoed *Tea and Sympathy.* Shurlock opened the door that Breen
had slammed shut, but asked that MGM drop all reference to
homosexuality; the studio quickly complied. Metro production
chief Dore Schary knew that audiences would have little trouble
reading the picture's subtext, and besides, as part of the deal, he got
to keep the act of adultery. MGM ads promoted the 1956 feature as
the "Love Story of a Teenage Boy and an Understanding Woman"
and asked "When Does a Woman's Sympathy End and Her Indiscretion Begin?" Metro reached a similar agreement two years later
on *Cat on a Hot Tin Roof;* the hero's homosexuality was barely
disguised, and the Code continued to crumble. When Shurlock
refused to certify *Suddenly Last Summer,* the tale of doomed homosexual poet Sebastian Venable, producer Sam Spiegel appealed to
the Motion Picture Association. He lost, but *Lolita* and the sheer
number of pictures that touched on "the homosexual angle" or
other "sex perversions" would soon make the rule almost impossible to enforce.

The Production Code Administration shouldered part of the
responsibility for the adultery, rape, fornication, and nymphomania
on-screen: "We have been told repeatedly that we are too lax and
too liberal," Shurlock told Darryl Zanuck, "and we are beginning
to believe it." But what could Shurlock do? He could no longer fine
the studios for releasing a picture without a Seal; he could not even
deny a Seal without fear of litigation. A Breen man throughout the
years, Shurlock had adopted the Irishman's unswerving faith in

self-regulation, yet Production Code enforcement had become not only frustrating but embarrassing. Some months before *Lolita* entered production, Shurlock had confided in Eric Johnston that he was "in terror" that the producers of *Never on Sunday* would apply for a Seal. "But the horrible part is that, in rejecting it, we would probably have to adduce perforce exactly the same reasons as did the Atlanta censor board." A television program had just lambasted the Georgia censors as parochial crackers, and Shurlock hated "the idea of our Code operation being equated in the public mind" with Southern bigotry.

With *Lolita* under way and the balance of power tipped toward the producers, the former Breen man turned wistful. "In trying to hew to the classic tradition," he told Johnston, "the Code may often seem cumbersome and, to use a word which is by now becoming hackneyed, 'hackneyed.' We will simply have to struggle along and do our best to make the pictures (in our favorite escape-hatch phrase) reasonably acceptable to the reasonable members of our modern-day audience." *Lolita* would pose an insurmountable challenge, however, for no matter how much Shurlock tinkered, he could not elude the premise of children and sex, a premise that could have dire consequences for an agency committed to precedent.

By December 1960, Kubrick had a shooting script. Shurlock apparently preferred not to read it. He wanted to keep himself "free-handed," and hoped that Kubrick would make whatever picture he wished without consulting—and thus potentially compromising—the Production Code Administration. Working in London, though, the producers sent the *Lolita* script to the British Board of Film Censors, then to Shurlock, for Seven Arts was convinced that with the necessary approvals *Lolita* could produce a box office bonanza. The British readers called the screenplay a "botched up pastiche" of "smutty juvenilia and Teutonic lavatory humour" and prompted British Board director John Trevelyan to mark every offensive passage for the producers. Trevelyan wrote Shurlock:

I have taken rather a strong line with Kubrick, and there is little that I have left out, because I want to cover ourselves in the event of our having to refuse a certificate when the film is completed. You can imagine that if we had to do this it would create a major press sensation, but I feel sure that a great many people, including many who have not read the book, would be on our side. Of course the intellectuals would tear us apart.

Shurlock would object to the same elements of the script that concerned Trevelyan: the double entendres about "having a cavity filled," the gags whose punch lines turned on "erector sets" and "limp noodles," the moment when Humbert "plunges his face into a heap of crumpled things that had touched her." Once Seven Arts executives saw the report from Trevelyan, they could anticipate the report from Shurlock. The young *Lolita* needed a ward, someone who could protect her from the lash of the Production Code Administration. They turned to an elder statesman of the motion picture industry.

While Kubrick and Harris saw Martin Quigley as a sweet old man, Breen and Shurlock had another view. Breen had hated the *Motion Picture Herald* editorials that chastised him or the Production Code Administration. He would never have alienated Quigley, though, for the *Herald* had the eyes and Quigley the ears of the company presidents. Breen and Shurlock had both heard stories of how Quigley paraded through the Plaza Hotel Oak Room at one o'clock on weekdays, a Legion of Decency prelate on each arm, the better to impress the New York moguls who regularly lunched there. They had seen how disruptive Quigley could be, and also resented him. But Shurlock was no pushover. When executive secretary Rae Taylore reminded Shurlock once too often of her former boss and the way that he ran the Production Code Administration, Shurlock demeaned her: he answered his own phone calls and typed his own letters. "It was cheap and cowardly," Jack Vizzard recalled, but the strategy worked; Taylore quit. Quigley would later know how Taylore felt.

In 1956, Martin Quigley had named his son editor-in-chief of the *Motion Picture Herald;* thereafter the winds of change cost the publisher and the paper their influence. As *Streetcar* had demonstrated, Quigley had been active behind the scenes at the Legion of Decency and had sometimes pressed the buttons that insured cooperation from the Production Code Administration. The Legion turned more liberal in the early 1960s, however, and Quigley became less welcome at the Catholics' Manhattan headquarters. He had no vocation or avocation; he had only the cancer that would kill him and the need to play one more starring role before he died. An expert on how the Legion of Decency (or at least the *old* Legion of Decency) and the Production Code Administration worked, he became a full-time consultant to independent producers, a champion of lost censorship causes, a fixer. How perverse the symmetry appeared. As late as 1959, he had warned that "a Code that rolls with the punches, wobbles and winds up in expedient compromises will not do the job. It must not be allowed to degenerate into a hollow pretense, trying to appear as something it is not." Less than two years later, the author of the Code would represent Seven Arts and the inflammatory *Lolita* before the Production Code Administration.

In correspondence with Kubrick and Harris, though, Quigley attempted to protect the Code and tone down the *Lolita* script. He predicted that both men would "gag over" some comments, and they must have. Quigley warned the producers that the "tongue-in-ear business" (the method of seduction that Lolita chose for Humbert) "cannot be used without arousing *erotically* the susceptible members of any audience, anywhere any time." He also told the producers that an "odor of disgust" would adhere to the "toe-painting business." But he soon learned that the producers wanted no script doctor. Much of the revised screenplay that they asked Quigley to send Shurlock in mid-January 1961 had already been shot, including the "cavity" and "noodle" lines. The Production Code Administration could not shape the narrative but only hope to make the picture "reasonably acceptable to the reasonable members of our modern-day audience."

Shurlock red-pencilled all that Trevelyan had, then warned Quigley that the Clare Quilty murder (because of the potential for screen violence) along with the age of Lolita and the seduction scene at the Enchanted Hunters could all block a Seal. Quigley told the producers that he found Shurlock more than reasonable. Had Kubrick and Harris not been thwarted by United Artists, Warners, and Columbia, had they not been pressured by Seven Arts, or had they been more experienced as independent producers, they might have rebelled. But the partners were not as "presumptuous and arrogant" about censorship matters as they had been about financing; besides, they believed that they were making a *Lolita* far more benign than the Nabokov novel. To secure a wide release and the necessary Code Seal, they were prepared (Quigley reported) to take "this notorious story out of the gutter." The Quilty murder would not be brutal, Harris promised, and Sue Lyon would photograph older than her thirteen years; the seduction scene would costume Lolita in a "heavy flannel, long sleeved, high-necked, full-length nightgown and Humbert not only in pajamas, but bathrobe as well." Long before they retained Quigley, the producers had made these alterations, and Shurlock could only hope that the finished picture would reflect them.

By August 1961, Kubrick and Harris had a cut of *Lolita* to screen for Shurlock. The cerebral touch of Stanley Kubrick was everywhere apparent. *Lolita* opens with a foot descending against a satin backdrop into the frame. The small foot falls with coolness and grace, and rests on air. A hand moves into the frame and tenderly palms the suspended foot. The credits continue as the other hand presses cotton between two toes and starts to apply nail gloss, from the largest toe to the smallest. Kubrick had found the essence of Nabokov; he had also created an image that could not only tickle audiences but please Shurlock: the pedicure conveys the obsession and the devotion, the subjugation and the tenderness, the dream and the nightmare of Humbert Humbert.

The narrative proper starts with the Quilty murder. Nosing around Pavor Manor, the Quilty estate, Humbert Humbert discovers his nemesis—already ghostlike—beneath one of many sheets thrown over the furniture. The men play a mad Ping-Pong game (a Peter Sellers invention), then Humbert drives Quilty upstairs where the playwright takes refuge behind an imitation Gainsborough, a portrait of a demure young woman. Humbert sends bullets through the canvas. Shurlock could not only approve but applaud such circumspect treatment of murder. Like Boris Karloff, whose death had been suggested by dashed bowling pins in *Scarface*, Peter Sellers had taken the fall "offscreen," with no blood spilled. The urbane Shurlock could appreciate the shock cut from the Haze lawn to the drive-in horror movie, the tongue-lashing that the heavily mascaraed Lolita gives Humbert after he drags her home from the school play, the scene in which Humbert (rather like Edward G. Robinson in *Key Largo*) lolls in the bathtub while guests pay condolence calls following the death of Charlotte. *Lolita* contained the razor-sharp slant on humanity that would come to represent the Stanley Kubrick style.

Quigley had recommended that the producers screen *Lolita* for Shurlock in the afternoon, "at which time Geof. and his staff members may be in better spirits than perhaps in the forenoon." But the clock could not help the Kubrick-Harris production, for the cosmetic changes had not altered the lethal theme. Lolita sometimes looked mature, particularly in a black formal gown with two scoops of white that accented her breasts, but at other times she looked and behaved like a twelve-year-old child. And the child, not the adolescent, pecked Humbert's cheek, crawled onto his lap at a motel, and invited him to play games at the Enchanted Hunters. Shurlock could not change the subtext of *Lolita,* the love affair between man and child that the public would not fail to extrapolate. He could not even change much of the text. He could attempt to make the unacceptable "reasonably acceptable," though, and he could toss the picture into the barrel that he would soon roll toward the Association board to prompt passage of a Code amendment on cinema sex. He could also taunt Martin Quigley, who had screened the picture alongside Production Code associates. After some discussion about minor deletions, Shurlock focused on the seduction scene at the Enchanted Hunters. There Lolita suggests that she and Humbert play games. When the professor asks the nature of the games, she whispers in his ear. Kubrick had attempted to follow the Nabokov script.

> With a burst of rough glee she puts her mouth to his ear (could one reproduce this hot moist sound, the tickle and the buzz, the vibration, the thunder of her whisper?). She draws back. Kneeling above recumbent Humbert (who is invisible except for a twitching toe), she contemplates him expectantly. Her humid lips and sly slit eyes seem to anticipate and prompt an assent.

At once hesitant and aquiver, Humbert agrees to play the game. "If it's not too dangerous. If it's not too difficult. If it's not too—*Ah, mon Dieu!*" Shurlock saw how the moment could be made

acceptable—a fast fade-out on the whispered words and elimination of the dialogue that followed—then announced that he would
telephone producer James Harris to explain. "Wait a minute,"
Quigley cried. "You speak to *me!*" Heading for his office, Shurlock
asked Quigley: "Are *you* paying for the Certificate?" Shurlock
called Harris while Quigley contemplated the double humiliation
of having betrayed the Code and lost face with the producers; the
fact that Shurlock had focused on the "tongue-in-ear business" that
had so incensed Quigley completed the abasement.

The Seal on *Lolita,* a picture about a love affair between a man
and a child, compounded by an aura of incest, would cut another tie
to Breen and the Production Code Administration of the 1930s and
1940s. No matter what the deletions, the theme would undermine
the Production Code (especially the strict rule on "sex perversion")
and make others wonder whether a Code was operative at all.
Shurlock was ambivalent. He had proprietary feelings toward the
Production Code Administration, whose commercial and even
moral purpose still seemed viable. Yet he knew that many Hollywood producers—especially independent producers—respected
neither the agency nor its laws. The Production Code Administration could no longer patch and plaster. Board members must soon
remodel or raze the Code.

Shurlock sensed that even the religious community—which once
would have taken the Production Code boys to the woodshed over
Lolita—wanted change. Chaos and contradiction were rife in Hollywood, with Jews, Protestants, and Catholics torn between a commitment to freedom and a desire to control. The Protestant Motion
Picture Council rated the American musical *Gigi* for "Adults Only";
the American Jewish Committee (along with the National Congress
of Parents and Teachers) rated it suitable for children over twelve.
Tensions between liberals and conservatives within the faiths made
it hard for Shurlock to preach moderation to Hollywood. In 1960, a
National Council of Churches committee composed of such Protestant and Eastern Orthodox leaders as Bishop James Pike and Twentieth Century–Fox mogul Spyros Skouras had condemned the
"pathological preoccupation with sex and violence" in motion pictures. But when George Heimrich, the Hollywood liaison for the
Council, moved to establish a three-man board to evaluate every

script submitted to the Production Code Administration, the Council stopped him cold. A member of the Lutheran Film Board commented in words fit for a Hollywood sampler: "It is decidedly un-Christian, after a man has put millions of dollars into a picture, to tell people not to see it." The following year, Hollywood earned another respite when the General Assembly of the Southern Presbyterian Church refused to allow the Louisiana Presbyteria to discourage attendance at "immoral" pictures.

Even the Legion of Decency was softening: liberal membership was in the ascendant, and revisions made in 1957 had not only increased the number of laymen and broad-minded priests on the evaluation staff but made possible a number of acceptable ("A-II" or "B") ratings for pictures that in years past would have been condemned. Perhaps more important, some theaters that had once followed the Catholic standard now screened an occasional condemned picture. Many within the Church had warmed to the more serious adult pictures and, along with Father Patrick Sullivan, the Jesuit who had become assistant executive secretary of the Legion, rejected the notion that "the Catholic conscience" should be used "to control the output of Hollywood." Soon the Legion even offered parishioners a revised—and wholly voluntary—pledge: "I promise to promote by word and deed what is morally and artistically good in motion picture entertainment. I promise to discourage indecent, immoral and unwholesome motion pictures, especially by my good example and always in a responsible and civic-minded manner."

Yet Kubrick and Harris knew that the Legion of Decency could still bite. In 1959, Monsignor Little had almost condemned *Some Like It Hot*. "The subject matter of 'transvestism' naturally leads to complications," he told Shurlock; "in this film there seemed to us to be clear inferences of homosexuality and lesbianism. The dialogue was not only 'double entendre' but outright smut. The offense in costuming was obvious." The comedy that Shurlock called a lark from beginning to end earned a "B." An even more telling case involved *King of Kings*. While the Vatican heaped accolades on the solemn 1961 epic, the Legion awarded the picture a "Separate Classification," one that tabbed the Biblical spectacular inappropriate for the uninformed and thus reduced attendance.

Seven Arts was afraid that the Legion would condemn *Lolita* and, since the picture lacked the innocence of *The Moon Is Blue,* suburban exhibitors would shy away. Those sub-run bookings sometimes meant the difference between profit and loss, so the distributor asked Martin Quigley to run interference. Spited on the West Coast, Quigley was willing to serve but could hardly have assured the company that the Catholics would anoint *Lolita.* Some of the women from the International Federation of Catholic Alumnae, once the sole members of the evaluation staff, resented the dilution of their power as well as the new rules and the foreign films that had made them necessary; they may also have seen Quigley as a turncoat. Yet the publisher and the producers could reason that the new blood of the Legion would regard *Lolita* as a picture that deserved a "Separate Classification." And with such a dispensation from the Catholics, Kubrick and Harris could return to Shurlock and ask that he reconsider the mandated cuts.

Kubrick and Harris screened the same print for the Legion that they had for Shurlock. But while more than a third of the board (none of them Catholic Alumnae) voted to award *Lolita* a "Separate Classification," almost half (and half of them clergy) voted for "Condemned." The picture offered "two and a half hours of exposure to an unrelieved concentration upon the subject of sexual depravity," Monsignor Little told the producers. Not only was Lolita a younger adolescent, but the producers had countenanced "the moral corruption of a minor [Sue Lyon] for purposes of film making." The Monsignor reserved much of his wrath for Quigley. The "Legion people put Martin through the most meticulous paces," Vizzard wrote, "demanding that he scrub here and sandpaper there, in exactly the spots where he had negotiated compromises with the Code office." It was even worse than Vizzard imagined: the Catholics shunted Quigley and communicated directly with Seven Arts. What Quigley termed the "ordeals of tension" soon ended. The chastened producers—who perhaps shared Quigley's perception that the "C" had been awarded "to offset a long series of liberalistic classifications"—took the shears to *Lolita* and made the changes that Shurlock and the Legion ordered, from the "*mon Dieu*" fade-out to Humbert's offscreen bathroom grunts and "limp noodle" dialogue.

Meanwhile, Shurlock won the concession that would allow him to certify *Lolita* and buy some time for the Code. For months Hollywood had leaned on New York to bend the "sex perversion" clause of the Production Code. United Artists alone had three forthcoming releases— *The Best Man, Advise and Consent,* and *The Children's Hour*—that would touch on homosexuality, and UA president Arthur Krim had pleaded for a Code amendment that would permit serious treatment of such content. "We are most anxious to distribute these three pictures with a Code seal," he had told Eric Johnston in May 1961. Shurlock tacitly supported Krim, and perhaps used *Lolita* to pry a revision from board members. By October, the Association had broadened the Code so that producers could treat sex aberration.

For an industry whose 1930 Production Code saw the audience as the masses, "the cultivated and the rude, the mature and the immature, the self-respecting and the criminal," the new amendment was a remarkable step forward. In 1915, the Supreme Court had called the movies a business "pure and simple." But the *Miracle* case had been the prelude to a symphony of important decisions that recognized the movies as art and rendered the Production Code amendment almost mandatory. In June 1959, the United States Supreme Court found a section of the New York censorship law unconstitutional. "What New York has done," the Court ruled in the *Lady Chatterley's Lover* case, "is to prevent the exhibition of a motion picture because that picture advocates an idea—that adultery under certain circumstances may be proper behavior. Yet the First Amendment's basic guarantee is of freedom to advocate ideas. The State, quite simply, has thus struck at the very heart of constitutionally protected liberty." Courts declared the Pennsylvania and Atlanta censorship laws unconstitutional in the early 1960s. The Pennsylvania Supreme Court decision condemned not only censorship but the board's hidden agenda, the assessment of examination fees, "a plain attempt to tax the exercise of free speech." Resistance continued. Chicago police chief Vincent Nolan announced that if a picture "is objectionable to a child, the picture is objectionable—period!" Senator James Eastland proposed a constitutional amendment that would allow each state to govern "decency and morality." But the censors had seen the writing on the wall, and as they faded away, so did the fear of them that had once prompted Hollywood to heed the Production Code and shun pictures like *Lolita*.

In January 1962, after Shurlock passed the recut *Lolita* under the amended "sex perversion" rule, Kubrick and Harris returned to the Legion. Nine of twelve Catholic Alumnae who screened the picture still wanted to condemn *Lolita* but did not prevail. So vocal were they and some others, though, that Monsignor Little attached a proviso to the "Separate Classification" awarded the film: the Legion would have veto power over all advertising, and the distributor would add two captions to all ads for the picture: "This movie has been approved by M.P.A.A." and "For persons over 18 only."

The Legion wanted to control the ads because it feared that Seven Arts would pervert the "over 18 only" caveat. Like the Duke and the Dauphin from *Huckleberry Finn*, promoters understood the value of barring "women and children" from a dramatic performance. By 1961, the "Adults Only" tag had become so common a euphemism for sex that Russ Meyer could mimic it in ads for *The Immoral Mr. Teas*, a "nudie" picture "Not recommended for prigs, prudes, or Puritans." As the campaign for *Open City* had demonstrated, Hollywood carnival barkers sold even literate foreign films as exploitation items. *Les Liaisons Dangereuses* became *Les Liaisons Dangereuses 1960*, hawked as a story of contemporary immorality. A far more important picture, Kenzi Mizoguchi's *Utamaro, Painter of Women* opened in the States as *Utamaro, Painter of Nudes*.

Catholics who never went to the movies read the ads and drew conclusions. The layout for *Waltz of the Toreadors* had military man Peter Sellers with the bosoms of one woman in his face, the buttocks of another at his elbow. *Doctor in Love* played up "operation fun," a physician bent over a showgirl about to wrap her leg around his waist. A quote from Walter Winchell dominated newspaper layouts for *The Bramble Bush:* "It makes 'Peyton Place' read like a book of nursery rhymes." True to Hollywood, the promotional materials were more excessive than the pictures they advertised. At the end of *North by Northwest*, Cary Grant pulled Eva Marie Saint into the upper bunk of their Pullman roomette; Shurlock made Hitchcock cut before the couple fell backward in an embrace, but a promotional still caught them almost supine. On *Happy Anniversary*, the picture turned out more proper than the ads, which ballyhooed a new photographic process, something United Artists called "Sin-a-Scope." Seven Arts and *Lolita* had the potential for mischief. As Charlotte Haze introduced Professor Humbert to her bikini-clad daughter, she chattered on about the "peace" and "cherry pies" she would offer him, but the Legion veto would insure that such double entendres would not spill over from the picture to the ads.

Eric Johnston could gracefully accept the Legion veto but not the two captions, "This movie has been approved by M.P.A.A." and "For persons over 18 only." Should the Legion push the endorsement, Johnston wanted the "P.C.A."—not the "M.P.A.A."—to appear on posters. The Production Code Administration had "approved" the picture, and the "censorship" rather than the trade wing of the Association should take the heat. The Legion consented to the change. Johnston also had strong feelings about the restricted audience for the film, but those feelings he suppressed. The Association president spoke of motion picture classification only when spoken to.

Many in Hollywood thought that voluntary classification could end the game of tag between producers and the Production Code Administration. In 1959, screenwriter James Poe told *Look* that all his colleagues favored "this classification." Actress (and mother) Joan Crawford was "all for adult pictures" and hoped that "they don't go back to making those dull films nobody wants to see"; yet she too advocated "a system that would protect youngsters." The Association had supported classification *outside* the industry. It assisted groups that rated picture content for audiences; it also underwrote the monthly *Green Sheet,* the parents' guide to movies that had been published since the 1930s. But the Association so vigorously opposed classification *within* the industry that it would not allow the *Green Sheet* ratings to appear in film ads. "Could an 'adult only' system really work?" Eric Johnston asked congressmen in 1960. "Who could say what is suitable for an adult? Who could decree when someone becomes an adult?—at 14? or 16? or 18? or 21?" Whether voluntary or political, classification was censorship. And censorship, Johnston later added, was unconstitutional.

Beneath such golden platitudes lay base metal: the industry found classification far less unconstitutional than uneconomical. An

"Adults Only" picture often played only a downtown run; managers of neighborhood theaters, carefully attuned to community opinion and more susceptible to criticism than downtown exhibitors, rarely booked adult pictures that had been widely publicized *as* adult pictures. Exhibitors also scratched them from the occasionally lucrative double bill. The concessions stand mattered as much as the box office. After the British Board of Censors classified *Never on Sunday* "X" (for ages seventeen and above), the film attracted an older crowd that passed up the sweets, a major source of revenue for theaters.

The administrator of the Production Code felt differently. Shurlock hated the rows with producers, too many of whom now went around the Production Code Administration. And despite the amended rule on "sex perversion," the absence of classification meant that—nominally at least—pictures concerned with aberrant sex still had to treat it for the widest possible audience. Shurlock told the *New York Times'* Murray Schumach that in 1960 "there were more pictures than ever that should not have been seen by children under 16, unless accompanied by adults." Had Shurlock rather than Johnston made policy, America would have had voluntary classification well before *Lolita* entered production.

Throughout spring 1962, Monsignor Little vetoed captions and photographs that Loew's (Metro's distributor) submitted on *Lolita,* but he refrained from wholesale censorship. The poster and newspaper art for the picture featured Sue Lyon in heart-shaped sunglasses and little else, her tongue at her lollipop. Exploiting the widespread fame of the novel, Metro trimmed the verbal material to a single provocative question: "How did they ever make a movie of 'Lolita'?" Though Monsignor Little knew, he feared that parishioners would assume a different answer. "Ten years ago people went to the movies to be passively entertained," Little told the press, breaking the silence that usually followed the assignment of a rating. Now audiences are "more mature in the sense that they are more selective in film entertainment"; they are ready, he concluded, for *Lolita.* Censorship attorney Ephraim S. London had another view: "It is not so much the audiences which have grown up as the legion, and I applaud it for this."

On opening night in June 1962, to underscore the "Adults Only" content of *Lolita,* Metro stationed a man at the entrance of the Loew's State to keep out all children under nineteen. Naturally the guard turned away Sue Lyon, and naturally the Manhattan press was there. The caption beneath the *Herald Tribune* photograph read: "STUNT—Sue Lyon, only 15 and star of 'Lolita,' barred at N.Y. opening." Lyon eventually entered the theater and saw the picture. "For persons over 18 only" meant "for persons over 18 only unless accompanied by an adult"; an "adult" meant a parent, an older brother, or a John Doe on line who could pose as either. When author Paul Nathan later saw *Lolita,* he noted that "a considerable part of the audience was under age."

At the Manhattan premiere Nabokov found the "horrible seats" reserved for him, then settled down as the lights dimmed. Though the picture was less roguish than the novel, he understood how "infinite fidelity may be an author's ideal but can prove a producer's ruin." The critics were less generous. The *Los Angeles Times* charged that Kubrick had made Nabokov's wickedness seem mere naughtiness. With a left-handed compliment for the Production Code Administration, Philip K. Scheuer continued: "it isn't as though anybody is ever really happy or gets away with anything; moral compensations are left lying around all over the place." The Catholic *Our Sunday Visitor* called the picture "a great big shaggy dog story, saturated with slapstick and striving to get tastefully around a sickeningly abnormal relationship," while *Variety* compared it to "a bee from which the stinger has been removed. It still buzzes with a sort of promising irreverence, but it lacks the power to shock and, eventually, makes very little point either as comedy or satire." The *New York Times* (and many others) answered the oneliner in the ads, "How did they ever make a movie of 'Lolita'?": "They didn't."

Despite mixed reviews, *Lolita* opened to strong box office. At the Capri Theatre in Boston, where *The Birth of a Nation* and other pictures had been banned, the queue for *Lolita* snaked along Huntington Avenue east toward the Public Library and west toward the Christian Science Mother Church. Massaged by the ads and the novel's reputation, patrons anticipated the red hots. Yet Kubrick's forte was cool irony. *Lolita* was droll, absurd, even tragic, but not salacious. In retrospect, it seems a better picture than critics let on, one with occasional but authentic pleasures. It could not possibly have met contemporary expectations, though, and it was far from the commercial triumph that Seven Arts and Loew's had wanted. "In spite of the glowing financial report in the trade press," an associate told Monsignor Little a month after the picture opened, "I have the impression . . . that LOLITA is not measuring up to expectations at the boxoffice."

The picture nonetheless gave Stanley Kubrick the exposure that he desired. "If I could do the film over again," he later remarked, "I would have stressed the erotic component of their relationship with the same weight Nabokov did. But that is the only major area where I believe the film is susceptible to valid criticism." Shurlock wished that Kubrick and Harris had not produced *Lolita* at all. Since they had, though, he may also have wished that they had produced the *Lolita* that Nabokov had written. Had Kubrick and Harris been determined to photograph a seduction scene well beyond the boundaries of the Code and had they not backed off to insure the Seal, Shurlock would have rejected the picture. And had other producers offered Shurlock other pictures with censorable content, the Production Code Administration could perhaps have forced Eric Johnston to address the idea of classification.

Though Shurlock and *Lolita* may have been strange bedfellows, the Kubrick release was nonetheless perverse enough to serve a nascent goal of the Production Code director. The prospect of the nymphet, the passionate professor, and the sex-sparked characters of other features then in production had moved board members to amend the "sex perversion" clause of the Code and at least widen the escape-hatch for the besieged Shurlock. Perhaps even more valuable, the new license had in turn prompted the Legion of Decency to step up demands for classification.

"How did we produce such a little beast?" the widowed Charlotte Haze asked the portrait of her late husband, whose looks and name bore a passing resemblance to a jug-eared Hollywood legend. Will Hays had been dead for almost a decade in 1962, and the "little beast" that he and Hollywood had fathered—the Production Code Administration—now threatened few. Shurlock had watched the conservative Catholics galvanize the beast thirty years before, though, and on the eve of retirement he would watch the liberalistic element of the Church help destroy it.

11

Who's Afraid of Virginia Woolf?

IN *TROPIC OF CANCER*, the down-and-out narrator spends months on the skids. He sponges from American expatriates, pimps for French tarts, and concludes that civilization is doomed, that only art and sex—especially sex—matter. *Tropic of Cancer* (author Henry Miller noted) was about "the recording of all that which is omitted in books." At once funny and sexually explicit, the novel was published in France during the heyday of Mae West, and promptly divided the critics. Was it literature? Or high-toned graffiti? Americans could only speculate, for the government had banned the novel. In 1961, however, Grove Press published an American edition. The legal battles that followed led not only to an important Supreme Court decision but to the predictable announcement that Hollywood would produce *Tropic of Cancer* for the screen.

Moviemaker Joseph E. Levine promised Shurlock to cut the four-letter words from the novel, yet he told *Variety* that he intended to preserve the "humor, anger, art and sex that made it internationally controversial." The Production Code Administration doubted that the picture could be made at all. But when the Supreme Court ruled that only worthless matter could be judged constitutionally obscene, the era of plain-brown-wrappers ended and *Tropic of Cancer* edged closer to Hollywood. Wizened by disease, Joe Breen would not have read *Tropic of Cancer*, though he would have had an opinion about Levine and his plans for the novel. Serious literature? Breen would have snorted. Henry Miller was one more wildcat, no better than the Hollywood lions the Irishman had once whipped. "They'd put fucking in Macy's window," Breen told an associate, "and they'd argue till they were blue in the face that it was 'art.' "

Meanwhile, Edward Albee had opened his own monument to art and candor, *Who's Afraid of Virginia Woolf?* The play fused the realism of Arthur Miller, the poetry of Tennessee Williams, and the symbolism of Eugene O'Neill. Yet Albee spoke with an original voice, one that echoed the courts' renewed commitment to free expression. The characters were witty and neurotic; Martha and George were a postnuclear American first family, their crisp dialogue was seasoned with profanity and blasphemy. The blue language would have roused Breen from his wheelchair, but Broadway audiences of 1962 and 1963 hailed the atonal drama of wedded hell that begins with Martha and George coming home from the party hosted by her father, the president of the college where George teaches history. Martha has invited Nick and Honey, a new professor and his wife, for a nightcap. Martha and George quarrel. When he swings open the front door to welcome the guests, she yells at him, "Screw you!"

The Walpurgisnacht wears on, the alcohol flows. The younger couple see George and Martha bicker and taunt each other; they watch them play games, tell secrets, and prick illusions. In a round of "Get the Guests," George betrays what Nick has shared in confidence, that Honey may not have children because she's "slim-hipped." In "Hump the Hostess," Martha lures Nick upstairs to bed. But the young biology professor cannot satisfy Martha. She later confesses that only George can. Behind the Sturm und Drang of George and Martha lies an odd mutual need, a trust and even love somehow related to an absent child, a son. George rallies Honey, Nick, and Martha for one more game. While Nick and Martha were away, George announces, Western Union delivered a wire: "the little bugger" (the adolescent son) has died in an automobile accident. Martha protests that George may not kill the dream that binds them, the imaginary child. Yet George prevails. He sends Nick and Honey home, then tenderly reprises the punch line of a joke. " 'Who's afraid of Virginia Woolf?' " he sings. "I am, George," Martha says. "I am." The curtain falls.

When *Who's Afraid of Virginia Woolf?* opened, it proved almost as controversial as *Tropic of Cancer.* "Whether such a dramatic ordeal will be successful may be questionable," *Variety* observed; "whether it would be suitable for the road or pictures may be dubious." Six weeks after the October 1962 premiere, though, *Virginia Woolf* had already shown a profit. Despite the three-hour running time, the problematic imaginary child, and the profane and blasphemous dialogue, the play became an attractive road property. Touring companies brought investors almost $1.5 million—along with some problems. In Boston, the censor forced the producers to eliminate references to "Jesus" and "Christ," and to change the opening line from "Jesus H. Christ" to "Mary H. Magdalen." Indianapolis and St. Paul also offered resistance, and the producers dropped a number of conservative stops from the American tour. Apparently without incident, Ingmar Bergman directed a production in Stockholm, Franco Zeffirelli in Venice. But the Lord Chamberlain threatened to block the English production until Albee made sixty-seven cuts; over nine months, the producers whittled the demands to two. Meanwhile, the Pulitzer Prize jury cited the rough language and denied *Virginia Woolf* a Best Play award; two well-known Pulitzer judges resigned over the incident.

Jack Warner knew "art" when he saw it. In March 1963, he optioned *Virginia Woolf* and sent the Production Code Administration a copy of the playscript. Shurlock no longer blanched over "damn" and "hell." *Lolita* and other releases demonstrated that the Production Code Administration could tolerate strong language and even approve pictures about sexual aberration. On *Hud,* then in production, Shurlock allowed not only "damn" and "hell" but "bitch" and "bastard." Yet while the conservative Motion Picture Association had warmed to adult drama, board members still expected Shurlock to rule Hollywood as superego. On *Hud,* producer Martin Ritt crossed the line with "take the cock out of his doodle-doo," and Shurlock told him so. *Virginia Woolf* seemed pure id. In addition to seven "bastard"s and five "son-of-a-bitch"s, Shurlock and associates counted over fifteen "goddamn"s, thirteen references to Christ, and such piquant anatomical phrases as "ass" and "right ball," "angel boobs," and "melons bobbling." The Production Code Administration had bent the Code for *Hud;* it could not break it for *Who's Afraid of Virginia Woolf?*

In a brief letter, Shurlock advised Warner to remove "all the profanity and the very blunt sexual dialogue" from *Virginia Woolf.* He acknowledged that such action would "considerably reduce" the play's impact but concluded that "under the circumstances" he could not otherwise award the Seal. With *Virginia Woolf*—even a laundered *Virginia Woolf*—a potential cornerstone of the studio's expanded production schedule for 1964, Warners seemed compliant. The company turned to Edward Albee. Approaching the playwright through his agent, the studio expressed confidence that Albee was "sufficiently inventive and creative to substitute potent and pungent dialogue that could prove highly effective, even though possibly reducing somewhat the 'shock' impact of this highly regarded play." Beyond a handsome fee for the screen rights, however, Albee wanted nothing to do with Warners or its adaptation.

Talking to a *Variety* reporter but indirectly to Warners, Shurlock warned that a Motion Picture Association member company that attempted *Virginia Woolf* would be in for "some major headaches." By March 1964, though, Warners announced that it had purchased the play for $500,000 and a percentage of the gross. Along with the price tag, the announcement that Fred Zinnemann would direct alarmed Shurlock. The collaboration of Warner, screenwriter Ernest Lehman, and Zinnemann on a half-million-dollar property connoted a substantial budget. And the bigger the budget for *Virginia Woolf,* the more the potential for migraines on Beverly Boulevard.

Warner and Lehman were aware of Shurlock's resistance, so aware that they even considered circumventing the Production Code altogether. The obvious solution—as it was early on for *Lolita*—was to produce *Virginia Woolf* more for the art market and release it under the banner of a Warner Bros. subsidiary. Warners had no subsidiary, however. Like producers Kubrick and Harris on *Lolita,* Lehman and Warner also thought that *Virginia Woolf* merited distribution well beyond the art houses.

Another possible solution was the "theatrofilm." In summer 1964, Warner Bros. and the Electronovision company brought seven cameras into a Broadway theater to shoot two performances of Richard Burton's *Hamlet*. Cut primarily during principal photography, the kinescopelike finished print was ready a few days later. In early fall, the picture would play a two-day-only booking in 971 United States and Canadian theaters. A precursor of the theatrofilm was the 1948 Hitchcock-Warners *Rope*, whose static technique had been economical but dulling. Warners should have seen the downside of seamless photography with the commercial failure of *Rope*, but penny-pinchers since the 1920s, the studio considered Electronovision the road to easy profit. Then Jack Warner saw *Hamlet*. The fuzzy image (especially in long shots), the spotty lighting, and the hum and vibration of the voices were passable for a public domain Shakespearean tragedy but dicey for a $500,000 contemporary American play. Shurlock hoped that "nobody brings the script [of *Virginia Woolf*] to me—I wouldn't want to be the one to butcher it." But with the subsidiary route closed and theatrofilm rejected, Warners seemed certain to produce *Virginia Woolf* as a Hollywood blockbuster.

Lehman could have challenged Shurlock on the butcher issue ("all the profanity and the very blunt sexual dialogue"), for the *Tropic of Cancer* case had armed screenwriters to battle for free expression. Other cases in progress would soon alter the censor boards' procedures and end prior restraint; the outcomes would prompt attorney Ephraim London to remark that "any producer has the option of bypassing the board[s] altogether." What *Variety* once called "the Hollywood typewriter corps" knew that the courts and the culture would accept content that the Production Code had once forbidden. Screenwriters also knew that state and municipal censorship—the raison d'être for the Production Code—no longer threatened Hollywood. The censor boards had gradually drifted into backwaters. The state censors of New York, Maryland, Virginia, and Kansas as well as the municipal censors of Chicago, Detroit, and Memphis probably believed—as they had since the 1930s—that the movies should bar profanity and nudity, two demons that promoted evil. By the late 1950s, though, pluralism had moved America from a religious to a secular base, from a common

notion of evil to one more relative. One landmark court case after
another demonstrated that mainstream currents were too swift for
the censor boards and even the Church. The Legion of Decency still
flexed its muscle; it criticized neighborhood theaters that booked
adult fare, protested the drop in Hollywood family pictures, and
condemned more films in 1964 than in any single year since its
inception. Yet as the Catholic Alumnae fell away and the staff
expanded to include more young professionals, both laity and
priests, the Legion outlook became more and more positive. The
Catholics' response to a "documentary" called *Malamondo* was not
unusual. *Malamondo* showed an alcoholic orgy in a cemetery, some
nude skiers in Switzerland, and a rash of suicides among adolescents in Sweden. When the picture was imported in 1964, it bypassed the Catholics but earned only a slap on the wrist for
"depriving parents of the guidance they expect from the Legion."

   Malamondo and countless other pictures also went around Shurlock, whose office seemed more and more outmoded. A Los Angeles Methodist bishop compared the rules of the Production Code
to "a maiden aunt's fussy regulations," while the Legion continued
to badger Hollywood to adopt classification. Shurlock wanted to
oblige but found the industry paralyzed. Motion Picture Association president Eric Johnston had entered a Washington hospital in
June 1963 and died there two months later. He had run what *Variety*
called "a smoothly-functioning lobby" for Hollywood since 1945,
though the trade paper exaggerated when it called him the
spearhead for freedom of expression. Publishers and renegade
film distributors—not Johnston and the Association company
presidents—hauled the censors into court. With so much govern-
mental censorship routed, some board members wondered about
the philosophy and future of the Association. Walt Disney saw the
group as an unneeded anticensorship lobby and resigned; even
companies that released adult pictures thought the Association less
important than it had once been. The appointment of executive
secretary Ralph Hetzel as Johnston's temporary replacement meant
that Shurlock could not expect real leadership when he would
perhaps most need it: an executive secretary was not a president.

   The month that Johnston died, the wrecking ball fell across the
Hal Roach Studios, a part of motion picture history. Was yet an-

other period of transition—or perhaps anarchy—at hand? When Mike Frankovich became studio head at Columbia in 1964, he announced that the studio head was "expendable. No doubt about it. He is obsolete." Below the studio head lay the producer, and he too had become obsolete; from Kubrick to Hitchcock, the directors who ran Hollywood wanted no producers. The void bothered Shurlock, for most studio heads and producers were true Code allies, most directors mere fair-weather friends. Then there were the actors. Once muzzled by the front office, stars turned political in the 1960s. During the 1964 elections, Ronald Reagan stumped for Barry Goldwater, George Murphy ran for the United States Senate, and Connie Stevens and Marlo Thomas rallied votes for the Democrats. The National Association for the Advancement of Colored People agitated for more blacks on-screen; when the Student Nonviolent Coordinating Committee tossed a fund-raiser at The Daisy, actors Sidney Poitier, Richard Burton, and Marlon Brando anted up $5,000 each. Burt Lancaster supported an early school busing plan, while *Bonanza* star and Democrat Dan Blocker railed at Goldwaterite Hedda Hopper. Years before, conservative news hens Hopper and Louella Parsons would have slapped down the liberals in print, but the times encouraged actors to speak out.

Ernest Lehman understood as well as Shurlock that the Albee *Virginia Woolf* could not meet the Production Code; the profanity and blasphemy were too constant, too abusive. While Lehman wanted to preserve as much of the text as possible, he did not consider it sacrosanct. He dropped the moment when Martha (with encouragement from George) draws Nick to her bedroom, and underplayed the nonexistent child. He added some intimacy between George and Martha, a bedroom scene that showed "this had once been a marriage, and in fact still was a tiny bit of one." The bedroom and the characters echoed the past, Lehman recalled, because "you can't dramatize loss if you can't ever make an audience believe there ever was once something to lose." These changes occurred over multiple drafts, but the language posed the real hurdle.

Jack Warner expected Lehman to "substitute potent and pungent dialogue" for the profanity and blasphemy of *Virginia Woolf,* for he agreed with Sam Goldwyn (once an advocate of Code "modernization") that an "overemphasis on sex, violence, nudity or semi-nudity and similar gimmicks" as box office catnip could destroy Hollywood. Lehman ran the language through the washer. "God damn" became "gah damn"; "for Christ's sake," "for cry sake"; "Hump the Hostess," "Hop the Hostess"; and "you son of a bitch," "you dirty, lousy . . ." On the third draft, sensing that the bowdler-ization had sapped too much vitality from character and theme, the screenwriter restored much of the Albee text. Jack Warner read that script in March 1965 and circled, among other Code breaches, "god damn," "bastard," "chastity belt," "ineffectual sons of bitches," "mount her like a g.d. dog," and (shades of Joan Blondell and her bulbs) "with her melons bobbling." Warner expected the Shurlock boys to spit these back in his face like so many watermelon seeds.

In September 1964, the *Hollywood Reporter* told Patricia Neal and Henry Fonda to "go on hoping," but Jack Warner wanted Elizabeth Taylor and Jack Lemmon to star and John Frankenheimer to direct *Virginia Woolf.* Toward the end of the year, Warners opened negotia-tions with Taylor and Richard Burton. The larger-than-life Burtons came to *Virginia Woolf* from *Cleopatra,* a debacle for the stars and the studio. The million-dollar-plus contract that Jack Warner offered Taylor would help pay her lawyers. Twentieth Century–Fox had sued her for misconduct on *Cleopatra,* ex-husband Eddie Fisher had sued her for custody of their adopted daughter, and she and Fisher had countersued Fox for "mismanaged distribution" of *Cleopatra.* Burton, once England's angry young man, had meanwhile become an alcoholic. "I began having hangovers," he recalled. "I felt ill— shortness of breath. I thought I was having a heart attack. It creeps up on one." *Virginia Woolf* would advance the Burtons' celebrity. More important, with Burton almost on the wagon, it would reestablish them as serious actors. Sandy Dennis tested for Honey in February 1965, and when Robert Redford decided that the role of an impotent young man would compromise his screen persona, Warners cast George Segal as Nick. With the actors signed and a shooting script ready, Warner set principal photography for mid-August. He continued to vacillate on the characters' blue language, but the director soon made the decision for him.

The whimper that Dustin Hoffman used in *The Graduate* origi-nated with Mike Nichols. "I was told that I used to do that in meetings with Jack Warner," Nichols recalled. "Somebody said, 'When Mr. Warner is telling his jokes, you must stop whimpering.'" Nichols had no reason to whimper. He had three plays running concurrently in New York (*Barefoot in the Park, The Knack,* and *Luv*), had been chosen by the Burtons to direct *Virginia Woolf,* and negotiated a reported quarter-million-dollar contract for the picture. Though he was young and inexperienced, his Broadway reputation—as well as the hegemony of directors over studios in postwar Hollywood—gave him almost total control of *Virginia Woolf.* He worked on the screenplay with Lehman for eight weeks during spring 1965, and together, with Warner's reluctant approval, they permanently restored Albee's salty dialogue. The "clean but suggestive phrases" seemed worse than the profanity, Nichols later told *Life*.

> It reminded me of an old Gary Cooper movie when somebody said, "He's so poor he hasn't got a pot to put flowers in." Everybody in the audience got what was intended: echoes of wild talk, it seems to me, are deliberately titillating. People do certain things in bed that we all know they do, and people say certain things to each other that we all have heard. The whole point of the sexual revolution that's happening today is to let those things take their place and then go back into proportion. We feel the language in *Woolf* is essential to the fabric; it reveals who the people are and how they lived.

Nichols was "the domineering force on the picture," film editor Rudi Fehr recalled; what he wanted, Jack Warner gave him. The reverse did not hold true. Though Warner wanted protection footage for the strong language, he was afraid to alienate Nichols by pressing for it, and Nichols shot none.

The travails of *Virginia Woolf* could have made Pollyanna curse. On location at Smith College, the company stood idle as rain and fog canceled principal photography night after night. When cast and crew returned to Burbank in late autumn 1965, Nichols was already over budget. He shot the picture on a closed set, where he and Lehman handled Elizabeth Taylor like the racehorse she had once played opposite. They agonized during a shot when Burton threw her against a car and caused a contusion; in November, they monitored an eye injury she sustained as, two months before, they had monitored some minor bleeding. Nichols offered direction and friendly kisses in tandem, and when Lehman and Taylor quarreled one night, he apologized early the following morning. "To err is human," he wrote to her, "to forgive is . . . Elizabeth." Weeks into production, Nichols replaced cinematographer Harry Stradling and editor Doane Harrison (both studio veterans) with Haskell Wexler and Sam O'Steen. Along with the costly location-photography and the pampering of the high-priced stars, the personnel changes sent the picture thirty-six days behind schedule. As the budget soared, the Shurlock mien turned more mournful than usual.

Midway through production, Warners sent the Production Code Administration the *Virginia Woolf* shooting script. Shurlock found "a good deal of the profanity, the blunt sexual references, and the coarse and sometimes vulgar language which we noted in the original playscript when we first commented on it," he told Warner. Nichols had not attempted to conceal from anyone the boldness of the screenplay. An October 1965 *Saturday Evening Post* feature article reported that the picture would leave the earthy dialogue "virtually intact." Another director in another era would have wrestled Shurlock *in camera* over the potential Code violations, but Nichols apparently used the media as pressure on the Production Code Administration: Warners had been faithful to an award-winning play that only Geoff Shurlock could desecrate. With no classification system that would let him pass *Virginia Woolf,* Shurlock could only tell Warner that the screenplay remained "unapprovable under Code requirements." And as Nichols filmed the last shots of *Virginia Woolf,* the dawn of a new relationship between George and Martha, he cleared the path for a major confrontation between a producer and the Production Code Administration. It would be the second such confrontation in less than eighteen months.

In the early 1960s, former advertising man Roger Lewis bought the screen rights to Edward Wallant's *The Pawnbroker* and peddled the novel all over Hollywood. The story concerned a faithless Jew haunted by memories of the holocaust that took his wife and children. Sol Nazerman lives with Americanized relatives and runs a Harlem pawnshop, a front for a black racketeer; when a young

Puerto Rican dies while trying to save him, he apparently recovers the meaning of existence. The studios were timid. Could the pawnbroker be gentile? asked one. Could the references to concentration camps be cut? asked another. It soon became obvious that Lewis could make *The Pawnbroker* only as an independent production, with screenwriter, cinematographer, performers, and other artists working for minimal fees and profit participation. In autumn 1963, director Sidney Lumet shot the picture on location in Spanish Harlem and elsewhere in New York. The final cut contained two nude scenes: a modest shot of Nazerman's wife at the camps, and a bold one of a Negro prostitute who bares her breasts for the pawnbroker. On New Year's Eve 1964, Shurlock refused to certify the picture because of the nudity.

Throughout the 1960s, performers shed both their inhibitions and their clothes as the movies mirrored—and perhaps even stimulated—the "sexual revolution." A 1964 Supreme Court decision that concerned *The Lovers* (a French import with nudity intact) narrowed the scope of state authority to those films "utterly without social importance," and Hollywood soon aped French fashion. Though the Screen Actors Guild opposed nude scenes, afraid that actors who refused them would lose roles, producers continued to condone them. In 1964, Kim Novak appeared nude in *Of Human Bondage,* Carroll Baker in *The Carpetbaggers,* and (according to one account) Elizabeth Taylor in *The Sandpiper.* Producers trimmed them all to secure the Code Seal. A studio preview audience saw Natalie Wood nude in *Splendor in the Grass,* but Shurlock ordered Elia Kazan to trim the sequence from release prints. Nude scenes for *The Cincinnati Kid* and *The Americanization of Emily* also fell to the cutting room floor, though *Emily* producer Martin Ransohoff attacked the Code and vowed to restore the footage for European prints. In a 1965 report on the Legion of Decency, Monsignor Little boasted that "in the last two years 34 films, of which 20 were major American productions, would have been released with scenes employing nudity had not the producers realized that they would then have been condemned." Yet the filmmakers now had allies who, a decade before, would have been enemies. During a New York junket, Shurlock met two Protestant ministers who complained about the Production Code's "pruriently impure" rules on nudity.

The Code, they told him, promoted a "teasing" kind of undress far more offensive than nudity itself.

Personally, Shurlock admired *The Pawnbroker,* a picture that again showed how much America needed a classification system. But he could bend on nudity no more than he could on profanity. Nude scenes "call forth a great amount of protest from pressure groups," Shurlock told Ely Landau, the associate producer of *The Pawnbroker.* He also predicted that the Legion would not favor the release unless Landau cut the nudity. Because Allied Artists, a member of the Association, would handle the picture and wanted wide distribution, the producers appealed. The Production Code Review Board was now composed of independent producers and exhibitors as well as Association members. Should the board affirm Shurlock, Allied Artists could release through its arts subsidiary rather than cut the nude footage; the aftermath would further erode self-regulation. Should the board overturn Shurlock—not unlikely since nonmember producers Stanley Kramer, Joseph Mankiewicz, and others would hear the appeal to assure fair treatment for an independent—it would establish a precedent. Meanwhile Landau grumbled that he would consider antitrust action against the Association should *The Pawnbroker* not be awarded a Seal.

The Association met for over four hours in March 1965 to consider *The Pawnbroker.* Independent producer Joe Mankiewicz and Paramount president Barney Balaban led the forces of pro and con. Mankiewicz defended *The Pawnbroker,* nude scenes and all; a unique picture, he argued, should always merit an exception from the rules. Balaban warned that the "harm resulting from this decision may prove to be incalculable." He also called any attempt to brand *The Pawnbroker* "unique" a "self-serving statement." When the debate ended, the board passed *The Pawnbroker.* One historian has speculated that racism influenced the vote, for "films have always regarded the exposure of dark skins more indulgently than white." Industry conditions certainly had an effect, for Hollywood had wandered into the wilderness, unsure from one picture to the next what the audience—no longer so monolithic—wanted. Even some older board members may have reasoned that the independents and the younger producers had answers, and a flash of bare breasts seemed a small price to discover whether a picture with nudity could restore box office health or send Hollywood into the jaws of an angry press and public. In tortured prose, the board told Landau that it had "upheld and affirmed" Shurlock but granted a "special exemption" for *The Pawnbroker*—once the producers had reduced "the length of the scenes which the Production Code Administration found unapprovable." Landau reedited several ways, then told Shurlock that the producers could eliminate only a few frames from the picture. "That's cuts," the Production Code administrator responded, "and what they asked for is cuts. Technically that should suffice. I'll be able to tell them you made cuts as requested." Shurlock seemed no less eager than the board to find out how *The Pawnbroker* would fare.

The outcome of *The Pawnbroker* appeal troubled the Legion of Decency. Monsignor Little feared that the Seal and the excellent notices certain to follow would "open the door to substantial abuse in future American motion picture production." The Catholics were torn; while they respected the humanism of *The Pawnbroker,* they also wanted to halt "the effort by producers to introduce nudity into American films." The picture had been running for several weeks in major theaters in Los Angeles and New York when Little finally announced the verdict: the Legion condemned *The Pawnbroker,* not because it "was in itself obscene, but because the Legion has a principle according to which nudity, for whatever reason, will not be accepted in motion picture treatment—and this for the common good." Perhaps hurt more by its art house reputation than the Legion "C," *The Pawnbroker* failed to meet the producers' commercial expectations. Yet the problems that both the Motion Picture Association and the Legion addressed—and the narrow votes that apparently followed—suggested just how close Hollywood had come to the freedom of expression it so wanted. *Variety* called the condemnation of *The Pawnbroker* "perhaps the mildest ever offered," and the liberal Catholic press saluted the picture. When the bare breasts of *The Pawnbroker* became the "angel tits" of *Virginia Woolf,* Hollywood would have an ultimate test.

Once Mike Nichols completed *Virginia Woolf,* Warners locked up the print and denied access to the press, exhibitors, and even high-ranking studio personnel. In early May 1966, though, Shurlock finally saw the picture. As he had feared, he found it unacceptable. Jack Warner could appeal and hope for the victory that *The Pawnbroker* had enjoyed one year before. If he lost, which seemed possible because of the volume of profanity in *Virginia Woolf*, he had two alternatives: he could cut the film or resign from the Motion Picture Association. Nichols had no protection footage, so the former course was practically impossible; it would also have subjected Warners to what *Variety* termed "a good deal of criticism for 'knuckling under to the blue-noses' " in mutilating a " 'class' offering" that had won the New York Drama Critics Circle citation, earned a Tony Award, and contended for the Pulitzer Prize. The other alternative—resignation—would have sparked even more censure, for it would have turned the Motion Picture Association into a revolving door, with membership tied to the release of the moment. For Warners, *Virginia Woolf* was *Streetcar* revisited.

Classification or at least a more liberal Production Code, both of which Shurlock endorsed, could have loosened the Gordian knot. Less than a week after the *Pawnbroker* appeal in spring 1965, Ralph Hetzel had told the press that the Association would soon enact a new code "more in line with present-day thinking." What was "present-day thinking"? For the midsixties counterculture, it was civil rights marches, campus sit-ins, and communal free sex; it was Timothy Leary's League for Spiritual Discovery, which sought God through LSD, and other cults who found truth in Eastern metaphysics. For some theologians, God was dead; for others, She was irrelevant. A new generation wanted—and demanded—social and sexual freedom. And despite the outrage of conservatives, the Supreme Court continued to bless such free expression. The Motion Picture Association had only a modest proposal on the drawing board. The new code would ease restrictions on drugs, nudity, profanity, aberrant sex, and abortion, and cast morality in a supporting—but not leading—role. "What the code administration should do," one Hollywood executive thought, "is to function as an arbiter of good taste to censor offensive scenes but not to impose narrow puritanical restrictions." Though many agreed, the long gestation of the new code revealed anew the industry paralysis.

The Association examined and reexamined that new code

throughout 1965 and into 1966. In February 1966, the Legion of Decency scanned the document and tacitly approved even the abortion rule; still, board members would not formally adopt the code. A Motion Picture Association president could have moved them, an executive secretary could not. The board needed leadership.

When Motion Picture Association members Arthur Krim, Lew Wasserman, and Paramount éminence grise Ed Weisl called on Jack Valenti in spring 1966, he was special assistant to Lyndon Johnson. A manicured shrub next to Johnson honeysuckle, Valenti served the administration with the supreme loyalty that the Texas president demanded. Johnson "did not want me to leave," Valenti recalled, "so I was in a quandary for about three months." The president finally relented, though, and may well have helped engineer the Association's $170,000-plus annual contract offer, which fellow Texan Valenti soon accepted. In Manhattan, an Association staff member smiled when he heard President Valenti speak of "energy" and "vigor," words "that all of us needed to hear." In Los Angeles, Jack Vizzard found Jack Valenti sartorially splendid, with a fast smile, luminous dark eyes, and a resemblance to Governor George Wallace. Yet board members wanted someone to lead not through confrontation—the Wallace touch—but reason and tact, intelligence and firmness. According to one press account, they wanted someone to "prepare the public for news of a new Code revision." And on the eve of Walpurgisnacht, they wanted someone to tell them whether they should be afraid of *Virginia Woolf.*

Hoping that Valenti and the Association would favor the *Virginia Woolf* appeal, Jack Warner sent the East Coast Association some promotional materials that contained two messages: the picture was high-octane drama, and was intended for adults. Members of the Advertising Code Administration, who oversaw Hollywood promotional campaigns, noted the "excessive exposure" of Elizabeth Taylor in some art work, and the phrase "shove it" in a one-minute radio spot. They also noted a prominent announcement in the copy: No admission of the under-eighteen patron without mother or father. Unprecedented as well, Warners stated in the press book that exhibitors must honor the box office ban. No one—producer, distributor, exhibitor, or patron—thought that age could lock the turnstile, but Warners' *Virginia Woolf* "literally forces the movie industry into classification of films," the *Hollywood Reporter* wrote, "something strongly opposed in the past." No one at Association headquarters asked *why* Warners had painted a large segment of the audience out of the picture; everyone knew. Since the advent of adult films, the American Catholic hierarchy had urged Hollywood to adopt voluntary classification. On *Virginia Woolf*, the Church had forced the issue.

The passing years had taught the Legion of Decency that inflammatory rhetoric and demonstrating pickets would not stem the flow of problematic films. As the Legion became more sympathetic to adult fare, it preached classification to Hollywood. In November 1961, a Catholic bishops' committee had predicted "an understandable popular demand for mandatory classification should the industry refuse to regulate itself," yet neither Johnston nor Hetzel had responded. Though finally the Legion supported laws for advisory film classification, the Catholic fathers hoped that through example rather than political pressure they could influence the industry.

After three decades, the Legion had a new purpose—not to censor, but to offer "an intelligent and discriminating moral guide to moviegoers." The advisory labels that producers had added to such pictures as *Elmer Gantry, La Dolce Vita, Lolita,* and *Long Day's Journey Into Night* bore the Legion mark. The affirmative approach continued with cosmetic changes (the "Separate Classification" [awarded *Lolita*] became the less onerous "A-IV") as well as the publication of a biweekly *Catholic Film Newsletter* and the continued expansion of the review board. By 1965, priests, teachers, writers, admen, scholars, graduate students, movie critics, and business people screened pictures alongside a diminished cadre of older Catholic women. The number of consultors and their frequency at screenings rose as, conversely, the number of Alumnae fell. Legion consultor William Mooring felt that he belonged to a "hopelessly outnumbered minority of moderates and conservatives" and resigned. The liberal wave continued. The Legion not only pondered the death of the "Condemned" rating but established annual awards to honor and thus promote distinguished films for "Youth," "General Audiences," and, significantly, "Mature Audiences." After 1965, the organization that comedian George Jessel called "the Legiotency" became the National Catholic Office for Motion Pictures. Slowly the band of religious and civic groups that had marched on Hollywood with the Legion as drum major packed up and started home.

Nonetheless, in 1966, Jack Warner continued to fret about the Catholics and *Virginia Woolf.* "It might be well to obtain Catholic technical advice," Shurlock had told Warner over three years before, "in order to avoid anything offensive regarding the Latin prayers" in George's Dies Irae for the imaginary son. If the Legion paled on "goddamn," Rudi Fehr warned, it might black out on "Jesus": the Lord's name was "not approved when used lightly." Though the sober theme would carry *Virginia Woolf* far, the moderates of the National Catholic Office could pin down the liberals over the profane dialogue or Martha and Nick's wild dance at a roadhouse. And with no protection footage, Warners' *Virginia Woolf* became an all-or-nothing affair. A "Condemned" would not have been catastrophic. While some theater chains shunned "C" pictures, others needed product enough to overlook the stigma. Yet Warners wanted any "C" stamped on *Virginia Woolf* to denote "Class." A "Condemned" would have not only obscured the artistry of the picture but—perhaps more important—narrowed the distribution channels.

In June 1966, as the meeting with the Catholics neared, Warner became punchy. Would one too many "Christ"s or "goddamn"s offend the liberals? Would the "little old ladies in tennis shoes" (the Alumnae) oppose the picture and sway others? "Don't worry," advertising vice-president Richard Lederer assured him, "the film's artistic." Lederer was right. Only days before the Warners appeal came before the Association Review Board, the National Catholic Office for Motion Pictures reached a decision. The consultants believed that—properly restricted—*Virginia Woolf* could be approved for mature Catholic filmgoers. The Alumnae and some churchmen vigorously disagreed. After Martha and George invoked "Christ" for the second or third time, Reverend Thomas B. Coyne asked: "Why can't these people say 'Jack Warner' and leave the Sacred Name to those who revere It?" In spite of the high stakes on *Virginia Woolf,* the debate produced an echo of the *Lolita* vote. Ten percent of the consultants and sixty percent of the Alumnae voted to condemn *Virginia Woolf.* The consultants prevailed, though, for the picture earned a benign "A-IV" rating—without cuts. "We asked for nothing," Monsignor Little told the press when questioned about age and parental restrictions on *Virginia Woolf,* yet Father Patrick Sullivan, an associate of Monsignor Little, later admitted that the National Catholic Office had been "directly instrumental" in Warners' box office policy: No admission of anyone "under the age of 18 unless accompanied by his parent." The vote sent an emphatic message to Hollywood. With classification, motion pictures and free expression could coexist.

"As responsible film-makers, we undertook to make 'Virginia Woolf' for the over-18 section of our audience," Jack Warner crowed, reading from a statement prepared for him by the National Catholic Office. "Now, we have reached the point where we are getting ready to put our film before the public and we are determined to display the same responsibility and care in this phase of our work, by refraining from any suggestion of sensationalism in our advertising and by thoroughly enforcing the contractual obligation which every exhibitor will have to undertake if he wishes to show our picture." Behind the scenes, to keep Warner honest, the Valenti office used orange crayon on the mock-up ads to show where the studio must cover up the "excessive exposure" of Elizabeth Taylor. Valenti and the company presidents meanwhile discussed the Catholics' response to *Virginia Woolf.*

With the *Virginia Woolf* appeal, Valenti and the Association could advance both motion picture art and the motion picture industry; they could also cast off the shade of Joe Breen that still haunted Shurlock. United Artists' Max Youngstein told Shurlock in 1962 that the "Association has provided no yardstick for an ethical, moral base for the judgment of the in toto effect of motion pictures, and until you do, you are going to find yourself on both sides of every argument, accomplishing nothing for our business." Classification could lead Shurlock out of the maze, but resistance came from without and within the Production Code Administration. When the agency passed *Irma La Douce,* the story of a French streetwalker, independent producer Hal Wallis told Shurlock that while he admired Billy Wilder, "the only thing I admired in this one was his ability to pull the wool so far over your eyes as to enable him to get a Seal on this picture. This is without a doubt the filthiest thing I have ever seen on the screen." Shurlock responded that de facto classification had made the Seal possible, since United Artists promised that the picture would "be sold and advertised as a strictly adult film." Wallis wanted moral pictures, not "adult" pictures. Classification would only have angered him more.

Jack Vizzard, even-money to become the next Production Code administrator, tended to agree with Wallis. The former Jesuit thought that Shurlock had compromised his standards to retain power, that he had played the "maturing liberal" to demonstrate that old age had not calcified him. The approval of "Pussy Galore," a character in *Goldfinger,* seemed to Vizzard more an act of non compos mentis than good sense. In 1965, Shurlock had approved *Kiss Me, Stupid.* When the Legion condemned it as "morally repul- sive," *Life* charged producer Billy Wilder and Shurlock as perpetra- tors. "The jury is still out on this picture," the Shurlock defense went. "We must wait to see how the audiences react." Even a boycott of the theaters would not have stemmed the flow of sex farces, however; the industry wanted them, the culture accepted them, the courts encouraged them. For Vizzard, classification would mark "the end of an era." For Shurlock, it would mark the dawn of another. According to *Variety,* the Production Code direc- tor looked forward "to the day when there will be no need for a Code, that is, when producers will take it upon themselves to do what the Code now does." Classification could hasten that mo- ment. "Let 'em make whatever they want," Shurlock told an asso- ciate, and we will "call 'em whatever they are." He sensed, as the more conservative Vizzard had not, that classification could at once slay and salvage the Production Code Administration. With *Vir- ginia Woolf,* the opportunity ripened.

In late May, Warners screened *Virginia Woolf* for Jack Valenti. The Association president understood that exemption from Code law would support classification, while enforcement would show how holier-than-Catholics board members had apparently become. To complicate matters further, Warners had not produced *Virginia Woolf* with shoestring capital and salary deferrals. In December 1965, the Burtons had tossed a $12,000 wrap party at their $4,000- a-month rented home, the thousands a mere scintilla of the *Virginia Woolf* budget. As the appeals board knew, *Virginia Woolf* was not just a movie but a $7.5 million investment, "near a high for a non-spec[tacle] studio film." Money governed most Hollywood decisions, and *Virginia Woolf* could conceivably earn an exemption on dollars alone.

A *Life* photo story that hit the newsstands days before the appeals board met was headlined RAW DIALOGUE CHALLENGES ALL THE CENSORS, and featured a production still of Taylor and Segal's dance, "a scorching, sexual frug." Though two of the photographs screamed exploitation, author Thomas Thompson noted between the lines that *Virginia Woolf* was a serious picture with a serious theme. After "more soul-searching than they had ever done on an American film," the National Catholic Office had passed *Virginia Woolf*, Thompson reported. He seemed to approve the decision, wanted the Association to concur, and called Geoff Shurlock as defense witness. "I think it is a marvelous film," the Production Code administrator told *Life*. "Right now it is the one to beat for the Academy Award; anyone who thinks otherwise would be an idiot." Association board members who could read could read that one: they must confer the Code Seal on *Virginia Woolf*; to have an American Oscar contender become an Oscar winner without the Code Seal could tumble the house of cards.

On the morning of June 10, 1966, Valenti and the men of the appeals board met in Warners' New York screening room to see *Who's Afraid of Virginia Woolf?* Most were impressed with the picture, which promised to become not only an Oscar favorite but a major commercial and critical success.

Virginia Woolf produced some "lonely soul-searching" in Jack Valenti. *Variety* reported that "the biggest stumbling block to granting an 'exception' [to *Virginia Woolf*] won't be Valenti but the probable reluctance, on the part of the other company presidents, to encourage [the] trend toward 'voluntary classification.'" But more than *Variety* admitted, Valenti *was* the linchpin. Like board members, he understood that voluntary classification could lessen box office revenues. Like Geoff Shurlock, though, he also understood that time had passed the Association by, that events controlled the Association, not vice versa. Voluntary classification was more wave than trend. The Association must ride the wave or go under.

After screening *Virginia Woolf*, board members lunched, then reconvened in a private suite at the St. Regis. There Geoff Shurlock told them that both the Legion and *Life* had recognized the merit of *Virginia Woolf;* the Production Code Administration must henceforth have the power of "making exemptions on our own and approving a picture without having to call this entire Board into session." Warners' Richard Lederer spoke next. He highlighted the theme of the film, the voluntary classification, and the studio's general responsibility to its public. He also noted—lest the board nod—that Warners had "a lot of money invested in [*Virginia Woolf*]."

Valenti needed the support of at least six of the ten board members assembled; only one of those present was an independent producer, and at least three of them were personally disturbed by the language and content of *Virginia Woolf.* Valenti marshaled the arguments carefully. The Warners release was "a superior picture," he told the company presidents, and an exemption would apply *only* to *Virginia Woolf,* not to films of lesser quality. Perhaps as a sop to conservative board members, he also noted that he had convinced Warners to make two important changes; the studio had deleted the word "frigging" and changed Martha's party-opener from "screw you" to "goddamn you." Valenti then recommended an exemption from Production Code rules for *Virginia Woolf,* and opened the debate.

Most Association board members knew that the Production Code had become as much a fantasy—and as ripe for destruction— as George and Martha's "little bugger," yet the debate released pent-up frustrations. White-hot during the *Pawnbroker* challenge, Barney Balaban understood that the board must favor the appeal; still, the prospect of change made him uncomfortable. Sherrill Corwin, representing fifteen thousand theater owners, noted that exhibitors had successfully handled mature films in the past with no mandatory "adults-only" clause inserted in the contract: "We feel we can police our theatres for pictures that need policing." Only moments before, "speaking confidentially," Valenti had told board members that while he knew little about classification, "I intend to know more." The ominous statement suggested that once he knew more, Valenti would become police chief and move the Association toward the voluntary classification system that the independent producers, the Catholics, and Geoff Shurlock supported. Corwin and others could delay—not stop—classification.

Spyros Skouras objected to *Virginia Woolf* on moral grounds. The bearlike Skouras had run Twentieth Century–Fox until 1962, when *Cleopatra* toppled him. He moved from Hollywood production head to board chairman, with no goodwill toward the Burtons. "Elizabeth Taylor added five million dollars to our [*Cleopatra*] budget in Italy," a bitter Skouras recalled. "She tried to commit suicide four times because she believed Burton was losing interest in her and she wanted to frighten him. On one occasion she almost succeeded—if they hadn't left the car roof open on a drive to Rome from her villa she *would* have died." Like Balaban on *The Pawnbroker,* Skouras praised the artistry of *Virginia Woolf* but wanted deletions: "Goddamn," "son of a bitch," "Hump the Hostess," and others. Retaining the language, he argued, would not only scuttle the Code but injure society. The Association then voted. All supported Valenti except Skouras. The board chairman chastised Shurlock and Warners: Shurlock should have communicated more often with the studio, Warners should have made "replacement scenes for the ones that the Code Authority was bound to oppose." As a result of joint negligence, he concluded, Warners and Shurlock had opened the floodgates. Valenti assured Skouras that in the future the Association was "going to be stronger and tougher," that Shurlock would "get scripts, dialogue, etc., before a picture is completed and before a lot of money is invested."

Board members were not idiots. All present at the *Virginia Woolf* appeal sensed that the movies—and the industry—would change. The match had been struck, the old Production Code would burn, the phoenix of classification would rise. Would the phoenix be an Audubon watercolor or a Hitchcock horror? Some predicted that what happened to Bodega Bay in *The Birds* would happen to Hollywood. In a June 1966 letter to Monsignor Little, British Board chairman John Trevelyan anticipated that between classification and the pending retirement of Geoff Shurlock, Hollywood would step up "the number of trashy and semi-pornographic pictures" produced. Back across the Atlantic, Valenti confidant and Association counsel Louis Nizer believed that classification could open "the door for possible State and City classification laws."

But the movies—and the industry—had *already* changed. The moguls would surrender to classification much as they had surrendered to the banks, the agents, and the unions. *Virginia Woolf* bore traces of that new Hollywood. After the *Paramount* case closed the smooth path from production to distribution and exhibition, bankers forced the studios to build pictures around balance sheets, cost analyses, negative income, and other economic factors that had more to do with shopping center construction than filmmaking. The agents who managed the stars, directors, and writers—the heart of the movie-as-mall phenomenon—became more powerful than the studios, so much so that the Justice Department threatened to intervene. The family ties on *Virginia Woolf* started with the William Morris agency, which managed both Edward Albee and Ernest Lehman. After Warners had signed Elizabeth Taylor for Martha, Hugh French, her agent, pestered the studio to hire other clients of his to direct and costar. Tell "French [to] let us make Picture," a frustrated Jack Warner scribbled in a March 1965 note to Lehman. Throughout the 1960s, the unions under contract to Warners and other companies worked hard to protect the advances of the 1930s and 1940s; they virtually shut the door on new members, and even as production starts diminished and overseas shooting became common, they bargained for wage hikes. The astronomical price tag on *Virginia Woolf* reflected not only the Burtons' salaries but those of organized labor. Compared to agents and unions—crosses that called for a Steve Reeves—classification would seem a manageable burden.

Perhaps motion pictures could weather classification as they had weathered much else, from the municipal and state censors to television. As the censor boards fell, Hollywood and television became partners. By 1966, every major studio had sold post-1948 features to television. Some studios (especially Universal and Twentieth Century–Fox) had entered television production; many had network prelicensing agreements that produced front money for theatrical motion pictures. As long as the finished product bore the Motion Picture Association Seal—whether the mechanism was Code or classification—the broadcasters were happy.

Beyond the boardroom, the *Virginia Woolf* appeal produced lamentation and jubilation. It was "pointless to consider whether the

Code expired when the decision was made to film the play without regard to the Code, or when the decision was made by the Review Board to grant the picture an 'exemption' from the Code," Martin Quigley, Jr., wrote in a caustic 1966 *Motion Picture Herald* editorial. The "high quality" and "great cost" of *Virginia Woolf* triumphed over its torrent of "blasphemy, profanity and obscenity." Quigley titled the editorial, "The Code Is Dead." Former comedian Mike Nichols found it hard to suppress laughter at the funeral. "I was not at all concerned about whether or not the Motion Picture Association gave 'Who's Afraid Of Virginia Woolf' a Production Code Seal or not," Nichols told *Variety*. Neither did he "care what people think of the language in the film." Misquote! Nichols cried, but even his letter to *Variety* celebrated the consequences of the *Virginia Woolf* decision: "The Motion Picture Association of America has my respect and gratitude as a group," Nichols wrote. "I would be foolish indeed if at this happy point I bit the hand that freed us." In Hollywood, Shurlock turned a corner, at once apprehensive and relieved. Though he too had reservations about an onslaught of "trashy and semi-pornographic pictures," he had won what he wanted, the right to approve pictures without board members' intervention.

Less than a month after the *Virginia Woolf* appeal, Jack Valenti showed three hundred studio executives, directors, and performers the new Production Code. General Hays had sold the Wild West moguls a Production Code that tamed them; now Valenti offered them one that favored the schoolmarm no more than the dance-hall girl. The old principles had ruled that "no picture shall be produced which will lower the moral standards of those who see it." The new one recommended that movies "keep in closer harmony with the mores, the culture, the moral sense and the expectation of our society." Valenti had had enough of the "excessive exposure" wars. He and Jack Warner had argued over "screw you" and "Hump the Hostess" for three hours, and it "seemed wrong that grown men should be sitting around discussing such matters. More, I was uncomfortable with the thought that this was just the beginning of an unsettling new era in film, in which we would lurch from crisis to crisis, without any suitable solutions in sight." The new Code replaced rules on murder, drug addiction, and nudity with more general rules that preached *caution* on scenes of violence, exposure, criminal behavior, and sexual intimacy. Most important, it gave Shurlock the power to label certain pictures "Suggested for Mature Audiences."

In autumn 1966, Valenti publicly unveiled the new Production Code, which *Newsweek* called "a glittering diadem of hypocrisy." While the press echoed the scorn that had greeted the original Production Code in 1930, the Association looked toward the future. *The Pawnbroker, Who's Afraid of Virginia Woolf?,* and a few others had, as Spyros Skouras foretold, opened the floodgates; with the "Mature Audiences" label, classification had rushed in. Even *Alfie,* a Paramount import with an abortion sequence, won approval from an Association review board, the final tally a vote of confidence for Shurlock and the new powers of the Production Code Administration. "Everything expressly prohibited in the Production Code apparently is to be approved, one way or other," wrote the *Motion Picture Herald.*

The more Code staffer Jack Vizzard saw of the change, the more he thought it deserved *Newsweek*'s contempt. Though the "mature audiences" tag would reduce conflict between the producers and the Production Code Administration, Vizzard wondered about the high price in screen morals. Had Geoff Shurlock no concern about the fall of self-regulation? The Production Code director was "an ineffective, little feckless guy to start with," Vizzard recalled. "He grew strong, then he burned out." But Shurlock would not retire. Over seventy, he would not pass the reins to heir-apparent Vizzard. Toward the end of the decade, as Shurlock made concession after concession, Vizzard feared that there would be only reins—no horse—to pass along.

When, though, had Hollywood ever taken censorship commitments seriously? By September 1966, *Virginia Woolf* had entered second runs. At some theaters, "No One Under 18 Admitted Without Parent" became "Not Recommended for Children." At some drive-ins, exhibitors dropped the caveat, while at others they left posted an old sign, "Children Under 12 Free." How Breen would have paled.

In early December 1965, though, Joe Breen had died. Survivors from the Breen era had attended the funeral and the Irish wake—

which ended when Mary Breen tongue-lashed the wife of one of her husband's cronies—but many of the moguls who had fought the Production Code wars were gone. Old Hollywood had become New Hollywood, and in the years ahead, Shurlock and the nascent classification system would confront some of the most controversial and evocative motion pictures in American history.

AFTERMATH

TWO MOBSTERS ONCE formed a partnership to take over gambling—and more—in Havana. They met with Cuban officials who blessed the merger, then celebrated on the terrace of a luxury hotel suite. Florida kingpin Hyman Roth called the moment historic. "We have now what we have always needed," he told Michael Corleone, heir to the Corleone family and the Havana operation, "real partnership with a government." As the gangsters cut a birthday cake shaped to represent Cuba, Roth and Corleone contemplated the rewards of an Olympian blend of private and public interests. "Michael," Roth mused, "we're bigger than U.S. Steel."

The Godfather, Part II caught the pulse of the age of conglomerates, an age that touched motion pictures and motion picture regulation. Though like companies had merged before World War II—dry cleaners with other dry cleaners, manufacturers with other manufacturers—diversification became the corporate watchword of the 1960s. Hollywood had come through the 1950s battered and bruised, but was less *Irma La Douce* than *Belle de Jour,* less the streetwalker than the mistress with whom a conglomerate looking for variety could find pleasure and fulfillment. Her stocks were undervalued, her film libraries vast, her southern California real estate prime. Soon the corporate giants lined up. In 1966, Gulf & Western acquired Paramount; in 1967, TransAmerica merged with

United Artists; in 1969, Kinney Services took over Warner Bros. "There is a tremendous future in the leisure field," Gulf & Western president Charles Bluhdorn told *Life* in 1970. "Movies in cassettes for home viewing will open a tremendous market. Satellites some-day will relay first-run movies into millions of homes. It's a great challenge."

Bluhdorn saw movies as widgets, as a business "pure and sim-ple," and the men such new moguls hired were company men. They ran the studios at some distance from the producers, and deferred to them on censorship matters, perhaps because screen candor had become both juggernaut and box office lure—as the case of *Blow Up* shows. In November 1966, MGM had asked Geoff Shurlock to screen the Michelangelo Antonioni film about a photographer who snaps shots of a murder. Shurlock told MGM that several nude scenes crossed the bounds of the revised Produc-tion Code and must be trimmed to earn the Seal, but the company declined to alter the film. "Good directors are at such a premium," the Metro representative told Shurlock and Jack Vizzard, "that they can set their own terms. The company's afraid if it doesn't give him what he wants, he'll take his picture elsewhere." Neither the Cath-olics' "Condemned" nor the absence of a Seal hampered bookings. Released through a Metro subsidiary, *Blow Up* played theaters that even two years before would not have touched a twice-cursed feature. Americans could also produce adult films for adult audi-ences: along with *Blow Up, Bonnie and Clyde* and *The Graduate* contributed to the first box office boom since 1946. Shurlock saw more sex and violence on the horizon, and since the conglomerates were engrossed in balance sheets and the Association refused to close the subsidiary loophole, he pinned the survival of the Produc-tion Code on accommodation. Less than a year after the Antonioni release opened, almost sixty percent of the pictures with Seals bore a "Mature Audiences" tag.

Though Hollywood had an inchoate classification system by 1967, two Supreme Court decisions led to the formal adoption of one. A Bellemore, Long Island, mother had sent her sixteen-year-old to Sam's Stationery and Luncheonette to buy a "girlie maga-zine"; when the boy exited the store with his purchase, the woman sued the owner for selling matter "harmful to minors." Meanwhile, a Dallas exhibitor had taken municipal censors to court for banning under-sixteens from *Viva Maria,* a Western spoof with Jeanne Moreau and Brigitte Bardot. On the same day in spring 1968, the Supreme Court ruled on the two cases. *Ginsberg* v. *New York* decreed that the government could protect minors (though not adults) from sexually graphic materials; *Interstate Circuit* v. *Dallas* found the municipal censorship ordinance too vague to enforce. *Ginsberg* and *Dallas* in tandem suggested that with carefully worded laws, state legislatures could close the box office to minors. The Catholics had made a decision for Hays thirty years before; the Court made one for Valenti. Under the shadow of *Ginsberg* and *Dallas*—and despite exhibitor resistance—Valenti convinced board members to adopt classification. Stuart Byron, the *Variety* reporter who covered the Association, called Valenti a miracle worker: the Texan had established a rating system "before a single state had had time to pass a classification bill in the wake of the *Dallas* ruling." Years later, Byron still considered Valenti the "hero who saved the film industry and its artists from a terrible fate."

The ratings system had two goals: to "encourage artistic expression by expanding creative freedom" and to "insure that the freedom which encourages the artist remains responsible and sensitive to the standards of the larger society." Had the ratings system been legal rather than voluntary, it would not have passed the *Dallas* test. But it *was* voluntary. Hollywood had lived long enough with the crossed t's and dotted i's of the Production Code to appreciate some flexible rules, while the conglomerates were so pinched by federal regulations that they must have found self-regulation a boon.

The Production Code and the sole "Mature Audiences" tag yielded to four ratings: "G" (for general audiences of all ages); "M" (suggested for adults and mature young people); "R" (persons under sixteen restricted unless accompanied by parent or adult); and "X" (no one under sixteen admitted). ("M" became "GP," then "PG" [used henceforth] for parental guidance recommended.) Though Valenti wanted only "G" through "R," theater owners fought for "X" because they feared criminal prosecutions under *Ginsberg*. Pictures rated "X" would bear no Seal and suffer the consequences. Child psychologist Jacqueline Bouhoutsos, a late-1968 appointee to the newly formed Code and Rating Administration, called "X" releases "garbage, pictures that shouldn't have been made for anybody, films without any kind of artistic merit, poor taste, disgusting, repulsive." Directors who walked the thin line between "R" and "X" (and even "PG" and "R") would soon wonder whether the ratings system was the Production Code reborn.

With the ratings a fait accompli, Geoff Shurlock finally stepped down. Powerful mainstream producers such as Freddie Brisson had assumed that Jack Vizzard would become the new chief administrator. "We chose a typewriter as [your] gift," Brisson and David Swift told the former Jesuit after his help on *Under the Yum Yum Tree* in 1963, "because we feel anyone who can express himself so beautifully should be writing, not editing!" Vizzard agreed: by 1968, he had left the agency to author a book about his years with the Production Code Administration. "At that time I thought I needed continuity," Valenti later commented, so he named Eugene "Doc" Dougherty—the senior member of the Production Code staff—director of the fledgling Rating Administration. Dougherty had worked under Joe Breen, then Geoff Shurlock; he was conversant with the Code and could horse-trade with producers. Al Van Schmus, who had been a Production Code staffer almost as long as Dougherty, would have been the better appointment. Less voluble than Dougherty, the self-effacing Van Schmus agreed with Shurlock that the producers should produce, the Rating Administration should rate. He would have provided direction; Dougherty provided only continuity.

After November 1, 1968, when classification formally began, the men who once enforced the Production Code became the men who ran the Code and Rating Administration. They huddled with Dougherty to review the daily agenda. They examined scripts, even early drafts, and offered producers advice on the outcome of the picture, whether "G," "PG," "R," or (rarely) "X." And of course they screened films. A young intern who served on the board found his colleagues "literal-minded," able to pinpoint "R" matter in "PG" pictures, "X" matter in "R." Though board members presumably based the classification on "the *accumulation* of a great number of elements—subject matter, the film's attitude toward complex and mature themes, explicitness of visuals and dialogue throughout an entire film"—producers could sometimes negotiate a less restrictive rating with only one or two minor cuts. In 1968 and 1969, the studios reedited a third of the pictures submitted to achieve the desired rating.

By 1970, despite protests from conservatives, nude scenes had become common, and actors scorched motion picture soundtracks with the words "bitch," "goddamn," and "shit." The slave to contemporary mores, the Rating Administration allowed what had been "X" to become "R," and what had once been "R" to become "PG" (which cynics called "Pretty Gamy" and "Pretty Gory"). In 1970, United Artists had itself applied an "X" to *Midnight Cowboy,* but when UA asked for a rating in January 1971, seven months after the New York premiere, the Dougherty office assigned an "R." The "R" continued to absorb "shock" elements, from explicit sex to words like "fuck" and "cunt." Though some conservative moviemakers blamed the Rating Administration for four-letter "artistic expression," the Hollywood Turks condemned it for another reason: cuts suggested by the Rating Administration and mandated by the studios—cuts needed to move an "X" to "R" or an "R" to "PG"—were censorship. Like Breen and Shurlock, Dougherty found himself in the cross fire.

A Catholic, Dougherty had neither the presence of Joe Breen nor the liberal commitment of Geoff Shurlock. Independent producers saw him as the studios' pawn. Metro's *The Magic Garden of Stanley Sweetheart* concerned the tawdry sex-and-drug adventures of a wayward college student. After the board rated the picture "X," Dougherty met with the MGM brass, and, two minor cuts later, awarded the release an "R." He sent Avco's *Soldier Blue* along the same road from "X" to "R." But independent producers unaffiliated with the major companies charged that once Dougherty branded a low-budget picture "X," the "X" stuck.

The studios had another perspective on Dougherty. Even after director Robert Aldrich offered to cut the lesbian seduction scene from *The Killing of Sister George,* his "old friend" Dougherty told him that the "X" must remain. Months later, when Dougherty assigned MGM's *Ryan's Daughter* an "R," studio president James Aubrey appealed. He constructed a defense based not on screen content, but on box office dollars: Metro needed the "PG" to survive. Association board members acceded, and Valenti later called the *Ryan's Daughter* case "one of the tarnishing marks of the rating system." The two student interns whom Valenti appointed to the board—products of the turbulent late 1960s—had still another perspective. They clashed with Dougherty over the "R"s awarded *Woodstock, Alice's Restaurant,* and other youth-oriented pictures of the era. UCLA cinema graduate (and Rating Administration intern) Stephen Farber thought that both *Woodstock* and *Alice's Restaurant* should have been rated "PG." Dougherty had heard the word "fuck" over fifty years before, he told Farber, but when Country Joe McDonald "gets up in front of a crowd of people and has them spell out the word 'fuck,' is that supposed to be clever? Is that cute? I think this is a sick mentality." Some newspapermen sided with Farber. "The ghost of the late Joe Breen (the first Code chief with any power, the man who used to worry about the extent to which Jane Russell's breasts bounced when she danced) will not rest," the *New York Times'* Vincent Canby wrote in 1970. "Perhaps naively, I had expected the film classification system to act as an exorcism."

Jack Valenti wanted to rejuvenate and professionalize the board much as the Catholics had done with the Legion of Decency some years before; the appointment of the two interns had brought only discord, though, perhaps because Stephen Farber and Estelle Changas trusted no one over thirty. Valenti reasoned that a younger and more vigorous Rating Administration director could lay the Breen ghost to rest and—as Breen had in 1934—sell Hollywood and the press on self-regulation. When Dougherty became ill, the Association offered him a sinecure, then a meager settlement, so meager that when Valenti later asked what caused Dougherty's unexpected death, Association treasurer Robert Watkins replied: "They're suspecting it was a broken heart." With Dougherty gone and Al Van Schmus the only Production Code veteran, forty-five-year-old psychiatrist Aaron Stern became the new Rating Administration director.

Stern found a Rating Administration under Catholic indictment. In 1966, Monsignor Little had retired from the National Catholic Office. "I want to die in the Stations of the Cross," he said, "not looking at Gina Lollobrigida." Patrick Sullivan, an urbane Jesuit, succeeded Little, and in 1967 condemned seventeen pictures, more than the Legion or the National Catholic Office had ever condemned in one year. Throughout the late sixties and early seventies—the period of the "R"-rated *M★A★S★H, Fellini Satyricon, The Love Doctors,* and *The Boys in the Band*—Father Sullivan chastised the Rating Administration for the "growing number of films unsuitable for the young, coupled with the clearly unrealistic ratings handed out." In May 1971, only a month before Stern became director, Sullivan withdrew Catholic support from the Rating Administration: except in name, the priest charged, the organization had abandoned the Code. The announcement was kindling for the movies' foes, and may even have prompted Stern to make his name his motto.

While Valenti worked by consensus, Stern apparently preferred confrontation. Intern Evelyn Renold encountered Stern in August 1971, on her second day at work. He "informed me that I was part of a narcissistic, power-hungry generation," she told Stephen Farber. "Things sort of went downhill from there." Producers who shared her ideals found Stern tough. Four months after Stern became director, the *New York Times* reported on a "general feeling within the industry that practices have become more restrictive since the appointment of Dr. Stern last July 1." No less certain than Dougherty about what picture belonged in what category, Stern wanted to restore the outlook of the Production Code Administration. "You can have a love scene," he told the *Hollywood Reporter* a month after he was appointed, "but as soon as you start to unbutton or unzip you must cut. Afterward, you can show the two in bed, clothed. Anything else and you are going out of the GP rating." "Right on!" Breen would have cheered. But producers who wanted both screen freedom *and* box office queues continued to press Stern for "PG" ratings on "R" pictures. Meanwhile, as conservatives despaired, the courts ruled for those who showed the flesh behind the buttons and zippers.

One East Coast theater sold no popcorn. In a District of Columbia basement the Supreme Court watched movies whose candor would affect Hollywood. In 1970, the justices filed into the basement screening room to watch *I Am Curious (Yellow)*, the story of an actress whose oral-genital activity had already grossed over $8

million and spawned litigation in a dozen states. The potential for
drollery seemed endless. "Did Lena actually kiss [her lover's]
penis?" a government lawyer had once asked Swedish director
Vilgot Sjöman. "Do you mean if her lips actually touched his
penis?" Sjöman responded. "I can't answer that because I wasn't
that close. . . . I have a feeling it was possible for her just to have her
lips a couple of millimeters above the penis." A kiss was once a kiss,
a sigh was once a sigh. No more. The Court split 4–4, which
affirmed a Maryland Supreme Court decision that the picture was
obscene. By 1970, though, the hundreds of obscenity petitions on
the Supreme Court annual docket showed not only how available
sexually oriented materials had become but how much public acceptance they enjoyed. More important, the pressure meant that
Aaron Stern could not hold firm an arbitrary "PG"/"R" line.

Deep Throat, The Devil in Miss Jones, and other "triple-X" pictures
went well beyond the valley of the dolls; they went beyond nude
couples and pantomimed intercourse to show close-ups of genitals
as well as oral and anal penetration, heterosexual and homosexual
sex. Screen sex had become so popular that both Deep Throat and
The Devil in Miss Jones popped up among the twelve top-grossing
pictures of 1973, while I Am Curious became an art house smash.
But who—Hollywood wondered—could top Linda Lovelace and
Lena the Swedish Hummingbird?

In Last Tango in Paris, Bernardo Bertolucci brought explicit sex to
the commercial art film. The Marlon Brando picture included
profane language, frontal nudity, masturbation, and even sodomy.
Paul (Brando) showed all—and more—that Stanley Kowalski had
been forced to suppress two decades before. United Artists applied
an "X" to the Catholic "Condemned" feature: "It's the rating we
should get," UA president David Picker said; "no one under seventeen should see this film."

The reviews of Last Tango were generally good. "If Deep Throat is
a cost of the new freedom," the Los Angeles Times' Charles Cham-
plin wrote, "Last Tango is a reward, an examination in recognizable
individual terms of some of the most guarded but universal fears,
fantasies, desires and pains in human nature." Newsweek and Time
devoted cover stories to the picture, the Motion Picture Academy
nominated both Brando and director Bernardo Bertolucci for Os-

cars, and *Last Tango*—a $100-million box office victory—became the Hollywood beachhead of the 1970s and 1980s.

"I don't want psychologists, psychiatrists, Ph.D.'s, [and] novelists" on the ratings board, Valenti told a congressional committee; he wanted parents. In summer 1974, when Valenti replaced Aaron Stern with Rutgers University professor Richard Heffner, the Association stressed that members of the Rating Administration— even the interns—were mothers and fathers. Heffner commuted between New Jersey and southern California, with Al Van Schmus chief West Coast administrator. Van Schmus's mentor was Geoff Shurlock, who now suffered from ischemia and would later die at the Motion Picture Home in April 1976. After Stern, whom Valenti interns saw as a despot, the low-key authority of Van Schmus seemed blessed. Unlike Dougherty and Stern, Van Schmus "had more respect for the film-makers," Stephen Farber wrote, "and [was] more reluctant to interfere." Producers also admired him. Jonathan Dana earned an "X" for *Sandstone,* a documentary about group sex, yet was told that Van Schmus would not "be offended if we made hay of him in the trades." The remark was an exaggeration, perhaps even a distortion. Dana spoke for others, though, when he commended Van Schmus for "doing his best in a difficult, even intolerable role."

The Vietnam War ended. The flower children became parents of preteens, and Americans turned from protest movements to the "culture of narcissism." Some thought that the ratings had shackled free expression, others that they had lowered "the standards of the larger society." Most thought nothing: they were no longer moviegoers and no longer cared. When the Code and Rating Administration became the Classification and Rating Administration in 1977, few noticed. Even when "X" sired the unofficial "Hard 'R,' " the Church looked away. The National Catholic Office for Motion Pictures closed in 1980, while fundamentalists spotted the devil in secular humanism, pornography, and television—not Hollywood features. The carnal mind remained "enmity against God," but the jeremiads against the movies almost vanished in the 1970s and 1980s.

Though the industry embraced the ratings as triumph, some screenwriters and directors grumbled about them; naturally the Heffner agency was sometimes challenged. The producers of *Cruising,* a police story that outraged homosexuals (and many heterosexuals), promised cuts, then released prints without them; certain other pictures (*Dawn of the Dead, The Chant of Jimmie Blacksmith*) were released unrated. According to one *Los Angeles Times* reporter, the ratings were an alphabet soup that spelled out nothing; in 1977, the paper began its own "Family Film Guide," a gloss for parents. In the early 1980s, faced with the violence of *Gremlins, Indiana Jones and the Temple of Doom,* and other releases, Valenti created "PG-13," an intermediate rating between "PG" and "R" that meant "Parents Strongly Cautioned." The announcement could have occasioned widespread debate or attacks on classification, but did not. The ratings had the tensile strength of the Production Code.

When Al Van Schmus—the last of the Breen boys—retired, the Classification and Rating Administration lost all resemblance to the Production Code Administration. Or did it? "I am not very proud of some of the pictures Hollywood is putting out," President Ronald Reagan noted in 1986. "I don't even think the letter rating system is very effective." Neither do the civil libertarians who would gladly perform one for the Gipper and boot the ratings out of the stands. Why avoid "one set of censors by submitting to more extensive censorship at the hands of another?" one vocal opponent of the ratings asks. "The true test of a democracy's commitment to freedom of expression comes in hard times, not easy; it is measured by resistance to censorship's threat, not acquiescence."

Despite arguments as old as the movies, the public and the producers seem to have accepted classification. On orders from the studio and hints from the Rating Administration, Sam Peckinpah recut the "X"-rated *Straw Dogs* to win an "R." "I detest censorship in any form," he wrote some months later, "but like subsidies, suppositories, taxes and the Nixon Administration, it seems to be part of the American way of life, and has to be dealt with." Contemporary filmmakers are no less philosophical. *Footloose* producer Craig Zadan once stood on the border between "R" and "PG." Would the picture "be O.K. if we took out those 'fucks'?" he asked a Heffner spokesman. " 'Well, we can't promise anything, but yeah,' " the man responded. "It's all done in a sort of code, with a wink," Zadan told the press.

For Albert Brooks, whose *Modern Romance* and *Lost in America* concern the acceptance of limits, the ratings are matters of fact, as plain and straightforward as the story of the birds and the bees: "If you say, 'I'm going to fuck you over,' that's a PG–13. If you say, 'I'm going to fuck you over the desk,' that's an R." And from a dark corner of the Warner Bros. vault, ten scenes into a film covered with the dust of half a century, the dame in the kimono smiles.

APPENDIX:
THE MOTION PICTURE
PRODUCTION CODE

The Motion Picture Production Code was adopted by the Association of Motion Picture Producers, Inc. (the West Coast producers) in February 1930, and by the Motion Picture Producers and Distributors of America the following March. The initial document included a summary of the code version drafted by Daniel Lord and Martin Quigley as well as a "Resolution for Uniform Interpretation" (Hays Papers, 17 February 1930). Before Hays published the Code, the Association changed "the lower and baser element" to "the lower and baser emotions." In 1931, the "Resolution for Uniform Interpretation" was altered to require the submission of scripts, and in 1934, the Production Committee (the "Hollywood Jury") was eliminated so that appeals from decisions of the Code Administration went directly to the Association board.

After the *Motion Picture Herald* published the full text of the original Lord-Quigley document in 1934, the Hays Office sought to fuse the two versions by adding the philosophic sections authored by Lord and Quigley to the end of the 1930 summary released by Hays. In the process, the Lord-Quigley original became the "Reasons Supporting Preamble of Code," the "Reasons Underlying the General Principles," and the "Reasons Underlying Particular Applications." Over the years, the Association amended the Code several times and added major sections on crime (1938), costumes (1939), profanity (1939), and cruelty to animals (1940).

The undersigned members of the Association of Motion Picture Producers, Inc. hereby subscribe to and agree faithfully to conform to the provisions of the following

CODE
TO GOVERN THE MAKING OF
TALKING, SYNCHRONIZED AND SILENT MOTION PICTURES
Formulated by

Association of Motion Picture Producers, Inc. and The Motion Picture Producers and Distributors of America, Inc.

Motion picture producers recognize the high trust and confidence which have been placed in them by the people of the world and which have made motion pictures a universal form of entertainment.

They recognize their responsibility to the public because of this trust and because entertainment and art are important influences in the life of a nation.

Hence, though regarding motion pictures primarily as entertainment without any explicit purpose of teaching or propaganda, they know that the motion picture within its own field of entertainment may be directly responsible for spiritual or moral progress, for higher types of social life, and for much correct thinking.

During the rapid transition from silent to talking pictures they have realized the necessity and the opportunity of subscribing to a Code to govern the production of talking pictures and of reacknowledging this responsibility.

On their part, they ask from the public and from public leaders a sympathetic understanding of their purposes and problems and a spirit of cooperation that will allow them the freedom and opportunity necessary to bring the motion picture to a still higher level of wholesome entertainment for all the people.

GENERAL PRINCIPLES

1. No picture shall be produced which will lower the moral standards of those who see it. Hence the sympathy of the audience should never be thrown to the side of crime, wrongdoing, evil or sin.
2. Correct standards of life, subject only to the requirements of drama and entertainment, shall be presented.
3. Law, natural or human, shall not be ridiculed, nor shall sympathy be created for its violation.

PARTICULAR APPLICATIONS

I—Crimes Against the Law

These shall never be presented in such a way as to throw sympathy with the crime as against law and justice or to inspire others with a desire for imitation.

1. *Murder*
   a. The technique of murder must be presented in a way that will not inspire imitation.
   b. Brutal killings are not to be presented in detail.
   c. Revenge in modern times shall not be justified.
2. *Methods of Crime* should not be explicitly presented.
   a. Theft, robbery, safe-cracking, and dynamiting of trains, mines, buildings, etc., should not be detailed in method.
   b. Arson must be subject to the same safeguards.
   c. The use of firearms should be restricted to essentials.
   d. Methods of smuggling should not be presented.
3. *Illegal drug traffic* must never be presented.
4. *The use of liquor* in American life, when not required by the plot or for proper characterization, will not be shown.

II—Sex

The sanctity of the institution of marriage and the home shall be upheld. Pictures shall not infer that low forms of sex relationship are the accepted or common thing.

1. *Adultery,* sometimes necessary plot material, must not be explicitly treated, or justified, or presented attractively.
2. *Scenes of Passion*
   a. They should not be introduced when not essential to the plot.
   b. Excessive and lustful kissing, lustful embraces, suggestive postures and gestures, are not to be shown.
   c. In general passion should so be treated that these scenes do not stimulate the lower and baser element.
3. *Seduction or Rape*
   a. They should never be more than suggested, and only when essential for the plot, and even then never shown by explicit method.
   b. They are never the proper subject for comedy.
4. *Sex perversion* or any inference to it is forbidden.
5. *White-slavery* shall not be treated.
6. *Miscegenation* (sex relationships between the white and black races) is forbidden.
7. *Sex hygiene* and venereal diseases are not subjects for motion pictures.
8. Scenes of *actual child birth,* in fact or in silhouette, are never to be presented.
9. *Children's sex organs* are never to be exposed.

III—Vulgarity

The treatment of low, disgusting, unpleasant, though not necessarily evil, subjects should be subject always to the dictates of good taste and a regard for the sensibilities of the audience.

IV—Obscenity

Obscenity in word, gesture, reference, song, joke, or by suggestion (even when likely to be understood only by part of the audience) is forbidden.

V—Profanity

Pointed profanity (this includes the words, God, Lord, Jesus, Christ—unless used reverently—Hell, S.O.B., damn, Gawd), or every other profane or vulgar expression however used, is forbidden.

VI—Costume

1. *Complete nudity* is never permitted. This includes nudity in fact or in silhouette, or any lecherous or licentious notice thereof by other characters in the picture.
2. *Undressing scenes* should be avoided, and never used save where essential to the plot.
3. *Indecent or undue exposure* is forbidden.
4. *Dancing costumes* intended to permit undue exposure or indecent movements in the dance are forbidden.

VII—Dances

1. Dances suggesting or representing sexual actions or indecent passion are forbidden.
2. Dances which emphasize indecent movements are to be regarded as obscene.

VIII—Religion

1. No film or episode may throw *ridicule* on any religious faith.
2. *Ministers of religion* in their character as ministers of religion should not be used as comic characters or as villains.
3. *Ceremonies* of any definite religion should be carefully and respectfully handled.

IX—Locations

The treatment of bedrooms must be governed by good taste and delicacy.

X—National Feelings

1. *The use of the Flag* shall be consistently respectful.
2. *The history,* institutions, prominent people and citizenry of other nations shall be represented fairly.

XI—Titles

Salacious, indecent, or obscene titles shall not be used.

XII—Repellent Subjects

The following subjects must be treated within the careful limits of good taste:

1. *Actual hangings* or electrocutions as legal punishments for crime.
2. *Third Degree* methods.
3. *Brutality* and possible gruesomeness.
4. *Branding* of people or animals.
5. *Apparent cruelty* to children or animals.
6. *The sale of women,* or a woman selling her virtue.
7. *Surgical operations.*

RESOLUTION FOR UNIFORM INTERPRETATION 1930

The undersigned members of the Association of Motion Picture Producers, Inc. hereby subscribe to and agree faithfully to conform to the provisions of the following resolution:

WHEREAS, we, the undersigned have this day subscribed and agreed faithfully to conform to a

CODE
TO GOVERN THE MAKING OF
TALKING, SYNCHRONIZED AND SILENT MOTION PICTURES
Formulated by

Association of Motion Picture Producers, Inc., and The Motion Picture Producers and Distributors of America, Inc.

AND WHEREAS, a uniform interpretation of such Code is essential, and for the promotion of such uniform interpretation and consequent universal conformance by ourselves and the personnel of our respective studios it is believed necessary that additional facilities and procedure be established and maintained;

THEREFORE BE IT RESOLVED that we hereby agree to the following methods of operation:

1. When requested by production managers the Association of Motion Picture Producers, Inc. shall secure any facts, information or suggestions concerning the probable reception of stories or the manner in which in its opinion they may best be treated.

2. That each production manager may submit in confidence a copy of each or any script to the Association of Motion Picture Producers, Inc. The Association of Motion Picture Producers, Inc. will give the production manager for his guidance such confidential advice and suggestions as experience, research and information indicate, designating wherein in its judgment the script departs from the provisions of the Code, or wherein from experience or knowledge it is believed that exception will be taken to the story or treatment.

3. Each production manager shall submit to the Association of Motion Picture Pro-

ducers, Inc. every picture he produces before the negative goes to the laboratory for printing. The Association of Motion Picture Producers, Inc. having seen the picture shall inform the production manager in writing whether in its opinion the picture conforms or does not conform to the Code, stating specifically wherein either by theme, treatment or incident the picture violates the provisions of the Code. In such latter event the picture shall not be released until the changes indicated by the Association of Motion Picture Producers, Inc. have been made; provided, however, that the production manager may appeal from such opinion of the Association to the Production Committee of the Association of Motion Picture Producers, Inc.

In the event the Production Committee concurs in the judgment of the Association and the production manager still believes that such picture conforms to the spirit and the letter of the Code, he may appeal to the Board of Directors of the Motion Picture Producers and Distributors of America, Inc. whose findings shall be final and such production manager and company shall be governed accordingly.

The Production Committee shall be constituted as follows:

Charles H. Christie	William R. Fraser	Warren Doane
Cecil B. De Mille	Sol Lesser	John A. Waldron
E. H. Allen	Irving Thalberg	Joseph M. Schenck
Hal B. Wallis	Ben Schulberg	Carl Laemmle, Jr.
Sol Wurtzel	Charles Sullivan	J. L. Warner
Abraham Lehr	William LeBaron	

The Board of Directors of the Association of Motion Picture Producers, Inc. may from time to time by unanimous vote make changes in the personnel of this Committee.

When a production manager appeals from a decision of the Association of Motion Picture Producers, Inc. he will so inform its Secretary, who will in rotation designate from the above named Production Committee three members who will immediately examine the picture in question and render its opinion, as provided for above. The Secretary of the Association of Motion Picture Producers, Inc., in designating the members of any such committee will not include members from studios with business alliances with each other or with the studio whose picture is being examined. In the event any of the three so designated are unavoidably absent from the city, the member or members next in order will be selected, under the same provisions. Any such member so unavoidably out of the city when so designated shall be considered at the head of the list subject to the next call for service.

REASONS SUPPORTING PREAMBLE OF CODE

I. Theatrical motion pictures, that is, pictures intended for the theatre as distinct from pictures intended for churches, schools, lecture halls, educational movements, social reform movements, etc., are primarily to be regarded as ENTERTAINMENT.

Mankind has always recognized the importance of entertainment and its value in rebuilding the bodies and souls of human beings.

But it has always recognized that entertainment can be of a character either HELPFUL or HARMFUL to the human race, and in consequence has clearly distinguished between:

    a. Entertainment which tends to improve the race, or at least to re-create and rebuild human beings exhausted with the realities of life; and

    b. Entertainment which tends to degrade human beings, or to lower their standards of life and living.

Hence the MORAL IMPORTANCE of entertainment is something which has been universally recognized. It enters intimately into the lives of men and women and affects them closely; it occupies their minds and affections during leisure hours; and ultimately touches the whole of their lives. A man may be judged by his standard of entertainment as easily as by the standard of his work.

So correct entertainment raises the whole standard of a nation.

Wrong entertainment lowers the whole living conditions and moral ideals of a race.

Note, for example, the healthy reactions to healthful sports, like baseball, golf; the unhealthy reactions to sports like cockfighting, bullfighting, bear baiting, etc.

Note, too, the effect on ancient nations of gladiatorial combats, the obscene plays of Roman times, etc.

II. Motion pictures are very important as ART.

Though a new art, possibly a combination art, it has the same object as the other arts, the presentation of human thought, emotion, and experience, in terms of an appeal to the soul through the senses.

Here, as in entertainment,

Art enters intimately into the lives of human beings.

Art can be morally good, lifting men to higher levels. This has been done through good music, great painting, authentic fiction, poetry, drama.

Art can be morally evil in its effects. This is the case clearly enough with unclean art, indecent books, suggestive drama. The effect on the lives of men and women is obvious.

Note: It has often been argued that art in itself is unmoral, neither good nor bad. This is perhaps true of the THING which is music, painting, poetry, etc. But the thing is the PRODUCT of some person's mind, and the intention of that mind was either good or bad morally when it produced the thing. Besides, the thing has its EFFECT upon those who come into contact with it. In both these ways, that is, as a product of a mind and as the cause of definite effects, it has a deep moral significance and an unmistakable moral quality.

Hence: The motion pictures, which are the most popular of modern arts for the masses, have their moral quality from the intention of the minds which produce them and from their effects on the moral lives and reactions of their audiences. This gives them a most important morality.

1. They reproduce the morality of the men who use the pictures as a medium for the expression of their ideas and ideals.

2. They affect the moral standards of those who, through the screen, take in these ideas and ideals.

In the case of the motion pictures, this effect may be particularly emphasized because no art has so quick and so widespread an appeal to the masses. It has become in an incredibly short period the art of the multitudes.

III. The motion picture, because of its importance as entertainment and because of the trust placed in it by the peoples of the world, has special MORAL OBLIGATIONS:

A. Most arts appeal to the mature. This art appeals at once to every class, mature, immature, developed, undeveloped, law abiding, criminal. Music has its grades for different classes; so has literature and drama. This art of the motion picture, combining as it does the two fundamental appeals of looking at a picture and listening to a story, at once reaches every class of society.

B. By reason of the mobility of a film and the ease of picture distribution, and because of the possibility of duplicating positives in large quantities, this art reaches places unpenetrated by other forms of art.

C. Because of these two facts, it is difficult to produce films intended for only certain classes of people. The exhibitors' theatres are built for the masses, for the cultivated and the rude, the mature and the immature, the self-respecting and the criminal. Films, unlike books and music, can with difficulty be confined to certain selected groups.

D. The latitude given to film material cannot, in consequence, be as wide as the latitude given to book material. In addition:

    a. A book describes; a film vividly presents. One presents on a cold page; the other by apparently living people.

    b. A book reaches the mind through words merely; a film reaches the eyes and ears through the reproduction of actual events.

    c. The reaction of a reader to a book depends largely on the keenness of the reader's imagination; the reaction to a film depends on the vividness of presentation.

Hence many things which might be described or suggested in a book could not possibly be presented in a film.

E. This is also true when comparing the film with the newspaper.

    a. Newspapers present by description, films by actual presentation.

    b. Newspapers are after the fact and present things as having taken place; the film gives the events in the process of enactment and with apparent reality of life.

F. Everything possible in a play is not possible in a film:

    a. Because of the larger audience of the film, and its consequential mixed character. Psychologically, the larger the audience, the lower the moral mass resistance to suggestion.

    b. Because through light, enlargement of character, presentation, scenic emphasis, etc., the screen story is brought closer to the audience than the play.

    c. The enthusiasm for and interest in the film actors and actresses, developed beyond anything of the sort in history, makes the audience largely sympathetic toward the characters they portray and the stories in which they figure. Hence the audience is more ready to confuse actor and actress and the characters they portray, and it is most receptive of the emotions and ideals presented by their favorite stars.

G. Small communities, remote from sophistication and from the hardening process which often takes place in the ethical and moral standards of groups in larger cities, are easily and readily reached by any sort of film.

H. The grandeur of mass settings, large action, spectacular features, etc., affects and arouses more intensely the emotional side of the audience.

In general, the mobility, popularity, accessibility, emotional appeal, vividness, straightforward presentation of fact in the film make for more intimate contact with a larger audience and for greater emotional appeal.

Hence the larger moral responsibilities of the motion pictures.

REASONS UNDERLYING THE GENERAL PRINCIPLES

I. No picture shall be produced which will lower the moral standards of those who see it. Hence the sympathy of the audience should never be thrown to the side of crime, wrong-doing, evil or sin.

    This is done:

    1. When evil is made to appear attractive or alluring, and good is made to appear unattractive.

    2. When the sympathy of the audience is thrown on the side of crime, wrong-doing, evil, sin. The same thing is true of a film that would throw sympathy against goodness, honor, innocence, purity or honesty.

Note: Sympathy with a person who sins is not the same as sympathy with the sin or crime of which he is guilty. We may feel sorry for the plight of the murderer or even understand the circumstances which led him to his crime: We may not feel sympathy with the wrong which he has done. The presentation of evil is often essential for art or fiction or drama. This in itself is not wrong provided:

a. That evil is not presented alluringly. Even if later in the film the evil is condemned or punished, it must not be allowed to appear so attractive that the audience's emotions are drawn to desire or approve so strongly that later the condemnation is forgotten and only the apparent joy of the sin remembered.

b. That throughout, the audience feels sure that evil is wrong and good is right.

II. Correct standards of life shall, as far as possible, be presented.

A wide knowledge of life and of living is made possible through the film. When right standards are consistently presented, the motion picture exercises the most powerful influences. It builds character, develops right ideals, inculcates correct principles, and all this in attractive story form.

If motion pictures consistently hold up for admiration high types of characters and present stories that will affect lives for the better, they can become the most powerful natural force for the improvement of mankind.

III. Law, natural or human, shall not be ridiculed, nor shall sympathy be created for its violation.

By natural law is understood the law which is written in the hearts of all mankind, the great underlying principles of right and justice dictated by conscience.

By human law is understood the law written by civilized nations.

1. The presentation of crimes against the law is often necessary for the carrying out of the plot. But the presentation must not throw sympathy with the crime as against the law nor with the criminal as against those who punish him.

2. The courts of the land should not be presented as unjust. This does not mean that a single court may not be represented as unjust, much less that a single court official must not be presented this way. But the court system of the country must not suffer as a result of this presentation.

REASONS UNDERLYING PARTICULAR APPLICATIONS

I. Sin and evil enter into the story of human beings and hence in themselves are valid dramatic material.

II. In the use of this material, it must be distinguished between sin which repels by its very nature, and sins which often attract.

a. In the first class come murder, most theft, many legal crimes, lying, hypocrisy, cruelty, etc.

b. In the second class come sex sins, sins and crimes of apparent heroism, such as banditry, daring thefts, leadership in evil, organized crime, revenge, etc.

The first class needs less care in treatment, as sins and crimes of this class are naturally unattractive. The audience instinctively condemns all such and is repelled.

Hence the important objective must be to avoid the hardening of the audience, especially of those who are young and impressionable, to the thought and fact of crime. People can become accustomed even to murder, cruelty, brutality, and repellent crimes, if these are too frequently repeated.

The second class needs great care in handling, as the response of human nature to their appeal is obvious. This is treated more fully below.

III. A careful distinction can be made between films intended for general distribution, and films intended for use in theatres restricted to a limited audience. Themes and plots quite appropriate for the latter would be altogether out of place and dangerous in the former.

Note: The practice of using a general theatre and limiting its patronage during the showing of a certain film to "Adults Only" is not completely satisfactory and is only partially effective.

However, maturer minds may easily understand and accept without harm subject matter in plots which do younger people positive harm.

Hence: If there should be created a special type of theatre, catering exclusively to an adult audience, for plays of this character (plays with problem themes, difficult discussions and maturer treatment) it would seem to afford an outlet, which does not now exist, for pictures unsuitable for general distribution but permissible for exhibitions to a restricted audience.

I. Crimes Against the Law

The treatment of crimes against the law must not:

1. Teach methods of crime.
2. Inspire potential criminals with a desire for imitation.
3. Make criminals seem heroic and justified.

Revenge in modern times shall not be justified. In lands and ages of less developed civilization and moral principles, revenge may sometimes be presented. This would be the case especially in places where no law exists to cover the crime because of which revenge is committed.

Because of its evil consequences, the drug traffic should not be presented in any form. The existence of the trade should not be brought to the attention of audiences.

The use of liquor should never be excessively presented. In scenes from American life, the necessities of plot and proper characterization alone justify its use. And in this case, it should be shown with moderation.

II. Sex

Out of regard for the sanctity of marriage and the home, the triangle, that is, the love of a third party for one already married, needs careful handling. The treatment should not throw sympathy against marriage as an institution.

Scenes of passion must be treated with an honest acknowledgment of human nature and its normal reactions. Many scenes cannot be presented without arousing dangerous emotions on the part of the immature, the young or the criminal classes.

Even within the limits of pure love, certain facts have been universally regarded by lawmakers as outside the limits of safe presentation.

In the case of impure love, the love which society has always regarded as wrong and which has been banned by divine law, the following are important:

1. Impure love must not be presented as attractive and beautiful.
2. It must not be the subject of comedy or farce, or treated as material for laughter.
3. It must not be presented in such a way as to arouse passion or morbid curiosity on the part of the audience.
4. It must not be made to seem right and permissible.
5. In general, it must not be detailed in method and manner.

III. Vulgarity; IV. Obscenity; V. Profanity; hardly need further explanation than is contained in the Code.

VI. Costume

General principles:

1. The effect of nudity or semi-nudity upon the normal man or woman, and much

more upon the young and upon immature persons, has been honestly recognized by all lawmakers and moralists.

2. Hence the fact that the nude or semi-nude body may be beautiful does not make its use in the films moral. For, in addition to its beauty, the effect of the nude or semi-nude body on the normal individual must be taken into consideration.

3. Nudity or semi-nudity used simply to put a "punch" into a picture comes under the head of immoral actions. It is immoral in its effect on the average audience.

4. Nudity can never be permitted as being necessary for the plot. Semi-nudity must not result in undue or indecent exposures.

5. Transparent or translucent materials and silhouette are frequently more suggestive than actual exposure.

VII. Dances

Dancing in general is recognized as an art and as a beautiful form of expressing human emotions.

But dances which suggest or represent sexual actions, whether performed solo or with two or more; dances intended to excite the emotional reaction of an audience; dances with movement of the breasts, excessive body movements while the feet are stationary, violate decency and are wrong.

VIII. Religion

The reason why ministers of religion may not be comic characters or villains is simply because the attitude taken toward them may easily become the attitude taken toward religion in general. Religion is lowered in the minds of the audience because of the lowering of the audience's respect for a minister.

IX. Locations

Certain places are so closely and thoroughly associated with sexual life or with sexual sin that their use must be carefully limited.

X. National Feelings

The just rights, history, and feelings of any nation are entitled to most careful consideration and respectful treatment.

XI. Titles

As the title of a picture is the brand on that particular type of goods, it must conform to the ethical practices of all such honest business.

XII. Repellent Subjects

Such subjects are occasionally necessary for the plot. Their treatment must never offend good taste nor injure the sensibilities of an audience.

NOTES

Archival materials, personal interviews, contemporary newspapers, and other second-ary works formed the research base for *The Dame in the Kimono*. The following notes provide sources for almost all quotations in the text; where only author and page number are listed below, the reader should consult the Selected Bibliography.

The authors have not cited—except when unattributed within the text—quotations from their personal (P) or telephone (T) interviews: Pandro Berman (T), 19 January 1986; Niven Busch (T), 8 December 1985; J. J. Cohn (P), Los Angeles, 23 May 1985; William Dozier (T), 11 May 1986; Philip Dunne (T), 3 November 1987; Rudi Fehr (T), 22 June 1979; James B. Harris (T), 16 September 1988; John Michael Hayes (P), Los Angeles, 14 May 1985; Stanley Kramer (T), 2 November 1987; Ely Landau (T), 19 May 1980; Arthur Laurents (T), 8 June 1986; Ernest Lehman (P), Los Angeles, 30 July 1981; Luigi Luraschi (P), London, 18 July 1985; Frank McCarthy (P), Los Angeles, 21 May 1985; Patrick J. Sullivan, S.J. (T), 16 November 1988; Daniel Taradash (P), Stillwater, Oklahoma, 4 April 1985; Jack Valenti (T), 18 November 1988; Al Van Schmus (P), Laguna Niguel, California, 18 May 1985, and (T), 2 July 1988; Jack Vizzard (P), Los Angeles, 14 August 1987; Robert M. W. Vogel (P), Los Angeles, 20 May 1985; Robert Watkins (P), Los Angeles, 12 August 1987.

The authors have also not cited paraphrased facts and opinions; quotations from contemporary reviews or advertisements of motion pictures; quotations from novels or plays (for example, *Gone With the Wind* or *Who's Afraid of Virginia Woolf?*) on which films were based; or, unless otherwise indicated, quotations from the Production Code or from treatments, screenplays, or motion picture sound tracks.

PREFACE

xi "BREASTS PARTIALLY EXPOSED": R. E. Plummer to Jason Joy, 29 May 1931, *The Maltese Falcon* file, Production Code Administration (PCA) Collection, Margaret Herrick Library, Academy of Motion Picture Arts and Sciences, Beverly Hills, California. The *Falcon* was released in 1931; it was rereleased for television under the title *Dangerous Female*.

xii "I AM SO ENTHUSIASTIC": Joseph Breen to Will Hays, 9 November 1930, Will Hays Papers, Part II, ed. Douglas Gomery, University Publications of America. Hays was president of the Motion Picture Producers and Distributors of America, which later was called the Motion Picture Association of America; throughout, we refer to the organization as "the Association."

xii "SOME HELP IN CLEANING UP": Joy to Hays, 15 April 1931, *The Maltese Falcon* PCA file.

xii "THE PEST HOLE": The National Catholic Welfare Conference, cited in "The Legion of Decency," *Commonweal*, 18 May 1934: 58.

xiii "ADROIT INDIRECTION": Philip Dunne, "Blast It All," *Harvard Magazine*, September–October 1987: 8.

xiii "WE LIKE TO THINK": Breen to Arthur H. DeBra, 20 April 1944, copy provided to the authors by Al Van Schmus.

xiv ELEVEN "TOUGH CASES": *She Done Him Wrong, I'm No Angel,* and *Belle of the Nineties* are curtain-raisers for the story of the Production Code Administration. Because they involved important Motion Picture Association board challenges, *Gone With the Wind, The Outlaw, The Bicycle Thief,* and *The Moon Is Blue* seemed indispensable as four of the eleven case studies. The other seven films—remarkable for their content, their artistry, or their exposure of the Hollywood system—show how the Production Code Administration responded to pressure and changed over time. The authors recognize that many

other films, from *Scarface* and *Scarlet Street* to *Duel in the Sun, Double Indemnity,* and *Baby Doll* stirred the dust around Breen and Shurlock. For *The Dame in the Kimono,* however, no picture was as important as the issues it raised or the insights it provided into Code operations.

THE PRODUCTION CODE, 1922–1934

Welcome Will Hays!

4 "AN EAR-REDUCTION LENS": *New York Times,* 7 March 1937.

5 "PUBLIC DEMANDS AND MORAL STANDARDS": Howard T. Lewis, *The Motion Picture Industry* (New York: D. Van Nostrand, 1933), 372.

5 "EXERCISE EVERY POSSIBLE": Moley, 58.

5 "DECORATED WITH BUNTING": Hays, 342.

5 "THE ARTIST AGREES": John Gilbert contract, Metro Pictures Corporation, 2 May 1924, Museum of the Moving Image, London.

5 "WE ARE AGAINST": quoted in A. A. Hopkins, "Charlie Chaplin, et al. / COMMUNIST ACTIVITIES," FBI Report, 15 August 1922.

6 "STUDIES IN DIMINISHING": William De Mille, cited in de Grazia and Newman, 29.

6 "ALL OF HER LEGS": *Variety,* 23 June 1926.

6 "DAVID THOUGHT": Irene Mayer Selznick, *A Private View* (New York: Knopf, 1983), 103.

6 "NAMBY-PAMBY": Laemmle, quoted in Robert Cochrane to Hays, 6 April 1927; cited in Robert F. Martin III, "Celluloid Morality: Will Hays' Rhetoric in Defense of the Movies, 1922–1930" (Ph.D. dissertation, Indiana University, 1974), 245.

7 "CUTTING HAS OFTEN": *Variety,* 7 March 1928.

7 "THE MOTION PICTURE INDUSTRY": Charles C. Pettijohn to Hays, 21 March 1927; cited in Martin, "Celluloid Morality," 236.

7 "IN SITUATIONS WHERE": David D. Jones (President, Bennett College for Women, Greensboro, North Carolina) to Joy, 2 August 1930, *The Birth of a Nation* PCA file.

8 "A FIGHT BETWEEN": Brookhart, quoted in Jerry A. Matthews to Maurice McKenzie, 26 August 1929, Hays Papers.

8 "MORE THAN FIFTY": Pettijohn to Hays, 2 April 1929, Hays Papers.

9 "CLEVER IRISH POLITICKING": Jack Vizzard interview.

9 "TIED UP THE PICTURE": Review of *Eucharistic Congress, Variety,* 10 November 1926.

9 "I DO NOT WANT": Martin Quigley to Father Daniel Lord, S.J., 3 January 1930, Martin J. Quigley Papers, Box 1, Folder 18 (hereafter 1:18), Special Collections Division, Georgetown University, Washington, D.C.

9 "WELL INTO THE MID-NIGHT": Breen to Quigley, 19 June 1937, Quigley Papers (1:19).

10 "THINGS INIMICAL": Joy to Hays, 12 November 1929, Hays Papers.

10 "NO PICTURE SHOULD": "Adopted Code to Govern the Production of Motion Pictures" (undated, c. 1929), "Production Code Administration" file, David O. Selznick Collection, Hoblitzelle Theatre Arts Library, Humanities Research Center, University of Texas at Austin.

10 "THE POWERFUL MAN": Lord to Quigley, 2 January 1930, Quigley Papers (1:18).

10 "MY EYES NEARLY": Hays, 439. Others agreed that Hays went bug-eyed, though for another reason. Joe Breen recalled "distinctly" how Quigley told him, "with considerable dramatic effect, about Mr. Hays' reaction to the whole thing—his failure, seemingly, to understand just what it was all about" (Breen to Quigley, 19 June 1937, Quigley Papers [1:19]). Less church mouse than he appeared, Hays dropped "hotdamn"s into conversation and gambled at backgammon; he may have been unprepared for so punctilious a Code,

one whose Catholic origins were complemented by dinned references to "MORAL IMPORTANCE" and "MORAL OBLIGATION."

11 "THAT HIS COMPANY": Joy to Hays, 22 October 1929, *Shanghai Gesture* PCA file.

11 "PATRIOTIC GENTILE": William Sheafe Chase, *Catechism on Motion Pictures in Inter-State Commerce* (New York: The New York Civic League, 1922), 116.

12 "PROMOTE A NOMINAL": "Hollywood Promises," *Commonweal,* 16 April 1930: 668.

12 "WHAT WITH SOUND FILMS": "Morals for Movies," *Outlook and Independent,* 16 April 1930: 612.

13 "ENTIRE OFFICE": Fred Beetson to Hays, 3 May 1930, Hays Papers.

13 "SERIOUS AND DETERMINED": *Exhibitors Herald-World,* 11 October 1930.

13 "POSTWAR PREOCCUPATION": *New York Times,* 31 March 1931.

13 "DURING THE FIRST": Joy to John A. Cooper, 21 February 1931, *Little Caesar* PCA file.

13 "WERE BASED ON": *Variety,* 31 December 1930.

14 "WASTE CEASED": *Variety,* 31 December 1930.

14 "A COMMUNITY TORN": French, 43.

14 "A GREAT CHAMPION": Breen to Hays, 7 November 1930, Hays Papers.

14 "I CAN UNDERSTAND": Breen to McKenzie, 6 March 1931, Hays Papers.

15 OTHER BOARDS ALSO SCISSORED: The boards' "preview" fees made Hollywood suspicious; one Hays associate called a proposed Minneapolis censorship law "a shake-down" whose sole purpose, according to the mayor, was "to *raise revenue* for the city" (Report [unsigned], October 1933, Hays Papers). Censor board members were concerned not with dollars but morals. At their headquarters in the Kansas City Fire Department Building, Jessie Hodges and the two other women who constituted the Kansas Board of Review screened pictures for six hours each weekday.

They sat at small desks and each time the action or dialogue breached their unpublished guidelines, they rang small bells; the projectionist marked the bell points for later discussion. Though the women strove for unanimity, they cut by consensus. And what they deemed proper for Kansans to see—and *only* what they deemed proper for Kansans to see—Kansans saw. For more on the rules, operation, and constitutionality of the state and municipal boards, see the Carmen and Randall entries in the Selected Bibliography.

15 "WE HAD TO STOP IN THE MIDDLE": Captain Robert Pearson (Chief Censor of Edmonton, Alberta) to Joy, 10 March 1931, *Little Caesar* PCA file.

15 "WHOLESALE" deletions: Joy to Breen, 25 September 1931, *Waterloo Bridge,* PCA file.

15 "SMALL, NARROW": Joy to Cooper, 21 February 1931, *Little Caesar* PCA file.

15 "BOLDNESS AND TRUTHFULNESS": Joy to Carl Laemmle, Jr., 21 August 1929, *All Quiet on the Western Front* PCA file.

15 "DESTROY THE MORAL VALUE": Joy to James Wingate (State of New York Education Department, Motion Picture Division), 5 February 1931, *Little Caesar* PCA file.

15 "HE WAS ALL HYPED UP": Quoted in Leonard Mosley, *Zanuck: The Rise and Fall of Hollywood's Last Tycoon* (Boston: Little, Brown, 1984), 115.

"You Can Be Had"

17 "THIS BURG": Breen to Hays, 29 August 1931, Hays Papers.

17 "FOR EXAMPLE": Breen to Hays, 29 August 1931, Hays Papers.

18 "RIGHT STUFF": Breen to Hays, 29 August 1931, Hays Papers.

18 "TO SERIOUSLY TAKE": Breen to Hays, 29 August 1931, Hays Papers.

18 "THOROUGHLY IN HAND": Breen to McKenzie, 29 January 1932, Hays Papers.

19 "GENERAL INDICTMENTS": Motion Picture Producers and Distributors of

America, Inc., Annual Report, 11 April 1932: 4, 22.

19 " 'OHS,' 'AHS' AND": *New York Times,* 27 April 1926.

19 "THE GREAT MAJORITY": Cited in Jon Tuska, *The Films of Mae West* (Secaucus, New Jersey: Citadel, 1973), 32.

19 "A SET OF PORNOGRAPHIC": Cited in Tuska, *Films of Mae West,* 37.

19 "IT IS DIFFICULT": Krutch, *The Nation,* 30 September 1931: 344.

19 "DEGENERATE SHRIEKS": Cited in Tuska, *Films of Mae West,* 46.

20 "VULGAR DRAMATIC SITUATIONS": Joy, Memorandum of Record, 11 January 1930, *She Done Him Wrong* PCA file.

20 "DISCOURAGED THE IDEA": Joy, Memorandum of Record, 11 January 1930, *She Done Him Wrong* PCA file.

20 "TO AVOID THE PICTURIZATION": "Agreement executed between the Authors' League of America, the Dramatists' Guild of the Authors' League, the Authors' Guild of the Authors' League and the Motion Picture Producers and Distributors of America, Inc., December 15, 1927," cited in Moley, 239.

20 "I SAT AROUND": John Kobal, *People Will Talk* (New York: Alfred A. Knopf, 1985), 163–64.

20 "A CREAKY, DATED": Quoted in Weales, 44.

22 "TO STAND BY ME": Breen to McKenzie, 29 January 1932, Hays Papers.

22 "NOT SINCE I HAVE BEEN": Lamar Trotti to McKenzie, 27 April 1932, *Red Headed Woman* PCA file.

22 "ASSOCIATE AND BODYGUARD": Carl E. Millikin to Hays, 25 June 1932, Hays Papers.

22 "UTTERLY IMPOSSIBLE": Trotti to Hays, 30 April 1932, *Red Headed Woman* PCA file.

23 "DETERMINED TO PUT ASIDE": Joy to Hays, 25 July 1932, *A Farewell to Arms* PCA file.

23 "WHETHER I CAN": Harry M.

Warner to Hays, 19 October 1932, *She Done Him Wrong* PCA file.

23 "OUT HERE": *New York Times,* 9 June 1935.

23 "I THINK THAT": Cited in Tuska, *Films of Mae West,* 126.

24 "WASH-OUT": Quigley to Hays, 4 August 1932, Hays Papers.

25 "TEARING OFF": Jack Jacobs, "The Dandy Who Directed: Lowell Sherman," *Focus on Film,* no. 23 (Winter 1975/76): 43.

25 "WATCHED MOST CAREFULLY": "JPH" to Joy, 5 November 1932, *She Done Him Wrong* PCA file.

26 "SET IN HIS WAYS": James M. Wall, "Oral Interview with Geoffrey Shurlock," Louis B. Mayer/American Film Institute Film History Program, July 1970, 89.

26 "BY ALL MEANS": Hays to Adolph Zukor, 23 November 1932, *She Done Him Wrong* PCA file.

26 "SICKENING . . .": Trotti to Milliken, 6 June 1930, *The Story of Temple Drake* PCA file.

26 "SUITABLE MATERIAL": Notes, MPPDA Board Meeting, 28 November 1932, *She Done Him Wrong* PCA file.

27 "SORDID REALISM": Wingate to Hays, 2 December 1932; Geoffrey Shurlock, Memorandum of Record, 30 November 1932; *She Done Him Wrong* PCA file.

27 "SUGGESTIVE AND VULGAR": Wingate to Harold Hurley, 6 December 1932, *She Done Him Wrong* PCA file.

28 "FAIRY SWEET FLOWER": "RRH" to H. Cass, 30 August 1932, *Red Headed Woman* PCA file. Regal Films' "RRH" represented Metro in British Columbia, where the censors had worked over *Woman;* he expected more rough treatment from the tough Ontario board: "There is not anything comical in the minds of our Methodists in the modest and fairy sweet flower of sex grown suddenly to sunflower proportions and surrounded by blades of sex grass that look like corn stacks. I lay you a bet that you do not get the picture by in Ontario

but I have hopes that I can get it by here in such form as will rake in a few shekels for 'Ye Old Regal.' "

28 "THE IDEA OF BABY": Howard Smith to Darryl Zanuck, 11 November 1932; Behlmer, *Inside Warner Bros.,* 8.

29 "A THROBBING, VIBRANT": Quoted in "Haysiana," *American Spectator,* November 1932.

29 "ONE OF HEARTY": Wingate to Hays, 13 January 1933, *She Done Him Wrong* PCA file.

30 "A CINEMATIZATION": *New York Times,* 12 February 1933.

30 "WHICH EVERYBODY KNOWS": Lord to Hays, 20 February 1933, Quigley Papers (1:18).

30 "THE WORST PICTURE": Sidney Kent to Hays (undated), *She Done Him Wrong* PCA file.

32 "THE STRICTEST SUPERVISION": Hays to Wingate, 7 February 1933, *The Story of Temple Drake* PCA file.

32 "EVERY SENSE": Quoted in Hays to Wingate ("Personal and Confidential"), 9 February 1933, *The Story of Temple Drake* PCA file.

Welcome Joe Breen!

33 "JUST DUMB ENOUGH": Robert Watkins interview.

33 "MY DEAR BOZO": Breen to Msgr. Joseph M. Corrigan, 17 October 1930, Hays Papers.

34 "THE CONFUSION WE HAD": Breen to Hays, 29 August 1931, Hays Papers.

34 "NOTHING TO COMPARE": Breen to Hays, 29 August 1931, Hays Papers.

35 STRONGER COMPLIANCE: West Coast executives supported the local trade press through ads, but they so underfed Quigley Publications' *Hollywood Herald* that Quigley closed the paper in March 1932. "I know exactly what [the studios'] attitude is," Quigley told an associate. "They would like to have a paper there for their own aggrandizement from time to time, and again they would like to have no paper there in the event of a possibility it might criticize them." Resentment as well as moral scruple may have fueled the

Motion Picture Herald campaign against screen sex (Quigley to Leo Meehan, 7 March 1932, Hays Papers).

35 "Q. IS VERY MUCH": Breen to Hays, 2 March 1933, Hays Papers; cited in Maltby, 39.

35 "VILE AND OFFENSIVE": Breen to Wingate, 5 May 1933, *Ann Vickers* PCA file.

35 "DEFINITELY INCORRECT": Breen to Wingate, 17 March 1933, *The Story of Temple Drake* PCA file.

35 "THE WRONG KIND": Breen to Wingate, 22 May 1933, *Of Human Bondage* PCA file.

35 "I THINK THE QUICKER": Kent to Winfield Sheehan, 7 March 1933, *The Power and the Glory* PCA file.

36 "WOMEN'S PICTURES": Wingate to Hays, 28 February 1933, *Baby Face* PCA file; cited in Maltby, 38.

36 "SEX IN THE LUSCIOUS": *New York Times*, 11 March 1934.

36 "A LAND-OFFICE": *Atlanta Journal*, 13 April 1933.

37 "THAT THE MOVIES": Frank K. Shuttleworth and Mark A. May, *The Social Conduct and Attitudes of Movie Fans* (New York: Macmillan, 1933), 92–93.

37 "RIDING THE MOVIES": Lupton A. Wilkinson to Hays, 29 October 1932, Hays Papers; cited in Maltby, 39.

37 "PAYNEFUL STUDIES": Kirk L. Russell to Hays, 2 May 1933, Hays Papers.

37 "TENDENCY TOWARD": Moley, 252.

37 "THE MAGNA CHARTA": Moley, 78.

37 "UPWARDS OF ONE THOUSAND": Harry Zehner, Memorandum of Record, 26 May 1933, Universal Collection, Special Collections, University Library, University of Southern California, Los Angeles.

38 "DEFINITE DECISION": Wingate to Hays, 8 May 1933, *The Story of Temple Drake* PCA file.

38 "FOR GOD'S SAKE": Hal Wallis to Michael Curtiz, 21 October 1933; Behlmer, *Inside Warner Bros.*, 14.

38 "WE MUST PUT BRASSIERES": Jack Warner to Wallis, 5 October 1933;

Behlmer, *Inside Warner Bros.*, 15. (Unless otherwise indicated, all "Warner" citations below refer to Jack Warner.)

38 "MAY PRESENT EVEN": Wingate to Hays, 20 September 1933, *Nana* PCA file.

39 "CONTINUE TO PRESENT": Wingate to Hays, 8 May 1933, *Ann Vickers* PCA file.

39 "WHY COMPANIES": Wingate to McKenzie, 22 May 1933, *Ann Vickers* PCA file.

39 "AT ONCE WRITE": C. F. Morgan, "Climax of the Movie Tragedy Approaches," *Magazine of Wall Street*, 15 April 1933: 671.

39 "MAE COULDN'T": Review of *She Done Him Wrong*, *Variety*, 14 February 1933.

40 "A TWO-WOMAN CAMPAIGN": *New York Times*, 13 June 1937.

40 "I CONCENTRATE ON": Mae West Interview, *Playboy*, January 1971: 80.

40 "I CONSIDER": Alice Ames Winter to Hays, 10 July 1933, Hays Papers.

41 "THAT THE PICTURE": Wingate to A. M. Botsford, 18 September 1933, *I'm No Angel* PCA file.

41 "A KNOCKOUT": Vincent Hart to McKenzie, 4 October 1933, *I'm No Angel* PCA file.

41 "THE GENERAL FLAVOR": Winter to Hays, 21 November 1933, Hays Papers.

42 "MAE PACKS 'EM IN": "The President and the Movie Code," *Christian Century*, 25 October 1933: 1327.

42 "MUCH OF THIS EFFORT": Quigley to Patrick F. Scanlan, 4 August 1936, Quigley Papers (1:19).

42 "FIRE IN HIS EYES": Breen to Wilfrid Parsons, S.J., 11 August 1933; quoted in Facey, 45.

43 "CATHOLICS ARE CALLED": *New York Times*, 2 October 1933.

43 "TIME CAN BE TAKEN": John T. McNicholas (Archbishop of Cincinnati) to John J. Cantwell (Bishop of Los Angeles and San Diego), 4 December 1933, Hays Papers.

43 "PRETTY WELL SWAMPED": Wingate

to Hays, 25 November 1933, *Of Human Bondage* PCA file.

43 "VILE, FILTHY": Report, 9 January 1934, Hays Papers.

43 "SINISTER EFFECTS": *Boston Sunday Post,* 31 December 1933.

44 "SOMETHING OF A CLASSIC": Breen, Memorandum of Record, 10 February 1934, *Of Human Bondage* PCA file.

44 "AFTER CONSIDERABLE PRESSURE": Breen, Memorandum of Record, 1 February 1934, *Heat Lightning* PCA file.

44 "NOTHING TO WORRY ABOUT": Breen to Warner, 5 March 1934, *Wonder Bar* PCA file.

44 "ONE ITEM WHICH": McKenzie to Breen, 1 March 1934, *Wonder Bar* PCA file.

44 "IT IS QUITE EVIDENT": Breen to McKenzie, 13 March 1934, *Wonder Bar* PCA file.

44 "STROKES THE BEDROOM": Charles Higham and Joel Greenberg, eds., *The Celluloid Muse: Hollywood Directors Speak* (New York: New American Library, 1969), 155.

45 "I HAVE LEARNED": Breen to McKenzie, 16 March 1934, *George White's Scandals* PCA file.

45 "WHAT'S ALL THIS": Vizzard, 51.

45 "GLORIFYING A COMMUNIST": Breen, Memorandum of Record (undated), *Red Square* PCA file.

45 "WHEN I KNEW THAT": Kobal, *People Will Talk,* 159.

46 "COMPENSATING MORAL VALUES": While the phrase "compensating moral values" appeared nowhere in the Code, Breen normally justified his use of the concept by citing a clause that allowed the "presentation of evil" provided that in the end, "the audience feels that *evil is wrong and good is right."* Breen to DeBra, 20 November 1944.

46 "THE VILLAIN CAN LAY": Schumach, 166.

46 "YOU UNDERSTAND": Breen to Hays, 7 March 1934, *Belle of the Nineties* PCA file.

47 "WE NEED, I THINK": McNicholas

to Cantwell, 4 December 1933, Hays Papers.

47 "I WISH TO JOIN": Facey, 144.

48 "WE SAY 'DON'T GO' ": Lord to Quigley (undated), Quigley Papers (1:18).

48 "UNFIT TO BE SHOWN": Earl Bright to Breen, 16 May 1934, *Design for Living* PCA file.

48 " 'LUNATIC FRINGE' ": Breen Report to Producers, 9 May 1934, "Production Code Administration" file, Selznick Collection.

49 "THOSE TEETH": Lord to Quigley (undated), Quigley Papers (1:18).

49 "BOYCOTT UNWHOLESOME": Breen Report to Producers, 12 May 1934, "Production Code Administration" file, Selznick Collection.

49 "NOT A GOOD STORY": *New York Times,* 3 February 1935.

49 "ATTACKED JEWISH": Report, 13 March 1934, Hays Papers.

49 "THERE IS MUCH 'UNDER COVER' ": Breen to Hays, 2 June 1934, *Belle of the Nineties* PCA file.

50 "IF THEY THINK": Dayton, Ohio, *News-Week,* 7 July 1934.

51 "THE GENERAL SENTIMENT": Bulletin No. VII (formerly "Breen Report to Producers"), 24 May 1934, "Production Code Administration" file, Selznick Collection.

51 "WE DECIDED TO USE": George Cardinal Mundelein to Franklin D. Roosevelt, 8 June 1934; quoted in de Grazia and Newman, 44.

51 "WARNER BROTHERS NOT": Lord to Quigley (undated), Quigley Papers (1:18).

52 "CHURCH-DICTATED CENSORSHIP": Roy W. Howard to Hays, 29 June 1934, Hays Papers.

52 "LAEMMLE AND HARRY": Cochrane to Hays, 1 June 1934, Hays Papers.

52 "WHEN THE LATTER'S": *Variety,* 10 July 1934.

53 "DID PRAISE": Margaretta Tuttle to Julia Kelly (Hays' secretary), July 1934 [no date given], Hays Papers.

53 "YOU [HAVE] CONTINUED":

Wilkinson to Breen, 9 July 1934, Hays Papers.

53 "I AM EXTREMELY": Cited in de Grazia and Newman, 44.

53 "A TERRIFIC RAZZING": Joy, Memorandum of Record, 31 January 1931, *The Blue Angel* PCA file.

53 "SUPERB LATE WEDDING": Richard Meryman, "Mae West," *Life,* 18 April 1969: 61.

53 "EVERYTHING DETERIORATES": Meryman, 62C.

53 "THE CENSORS WOULDN'T": Mae West Interview, *Playboy:* 78.

54 "I BELIEVE IN CENSORSHIP": Mae West Interview: 82.

54 "THE GREAT AMERICAN": Cited in Weales, 35.

THE PRODUCTION CODE ADMINISTRATION, 1934–1966

Dead End

57 "A MERE HINDENBERG": Glyn Roberts, "The Hitler of Hollywood," *Film Weekly,* 31 August 1934: 11.

57 "THE RESPONSIBLE HEADS": Breen to Hays, 29 January 1931, Hays Papers.

57 "IT IS STILL A HELL": Pat Casey to McKenzie, 9 November 1934, Hays Papers.

58 "I AM LOOKING": Breen to Hart, 28 July 1934, *Outcast Lady* PCA file.

58 "LEAVE THE QUESTION": Quoted in Roberts, "Hitler of Hollywood," 11.

58 "SENSATIONALIZED SEX-MADNESS": Gastonia, North Carolina, *Gazette* (undated), cited in Motion Picture Producers and Distributors of America, Inc., Annual Report, 30 March 1936: 27.

58 "THE PICTURES": Denver *Rocky Mountain News* (undated), cited in MPPDA Annual Report, 30 March 1936: 29.

59 "CRIME AND VICE": Moley, 88.

59 "IF AN APPEAL": Breen to Hays, 7 October 1935, *She Done Him Wrong* PCA file.

60 "IT IS A SORDID STORY": Breen to John Hammell, 8 October 1935, *The Blue Angel* PCA file.

60 "BECAUSE OF ITS GROSS": Breen to D. Biederman, 22 April 1935, *Cock of the Air* PCA file.

60 "A HOOTCH DANCE": Milliken to Breen, 23 August 1935, *George White's Scandals* PCA file.

60 "DEFINITELY NOT": Breen, Memorandum of Record, 10 February 1936, *Klondike Annie* PCA file.

60 "IT ELIMINATES": Breen, Memorandum of Record, 10 February 1936, *Klondike Annie* PCA file.

60 "HIGHLY—EVEN OUTRAGEOUSLY": Breen to Hays, 28 July 1936, *Ecstasy* PCA file.

61 "THE DIRECTORS": Francis Harmon to Breen, 22 December 1937, *Ecstasy* PCA file.

61 "CLEANER THAN THE CLASSIC": Karl Lischka (draft), 25 September 1934, and Breen to Louis Mayer, 25 September 1934, *Anna Karenina* PCA file.

62 "A COMPLETELY VITIATED": David Selznick to Breen, 7 March 1935, *Anna Karenina* PCA file.

63 "GREATER LEEWAY": Val Lewton to Selznick, 27 October 1937, "Censorship" file, Selznick Collection.

63 "MR. BREEN GOES": Lewton to Selznick, 4 April 1939, "Censorship" file, Selznick Collection.

63 "WE HAVE TRIED": Gene Towne to Breen, 24 April 1935, *Shanghai* PCA file.

65 "NATURALLY ELIMINATED": Selznick, "Notes on Anna Karenina," September 1935; in Behlmer, *Memo,* 82.

65 "WANTED TO HEAR": de Rochemont, cited in Raymond Fielding, *The March of Time, 1935–1951* (New York: Oxford University Press, 1978), 238.

65 "IN MANY PLACES": Quigley to Breen, 10 January 1939, Quigley Papers (1:3).

67 "SO SINCERE": Unsigned and undated report (Marian Robertson the probable author), *Dead End* PCA file.

67 "AN INSURRECTION": *Los Angeles Times,* cited in Edward Robb Ellis, *A Nation in Torment* (New York: Coward, McCann & Geoghegan, 1970), 382.

68 "MONKEY BUSINESS": Hinkle C. Hays to Will Hays, 11 April 1935, Hays Papers.

68 "LIBERAL WITH LEFT-WING TENDENCIES": Edward Reed, "Personae Gratae," *Theatre Arts,* January 1936: 50.

69 "TO PERMIT ITS": Breen to Hays, 21 May 1934, Weekly Report, *Black Fury* PCA file.

69 "NOT PRODUCE": Hays to Harry Warner, 4 September 1934, *Black Hell* [*Black Fury*] file, Warner Bros. Archive, Special Collections, University Library, University of Southern California.

69 "THAT WORKING CONDITIONS": Breen to Warner, 12 September 1934, *Black Hell* file, Warner Bros. Archive.

69 "THE DISHONEST INTRIGUE": Breen to Hays, 20 September 1934, *Black Fury* PCA file.

69 "A FINE SOCIAL": Breen to Hays, 23 January 1935, *Black Fury* PCA file.

70 "THE UNIMPORTANT": Joy to Breen, 5 November 1935, *Dead End* PCA file.

70 "IMPORTANT SOCIAL DOCUMENT": Breen to B. B. Kahane, RKO, 6 November 1935; Breen to Jason Joy, Fox, 6 November 1935, *Dead End* PCA file.

70 "SO WHAT'S THE PROBLEM?": William Amos, *The Originals: An A–Z of Fiction's Real-Life Characters* (Boston: Little, Brown, 1985), 312.

71 "IF IT PLEASES": Goodman, 179.

71 "AFFIRMATIVELY ESTABLISH": Breen to Samuel Goldwyn, 23 April 1937, *Dead End* PCA file.

71 "BE LESS EMPHATIC": Breen to Goldwyn, 23 April 1937, *Dead End* PCA file.

72 "THE NEED FOR": Goldwyn, quoted in Breen, Memorandum of Record, 27 April 1937, *Dead End* PCA file.

72 "UPON COMPLETION": Breen, Memorandum of Record, 27 April 1937, *Dead End* PCA file.

73 "IT'S EASY": *New York Times,* 30 May 1937. Warners' *Angels With Dirty Faces,* which featured the Dead End

Kids as antisocial petty criminals, lacked the poetry of the Goldwyn original. When the cycle of youth pictures ended, the Kids descended to the "head-thwacking technique of the Three Stooges and the subtlety of the Ritz Brothers" (review of *Little Tough Guys in Society, New York Times,* 21 November 1938).

73 "MARVELOUS . . . 'CAUSE": Vincent Sherman, quoted in Kobal, *People Will Talk,* 550–551.

74 "TO JUXTAPOSE": Quoted in Axel Madsen, *William Wyler: The Authorized Biography* (New York: Crowell, 1973), 156.

74 "THE TALK OF THE TOWN": Madsen, *Wyler,* 156.

74 "THAT COULD BE CHEAP": Bob Coburn, quoted in Kobal, *People Will Talk,* 348.

74 "IN A PROPERLY": Lillian Hellman, *An Unfinished Woman—A Memoir* (Boston: Little, Brown, 1969), 122.

74 "ASSOCIATE GARBAGE": *New York Times,* 30 May 1937.

75 "THE STORY, AS YOU KNOW": Breen to Hays, 22 July 1937, *Dead End* PCA file.

76 "IT IS ANOTHER": Ken Clark to Breen, 13 August 1937, *Dead End* PCA file.

76 "WIDENED THE RANGE": Motion Picture Producers and Distributors of America, Inc., Annual Report, 28 March 1938: 6.

77 "A STRONG ARGUMENT": "Just Like the Movies," *Literary Digest,* 11 December 1937: 4.

77 "DEAL WITH PRESSING": Balio, *American Film Industry,* 222.

77 "OPENLY 'LEFT' ": Hortense Powdermaker, *Stranger and Friend: The Way of an Anthropologist* (New York: Norton, 1966), 214.

77 "I THINK THIS PICTURE": Warner to Hays, 8 April 1937, *John Meade's Woman* PCA file.

77 "WHY IS EVERYTHING": Cited in Lawrence J. Epstein, *Samuel Goldwyn* (Boston: Twayne, 1981), 53.

Gone With the Wind

79 "INTIMATE DETAILS": New York *Evening Post,* 21 November 1935.

79 "A DEROGATORY REFERENCE": Wingate to Breen, 6 August 1937, *Dead End* PCA file.

79 WOULD RATHER SULLY: Falk, quoted in "Cinema Censorship," *Current History,* March 1939: 47.

80 "IN TIMES PAST": Sandberg to Hays, cited in Los Angeles *Evening News,* 25 February 1938; reprinted in "Excerpts from Recent Comment on Motion Pictures," Motion Picture Producers and Distributors of America, Inc., October 1938: 17.

80 "RIDICULOUS THINGS": De Rochement, quoted in "Cinema Censorship": 47.

80 "WHAT STRANGE PASSION": Reed Harris, "Letters," *Life,* 8 August 1938: 3.

80 "YOU'VE HEARD A LOT": McEvoy, "The Back of Me Hand," 8, 48.

81 "TIMIDITY AND BAD TASTE": Dudley Nichols, quoted in New York *World-Telegram,* 10 June 1939.

81 "TO DEAL WITH": Quoted in Facey, 179.

81 "SEDUCTIVE ARGUMENTATION": M. M. Neely, "Anti 'Block-Booking' and 'Blind Selling' in the Leasing of Motion-Picture Films," Hearings on S. 280 Before a Subcommittee of the Committee on Interstate Commerce, United States Senate, Seventy-Sixth Congress, First Session, 5 April 1939: 134.

82 "SEX PERVERSION": Hart, Memorandum of Record, 23 November 1937, *Of Mice and Men* PCA file.

82 "BUT THEY DIDN'T": Quentin Reynolds, "That's How Pictures Are Born," *Collier's,* 6 January 1940: 14.

82 "WRITES TO NEW YORK": Islin Auster, Memorandum of Record, 8 February 1939, *Of Mice and Men* PCA file.

82 "A BRIEF ROMANTIC": Vizzard, 63.

83 "COULDN'T BEAR": Behlmer, *Memo,* xi.

84 "WORTHY PICTURES" . . .

"AGHAST": Behlmer, *Memo,* 81–82. Clemence Dane could not have been too shocked; since the early thirties, she had seen how the studios as well as the Code and the British Board of Film Censors had changed her novels and stories.

84 "THERE IS NO POINT": Behlmer, *Memo,* 82.

87 "NIGHTS OF LOVE": Selznick to Sidney Howard, 6 January 1937; Behlmer, *Memo,* 150.

87 "THE CHARACTER": Auster to Breen, 29 January 1937, *Gone With the Wind* PCA file; the authors consulted the *GWTW* file at the Motion Picture Association West Coast office in 1982.

87 "SIDNEY AND I": Selznick to Cukor, 25 February 1938; Behlmer, *Memo,* 159.

88 "*UNDUE EXPOSURE*": Breen to Selznick, 14 October 1937, *GWTW* "Censorship" file, Selznick Collection.

88 "TAKE [SCARLETT]": Breen to Selznick, 14 October 1937, *GWTW* "Censorship" file, Selznick Collection.

89 "*ANY SUGGESTION*": Breen to Selznick, 14 October 1937, *GWTW* "Censorship" file, Selznick Collection.

89 "A PECULIAR KIND": Marcella Rabwin interview (telephone), 20 July 1986.

89 "I CAN GO DOWN": Lewton to Selznick, 27 October 1937, *GWTW* "Censorship" file, Selznick Collection.

89 "JOE [WAS] MOST": Selznick to Lewton, 1 November 1937, *GWTW* "Censorship" file, Selznick Collection.

90 "MENZIES' SKETCH": "Technical Adviser: The Making of 'Gone With the Wind' The Hollywood Journals of Wilbur G. Kurtz," ed. Richard Barksdale Harwell, *The Atlanta Historical Journal,* 27 (Summer 1978): 37.

90 "BELIEVE ME": Lewton to Selznick, 25 February 1938, *GWTW* "Censorship" file, Selznick Collection.

90 "FEAR OF CENSORSHIP": Kate Corbaley to Selznick, "Notes: Verification of Telephone Conversation with Mr. Selznick," 19 June 1938,

GWTW Correspondence file, Selznick Collection.

90 "HONESTLY!" Susan Myrick to Margaret Mitchell (undated [c. January 1939]), Margaret Mitchell Marsh Collection, File 58:84, Hargrett Rare Book Room and Manuscript Library, University of Georgia, Athens.

91 "OMIT THE ACTION": Breen to Selznick, 10 January 1939, *Gone With the Wind* PCA file.

91 "UNACCEPTABLE UNDER": Breen to Lewton, 24 January 1939, *Gone With the Wind* PCA file.

91 "A DARK RED VELVET": Myrick, *White Columns in Hollywood: Reports from the GWTW Sets,* ed. Richard Harwell (Macon, Georgia: Macon University Press, 1982), 229.

92 "I ASKED IF": "Technical Adviser": 51.

92 "QUITE APART": Selznick to Henry Ginsberg, 19 May 1939; Behlmer, *Memo,* 215.

92 "PERFECTLY PERMISSIBLE": Lewton to Selznick, 7 April 1939, *GWTW* "Censorship" file, Selznick Collection.

92 "EXCITE THE LUSTFUL": Breen, quoted in Lewton to Selznick, 7 April 1939, *GWTW* "Censorship" file, Selznick Collection.

93 "INFLUENCES OF TRANSIENT": *Motion Picture Herald,* 7 February 1942.

93 "ENORMOUSLY OFFENSIVE": Breen to Lewton, 24 January 1939, *Gone With the Wind* PCA file.

93 "VAL LEWTON, THE CONTACT MAN": Victor Shapiro journal, 27 May 1939, Victor Shapiro Collection, Special Collections, University Research Library, University of California at Los Angeles.

94 "THERE SHOULD BE": Breen to Selznick, 13 May 1939, *Gone With the Wind* PCA file.

94 "SOUND THE SIREN!" Selznick to John Hay Whitney, 27 June 1939; Behlmer, *Memo,* 216.

94 "FIGURATIVELY LICKING" / "YAWNING": Lewton to Selznick, 18 September 1939 / 11 September 1939,

GWTW "Censorship" file, Selznick Collection.

94 "I CAN SHOW": Lewton to Selznick, 18 September 1939, *GWTW* "Censorship" file, Selznick Collection.

95 "THE BEST WRITTEN DARKIES": Howard to Mitchell, 18 November 1936, Marsh Collection (905).

95 "COLORED MAIDS": Victor Shapiro to Selznick, 10 February 1939, *GWTW* "Negro Problem" files, Selznick Collection.

95 "I COMPLAINED SO MUCH": Los Angeles *Globe,* 24 March 1981.

96 "INCREASINGLY I REGRET": Selznick to Lewton, 7 June 1939, *GWTW* Correspondence file, Selznick Collection.

96 "I AM NOT SURE": Lewton to Selznick, 7 June 1939, *GWTW* "Negro Problem" files, Selznick Collection.

96 "INTELLIGENT NEGRO": Lewton to Selznick, 9 June 1939, *GWTW* "Negro Problem" files, Selznick Collection.

96 "OKAY, WE'LL FORGET IT": Selznick to Lewton, 9 June 1939, *GWTW* "Negro Problem" files, Selznick Collection.

97 "REAL OLD SOUTHERN": Whitney to Selznick, 23 October 1939, "Profanity" file, Selznick Collection.

97 "WHIPPED HIMSELF UP": Lewton to Selznick, 25 August 1939, *Intermezzo* file, Selznick Collection.

97 "MY DEAR, I DON'T CARE": Lewton to Selznick, 1 June 1939, *GWTW* "Profanity" file, Selznick Collection.

98 "THE HELL THAT": Breen, quoted in Lewton to Selznick, 9 June 1939, *GWTW* "Profanity" file, Selznick Collection.

98 "THERE HAVE BEEN SOME": New York *World-Telegram,* 25 October 1939.

99 "WITHOUT DOUBT THE GREATEST": Lewton to Katharine Brown, 11 September 1939, *GWTW* Correspondence file, Selznick Collection.

99 "A HARD FIGHT": Lewton to Selznick, 11 September 1939, *GWTW* "Censorship" file, Selznick Collection.

99 "THE ALLEGEDLY CENSORABLE SCENES": Cited in Selznick to Russell

Birdwell, 29 September 1939,
GWTW "Censorship" file, Selznick
Collection.

99 "ON A SILLY POINT": Selznick
to Whitney, 12 October 1939,
GWTW Correspondence file, Selznick
Collection.

100 "BRETT'S LEAVING SCARLIT":
Unsigned card from Santa Barbara
GWTW preview, October 1939, Selznick
Collection.

100 "THIS DRAMATIC WORD": Selznick
to Hays, 20 October 1939; Behlmer,
Memo, 230–231.

100 "I HAVE STATED": Breen to Hays,
21 October 1939, *Gone With the Wind*
PCA file.

100 "THE IDEAL OCCASION": Selznick
to Whitney, 6 September 1939, *GWTW*
"Censorship" file, Selznick Collection.

101 "THEY CANNOT GIVE": Selznick to
Whitney and Lowell Calvert, 20 October
1939, *GWTW* "Profanity" file, Selznick
Collection.

102 "A GOOSER": Howard Strickling,
quoted in Ronald Haver, *David O.
Selznick's Hollywood* (New York: Knopf,
1980), 169.

102 "VERY STORMY": Calvert to
Selznick and Whitney, 27 October 1939,
GWTW "Censorship" file, Selznick
Collection.

102 "CARRIED [THE] BIBLE": Dan
O'Shea (who cites Lesser's wire)
to Selznick, 27 October 1939,
GWTW "Censorship" file, Selznick
Collection.

103 "TO LEAVE ["DAMN"]": Hal Roach
to Hays, 26 October 1939, *GWTW*
"Censorship" file, Selznick Collection.

104 "TRADE PRACTICES AND
HOLLYWOOD CONDITIONS": "Statement
Re: 'Gone With the Wind,' " 27 October
1939, *Gone With the Wind* PCA file.

105 "THIS ENDS THE CENSORSHIP":
Lewton to Selznick, 15 November 1939,
GWTW "Censorship" file, Selznick
Collection.

105 "IT WAS THE BEST LINE":
Schumach, 221.

105 "VERY BAD REPUTE": Hays to

Roach, 30 August 1939, *Of Mice and Men*
PCA file.

105 "ENORMOUSLY DANGEROUS":
Breen to Milestone, 30 January 1939, *Of
Mice and Men* PCA file.

106 "I SINCERELY HOPE": Harmon to
Breen, 25 November 1939, *Of Mice and
Men* PCA file.

106 "PURISTS . . . NAUGHTY,
NAUGHTY": *Los Angeles Times,* 25
December 1939.

106 "FALSE BUT UTTERLY
RIDICULOUS": Breen to Jimmie Fidler, 26
December 1939, *Gone With the Wind* PCA
file.

106 "WILD ABOUT THIS": Lewton to
Selznick, 28 December 1939, *GWTW*
Correspondence file, Selznick Collection.

106 "DAMAGE WILL BE DONE": *Motion
Picture Herald,* 30 December 1939.

106 "IN THE SECOND HALF": Haver,
309.

107 "PERSONALLY I'M NOT": London
Daily Mirror (undated), *Gone With the
Wind* PCA file.

107 "COMPARATIVELY LIBERAL
ATTITUDE": Selznick to Whitney, 6
September 1939, *GWTW* "Censorship"
file, Selznick Collection.

107 "PURITY CODE": *New York Times,*
21 April 1940.

107 "THERE IS A CAMPAIGN": Quigley
to Breen, 18 April 1940, Quigley Papers
(1:4).

107 "TO SATISFY EVERYONE": *Q
Magazine* (undated clipping, "Hays
Office" file, New York Public Library).

108 "LETTING DOWN A LITTLE": Al
Deane to Breen, 14 May 1940, *The
Primrose Path* PCA file.

108 "IS IT YOUR THOUGHT": Breen to
Deane, 16 May 1940, *The Primrose Path*
PCA file.

108 "FALSE, ATHEISTIC": Russell
Whelan, "The Legion of Decency,"
American Mercury, June 1945: 66.

108 "AND, LESS IMPORTANTLY": Breen
to Hays, 18 June 1938, *Personal History*
PCA file.

108 "GLAD [TO BE] OUT": Laemmle,
quoted in de Grazia and Newman, 55.

The Outlaw AND The Postman Always Rings Twice

110 "I HAVE BECOME": Breen to Hays, 25 March 1941, Joseph Breen File, RKO Archive, Los Angeles.

110 "IT IS DIFFICULT": Breen to Hays, 15 April 1940, *Dr. Ehrlich's Magic Bullet* PCA file.

110 "SOME OTHER WORK": Breen to Hays, 25 March 1941, Joseph Breen File, RKO Archive.

111 "LEGISLATIVE CENSORSHIP EPIDEMIC": Pettijohn to Hays and Breen, 17 February 1941, *The Philadelphia Story* PCA file.

111 "IN RECENT MONTHS": Breen to Hays, 29 March 1941, *The Outlaw* PCA file.

111 "IN MY MORE THAN TEN": Breen to Hays, 28 March 1941, *The Outlaw* PCA file.

112 "AN IMPORTANT WESTERN": Breen, Memorandum of Record, 19 April 1940, *The Outlaw* PCA file.

113 "HAVING SPENT": Tony Thomas, *Howard Hughes in Hollywood* (Secaucus, NJ: Citadel Press, 1985), 80.

114 "I 'SEE BY THE PAPERS' ": Breen to Howard Hawks and Howard Hughes, 3 December 1940, *The Outlaw* PCA file.

114 "ILLICIT SEX" . . . "QUESTIONABLE ANGLES": Breen to Hughes, 27 December 1940, *The Outlaw* PCA file.

115 "A FLASH OF HER BREASTS": Memorandum of Record (unsigned), 10 April 1941, *The Outlaw* PCA file.

115 "AGAINST BILLY'S THIGHS": Breen to Hughes, 27 December 1940, *The Outlaw* PCA file.

115 "IS IT THAT THE GOOSE": Wallis to Breen, 27 March 1941, *The Philadelphia Story* PCA file.

116 FOR THAT BONDAGE SCENE: "Hollywood: The Golden Years," British Broadcasting Company television documentary.

117 "DEFINITELY AND SPECIFICALLY": Breen to Hughes, 28 March 1941, *The Outlaw* PCA file.

118 "BREAST SHOT DELETIONS": Memorandum of Record (unsigned),

10 April 1941, *The Outlaw* PCA file.

119 "HOLLYWOOD'S CURRENT MYSTERY": "Passing of a 'No' Man," *Newsweek,* 12 May 1941: 60–61.

119 "NIGHTGOWNS AND FRILLY": New York *World-Telegram,* 1 April 1941.

119 "ALL SCENES": Breen to Mayer, 3 June 1941, *Dr. Jekyll and Mr. Hyde* PCA file.

120 "NOW HOLLYWOOD *REALLY*": Adela Rogers St. Johns, "Why Breen Resigned from the Hays Office," *Liberty,* 5 July 1941: 14.

120 "I WAS FEELING": James M. Wall, "Oral Interview with Geoffrey Shurlock," 240.

120 "AT LEAST ONE PICTURE": Harmon to Preston Sturges, 20 June 1941, Preston Sturges Collection, Special Collections, University Research Library, University of California at Los Angeles.

120 "IMMORAL AND UN-CHRISTIAN": Quoted in *Kansas City Star,* 30 November 1941.

121 "THERE WAS A LOT": Quoted in Haver, *David O. Selznick's Hollywood,* 329.

121 BREEN'S RETURN: While Breen was at RKO, Hays created a six-member committee of the board to study the operations of the MPPDA. In February 1942, the committee recommended that Hays tighten control over industry public relations, define a long-range labor policy for Hollywood, and return Breen to the PCA (Confidential Memo from the "Committee of Six" to Hays, 14 February 1942, Hays Papers).

122 "HERMAN SHUMLIN TOLD ME": Johnson to Harold Ross, 17 November 1949, *Letters of Nunnally Johnson,* selected and edited by Dorris Johnson and Ellen Leventhal (New York: Knopf, 1981), 50.

123 "RIGHT KIND OF MIDDY BLOUSE": Birdwell to Dale Armstrong, 24 June 1941, Russell Birdwell Collection, Box 8, Special Collections, University Research Library, University of California at Los Angeles.

123 "JANE'S BREASTS": Armstrong to Birdwell, 27 June 1941, Birdwell Collection (8).

123 "HER PICTURES ATTACK THE EYE": Alva Johnston, "Profiles: Public Relations—IV," *The New Yorker,* 9 September 1944: 33.

124 "A STRONG CANDIDATE": "Hughes's Western," *Time,* 22 February 1943: 85–86.

126 "CONSTANCY IS UNKNOWN": *Tennessee Williams' Letters to Donald Windham, 1940–1965,* ed. Donald Windham (New York: Holt, Rinehart and Winston, 1977), 94.

127 "HOW CAN I REMEMBER": Breen to Luigi Luraschi, 21 October 1942, *The Miracle of Morgan's Creek* PCA file.

127 "THE HAYS OFFICE": *Agee on Film* (New York: McDowell, Obolensky, 1958), 74.

127 "THE EARTH MOVING": Breen to Luraschi, 3 March 1943, *For Whom the Bell Tolls* PCA file.

127 "PICKLE PERSUADER": Breen to Hunt Stromberg, 3 December 1942, *Lady of Burlesque* PCA file.

127 "LOW TONE": Breen to Mayer, 10 October 1935, *Double Indemnity* PCA file.

127 "AN EMANCIPATION": Quoted in *New York Times,* 19 November 1944.

127 "HAVE GOT HEP": Lloyd Shearer, "Crime Certainly Pays on the Screen," *New York Times Magazine,* 5 August 1945: 37.

127 "CERTAIN PHASES OF DEPRAVITY": Breen to Warner, 29 September 1944, *The Big Sleep* PCA file.

127 "SORDID AND REPELLENT": Breen to Warner, 2 February 1944, *Mildred Pierce* PCA file.

128 "RAW STUFF": Breen to Harmon, 13 December 1945, *Forever Amber* PCA file.

128 "A STORY OF ILLICIT SEX": Breen to William Gordon (RKO), 2 August 1944, *Duel in the Sun* PCA file.

128 "ANTAGONIZING THE REMAINING": Quoted in Shearer, "Crime Certainly Pays": 37.

128 "THERE ARE SEVERAL": Gertrude Atherton, *New York American,* January 1935; cited in Roy Hoopes, *Cain* (New York: Holt, Rinehart and Winston, 1982), 245.

128 "THIS IS STRONG MEN'S MEAT": Cited in Hoopes, *Cain,* 596.

129 "A COUPLE OF JERKS": James Cain to Mrs. Danber, 11 March 1959; cited in Hoopes, *Cain,* 233.

129 "WOULD BE AN ASSET": *New York Times,* 18 February 1934.

129 "MORE LIKE THAT OF A FILM": William Plomer, "New Novels," *Spectator,* 8 June 1934: 900.

129 "AMERICAN DOSTOYEVSKY": Quoted in Hoopes, *Cain,* 246.

130 "PEOPLE THINK I PUT": Cain, "Postman Rings Thrice," *New York Times,* 21 April 1946.

131 "BREEN SAYS IT CAN BE DONE": Cain, "Postman Rings Thrice."

131 "THE OVERALL FLAVOR": Breen to Mayer, 20 April 1945, *The Postman Always Rings Twice* PCA file.

131 "A CUISINE LIBERALLY": John Douglas Eames, *The MGM Story* (New York: Crown, 1975), 206.

132 "STUDY IN WHITE": *New York Times,* 13 May 1945.

132 "TURNER DRESSED IN WHITE": "Tough Guy: James M. Cain Interviewed by Peter Brunette and Gerald Peary," *Film Comment,* May–June 1976: 57.

132 "THEY HAD THIS GIRL'S CAT": Quoted in Hoopes, *Cain,* 378.

133 "IS THIS GIRL SHACKING": "Tough Guy": 57.

133 "THAT'S WHEN TAY FELL": Lana Turner, *Lana: The Lady, the Legend, the Truth* (New York: Dutton, 1982), 102.

133 "A TORRID KISS": "Love at Laguna Beach," *Life,* 20 August 1945: 123.

134 "FROM THE TYPE OF PUBLICITY": Breen to Carey Wilson, 18 September 1945, *The Postman Always Rings Twice* PCA file.

134 "WILL CAUSE A STORM": *Hollywood Reporter,* 30 January 1946.

135 "PRESBYTERIAN POPE": Kenneth Macgowan, quoted in Sargent, 116.

135 "IT LOOKED LIKE": "Exit King Log," *Time,* 1 October 1945: 87.

135 "DARLING OF U.S. FREE ENTERPRISE": "Exit King Log," *Time,* 1 October 1945: 87.

135 "SMOOTH-MANNERED SUPER-SALESMAN": Thomas, 18.

135 "FROM HUMAN FALLIBILITY": *Variety,* 27 March 1946.

136 "FILMS WITH QUESTIONABLE": *Variety,* 16 January 1946. Krug rejected the job and Johnston later abandoned his plan to create a West Coast film czar.

136 "ON THE SACRED INTIMACIES": Breen to Goldwyn, 16 April 1946, *The Best Years of Our Lives* PCA file.

136 "WITH SORDIDNESS, DRUNKENNESS": Breen to Luraschi, 11 April 1946, *The Great Gatsby* PCA file.

136 "HIT THE KEYS": Dunne, "Blast It All," 8.

137 THE MUSIC HALL: Cited in Joseph C. Goulden, *The Best Years, 1945–1950* (New York: Atheneum, 1976), 197.

137 NOT A SCENE CUT: Cited in Mary Beth Haralovich, "Film Advertising, the Film Industry, and the Pin-up: The Industry's Accommodations to Social Forces in the 1940s," in *Current Research in Film: Audiences, Economics, and Law,* vol. 1, ed. Bruce A. Austin (Norwood, N.J.: Ablex, 1985), 150.

137 "PECTORAL CURIOSITY": Los Angeles *Herald Express,* 4 April 1946.

137 "WHEN AN AD": Zanuck to Breen, 2 April 1946, *The Outlaw* PCA file.

137 "OPENLY AND REPEATEDLY": Eric Johnston to Hughes, 9 April 1946, *The Outlaw* PCA file.

137 "IN A CONSPIRACY": Motion Picture Association Press Release (undated), *The Outlaw* PCA litigation file.

137 "IN FAVOR OF ONE": *Hughes Tool Co. v. Motion Picture Assn. of America,* 66 F. Supp. 1006 (S.D.N.Y. 1946).

138 "AS THINGS STAND NOW": *Variety,* 25 September 1946.

138 "BUILT UP": Breen to Johnston, 22 March 1946, *Wicked Lady* PCA file.

138 "THE AMERICAN PRODUCING COMPANIES": Breen to Johnston, 13 February 1946, *Wicked Lady* PCA file.

139 "HUNG OVER THE PICTURE": Quoted in Jowett, 397.

139 "MOVE TOWARD LIBERALIZATION": Quoted in de Grazia and Newman, 66.

139 NO CUTS BY CENSOR BOARDS: In July 1988, Turner Broadcasting advertised its colorized version of the 1946 *Postman* as a "movie so hot it was banned by the censors."

The Bicycle Thief

142 "IF YOU NEED": Laurence Leamer, *As Time Goes By: The Life of Ingrid Bergman* (New York: Harper & Row, 1986), 152.

142 "JOHNNY, KEEP": Cited in Goodman, 202.

142 "I HAVE ALWAYS BELIEVED": Jerry Wald to Curtiz, 4 September 1948, *Flamingo Road* file, Warner Bros. Archive.

142 "SORDIDNESS": Breen to Warner, 13 December 1946, *Flamingo Road* PCA file.

143 "UNLESS THE GOOD": Vincent Sherman to Warner, 14 May 1947, *Flamingo Road* file, Warner Bros. Archive.

143 "EMPHASIZING THE COMPLETE CORRUPTION": Breen to Warner, 13 December 1946, *Flamingo Road* PCA file.

143 "HIGH-CLASS ROADHOUSE": Sherman to Warner, 14 May 1947, *Flamingo Road* file, Warner Bros. Archive.

143 "CONTRARY TO EXPECTATIONS": *Variety,* 5 April 1949.

143 "HUMANITARIAN VIEW": Cited in Tom Stempel, "George Byron Who?" *Sight and Sound* 54 (Summer 1985): 213.

143 "THOUGHT NOT IN IDEOLOGICAL": Daniel J. Leab, "'The Iron Curtain' (1948): Hollywood's First Cold War Movie," *Historical Journal of Film, Radio and Television* 8 (1988): 176.

143 "WE DON'T PASS": New York *Herald Tribune,* 10 July 1949.

143 "A DIVORCED WOMAN": Breen to Joy, 23 May 1947, *Gentleman's Agreement* PCA file.

143 "FLAVOR OF ACCEPTANCE": Breen to Joy, 23 May 1947, *Gentleman's Agreement* PCA file.

144 "WHEN IT WAS OBTAINED": Breen to Joy, 23 May 1947, *Gentleman's Agreement* PCA file.

144 "I WAS RIGHT NOT TO SETTLE": Breen to Joy, 23 May 1947, *Gentleman's Agreement* PCA file.

144 "OUR JOB IS": New York *Herald Tribune,* 10 July 1949.

144 "AVOID PHYSICAL CONTACT": Breen to Joy, 28 February 1949, *Pinky* PCA file.

144 "HOLLYWOOD IS GUTLESS": Quoted in Goodman, 421–22.

144 "FRANKLY STEVE": Wald to Steve Trilling, 29 November 1947; Behlmer, *Inside Warner Bros.,* 293.

145 "WE HAVE A NEW AUDIENCE": Eric Hodgins, "A Round Table on the Movies," *Life,* 27 June 1949: 99.

145 "WHEN THESE PEOPLE TALK": New York *Herald Tribune,* 10 July 1949.

145 "AN INCESTUOUS ATTRACTION": Breen to Warner, 31 March 1949, *The Glass Menagerie* PCA file.

145 "THE BEST, MOST LYRIC": Williams to Warner, Wald, and Charles K. Feldman, 6 May 1950; Behlmer, *Inside Warner Bros.,* 322.

146 "WE ARE REALLY": Breen to Quigley, 29 November 1949, *Beyond the Forest* PCA file.

146 "TO FIGHT THE CODE": Breen to Quigley, 29 November 1949, *Beyond the Forest* PCA file.

147 "NOT DESERVE TWO LINES": Bazin, vol. 2, 50.

147 "THE PERFECT AESTHETIC ILLUSION": Bazin, vol. 2, 60.

147 "A CAREFULLY ORCHESTRATED TOUR": Ted Perry, "Vittorio De Sica," in *Cinema: A Critical Dictionary, The Major Filmmakers,* vol. 1, ed. Richard Roud (n.p.: Nationwide Book Services, 1980), 274.

147 "AN EXCEEDINGLY HANDSOME MAN": Winthrop Sargeant, "Profiles: Bread, Love, and Neo-Realismo I," *New Yorker,* 29 June 1957: 40.

147 "BRIDES LEFT THEIR HUSBANDS": Sargeant, "Profiles": 55.

147 MAGGIORANI PUMMELED DE SICA: Sargeant, "Profiles": 44.

148 DE SICA AND SELZNICK: In 1953, De Sica finally agreed to direct a film for Selznick. The contract specified the leads, Jennifer Jones and Montgomery Clift, and required that De Sica abide by the Production Code. Critics frequently cite the result, *Indiscretion of an American Wife,* as De Sica's worst picture.

148 "POET OF POVERTY": Douglas McVay, "Poet of Poverty," *Films and Filming,* November 1964: 12–13.

149 "A SPICY LESBIAN TALE": Arthur Mayer, *Merely Colossal: The Story of the Movies from the Long Chase to the Chaise Longue* (New York: Simon and Schuster, 1953), 226.

149 "SEXIER THAN HOLLYWOOD": Mayer, *Merely Colossal,* 233.

149 "TO TAP THE SADIST TRADE": Mayer, *Merely Colossal,* 233.

149 "MORE VICTOR MATURES": Mayer, *Merely Colossal,* 231.

151 "YOU PASS STUFF LIKE THAT": Vizzard, 87.

151 "CERTAIN PLACES": The original Quigley-Lord version of the Code— before the Hays Office restructured and edited the document—contained a specific provision on brothels. It warned that houses of ill-fame were "dangerous and bad dramatic locations" but allowed that "sometimes their use may be necessary." The provision was dropped from the official version Hays released to the press in March 1930 ("Adopted Code to Govern the Production of Motion Pictures" [undated c. 1929], "Production Code Administration" file, Selznick Collection).

152 "SNIGGERING CENSORSHIP": "Rome's New Empire," *Time,* 14 July 1952: 86.

152 "GROSS ILLICIT SEX": Breen to

William Shelton, 17 December 1948, *Devil in the Flesh* PCA file.

153 "EXTRANEOUS MATTERS": Breen, Memorandum of Record, 9 February 1950, *Devil in the Flesh* PCA file.

153 *THE OUTLAW:* After minor cuts and new promises regarding the ad campaign, the Motion Picture Association reissued the Seal for *The Outlaw* in October 1949 (Gordon White to Ned E. Depinet, 20 October 1949, *The Outlaw* PCA file).

154 "A SUBTLE FORM OF SABOTAGE": Quoted in "Censor's Censor," *Time,* 13 March 1950: 94.

154 "A SHOCKING DEMONSTRATION": Cited in *New York Times,* 6 March 1950.

154 "PUT THEIR MINDS": *New York Times,* 5 March 1950.

154 "ONE OF THE FINEST": "The Evil-Minded Censors," *Life,* 13 March 1950: 40.

154 "A PICTURE FOR EVERYONE": Cited in *New York Times,* 12 March 1950.

155 "IN MY OPINION": Fred Niblo, Jr., to Breen, 21 March 1950, *The Bicycle Thief* PCA file.

155 "IF A PICTURE COMES ALONG": *Variety,* 25 January 1950.

156 "THE MAD DOGS": Quoted in *New York Times,* 15 March 1950.

157 "CONTEMPT FOR PUBLIC": Cited in "The Purity Test," *Time,* 27 March 1950: 99.

157 "PERSONS OF ILL REPUTE": Cited in *New York Times,* 15 March 1950.

157 "A 20 MINUTE TRAVELOG": *Variety,* 1 February 1950.

157 "BERGMAN UNDER THE INSPIRED DIRECTION": *Variety,* 22 February 1950.

157 "EVEN 10% OF THE SPACE": *Variety,* 22 February 1950.

157 "THE UNRELENTING PRESSURE": White to Johnston, 27 February 1950, *Stromboli* PCA file. In 1932, the Association board pledged its member companies to abide by an advertising code containing provisions and penalties similar to the Production Code.

158 "NARCOTICS ADDICT": Quoted in *Variety,* 29 March 1950.

158 "COMMON LOVE THIEF": Quoted in "Purity Test," *Time,* 27 March 1950: 99.

158 "POLICE STATE BILL": Cited in "Purity Test," *Time,* 27 March 1950: 99.

158 "HOLLYWOOD TEN": In October 1947, the House Un-American Activities Committee conducted eight days of public hearings on communism in the film industry. These widely publicized sessions featured the testimony of a number of stars and studio executives, each denouncing Communist efforts to infiltrate the movie colony, and ten "hostile" screenwriters and producers who condemned the Committee for intruding on First Amendment rights. The ten hostile witnesses were cited for contempt of Congress.

158 "HUNDREDS OF CASES": Breen notes for presentation to the board, 21 March 1950, *The Bicycle Thief* PCA file.

159 JOHNSON HEARINGS: *Stromboli* bombed in the theaters, and Senator Johnson quickly lost interest in his morals crusade. After receiving assurances that the studios would police their stars more vigorously, he canceled the hearings.

160 "UNKINDEST CUT": *New York Times,* 2 April 1950.

160 "ILL-ADVISED SUPER-PRUDISHNESS": Herbert M. Levy, "The Case Against Film Censorship," *Films in Review,* April 1950: 40.

160 "UTTERLY FALSE": PCA press release (undated), *The Bicycle Thief* PCA file.

161 "PEOPLE LIKE BURSTYN": Breen to White, 9 August 1950, *The Bicycle Thief* PCA file.

161 "CHINK IN THE CODE'S ARMOR": Arthur Knight, "Ring Around *The Moon Is Blue,*" *Saturday Review,* 27 June 1953: 33.

161 "THE CODE BAN": *Variety,* 14 June 1950.

Detective Story AND A Streetcar Named Desire

162 "MR. VILLY VYLER": Quoted in Elia

Kazan, *Elia Kazan: A Life* (New York: Knopf, 1988), 391.

162 "WE SAVED THE GUILD": Quoted in Kazan, *A Life*, 393.

163 "REGROUPING IN THE SHADOWS": Kazan, *A Life*, 393.

163 "MAROONED SAILORS": Quoted in John Cogley, *Report on Blacklisting*, vol. 1 (New York: Fund for the Republic, 1956), 92.

163 "SIGN IT NOW": Cited in Victor S. Navasky, *Naming Names* (New York: Viking, 1980), 181.

163 "TIME OF THE TOAD": Dalton Trumbo, *The Time of the Toad: A Study of Inquisition in America* (New York: Harper & Row, 1972). The next round of HUAC hearings would begin in March 1951, and over the course of the year, thirty Hollywood witnesses would name over three hundred former colleagues as part of the Communist conspiracy (David Caute, *The Great Fear: The Anti-Communist Purge Under Truman and Eisenhower* [New York: Simon and Schuster, 1978], 501).

164 "THE MOST SIGNIFICANT BREAK": *Variety*, 25 October 1950.

165 "A TERRIFIC EXPLOSION": Breen to White, 5 October 1950, *Bitter Rice* PCA file.

165 "IT'S NOT THE BUSINESS": *Variety*, 6 February 1952.

165 "GRIM AND GROTESQUE . . . WACKY COMPLAINANTS": *Time*, 4 April 1949: 75; *Life*, 2 May 1949: 131.

166 "THE DANGER INHERENT": Quoted in Joseph Wood Krutch, rev. of *Detective Story*, *The Nation*, 9 April 1949: 425.

166 "WILLY HAS THIS": Larry Swindell, "William Wyler: A Life in Film," *American Film*, April 1976: 7.

167 "SOMBER" AND "PAINFUL": Olivia de Havilland interview (personal), Paris, 9 July 1985.

167 "HE THINKS HE'S ALL-KNOWING": *Christian Science Monitor*, 3 April 1951.

168 "I TELL THEM": Quoted in Madsen, *William Wyler*, 305.

169 "REPELLENT SUBJECTS": Robert M. W. Vogel to Eric Johnston, 13 April 1949, *The Doctor and the Girl* PCA file.

169 "WE MUST STRIVE": Breen to Johnston, 15 April 1949, *The Doctor and the Girl* PCA file.

170 "AN EXPLOITATION NATURAL": *Variety*, 14 September 1949.

170 "EVERY HOUR": "A Report on the Negotiations with the L[egion] of D[ecency] on the Occasion of the Condemnation of the Warner Bros. Picture 'Beyond the Forest' " (unsigned), *Beyond the Forest* PCA file.

170 "SUPPRESSED ANGER": "Report," *Beyond the Forest* PCA file.

170 "SORDID STORY": "Report," *Beyond the Forest* PCA file.

170 "INCITE A MORBID": "Report," *Beyond the Forest* PCA file.

170 "HE HAD A KIND OF LEER EYE": Jack Vizzard interview.

171 "MANY RULES IN THE CODE": Quoted in *Variety*, 6 February 1952.

171 "BABY FARM": Breen, Memorandum of Record, 23 June 1950, *Detective Story* PCA file.

172 "THE EVIL OF THE ABORTION": Breen to Johnston, 4 August 1950, *Detective Story* PCA file.

172 "CERTAIN SUBJECTS": *New York Times*, 23 July 1950.

172 "THE LEADING PROGRESSIVE": Kazan, *A Life*, 373.

173 "I'D NEVER BE": Kazan, *A Life*, 373.

173 "IT WOULD BE LIKE MARRYING": Kazan, *A Life*, 383.

173 "[CLEAN] UP THE PLAY": Selznick, *A Private View*, 302.

173 "THE AUDIENCE WOULD BELIEVE": Mayer, quoted in Kazan, *A Life*, 345.

173 "CLEANED AND RUMPLED": Quoted in Selznick, *A Private View*, 328.

173 "ENTITLED TO RECEIVE": Contract dated 14 December 1949, *A Streetcar Named Desire* file, Warner Bros. Archive.

173 "JUST SHOOT THE PLAY": Quoted in Michel Ciment, *Kazan on Kazan* (New York: Viking, 1974), 67.

174 "1/ IT IS ABOUT THE THREE FS":

Kazan to Warner (undated), *A Streetcar Named Desire* file, Warner Bros. Archive.

174 "AN INFERENCE OF SEX PERVERSION": "From the Breen Office" to Warner Bros., 28 April 1950; Behlmer, *Inside Warner Bros.*, 323.

174 "AN EROTIC FLAVOR": "From the Breen Office" to Warner Bros., 28 April 1950; Behlmer, *Inside Warner Bros.*, 323.

174 "PIVOTAL, INTEGRAL TRUTH": Williams to Breen (undated); Behlmer, *Inside Warner Bros.*, 324.

174 "THE PLAY LOSES": Williams to Breen (undated); Behlmer, *Inside Warner Bros.*, 324.

175 "I WOULDN'T PUT THE HOMOSEXUALITY": Schumach, 74.

175 "WAS ACQUAINTED WITH": Teletype manuscript of UPI wire service story, 9 September [1950], *A Streetcar Named Desire* file, Warner Bros. Archive.

175 "YOU MEAN TO SAY": Kazan (quoting Feldman) to Warner, 19 October 1950; Behlmer, *Inside Warner Bros.*, 327.

176 "WAS JUST AN EMOTIONAL": Schumach, 76.

176 "GREAT CONCESSIONS": Williams to Breen (undated); Behlmer, *Inside Warner Bros.*, 324–25.

177 "IN SUCH A WAY": Quoted in the *Los Angeles Times*, 5 August 1951.

177 "BEGGED ME TO SEE": Kazan to Warner, 7 December 1950, *A Streetcar Named Desire* file, Warner Bros. Archive.

177 "FOR THE FIRST TIME": Schumach, 72.

177 "LOUSY PERFECTIONIST": Peter Lyon, " 'The Hollywood Picture' " (script of a CBS radio play, 3 November 1948), *Hollywood Quarterly* 3 (1947–48): 352.

177 "GOOD GOD, MAN": Quoted in Swindell, "William Wyler": 18.

178 "SAVE IT": Breen to Luraschi, 8 November 1950, *Detective Story* PCA file.

178 "LETTER OF THE CODE": Breen to Luraschi, 8 November 1950, *Detective Story* PCA file.

178 "UNLESS SUCH SCENES": Breen to Johnston, 20 November 1950, *Detective Story* PCA file.

179 "HAZY AND INDEFINITE": Breen to Johnston, 20 November 1950, *Detective Story* PCA file.

179 "SHOULD NEVER BE JUSTIFIED": Breen to Johnston, 20 November 1950, *Detective Story* PCA file.

180 "I AM MORE DISTURBED": Kazan to Trilling, 27 July 1951; Behlmer, *Inside Warner Bros.*, 331–32.

180 "HE IS CERTAINLY": Kazan, *A Life*, 432–33.

180 "TO DO ANYTHING NECESSARY": Kazan to Trilling, 27 July 1951; Behlmer, *Inside Warner Bros.*, 333.

180 "A BLASPHEMOUS": " 'The Miracle'—why it is blasphemous and sacrilegious" (undated draft), forwarded by the Rev. Patrick J. Masterson (Executive Secretary, National Legion of Decency) to Breen, 19 January 1951, *The Miracle* PCA file.

181 "GLORIFIED A THIEF": " 'The Miracle' and Related Matters," *Commonweal*, 2 March 1951: 507.

181 "FROM THE MOMENT": A. S. Howson to Vizzard, 11 July 1951, *A Streetcar Named Desire* file, Warner Bros. Archive.

181 "HIS FACE WORE": Vizzard, 177.

182 "TO SHOW STELLA'S": Elia Kazan, "Pressure Problem," *New York Times*, 21 October 1951.

182 "TOO CARNAL": Kazan (quoting an unnamed Legion of Decency representative), in Kazan, "Pressure Problem."

182 "THE CLEAR IMPLICATION": Kazan, "Pressure Problem."

182 "THE PLAIN FACT WAS": Kazan, *A Life*, 435.

182 "WORKED LIKE A DEMON": Kazan, *A Life*, 438.

182 "BY THE GLUTTONOUS POPE": Kazan, *A Life*, 438.

182 "WARNERS JUST WANTED": Schumach, 78.

183 "JOSEPH BREEN HAS EASED UP":
Boston *Evening American,* 24 October
1951.

183 "HIGH QUALITY AND
UNABASHED": Al Hine, "Polish
Up an Oscar," *Holiday,* October
1951: 25.

183 "A HELL OF AN UNDERSTANDING":
Los Angeles Times, 5 August 1951.

183 "CLOAK THE REAL ARGUMENTS":
Warner to Trilling, 29 November 1947,
Key Largo file, Warner Bros. Archive.
Scripted by Richard Brooks, *To the
Victor* concerned French collaborators on
trial for war crimes. Breen focused not
on the black market scenes or Gallic
jurisprudence, but sex. Among several
lines he circled: "Like the time I got
married. I fell for that typical succotash
. . . with every marriage a life of bliss!
Well, I went through the usual triple
play—elopement, honeymoon, divorce"
(Breen to Warner, 25 June 1947, *To the
Victor* PCA file).

184 "COURTEOUS" BUT INSISTENT:
FBI Bureau File 100-15732, 18 January
1949. Breen knew that the production
heads and company presidents were
concerned about Hollywood
Communists, particularly the
association of leftists with message
movies. Several years after he returned
to the Production Code Administration,
still bitter about the RKO experience,
he sent Hays a multipage ad from
Variety listing the supporters of the
"Writers Mobilization." He warned
Hays "to keep an eye on this group
because of the danger involved in any
film-making which seeks to teach and
preach." To further assist the General,
Breen starred the names of those who
were "either foreign born or Commies
or dark pinks" (Breen to Hays, 2
October 1944, Hays Papers). When
the Red Scare began, the studios
also compiled lists and mooted
the "Commies" problem for
Breen.

184 "LUSH HONORARIUMS": *Box
Office,* 30 June 1951.

The Moon Is Blue AND
The French Line

185 "PRETTY AND POPULAR": "Busy
Wife's Achievements," *Life,* 24
December 1956: 41, 43.

185 "BACHELORS OF MORE THAN":
Ferdinand Lundberg and Marynia F.
Farnham, M.D., *Modern Woman: The
Lost Sex* (New York: Harper, 1947), 365,
370.

186 "AMONG US MULES": Breen to
William Gordon, 25 October 1951,
Universal Collection.

186 "SWEETHEART OF THE MONTH":
"What Makes Marilyn?" *Playboy,*
December 1953: 17–18.

186 "SWEET ANGEL": Hugh M. Hefner,
"Marilyn," *Playboy,* January 1987: 215.

186 BREEN OFFICE LOSING: *Variety,*
4 March 1953.

186 "TURNING POINT": *Variety,*
4 March 1953.

187 "BURSTYN'S LATEST": Breen to
Clark, 11 January 1951, *The Miracle* PCA
file.

187 "GENTLEMAN'S AGREEMENT":
Variety, 14 June 1950.

188 "A SORT OF PRIMITIVE U.S.O.": *New
York Times,* 14 June 1953.

188 "A STRONG VOICE FOR MORALITY":
Breen to Cohn, 4 August 1952, *From
Here to Eternity* PCA file.

189 "THAT GIVEN SUFFICIENT
ABILITY": *Motion Picture Herald,* 15
August 1953.

189 "WE'VE FOUND THE WAY": *Variety,*
4 February 1953.

189 "MANGLE THE MUSE": Andrew
Sarris, "Preminger's Two Periods," *Film
Comment,* Summer 1965: 13.

189 "HE SHOUTS EVEN LOUDER":
David Niven, *The Moon's a Balloon* (New
York: Putnam, 1972), 324.

189 "THE PERFECT EXAMPLE": From
screenwriter Ben Hecht's introduction to
the published play.

191 "ONE OF THE MOST IMPORTANT":
Vizzard, 153.

191 "A MATTER OF MORAL
INDIFFERENCE": Vizzard,
153.

192 "HOLDEN IS IN CONSTANT": Goodman, 254.

192 "IT'S AN ODD QUALITY": Goodman, 255.

192 "IMMORAL PHILOSOPHY": Shurlock, Memorandum of Record, 6 January 1953, *The Moon Is Blue* file, Motion Picture Association of America, New York, New York.

192 "SMALL ROUNDISH MAN": Murray Schumach, "The Censor as Movie Director," *New York Times Magazine*, 12 February 1961: 36.

192 "SWELL": Wall, "Oral Interview with Geoffrey Shurlock," 156.

193 "IDIOTIC": Wall, "Oral Interview with Geoffrey Shurlock," 142.

193 "DRAWING A LONG BOW": Vizzard, 155.

193 "COLD AND DEFINITE REBUFF": Breen to Quigley, 26 January 1953, *The Moon Is Blue* file, Motion Picture Association.

193 "WOULD NOT BE PUSHED": Al Van Schmus interview.

193 "IF KRIM FEELS": Breen to Quigley, 26 January 1953, *The Moon Is Blue* file, Motion Picture Association.

194 "CREATIVE AUTONOMY": Murray Teigh Bloom, "What Two Lawyers Are Doing to Hollywood," *Harper's* magazine, February 1958: 42.

194 "WHERE THE WRITER": Bloom, "Two Lawyers," 42.

194 "UNACCEPTABLY LIGHT ATTITUDE": Breen to Preminger, 10 August 1953, *The Moon Is Blue* file, Motion Picture Association.

194 "LEANED OVER BACKWARD": Preminger to Breen, 13 April 1953, *The Moon Is Blue* file, Motion Picture Association.

195 "FURY, VIOLENCE, LAWLESSNESS": Vizzard, Memorandum of Record, 17 December 1952, *The Wild One* PCA file.

195 "SORDID AND IMMORAL RELATIONSHIP": Breen [Shurlock] to John Huston, 15 May 1952, *Moulin Rouge* PCA file.

196 "HIGHLY OFFENSIVE TO MANY": GSW [Gordon White], "notes for

argument at appeal hearing," 21 May 1953, *The Moon Is Blue* file, Motion Picture Association.

197 "PASSIONATE APPEAL": Wall, "Oral Interview with Geoffrey Shurlock," 157.

197 "I WOULDN'T LET MY DAUGHTER": Quoted in de Grazia and Newman, 86.

198 "SO HARD AS TO DROWN": *Motion Picture Herald*, 13 June 1953.

198 "SQUIRMED IN EMBARRASSMENT": *Motion Picture Herald*, 13 June 1953.

198 "OUTRAGED": Otto Preminger, *Preminger: An Autobiography* (Garden City, N.Y.: Doubleday, 1977), 109.

198 "AN ODD LOOKING": Bosley Crowther, *New York Times*, 12 July 1953.

198 "HYPOCRITICAL INTERPRETATION": *Variety*, 10 June 1953.

199 PRIVATE AND CONFIDENTIAL: Msgr. Thomas F. Little to Diocesan Directors, Legion of Decency, 11 June 1953, *The Moon Is Blue* file, Legion of Decency Archive, Department of Communication, United States Catholic Conference, New York, New York.

199 "SO FRANTIC": Preminger, 105–106.

200 "BEHAVED VERY WELL": Preminger, 109.

200 "WHOLEHEARTED COOPERATION": Little to the Rev. Walter J. Tappe, Director, Legion of Decency, San Francisco, 11 June 1953, *The Moon Is Blue* file, Legion of Decency Archive.

200 "AN OCCASION OF SIN": *New York Times*, 25 June 1953; *Variety*, 8 July 1953.

201 "ROUGH SAILING AHEAD": *Variety*, 15 July 1953.

201 "WITHOUT EXCEPTION": Cited in *Motion Picture Herald*, 15 August 1953.

201 "REPORTS THAT PRODUCERS": *Motion Picture Herald*, 15 August 1953.

202 "IT DOES SEEM A PITY": *Variety*, 2 September 1953.

202 "RATHER GRUDGING": Breen to Sidney Schreiber, 23 November 1953, *Cease Fire* PCA file.

202 "BEAR IN MIND": Cited in *Motion Picture Herald*, 28 November 1953.

202 "SOPHISTICATED SMUT": A parish weekly bulletin in St. John,

Nebraska, quoted in *Variety*,
2 September 1953.

202 "IMMORAL": *Variety*, 28 October
1953.

202 "OBSCENE, INDECENT": *New York
Times*, 15 October 1953.

203 "TOTALLY INNOCUOUS": Patrick
Sullivan interview.

204 "SPECIFICALLY": Breen to William
Feeder (RKO), 25 March 1953, *The
French Line* PCA file.

204 "PROFESSOR OF LOVE": Breen to
Feeder, 25 March 1953, *The French Line*
PCA file.

204 "ALREADY I HAVE": Breen to
Feeder, 14 May 1953, *The French Line*
PCA file.

204 "YOU'RE LUCKY": Breen to Feeder,
3 June 1953, *The French Line* PCA file.

205 "INTENTIONALLY DESIGNED":
Memorandum of Record (unsigned), 13
January 1954, *The French Line* PCA file.

205 "I FOUGHT": Quoted in "Fusses
over Ladies and a Ladies' Man," *Life*,
11 January 1954: 24.

205 "BIG BROWN": Memorandum of
Record (unsigned), 13 January 1954, *The
French Line* PCA file.

205 "STRIP-TEASE SANTA": "Fusses over
Ladies": 24.

205 "DID NOT HAVE A LOW-CUT":
"Fusses over Ladies": 24.

206 "WHAT WAS AT STAKE": Vizzard,
173–74.

206 "SOFT-SPOKEN BUT FEARLESS":
Vizzard, 174.

207 "SPECIAL EMERGENCY": Cited in
Donald L. Barlett and James B. Steele,
*Empire: The Life, Legend, and Madness of
Howard Hughes* (New York: W. W. Norton, 1979), 196.

207 "UNDER PENALTY": Cited in
Variety, 13 January 1954.

207 "THE THOUGHT THAT": Vizzard,
175.

207 "A FRONT BOX SEAT": *Variety*,
6 January 1954.

207 "MODERNIZATION": Cited in
Motion Picture Herald, 2 January 1954.

207 "OPEN SEASON": *Variety*,
13 January 1954.

207 "ALMOST UNANIMOUSLY": *Variety*,
30 December 1953.

208 "DIGNITY, FORCE": Quoted in
Patrick Sullivan interview.

208 "CONTINUING CABAL": Quigley
editorial, *Motion Picture Herald*,
2 January 1954.

208 "SCREEN FREEDOM LIBERALS":
Variety, 13 January 1954.

208 "THE CODE HAS BEEN DEFIED":
Quoted in *Variety*, 13 January 1954.

209 "THE THIN EDGE": Vizzard, 87.

209 "THE FLY-BY-NIGHTERS": *Variety*,
20 January 1954.

209 "DEFINITELY AND SPECIFICALLY":
Breen to James R. Grainger, 15 January
1954, *The French Line* PCA file.

209 "TO RESPECT THE PRINCIPLES":
Quoted in *Motion Picture Herald*,
23 January 1954.

209 "WOULD BE RUINOUS": Quoted in
Motion Picture Herald, 30 January 1954.

210 "SOUND IN PRINCIPLE": Quoted in
Variety, 17 February 1954.

210 "CHANGES OR REVISIONS": The full
board statement was reprinted in *Variety*,
17 February 1954.

210 "RESULT IN A MAJOR MIGRAINE":
Variety, 13 January 1954.

210 "LIST OF UNACCEPTABLE": Breen,
Memorandum of Record, 17 February
1954, *The French Line* PCA file.

210 "A TREMENDOUS THING": Clark to
Breen, 19 February 1954, *The French Line*
PCA file.

211 "THERE'S NO USE": *New York
Times*, 15 May 1954.

212 "TO JOSEPH I. BREEN": Cited in
Variety, 7 December 1965.

Lolita

215 "ROOTED IN THE TREMENDOUS":
Douglas T. Miller and Marion Nowak,
The Fifties: The Way We Really Were
(Garden City, N.J.: Doubleday, 1977),
286.

215 "FACELESS DORMITORIES": Joseph
M. Siracusa, *The Changing of America:
1945 to the Present* (Arlington Heights,
Ill.: Forum Press, 1986), 43.

215 "A GREAT RELIEF": Margaret

McDonell to Selznick, 19 June 1944, *Spellbound* Correspondence file, Selznick Collection.

216 "TO BROADEN HIS EDUCATION": Robert Watkins interview.

217 "A SHORT NOVEL": *The Nabokov-Wilson Letters,* ed. Simon Karlinsky (New York: Harper & Row, 1979), 180.

218 "A FLOCK OF HUNGRY BEASTS": Cited in Kathy Merlock Jackson, *Images of Children in American Film: A Sociocultural Analysis* (Metuchen, N.J.: Scarecrow, 1986), 57.

218 "PRECOCIOUS" AND "VOLUPTUOUS": *Graham Greene on Film: Collected Film Criticism, 1935–1940,* ed. John Russell Taylor (New York: Simon and Schuster, 1972), 92.

219 "TWO-VOLUME, SEWER-GREEN-COVERED": Brock Brower, *Nabokov: Criticism, Reminiscences, Translations and Tributes,* ed. Alfred Appel, Jr., and Charles Newman (Evanston: Northwestern University Press, 1970), 357.

219 "*LOLITA* IS PORNOGRAPHY": Reviews cited in "The *Lolita* Case," *Time,* 17 November 1958: 102.

220 "IT'S THE TREATMENT": "It's the Treatment That Counts," Shurlock speech, Theatre Owners of America annual convention, 29 October 1965; reprinted by the Motion Picture Association, New York, New York (undated).

220 "WE PRIDE OURSELVES": *New York Times,* 9 July 1961.

220 "HE'LL BE A FINE DIRECTOR": *New York Times,* 2 November 1960.

221 "NEVER HAVING READ": Jack Rose and Melville Shavelson, quoted in *New York Times,* 9 November 1958.

222 "OUTSMART THE CODE": Jack Hamilton, "Hollywood bypasses the Production Code," *Look,* 29 September 1959: 83.

222 "ONE OF THE MOST PRESUMP-TUOUS": Cited in Balio, *United Artists: The Company That Changed the Film Industry,* 159.

222 "POSSIBLE ADVERSE REACTIONS":

Shurlock, Memorandum of Record, 18 March 1959, *Lolita* PCA file.

223 "THE CODE HAS BECOME": Quoted in Hamilton, "Hollywood Bypasses": 80.

223 "INFANTILE": *New York Times,* 7 February 1960.

223 "DID NOT MAKE MUCH": Stanley Kubrick to Shurlock, 9 February 1960, *Lolita* PCA file.

223 "BLOOMING CANYON": *The Nabokov-Wilson Letters,* 330.

224 "HEED MY WHIMS": Nabokov, Foreword, *Lolita: A Screenplay,* ix.

224 "I DIDN'T HAVE TO PLAY IT": *New York Times,* 13 December 1970.

224 "YOUNGER AND GRUBBIER": Nabokov, *Lolita: A Screenplay,* xi.

225 "KNOW WHAT GEOFF DOES": *Los Angeles Times,* 5 February 1962.

225 "WE DO NOT PLAY": Richard Brandt, "Self-Policing of the Movie and Publishing Industry," Hearing Before the Subcommittee on Postal Operations of the Committee on Post Office and Civil Service, House of Representatives, Eighty-Sixth Congress, Second Session, 2 February 1960: 89.

225 "AN ORGY OF SIN": Wald, "Movie Censorship: The First Wedge," *Saturday Review,* 8 April 1961: 54.

225 "EVERY KIND": Hamilton, "Hollywood Bypasses": 80.

225 "A MOVIE ABOUT A YOUNG MAN": Quoted in William K. Zinsser, "The Bold & Risky World of 'Adult' Movies," *Life,* 29 February 1960: 79.

226 "VERY DIFFICULT ABOUT": Russo, 114.

226 "WE HAVE BEEN TOLD": Shurlock to Zanuck, 2 June 1961, *The Chapman Report* PCA file.

227 "IN TERROR": Shurlock to Johnston, 25 May 1961, *Butterfield 8* PCA file.

227 "IN TRYING TO HEW": Shurlock to Johnston, 25 May 1961, *Butterfield 8* PCA file.

227 "FREE-HANDED": Quigley to James Harris, 10 February 1961, Quigley Papers (3:7).

227 "BOTCHED UP PASTICHE": John

Trevelyan to Kubrick, 7 December 1960, *Lolita* PCA file.

227 "I HAVE TAKEN RATHER": Trevelyan to Shurlock, 14 December 1960, *Lolita* PCA file.

229 "A CODE THAT ROLLS": *Motion Picture Herald*, 14 November 1959; cited in Sargent, 182–183.

229 "GAG OVER": Quigley to Kubrick and Harris, 30 November 1960, Quigley Papers (3:5).

229 "TONGUE-IN-EAR BUSINESS": Quigley to Harris, 19 December 1960, Quigley Papers (3:5).

230 "THIS NOTORIOUS STORY": Quigley to Shurlock, 2 February 1961, *Lolita* PCA file.

230 "HEAVY FLANNEL": Harris to Quigley, 30 January 1961, *Lolita* PCA file.

231 "AT WHICH TIME": Quigley to Harris, 24 July 1961, Quigley Papers (3:8).

232 "WAIT A MINUTE": Vizzard, 271.

232 "PATHOLOGICAL PREOCCU-PATION": *New York Times*, 2 June 1960.

233 "IT IS DECIDEDLY UN-CHRISTIAN": H. K. Rasbach, quoted in "Hollywood," *Time*, 7 September 1959: 50.

233 "I PROMISE TO PROMOTE": *New York Times*, 26 November 1960.

233 "THE SUBJECT MATTER": Little to Shurlock, 5 March 1959, *Some Like It Hot* PCA file.

234 "TWO AND A HALF HOURS": Little to David B. Stillman (Seven Arts Associated Corporation), 16 October 1961, Quigley Papers (3:7).

234 "LEGION PEOPLE": Vizzard, 271.

234 "ORDEALS OF TENSION": Quigley to Kubrick, 7 May 1962, Quigley Papers (3:10). Quigley wrote Kubrick to decline an invitation to the *Lolita* premiere: "I will plan on not being present, because I have recently had quite enough in the way of ordeals of tension."

234 "TO OFFSET A LONG SERIES": Quigley to Francis Cardinal Spellman, 20 October 1961, Quigley Papers (3:7).

235 "WE ARE MOST ANXIOUS": Arthur Krim to Johnston, 10 May 1961, *The Children's Hour* PCA file.

235 TREAT SEX ABERRATION: In November 1961, when Shurlock and the board refused to issue a Seal for *Victim*, the frank and sympathetic story of a homosexual who challenges the British law against homosexuality, they showed that they would not go too far too fast. Exhibitors also feared that homosexuality could boomerang at the box office. An advertisement for *Oscar Wilde* prominently featured a bosomy woman, next to whom the following copy appeared: "This is the beautiful Mrs. Oscar Wilde . . . whose private life became public when her husband's controversial attitudes towards sex and love caused a national scandal." The ad neither mentioned homosexuality nor provided an illustration of Wilde himself.

235 "PURE AND SIMPLE": *Mutual Film Corporation v. Industrial Commission of Ohio*, 236 U.S. 230 (1915).

235 "WHAT NEW YORK HAS DONE": *Kingsley International Pictures Corp. v. Regents of the University of the State of New York*, 360 U.S. 684 (1959).

235 "A PLAIN ATTEMPT": *New York Times*, 13 August 1961.

235 "IS OBJECTIONABLE TO A CHILD": Hamilton, "Hollywood Bypasses": 84.

235 "DECENCY AND MORALITY": "High Court's Ruling on Sex in Movies," *U.S. News and World Report*, 13 July 1959: 50.

236 "NOT RECOMMENDED": Cited in "Self-Policing" Hearing: 15.

236 "IT MAKES 'PEYTON PLACE' ": *New York Times*, 21 January 1960.

237 "THIS CLASSIFICATION": Hamilton, "Hollywood Bypasses": 84.

237 "ALL FOR ADULT PICTURES": Cited in "Self-Policing" Hearing, 4 February 1960: 130.

237 "COULD AN 'ADULT ONLY' ": "Self-Policing" Hearing, 2 February 1960: 7.

237 "THERE WERE MORE PICTURES": *New York Times*, 12 February 1961.

238 "TEN YEARS AGO": New York *Herald Tribune*, 15 July 1962.

238 "IT IS NOT SO MUCH": New York *Herald Tribune*, 15 July 1962.

238 "STUNT—SUE LYON": New York *Herald Tribune*, 15 July 1962.

238 "A CONSIDERABLE PART": Paul Nathan, "Rights and Permissions," *Publishers Weekly*, 17 December 1962: 29.

238 "HORRIBLE SEATS": Nabokov, Foreword, *Lolita: A Screenplay*, xii and xiii.

240 "IN SPITE OF THE GLOWING": Patrick Sullivan, S.J., to Little, *Lolita* file, Legion of Decency Archive.

240 "IF I COULD DO THE FILM OVER": Joseph Gelmis, *The Film Director as Superstar* (Garden City, N.Y.: Doubleday, 1970), 300.

Who's Afraid of Virginia Woolf?

241 "THE RECORDING OF ALL": Miller, *Tropic of Cancer* (New York: Grove, 1961), 11.

241 "HUMOR, ANGER, ART": *Variety*, 26 December 1962.

242 "THEY'D PUT FUCKING": Vizzard, 36.

243 "WHETHER SUCH A DRAMATIC": Review of *Who's Afraid of Virginia Woolf?*, *Variety*, 17 October 1962.

243 "TAKE THE COCK": Shurlock to Edward Schellhorn, 15 March 1962, *Hud* PCA file, Motion Picture Association, New York, New York.

244 "ALL THE PROFANITY": Shurlock to Warner, 20 March 1963, *Virginia Woolf* PCA file, Motion Picture Association.

244 "SUFFICIENTLY INVENTIVE": Trilling to Abe Lastfogel, 29 March 1963, *Virginia Woolf* Papers, Box 19, Ernest Lehman Collection, Hoblitzelle Theatre Arts Library, Humanities Research Center, University of Texas at Austin.

244 "SOME MAJOR HEADACHES": *Variety*, 18 December 1963.

245 "NOBODY BRINGS": *Variety*, 18 December 1963.

245 "ANY PRODUCER": "Burdens on the Censor," *Newsweek*, 29 March 1965: 88. The Supreme Court ruled in March 1965 that the Maryland censorship law failed "to provide adequate safeguards against undue inhibition of protected expression." In the same case, it also ruled that when the political censors refused to certify a picture, they must assume the burden of proof and afford the distributor a prompt court hearing (*Freedman v. Maryland*, 380 U.S. 51 [1965]).

246 "DEPRIVING PARENTS": "Film Classification Defied," *America*, 5 December 1964: 730.

246 "A MAIDEN AUNT'S FUSSY": *New York Times*, 4 March 1965.

246 "A SMOOTHLY-FUNCTIONING": *Variety*, 28 August 1963.

247 "EXPENDABLE. NO DOUBT": *New York Times*, 15 March 1964.

247 "THIS HAD ONCE BEEN": Sharon Sue Rountree Hollenback, "Analysis of Processes Involved in Screenwriting as Demonstrated in Screenplays by Ernest Lehman," Ph.D. dissertation, University of Texas at Austin, 1980, 317.

248 "OVEREMPHASIS ON SEX": *New York Times*, 8 March 1964.

248 "GO ON HOPING": *Hollywood Reporter*, 8 September 1964.

248 "MISMANAGED DISTRIBUTION": Higham, 124.

248 "I BEGAN HAVING HANGOVERS": Barbara Gelb, "The Troubled Road Back to 'Camelot,'" *New York Times Magazine*, 6 July 1980: 30.

248 "I WAS TOLD": Gelmis, *The Film Director as Superstar*, 291.

249 "CLEAN BUT SUGGESTIVE": Thomas Thompson, "A Surprising Liz in a Film Shocker," *Life*, 10 June 1966: 92.

250 "TO ERR IS HUMAN": Ernest Lehman to Elizabeth Taylor, 6 August 1965, *Virginia Woolf* Papers (19), Lehman Collection.

250 "A GOOD DEAL": Shurlock to Warner, 9 October 1965, *Virginia Woolf* Papers (23B), Lehman Collection.

250 "VIRTUALLY INTACT": C. Robert Jennings, "All for the Love of Mike,"

Saturday Evening Post, 9 October 1965: 86.

250 "UNAPPROVABLE UNDER CODE": Shurlock to Warner, 9 October 1965, *Virginia Woolf* Papers (23B), Lehman Collection.

251 "UTTERLY WITHOUT": *Jacobellis* v. *Ohio,* 378 U.S. 184 (1964).

251 "IN THE LAST TWO YEARS": Little, "The Modern Legion and Its Modern Outlook," *America,* 11 December 1965: 746.

251 "PRURIENTLY IMPURE": *Variety,* 21 February 1962.

252 "CALL FORTH A GREAT AMOUNT": Shurlock to Ely A. Landau, 2 February 1965, *The Pawnbroker* PCA file, Motion Picture Association.

252 "HARM RESULTING": Barney Balaban to Ralph Hetzel, 29 March 1965, *The Pawnbroker* PCA file, Motion Picture Association.

252 "FILMS HAVE ALWAYS": Walker, 187.

253 "UPHELD AND AFFIRMED": Minutes of *The Pawnbroker* Appeal, 23 March 1965, *The Pawnbroker* PCA file, Motion Picture Association.

253 "THAT'S CUTS": Vizzard, 363.

253 "OPEN THE DOOR" . . . "THE EFFORT" . . . "WAS IN ITSELF": Little to "Your Excellency" (undated copy of letter), *The Pawnbroker* PCA file, Motion Picture Association.

253 "PERHAPS THE MILDEST": *Variety,* 12 May 1965.

254 "A GOOD DEAL OF CRITICISM": *Variety,* 8 June 1966.

254 "MORE IN LINE": *New York Times,* 7 April 1965.

254 "WHAT THE CODE ADMINISTRATION": *New York Times,* 7 April 1965.

255 "ENERGY" AND "VIGOR": *Variety,* 25 May 1966.

255 "PREPARE THE PUBLIC": *New York Times,* 26 April 1966.

255 "LITERALLY FORCES": *Hollywood Reporter,* 26 May 1966. In the wake of Catholic blacklists over thirty years before, Warner Bros. had announced a two-tier plan; it would classify its 1934 releases "A" for "Adult" and "F" for

"Family." Despite support from prominent Catholics, the experiment lasted only a few months.

256 "AN UNDERSTANDABLE POPULAR": *Variety,* 29 November 1961.

256 "AN INTELLIGENT AND": "Legion of Decency," *America,* 9 May 1964: 625.

256 "HOPELESSLY OUTNUMBERED MINORITY": Quoted in Gene D. Phillips, "No More Ratings?" *America,* 11 November 1967: 560.

257 "IT MIGHT BE WELL": Shurlock to Warner, 26 March 1963, *Virginia Woolf* PCA file, Motion Picture Association.

257 "NOT APPROVED": Fehr to Walter MacEwen, 4 August 1965, *Virginia Woolf* Papers (19), Lehman Collection.

257 "DON'T WORRY": Richard Lederer interview (telephone), 22 June 1979.

257 "WHY CAN'T THESE PEOPLE": *Virginia Woolf* file, Legion of Decency Archive.

258 "WE ASKED FOR NOTHING": *Variety,* 27 May 1966.

258 "DIRECTLY INSTRUMENTAL": Sullivan to complainant (unnamed), 28 June 1966, *Virginia Woolf* file, Legion of Decency Archive.

258 "AS RESPONSIBLE FILM-MAKERS": *Hollywood Reporter,* 26 May 1966.

258 "EXCESSIVE EXPOSURE": Advertising Code Administration notation on half sheet, 24 May 1966, *Virginia Woolf* PCA file, Motion Picture Association.

258 "ASSOCIATION HAS PROVIDED": Balio, *United Artists: The Company That Changed the Film Industry,* 228.

258 "THE ONLY THING": Wallis to Shurlock, 23 December 1963, *Irma La Douce* PCA file.

259 "BE SOLD AND ADVERTISED": Shurlock to Wallis, 6 January 1964, *Irma La Douce* PCA file.

259 "MATURING LIBERAL": Vizzard, 308.

259 "THE JURY IS STILL OUT": Thomas Thompson, "Wilder's Dirty-Joke Film Stirs a Furor," *Life,* 15 January 1965: 56A.

259 "THE END OF AN ERA": Vizzard, 304.

259 "TO THE DAY WHEN": *Variety*, 21 February 1962.
259 "LET 'EM MAKE WHATEVER": Robert Watkins interview.
260 "NEAR A HIGH": *Variety*, 4 May 1966.
260 "A SCORCHING" . . . "I THINK": Thompson, "A Surprising Liz": 88, 96.
260 "LONELY SOUL-SEARCHING": "Notes of Meeting of Production Code Review Board on Friday, June 10, 1966, at Hotel St. Regis (The Private Suite), New York, Following Screening at 10:00 A.M. of 'Who's Afraid of Virginia Woolf' at Warner Bros. Screening Room, 666 Fifth Avenue, New York," Motion Picture Association, 4.
260 "THE BIGGEST STUMBLING BLOCK": *Variety*, 8 June 1966.
261 "MAKING EXEMPTIONS": "Notes of Meeting," 3.
261 "A LOT OF MONEY INVESTED": "Notes of Meeting," 3.
261 "A SUPERIOR PICTURE": "Notes of Meeting," 4.
261 PERHAPS AS A SOP: Elizabeth Taylor was in Europe in May 1966, so Warners employed another actress to dub "goddamn you." By 1976, when Albee directed *Virginia Woolf* on Broadway, time had dulled the original "screw you"; Albee changed it to "fuck you."
261 "WE FEEL WE CAN POLICE": "Notes of Meeting," 8.
261 "SPEAKING CONFIDENTIALLY": Notes of Meeting," 4.
262 "ELIZABETH TAYLOR ADDED": Higham, 121–122.
262 "REPLACEMENT SCENES": Notes of Meeting," 11.
262 "GOING TO BE STRONGER": Notes of Meeting," 10.
262 "THE NUMBER OF TRASHY": John Trevelyan to Little, 28 June 1966, *Virginia Woolf* file, Office of the British Board of Film Censors, London.
262 "THE DOOR FOR POSSIBLE": *Variety*, 22 June 1966.
263 "FRENCH [TO] LET US": Warner to Lehman, *Virginia Woolf* third draft

screenplay, 14 March 1965, *Virginia Woolf* Papers (6), Lehman Collection.
263 "POINTLESS TO CONSIDER": *Motion Picture Herald*, 6 July 1966.
264 "I WAS NOT": *Variety*, 22 June 1966.
264 "THE MOTION PICTURE ASSOCIATION": *Variety*, 23 June 1966.
264 "KEEP IN CLOSER HARMONY": "Movies," *Time*, 30 September 1966: 61.
264 "SEEMED WRONG": Jack Valenti, "The Movie Rating System," Motion Picture Association (undated), 2.
265 "A GLITTERING DIADEM": "Hollywood: Three-and-a-half Square," *Newsweek*, 3 October 1966: 22.
265 "EVERYTHING EXPRESSLY PROHIBITED": *Motion Picture Herald*, 20 July 1966.
265 "NOT RECOMMENDED" / "CHILDREN UNDER 12 FREE": Cited in Ralph Hetzel to Tim Clagett, 15 / 22 September 1966, *Virginia Woolf* PCA file, Motion Picture Association.

AFTERMATH

269 "THERE IS A TREMENDOUS": "The Day the Dream Factory Woke Up," *Life*, 27 February 1970: 44.
270 "GOOD DIRECTORS ARE": Vizzard, 331.
270 "HARMFUL TO MINORS": New York Penal Law §484–h (1965).
271 "BEFORE A SINGLE STATE": Stuart Byron, "To the Editor," *Film Comment*, September–October 1986: 76.
271 "ENCOURAGE ARTISTIC": Farber, 15.
272 "GARBAGE, PICTURES THAT": Farber, 47.
272 "WE CHOSE A TYPEWRITER": Bresson and Swift to Vizzard (undated); courtesy of Jack Vizzard.
272 THEY HUDDLED WITH DOUGHERTY: Though the New York Association rated independent films and many imports, the Hollywood office had the heavy traffic; after 1971, the Hollywood office rated all films.
272 "LITERAL-MINDED" . . . "THE *ACCUMULATION*": Farber, 63.
273 "PRETTY GAMY" AND "PRETTY

GORY": *Los Angeles Times,* 1 November 1988.

273 "OLD FRIEND": Russo, 174.

274 "ONE OF THE TARNISHING MARKS": "Movie Ratings and the Independent Producer," Hearings Before the Subcommittee on Special Small Business Problems of the Committee on Small Business, House of Representatives, Ninety-Fifth Congress, First Session, 24 March 1977: 7.

274 "GETS UP IN FRONT": Farber, 40.

274 "THE GHOST OF THE LATE JOE BREEN": *New York Times,* 22 March 1970.

274 "THEY'RE SUSPECTING": Robert Watkins interview.

274 "I WANT TO DIE": Walker, 258.

275 "GROWING NUMBER": "Film Rating Fiasco," *America,* 29 May 1971: 557–558.

275 "INFORMED ME THAT I WAS": Farber, 95.

275 "GENERAL FEELING WITHIN": *New York Times,* 11 November 1971.

275 "YOU CAN HAVE A LOVE SCENE": *The Hollywood Reporter,* 24 August 1971; cited in Farber, 92.

276 "DID LENA ACTUALLY KISS": de Grazia and Newman, 124.

276 "IT'S THE RATING": Balio, *United Artists: The Company That Changed the Film Industry,* 289.

276 "IF *DEEP THROAT*": *Los Angeles Times,* 4 February 1973.

277 "I DON'T WANT PSYCHOLOGISTS": "Movie Ratings" Hearings: 7.

277 "HAD MORE RESPECT": Farber, 59.

277 "BE OFFENDED . . . DOING HIS BEST": Jonathan M. Dana, "Movie Ratings" Hearings, 12 May 1977: 139.

278 "I AM NOT VERY PROUD": *Stillwater NewsPress,* 6 March 1986.

278 "ONE SET OF CENSORS": "Lois P. Sheinfeld Replies," *Film Comment,* September–October 1986: 78.

278 "I DETEST CENSORSHIP": *New York Times,* 7 May 1972.

278 "BE O.K. IF WE TOOK": Paul Attanasio, "The Rating Game," *The New Republic,* 17 June 1985: 17.

279 "IF YOU SAY": Attanasio, "The Rating Game": 16.

SELECTED BIBLIOGRAPHY

Albee, Edward. *Who's Afraid of Virginia Woolf?* New York: Atheneum, 1962.

Ardrey, Robert. "Hollywood's Fall into Virtue." *The Reporter,* 21 February 1957: 13–17. "Letters," 4 April 1957: 4.

Ayer, Douglas, Roy E. Bates, and Peter J. Herman. "Self-Censorship in the Movie Industry: A Historical Perspective on Law and Social Change." *Wisconsin Law Review* 3 (1970): 791–838. Reprinted in Kindem, Gorham, ed. *The American Movie Industry: The Business of Motion Pictures.* Carbondale: Southern Illinois University Press, 1982. 215–253.

Balio, Tino, ed. *The American Film Industry.* Madison: University of Wisconsin Press, 1976.

————. *United Artists: The Company Built by the Stars.* Madison: University of Wisconsin Press, 1976.

————. *United Artists: The Company That Changed the Film Industry.* Madison: University of Wisconsin Press, 1987.

Bazin, André. *What Is Cinema?* Trans. and ed. Hugh Gray. 2 vols. Berkeley: University of California Press, 1967 and 1971.

Beaver, Frank Eugene. "Bosley Crowther: Social Critic of the Film, 1940–1967." Ph.D. dissertation, University of Michigan, 1970. New York: Arno Press, 1974.

Behlmer, Rudy. *America's Favorite Movies: Behind the Scenes.* New York: Frederick Ungar, 1982.

————. *Inside Warner Bros. (1935–1951).* New York: Viking, 1985.

————, ed. *Memo from David O. Selznick.* New York: Viking, 1972.

Bergman, Andrew. *We're in the Money: Depression America and Its Films.* New York: New York University Press, 1971.

Berman, Sam. "The Hays Office." *Fortune,* December 1938: 68–72+.

Biskind, Peter. *Seeing Is Believing: How Hollywood Taught Us to Stop Worrying and Love the Fifties.* New York: Pantheon Books, 1983.

Bordwell, David, Kristin Thompson, and Janet Staiger. *The Classical Hollywood Cinema: Film Style and Mode of Production to 1960.* New York: Columbia University Press, 1985.

Cain, James. M. *The Postman Always Rings Twice.* New York: Knopf, 1934.

Carmen, Ira H. *Movies, Censorship and the Law.* Ann Arbor: University of Michigan Press, 1966.

"Censorship of Motion Pictures." *Yale Law Review Journal* 49 (1939): 87–113.

Conant, Michael. *Antitrust in the Motion Picture Industry: Economic and Legal Analysis.* Berkeley: University of California Press, 1960.

Corliss, Richard. "The Legion of Decency." *Film Comment,* Summer 1969: 24–61.

De Grazia, Edward, and Roger K. Newman. *Banned Films: Movies, Censors and the First Amendment.* New York: R. R. Bowker Company, 1982.

Delpar, Helen. "Goodbye to the 'Greaser': Mexico, the MPPDA, and Derogatory Films, 1922–1926." *Journal of Popular Film and Television* 12.1 (1984): 34–41.

Deming, Barbara. *Running Away from Myself: A Dream Portrait of America Drawn from the Films of the 40's.* New York: Grossman, 1969.

Ernst, Morris, and Pare Lorentz. *Censored: The Private Life of the Movies.* New York: Jonathan Cape and Harrison Smith, 1930. New York: Jerome S. Ozer, 1971.

Facey, Paul W. "The Legion of Decency: A Sociological Analysis of the Emergence and Development of a Social Pressure Group." Ph.D. dissertation, Fordham University, 1945. New York: Arno Press, 1974.

Farber, Stephen. *The Movie Rating Game.* Washington, D.C.: Public Affairs Press, 1972.

Forman, Henry James. *Our Movie Made Children.* New York: Macmillan, 1933.

French, Philip. *The Movie Moguls: An Informal History of the Hollywood Tycoons.* Chicago: Henry Regnery, 1969.

Gardner, Gerald. *The Censorship Papers: Movie Censorship Letters from the Hays Office, 1934–1968.* New York: Dodd, Mead, 1987.

Giglio, Ernest David. "The Decade of the Miracle, 1952–1962: A Study in the Censorship of the American Motion Picture." D.SS. dissertation, Syracuse University, 1964.

Gomery, Douglas. "History of the (Film) World, Part II." *American Film,* November 1982: 53–57, 89.

_____ . *The Hollywood Studio System.* New York: St. Martin's, 1986.

Goodman, Ezra. *The Fifty-Year Decline and Fall of Hollywood.* New York: Simon and Schuster, 1961.

Hays, Will H. *The Memoirs of Will H. Hays.* Garden City, N.Y.: Doubleday, 1955.

Herbert, F. Hugh. *The Moon Is Blue.* New York: Random House, 1951.

Higham, Charles. *Hollywood at Sunset.* New York: Saturday Review Press, 1972.

Huettig, Mae D. *Economic Control of the Motion Picture Industry: A Study in Industrial Organization.* Philadelphia: University of Pennsylvania Press, 1944.

Inglis, Ruth. *Freedom of the Movies: A Report on Self-Regulation from the Commission on Freedom of the Press.* Chicago: University of Chicago Press, 1947.

The International Motion Picture Almanac. New York: Quigley Publishing Company, 1935–86.

Jacobs, Lea. "The Censorship of *Blonde Venus:* Textual Analysis and Historical Method." *Cinema Journal* 27.3 (Spring 1988): 21–31.

Jewell, Richard B., with Vernon Harbin. *The RKO Story.* New York: Arlington House, 1982.

Jowett, Garth. *Film: The Democratic Art.* Boston: Little, Brown, 1976.

Kingsley, Sidney. *Dead End.* New York: Random House, 1936.

————. *Detective Story.* New York: Random House, 1949.

Koppes, Clayton R., and Gregory D. Black. *Hollywood Goes to War: How Politics, Profits, and Propaganda Shaped World War II Movies.* New York: Free Press, 1987.

Lord, Daniel A., S.J. *Played by Ear.* Chicago: Loyola University Press, 1956.

MacCann, Richard Dyer. *Hollywood in Transition.* Boston: Houghton Mifflin, 1962.

McGilligan, Pat, ed. *Backstory: Interviews with Screenwriters of Hollywood's Golden Age.* Berkeley: University of California Press, 1986.

Maltby, Richard. " 'Baby Face,' or How Joe Breen Made Barbara Stanwyck Atone for Causing the Wall Street Crash." *Screen* 27.2 (1986): 22–45.

Martin, Olga J. *Hollywood's Movie Commandments.* New York: H. W. Wilson, 1937.

Mast, Gerald, ed. *The Movies in Our Midst: Documents in the Cultural History of Film in America.* Chicago: University of Chicago Press, 1982.

————. *A Short History of the Movies.* 4th ed. New York: Macmillan, 1986.

Mitchell, Margaret. *Gone With the Wind.* New York: Macmillan, 1936.

Moley, Raymond. *The Hays Office.* Indianapolis: Bobbs–Merrill, 1945.

Nabokov, Vladimir. *Lolita.* New York: Putnam, 1958.

————. *Lolita: A Screenplay.* New York: McGraw–Hill, 1974.

Nizer, Louis. *New Courts of Industry: Self-Regulation Under the Motion Picture Code.* New York: Longacre Press, 1935. New York: Jerome S. Ozer, 1971.

Peary, Gerald, and Roger Shatzkin, eds. *The Classic American Novel and the Movies.* New York: Frederick Ungar, 1977.

Phelan, John M., S.J. "The National Catholic Office for Motion Pictures: An Investigation of the Policy and Practice of Film Classification." Ph.D. dissertation, New York University, 1968.

Phelps, Guy. *Film Censorship.* London: Victor Gollancz, 1975.

Powdermaker, Hortense. *Hollywood: The Dream Factory.* Boston: Little, Brown, 1950.

Quigley, Martin. *Decency in Motion Pictures.* New York: Macmillan, 1937.

Randall, Richard S. *Censorship of the Movies: The Social and Political Control of a Mass Medium.* Madison: University of Wisconsin Press, 1968.

Robertson, James C. *The British Board of Film Censors: Film Censorship in Britain, 1896–1950.* London: Croom Helm, 1985.

Roddick, Nick. *A New Deal in Entertainment: Warner Brothers in the 1930s.* London: British Film Institute, 1980.

Roffman, Peter, and Jim Purdy. *The Hollywood Social Problem Film: Madness, Despair, and Politics from the Depression to the Fifties.* Bloomington: Indiana University Press, 1981.

Rosten, Leo. *Hollywood: The Movie Colony, The Movie Makers.* New York: Harcourt, Brace, and Company, 1941.

Russo, Vito. *The Celluloid Closet: Homosexuality in the Movies.* Rev. ed. New York: Harper & Row, 1987.

Samuels, Charles Thomas. *Encountering Directors.* New York: Capricorn, 1972.

Sargent, John Alan. "Self-Regulation: The Motion Picture Production Code, 1930–1961." Ph.D. dissertation, University of Michigan, 1963.

Schatz, Thomas. *The Genius of the System: Hollywood Filmmaking in the Studio Era.* New York: Pantheon Books, 1988.

Schumach, Murray. *The Face on the Cutting Room Floor: The Story of Movie and Television Censorship.* New York: Morrow, 1964. New York: Da Capo, 1975.

Sheinfeld, Lois P. "Ratings: The Big Chill." *Film Comment,* May–June 1986: 9–14. "Letters," September–October 1986: 72–80.

Short, K. R. M., ed. *Feature Films as History*. Knoxville: University of Tennessee Press, 1981.

Sklar, Robert. *Movie-Made America: A Social History of American Movies*. New York: Random House, 1975.

Thomas, Bob. "Those Good Old Bad Old Days." *Action*, March–April 1974: 18–22.

Thorp, Margaret. *America at the Movies*. New Haven: Yale University Press, 1939.

Trevelyan, John. *What the Censor Saw*. London: Michael Joseph, 1973.

Valenti, Jack. "Liberty Is Not License—The Artist Who Endures Is One Who Is Disciplined." *Action*, March–April 1968: 19–21.

Vizzard, Jack. *See No Evil: Life Inside a Hollywood Censor*. New York: Simon and Schuster, 1970.

Walker, Alexander. *Sex in the Movies: The Celluloid Sacrifice*. Baltimore: Penguin Books, 1968.

Wasko, Janet. *Movies and Money: Financing the American Film Industry*. Norwood, N.J.: Ablex Publishing, 1982.

Weales, Gerald. *Canned Goods as Caviar: American Film Comedy of the 1930s*. Chicago: University of Chicago Press, 1985.

Westin, Alan F. *The Miracle Case: The Supreme Court and the Movies*. Inter-University Case Program No. 64. [Tuscaloosa, Al.]: University of Alabama Press, 1961.

Williams, Tennessee. *A Streetcar Named Desire*. New York: New Directions, 1980.

Selected Filmography

She Done Him Wrong (Paramount, 1933; 66 minutes)

Producer	*William LeBaron*
Director	*Lowell Sherman*
Screenplay	*Harvey Thew and John Bright*
(based on the play *Diamond Lil,* by Mae West)	
Photography	*Charles Lang*
Editing	*Alexander Hall*
Music	*Ralph Rainger*
Lady Lou	*Mae West*
Captain Cummings ("The Hawk")	*Cary Grant*
Chick Clark	*Owen Moore*
Serge Stanieff	*Gilbert Roland*
Gus Jordan	*Noah Beery, Sr.*
Dan Flynn	*David Landau*
Russian Rita	*Rafaela Ottiano*
Spider Kane	*Dewey Robinson*
Sally	*Rochelle Hudson*
Chuck Connors	*Tammany Young*
Rag Time Kelly	*Fuzzy Knight*
Frances	*Grace La Rue*

Doheney	*Robert E. Homans*
Pearl	*Louise Beavers*
Pal	*Wade Boteler*
Mrs. Flaherty	*Aggie Herring*
The Bar Fly	*Arthur Housman*
Big Bill	*Tom Kennedy*
Pete	*James C. Eagle*
Mike	*Tom McGuire*
The Framed Convict	*Frank Moran*
Jacobson	*Les Kohlmar*
Steak McGarry	*Harry Wallace*
The Tout	*Mike Donlin*
The Janitor	*Michael Mark*
The Cleaning Woman	*Mary Gordon*
The Second Bar Fly	*Al Hill*
The Man in Audience	*Ernie Adams*
The Street Cleaner	*Henie Conklin*
The Patron (who hits girlfriend)	*Jack Carr*

I'm No Angel (Paramount, 1933; 87 minutes)

Producer	*William LeBaron*
Director	*Wesley Ruggles*
Screenplay	*Mae West*
(with suggestions by Lowell Brentano and continuity by Harlan Thompson)	
Photography	*Leo Tover*
Editing	*Otho Lovering*
Music	*Harvey Brooks*
(lyrics by Gladys duBois and Ben Ellison)	

Tira	*Mae West*
Jack Clayton	*Cary Grant*
Benny Pinkowitz	*Gregory Ratoff*
Big Bill Barton	*Edward Arnold*
Slick Wiley	*Ralf Harolde*
Kirk Lawrence	*Kent Taylor*
Alicia Hatton	*Gertrude Michael*
Flea Madigan ("The Barker")	*Russell Hopton*
Thelma	*Dorothy Peterson*
Ernest Brown ("The Chump")	*William B. Davidson*
Beulah	*Gertrude Howard*
A Maid	*Libby Taylor*
A Maid	*Hattie McDaniel*
Harry ("A Trapeze Artist")	*Nat Pendleton*
The Spectator	*Tom London*
Rajah	*Nigel de Brulier*
Bob ("The Attorney")	*Irving Pichel*
The Chauffeur	*Morrie Cohen*
The Judge	*Walter Walker*

Omnes	*George Bruggeman*
A Sailor	*Monte Collins*
A Sailor	*Ray Cooke*
The Reporter	*Dennis O'Keefe*
The Courtroom Spectator	*Edward Hearn*

Dead End (Samuel Goldwyn / United Artists, 1937; 93 minutes)

Producer	*Samuel Goldwyn*
Director	*William Wyler*
Screenplay	*Lillian Hellman*
(based on the play by Sidney Kingsley)	
Photography	*Gregg Toland*
Editing	*Daniel Mandell*
Music	*Alfred Newman*
Drina	*Sylvia Sidney*
Dave	*Joel McCrea*
"Baby Face" Martin	*Humphrey Bogart*
Kay	*Wendy Barrie*
Francey	*Claire Trevor*
Hunk	*Allen Jenkins*
Mrs. Martin	*Marjorie Main*
Tommy	*Billy Halop*
Dippy	*Huntz Hall*
Angel	*Bobby Jordan*
Spit	*Leo B. Gorcey*
T. B.	*Gabriel Dell*
Milty	*Bernard Punsly*
Philip	*Charles Peck*
Mr. Griswald	*Minor Watson*
Mulligan	*James Burke*
Mrs. Connell	*Elisabeth Risdon*
Mrs. Fenner	*Esther Dale*
Pascagli	*George Humbert*
The Governess	*Marcelle Corday*
Whitey	*Charles Halton*
The Doorman	*Ward Bond*

Gone With the Wind (Selznick International / Metro–Goldwyn–Mayer, 1939; 220 minutes)

Producer	*David Selznick*
Director	*Victor Fleming*
Screenplay	*Sidney Howard*
(based on the novel by Margaret Mitchell)	
Photography	*Ernest Haller, with Ray Rennahan and Wilfrid M. Cline*
Editing	*Hal C. Kern, with James E. Newcom*

Music	Max Steiner
Scarlett O'Hara	Vivien Leigh
Rhett Butler	Clark Gable
Melanie Hamilton	Olivia de Havilland
Ashley Wilkes	Leslie Howard
Mammy	Hattie McDaniel
Prissy	Butterfly McQueen
Gerald O'Hara	Thomas Mitchell
Jonas Wilkerson	Victor Jory
Ellen O'Hara	Barbara O'Neill
Suellen O'Hara	Evelyn Keyes
Carreen O'Hara	Ann Rutherford
Charles Hamilton	Rand Brooks
India Wilkes	Alicia Rhett
Pork	Oscar Polk
Big Sam	Everett Brown
Aunt "Pittypat" Hamilton	Laura Hope Crews
Dr. Meade	Harry Davenport
Belle Watling	Ona Munson
The Yankee Captain	Ward Bond
Bonnie Blue Butler	Cammie King
Brent Tarleton	George Reeves
Stuart Tarleton	Fred Crane
Frank Kennedy	Carroll Nye
Mrs. Meade	Leona Roberts
Mrs. Merriwether	Jane Darwell
Maybelle Merriwether	Mary Anderson
Uncle Peter	Eddie Anderson
Emmy Slattery	Isabel Jewell
Beau Wilkes	Mickey Kuhn

The Outlaw (Howard Hughes, 1943; 126 minutes)

Producer	Howard Hughes
Director	Howard Hughes
Screenplay	Jules Furthman
Photography	Gregg Toland
Editing	Wallace Grissell
Music	Victor Young
Billy the Kid	Jack Buetel
Rio	Jane Russell
Pat Garrett	Thomas Mitchell
Doc Holliday	Walter Huston
Aunt Guadalupe	Mimi Aguglia
Charley Woodruff	Joe Sawyer
Dolan	Emory Parnell
The Waiter	Martin Garralega
Pablo	Julian Rivero
The Stranger	Gene Rizzi
Shorty	Frank Darien

The Bartender	Pat West
The Minister	Carl Stockdale
Chito	Nena Quartero
The Boys	Dickie Jones
	Frank Ward
	Bobby Callahan
The Deputies	Ethan Laidlaw
	Ed Brady
	William Steele
The Bystander	Wally Reid, Jr.
Swanson	Ed Peil, Sr.
The Coach Driver	Lee "Lasses" White
The Guard	Ted Mapes
The Drunk Cowboy	William Newell
The Officer	Cecil Kellogg
The Dealer	Lee Shumway
The Salesmen	Arthur Loft
	Dick Elliott
	John Sheehan

The Postman Always Rings Twice (MGM, 1946; 113 minutes)

Producer	Carey Wilson
Director	Tay Garnett
Screenplay	Harry Ruskin and Niven Busch
(based on the novel by James M. Cain)	
Photography	Sidney Wagner
Editing	George White
Music	George Bassman
Cora Smith	Lana Turner
Frank Chambers	John Garfield
Nick Smith	Cecil Kellaway
Arthur Keats	Hume Cronyn
Kyle Sackett	Leon Ames
Madge Gorland	Audrey Totter
Ezra Liam Kennedy	Alan Reed
Blair	Jeff York

The Bicycle Thief (P.D.S. [Produzioni De Sica]/Mayer-Burstyn, 1949; 90 minutes)

Producer	Umberto Scarpelli
Director	Vittorio De Sica
Screenplay	Cesare Zavattini, with Oreste Biancoli,
(based on the novel by Luigi Bartolini)	Suso Cecchi d'Amico, Vittorio De Sica,
	Adolfo Franci, Gherardo Gherardi, Gerardo
	Guerrieri
Photography	Carlo Montuori
Editing	Eraldo Da Roma
Music	Alessandro Cicognini

Antonio Ricci	*Lamberto Maggiorani*
Bruno Ricci	*Enzo Staiola*
Maria Ricci	*Lianella Carell*
La Santona	*Elena Altieri*
The Thief	*Vittorio Antonucci*
Baiocco	*Gino Saltamerenda*

Detective Story (Paramount, 1951; 103 minutes)

Producer	*William Wyler*
Director	*William Wyler*
Screenplay	*Philip Yordan and Robert Wyler*
(based on the play by Sidney Kingsley)	
Photography	*Lee Garmes*
Editing	*Robert Swink*
Detective James McLeod	*Kirk Douglas*
Mary McLeod	*Eleanor Parker*
Detective Lou Brody	*William Bendix*
The Shoplifter	*Lee Grant*
Detective Dakis	*Bert Freed*
Detective Gallagher	*Frank Faylen*
Detective Callahan	*William Phillips*
Detective O'Brien	*Grandon Rhodes*
Joe Feinson	*Luis Van Rooten*
Susan Carmichael	*Cathy O'Donnell*
Lt. Monaghan	*Horace McMahon*
Endicott Sims	*Warner Anderson*
Dr. Schneider	*George Macready*
Arthur Kindred	*Craig Hill*
Charles Gennini (the First Burglar)	*Joseph Wiseman*
Lewis Abbott (the Second Burglar)	*Michael Strong*
Pritchett	*James Maloney*
Miss Hatch	*Gladys George*
Patrolman Barnes	*Russell Evans*
Patrolman Keogh	*Howard Joslyn*
Willie (the Janitor)	*Burt Mustin*
Tami Giacoppetti	*Gerald Mohr*

A Streetcar Named Desire (Warner Bros., 1951; 122 minutes)

Producer	*Charles K. Feldman*
Director	*Elia Kazan*
Screenplay	*Tennessee Williams*
(based on Oscar Saul's adaptation of the play by Williams)	
Photography	*Harry Stradling*
Editing	*David Weisbart*
Music	*Alex North*
Blanche DuBois	*Vivien Leigh*

Stanley Kowalski	*Marlon Brando*
Stella Kowalski	*Kim Hunter*
Mitch	*Karl Malden*
Steve	*Rudy Bond*
Pablo	*Nick Dennis*
Eunice	*Peg Hillias*
The Collector	*Wright King*
The Doctor	*Richard Garrick*
The Matron	*Ann Dere*
The Mexican Woman	*Edna Thomas*
The Sailor	*Mickey Kuhn*
The Street Vendor	*Chester Jones*
The Negro Woman	*Marietta Canty*
The Policeman	*Lyle Latell*
The Foreman	*Mel Archer*
A Passerby	*Charles Wagenheim*
A Passerby	*Maxie Thrower*

The Moon Is Blue (United Artists, 1953; 99 minutes)

Producer	*Otto Preminger*
Director	*Otto Preminger*
Screenplay	*F. Hugh Herbert*
(based on the play by Herbert)	
Photography	*Ernest Laszlo*
Editing	*Louis R. Loeffler and Otto Ludwig*
Music	*Herschel Burke Gilbert*

Patty O'Neill	*Maggie McNamara*
David Slater	*David Niven*
Donald Gresham	*William Holden*
Michael O'Neill	*Tom Tully*
Cynthia Slater	*Dawn Addams*
The Television Announcer	*Fortunio Bonanova*
The Taxi Driver	*Gregory Ratoff*
The Sightseer	*Hardy Kruger*
His Wife	*Johanna Matz*

The French Line (RKO, 1954; 102 minutes)

Producer	*Edmund Grainger*
Director	*Lloyd Bacon*
Screenplay	*Mary Loos and Richard Sale*
(based on a story by Matty Kemp and Isabel Dawn)	
Photography	*Harry J. Wild*
Editing	*Robert Ford*
Music	*C. Bakaleinikoff*
(songs by Josef Myrow, Ralph Blane, and Robert Wells)	
Mary Carson	*Jane Russell*

Pierre Duquesne	*Gilbert Roland*
"Waco" Mosby	*Arthur Hunnicutt*
Annie Farrell	*Mary McCarty*
Myrtle Brown	*Joyce MacKenzie*
Celeste	*Paula Corday*
Bill Harris	*Scott Elliott*
Phil Barion	*Craig Stevens*
Katherine Hodges	*Laura Elliot*
François	*Steven Geray*
The First Mate	*John Wengraf*
George Hodges	*Michael St. Angel*
Donna Adams	*Barbara Darrow*
Kitty Lee	*Barbara Dobbins*

Lolita (Seven Arts Productions and Metro-Goldwyn-Mayer, 1962; 153
minutes)

Producer	*James B. Harris*
Director	*Stanley Kubrick*
Screenplay	*Vladimir Nabokov*
(based on the novel by Nabokov)	
Photography	*Oswald Morris*
Editing	*Anthony Harvey*
Music	*Nelson Riddle*
("Lolita" theme by Bob Harris)	

Humbert Humbert	*James Mason*
Lolita Haze	*Sue Lyon*
Charlotte Haze	*Shelley Winters*
Clare Quilty	*Peter Sellers*
Jean Farlow	*Diana Decker*
John Farlow	*Jerry Stovin*
Mona Farlow	*Suzanne Gibbs*
Dick Schiller	*Gary Cockrell*
Vivian Darkbloom	*Marianne Stone*
The Physician	*Cec Linder*
Nurse Mary Lore	*Lois Maxwell*
Swine	*Bill Greene*
Potts	*C. Denier Warren*
Louise	*Isobel Lucas*
The Hospital Receptionist	*Maxine Holden*
Beale	*James Dyrenforth*
Lorna	*Roberta Shore*
Roy	*Eric Lane*
Mrs. Starch	*Shirley Douglas*
Bill	*Roland Brand*
Charlie	*Colin Maitland*
The Hospital Attendant	*Irvin Allen*
Miss Lebone	*Marion Mathie*
Rex	*Craig Sams*
Tom	*John Harrison*

Who's Afraid of Virginia Woolf? (Warner Bros., 1966; 129 minutes)

Producer	*Ernest Lehman*
Director	*Mike Nichols*
Screenplay	*Ernest Lehman*
(based on the play by Edward Albee)	
Photography	*Haskell Wexler*
Editing	*Sam O'Steen*
Music	*Alex North*
Martha	*Elizabeth Taylor*
George	*Richard Burton*
Nick	*George Segal*
Honey	*Sandy Dennis*

INDEX

ABOUT THE AUTHORS

LEONARD J. LEFF teaches film history and screenwriting in the English Department at Oklahoma State University. His books include the reference guide *Film Plots*, as well as *Hitchcock and Selznick* (published by Weidenfeld and Nicolson in 1987), which won the 1988 British Film Institute Book Award.

JEROLD L. SIMMONS teaches American constitutional history at the University of Nebraska at Omaha. He is the author of *Operation Abolition: The Campaign to Abolish the House Committee on Un-American Activities* and has published articles in such journals as *The Harvard Civil Rights/Civil Liberties Law Review, The Southern California Quarterly,* and *Mid-America*.